D1561546

The Transition to Democracy in Spain and Portugal

The Transition to Democracy in Spain and Portugal

HOWARD J. WIARDA
WITH THE ASSISTANCE OF
IÊDA SIQUEIRA WIARDA

AMERICAN ENTERPRISE
INSTITUTE FOR PUBLIC
POLICY RESEARCH
Washington, D.C.

Distributed by arrangement with

UPA, Inc.
4720 Boston Way
Lanham, MD 20706
3 Henrietta Street
London WC2E 8LU England

Library of Congress Cataloging-in-Publication Data

Wiarda, Howard J., 1939–
  The transition to democracy in Spain and Portugal / Howard J. Wiarda,
  with the assistance of Iêda Siqueira Wiarda.
    p. cm.—(AEI studies : 482)
  Includes index.
  ISBN 0-8447-3672-4.   ISBN 0-8447-3673-2 (pbk.)
  1. Representative government and representation—Spain.
  2. Representative government and representation—Portugal.
  3. Spain—Politics and government—1975– 4. Portugal—Politics and
  government—1974– I. Wiarda, Iêda Siqueira. II. Title.
    III. Series.
  JN8341.W53   1988
  320.946—dc19   88-19302
                                                                            CIP

AEI Studies 482

Printed in the United States of America

4-13-89
at

Contents

Preface

Since the mid-1970s, beginning with the Portuguese "Revolution of Flowers" in 1974 and Franco's death in 1975, Spain and Portugal have made remarkable strides toward democracy. Scholars and policy officials alike have devoted a great deal of attention to the transition to democracy in Iberia, both in its own right and as a model for other nations in transition to democracy, particularly those in Latin America.

The issue is loaded with emotional, intellectual, and ideological baggage. We all wish Spain and Portugal well and hope that they remain in the democratic camp. This is particularly so given Iberia's long and generally unhappy historical experience with democracy, the area's political culture and institutions which have not always been supportive of democratic precepts, and the particular experiences of the Franco and Salazar regimes which are often thought of as "fascistic" and as allied or sympathetic to the Nazi regime. We *want* very much for Spain and Portugal to succeed as democracies; all our literature and theoretical models, as well as our emotions, bias us toward hope that the democratic transition will be lasting and permanent. The literature we have tends to be celebratory rather than analytical.

But celebration cannot be used as a substitute for hard analysis, nor can wishful sociology and wishful political science be used to gloss over facts with which we may be uncomfortable. For the realities of the matter are that the Spanish and Portuguese democratic transitions are still incomplete, there are strong undercurrents and institutions in both countries that are not particularly democratic, it remains uncertain just how democratic the underlying political culture and society of both countries are, and there is at least as much continuity of old ways and institutions in the Spanish and Portuguese transitions as there has been change. This book emphasizes the continuities, the historical permanences in the Spanish and Portuguese systems, as contrasted with the transformations that so many other volumes have stressed, while also trying to arrive at some balanced conclusions.

This is, hence, a more skeptical and "darker" view of the Spanish and Portuguese transitions than is provided in most of the books on the subject. It is "dark" in the sense that my AEI colleague and former Assistant Secretary of Defense Richard Perle is referred to as the "Prince of Darkness" for his opposition to unrealistic and sometimes similarly wishful thinking about the Soviet Union. My book also comes down on the cloudier side in that, while recognizing the fundamental transformations that have occurred in Iberia and applauding the steps toward democracy, I remain uncertain how deeply the democratic ethos has been internalized within the Spanish and Portuguese political culture, whether democracy is viable there, how strongly it is wanted, and whether it will last. Iberia has had such a long and deep nondemocratic and even antidemocratic tradition that prudence alone should lead us to be circumspect in judging just how democratic these countries are or are likely to become.

In the last analysis, one needs to weigh and balance both the changes and the continuities, as well as the complex dynamics and frequent overlap between them. Most of the studies published so far emphasize the forces of change, the hopeful and celebratory side of the process. This book emphasizes the continuities, while not being unmindful of the transformations that have occurred, and shows how even the changes often lie within some quite traditional boundaries and institutions.

The papers and chapters contained in this book were all written during the past decade as the author sought to keep current on and interpret the fast-moving events in Spain and Portugal. They are published here in the order in which they were written. They have at their core the effort to understand change and continuity in Iberia following the Portuguese Revolution and the Spanish evolution after Franco. I had earlier published a long study (*Corporatism and Development: The Portuguese Experience,* University of Massachusetts Press, 1977) stressing the strength and continuity of authoritarianism and corporatism under the old regime of Salazar and Caetano in Portugal and had done similar research work and writing on the Franco regime in Spain.

But in the wake of the Portuguese Revolution and the romance with socialism and sometimes radical forms of democracy, a message stressing continuity was not what the Portuguese, or many American scholars similarly caught up in the spirit of the revolution, wanted to hear. They preferred to ignore this older and still often venerated history and culture. There is, however, now a new emphasis on continuity in Spain and Portugal and on those institutions once thought to be discarded (authoritarianism, corporatism, hierarchy, status preoccupations, traditional political behavior) but now revealed to be still very much present. The older interpretations stressing continuity as well as change are relevant again and are staging a comeback. Hence the effort in this book to wrestle once more, in a new and more open-minded context, with the question of just how much has changed in Spain and Portugal *and* how much remains the same.

Most of the chapters and papers included here were published earlier in other places. But because they were published in diverse and obscure formats, they can usefully be brought together under one cover. Some of the materials are out of print and no longer available. In addition, the continuing interest in the Spanish and Portuguese transitions to democracy, the influence of the Spanish and Portuguese cases on Latin America, the implications of all these changes for U.S. foreign policy, and the continuing importance of the main conceptual themes—authoritarianism, democracy, corporatism—justify a volume devoted to the subject. The reprinted articles and book chapters have been lightly edited to remove repetition and to bring them up to date; but in essence they appear as they were first written.

There needs to be a way by which authors recognize the enormous contributions of their spouses that goes beyond the usual "thanks" in the preface but which falls short of full co-authorships, which would not be accurate either. I am, for good or ill, the original author of all the chapters that follow, but Dr. Iêda Siqueira Wiarda prepared no less than thirty-four pages of written commentary on the original manuscript, served as indispensable critic and editor, provided a great deal of solid advice, and has long provided a family climate in which prodigious amounts of research and writing could be carried out—often to the detriment of her own professional career. It is very likely unfortunate that I have not always heeded the sound academic advice that I receive from this quarter; on the other hand, it is so valuable that the designation "with the assistance of" on the cover represents a modest acknowledgment of the immense support she has provided.

Thanks are also due the Tinker Foundation, which provided a major grant for the support of this book and an earlier companion volume (*The Iberian–Latin American Connection: Implications for U.S. Policy*, Westview Press and AEI, 1986) as part of a multifaceted project on the changes in Iberia, Iberian–Latin American relations, and U.S. foreign policy. I also wish to acknowledge the assistance of the AEI administrative and support staff, especially President Christopher DeMuth, without whose help over the years it would not be possible to continue such a vast and ambitious research agenda. It is certainly far easier to be productive when one's typists, research assistants, library facilities, and office support are as strong as they are at AEI; having one's editors (to say nothing of the dining room) right down the hall also helps a great deal! I am grateful for the marvelous opportunities this association provides; at the same time the ideas, arguments, and analysis included here are my responsibility alone.

Introduction

In April 1974, a cadre of young military officers launched a revolution to overthrow the authoritarian corporate regime put in place by Antonio Salazar and later headed by his intellectual and political heir, Marcello Caetano. Almost overnight what had begun as a military coup became a full-scale social revolution as sentiments for change bottled up for decades were unleashed and as the civilian population took to the streets. At first the revolution veered sharply to the left, but after 1975 it began to be more centrist. A series of elections held beginning that same year seemed to signal Portugal's successful transition to democratic rule.

Meanwhile, Francisco Franco, the long-time dictator of Spain, died in November 1975. Although Franco seemed to have made arrangements to continue his authoritarian corporate state after his death, in a series of moves under a courageous monarch and prime minister, Spain also undertook a democratic transition. A party system emerged, elections were held, and democratic political institutions came into existence. Whereas in Portugal the shift was dramatic and abrupt, in Spain the transition was peaceful and gradual; but in both countries a quite remarkable opening to democracy was undertaken and at least partially consolidated within a relatively short period of time.

These transitions have been justly celebrated in the literature.[1] We are all pleased at the success of the Iberian nations in building democracy. But there has been a lot of romantic and wishful writing about the degree and levels of institutionalization of democracy in Spain and Portugal; in addition, the literature has been skewed by its focus on the change and transforming currents in these two countries, with insufficient attention devoted to the question of what remains the same. The realities are—however uncomfortable these facts may leave us—that the democratic transitions in both these countries are still incomplete, democracy has not been fully consolidated and may not even now reach deeply into the society or its consciousness, and there are some powerful currents, attitudes, and institutions in Iberia that are not at all convinced that democracy is the best or only form of government.

I too wish Spain and Portugal all the best in their quests for democracy. But such wishes should not get in the way of the tough assessments and analysis that are necessary. Hence we need to focus on the authoritarian currents still coursing through Iberia as well as the democratic ones, the elements providing for the perpetuation of historic institutions as well as the rise of newer ones, and through all of this the change process itself, which most often involves the blending and fusion of traditional institutions with more democratic ones rather than the former superseding the latter.[2] Our analysis needs to be more balanced and therefore also more accurate than the democratizing focus alone has given us.

History and Political Culture

Spain and Portugal have long histories as nations, and very little of that history has been democratic. From the Greeks, Iberia took the notion not of a democratic *polis* but of a society organized in terms of its "natural" inequalities and classes. From Rome, under whose domination Iberia existed for six centuries, Spain and Portugal inherited their language and law as well as the organizing principles of an imperial state. From the Visigoths came the notion of an official state church, bolstering and reinforcing the civilian authority. The legacy of seven centuries of Islamic rule in Spain included a separate and glorified army and additional notions of inequality with regard to men and women. Feudalism in Spain and Portugal and the reconquest of the peninsula from the Moors created a structure of self-sufficient landed estates under warrior overlords, a legacy of separatism, and a rigidly hierarchical sociopolitical structure. Thomism, with its emphasis on authority, hierarchy, and the corporate organization of society, provided religious and absolutist legitimacy to this entire structure.[3]

These diverse historical strands came together in the sixteenth century, at the height of Spain's and Portugal's imperial importance and glory, into a structure of state and societal authority that may be termed the Hapsburgian model. The Hapsburgian model was authoritarian, hierarchical, elitist, corporatist, bureaucratic, absolutist, and—to add one more current—mercantilist or statist to its core. This model not only persisted in Spain and Portugal for the better part of the next five centuries (resurrected once again in the regimes of Franco and Salazar), but it was also carried over to Latin America where it similarly thrived and persisted. This would prove to be a model that would not die, fade away, or be overthrown easily.

The Hapsburgian model was not only a structure of political authority but also encompassed religious, social, economic, and personal relationships. It represented a very conservative political culture. This ethos penetrated deep into the society. Over the centuries it became an integral part of the political consciousness. It governed behavior, expectations, social relations, and ways of interacting with one's fellow citizens. Because it reached so deeply into society and was so pervasive, this authoritarian and elitist political culture would not be changed easily.

But beginning in the eighteenth century a fissure began to develop in the Iberian soul. The new current was more liberal, influenced by the Enlightenment, and with a social base in the emerging urban middle classes.[4] For a long time this liberal current remained a minority strain in both Spain and Portugal. Many serious analysts would argue it is still a minority strain.

From the eighteenth century there were two rival and competing forms of sociopolitical organizations, two Spains and two Portugals. One Spain and one Portugal were conservative, Catholic, traditional, closed, "semi-feudal," and centered in the historic countryside. The other Spain and Portugal were at least nascently liberal, urban, enlightened, oriented toward Europe, and concentrated sociologically in the major cities. Indeed much of the conflict, instability, and civil war that characterized Spanish and Portuguese histories during the nineteenth century (and into the twentieth) was due to these competing conceptions that were never resolved. They were not resolved by the brutal and devastating Spanish Civil War of 1936–1939 or by the long Franco era; and they were not resolved in Portugal by the incipient civil war and conflict of the first two decades of the twentieth century (more bombs per capita than any other country in Europe, according to historian Douglas Wheeler's calculations),[5] or by the Salazar-Caetano era or by the revolution of 1974. If they were not resolved in the course of these earlier traumas, it is unlikely that they are fully resolved now.

And that is of course the overriding question with which this book wrestles: to what extent (if at all) have Spain and Portugal now finally overcome their historic sources of discord and division and embarked on a new and consensually based course of democracy? Or are the old disputes, and therefore the possibilities for fragmentation and breakdown that usually lead to renewed authoritarianism, still with us?

3

A special word must be said here about the Franco and Salazar-Caetano regimes. In the United States and Western Europe these regimes are usually viewed as fascistic, backward-looking, and sympathetic, if not allied, to the Nazis. In my own earlier books on Spain and Portugal, I also conclude that these regimes exhibited many fascistic traits, held back the hands of time, failed to accommodate to changed circumstances, and therefore deserved to fall.[6]

But this conclusion should not blind us to the genuine popularity these regimes enjoyed in their primes or their efforts to fashion an indigenous, home-grown model of development. They did not rule, it is clear, by blood and totalitarianism alone. Rather, they stood for order, stability, nationalism, discipline, and social peace. In times of fear, chaos, or the potential for same that prevailed in Spain and Portugal in the 1920s and 1930s, these are revered and valued principles. Of course both regimes stayed in power too long and eventually lost support as the conditions and reasons for their coming to power in the first place changed. But should severe fragmentation and the potential for disintegration appear again, the allure of the Hapsburgian model, an authoritarian solution—the "wicked necessity," as sociologist Natalio Botana called it[7]—might reassert itself. Hence while the present circumstances would seem to be more or less propitious for the continuation of democracy in Spain and Portugal, one could conceive of circumstances in which that consensus could be quickly (or maybe only gradually) undermined.

Iberian Developmentalist Crosscurrents

Spain and Portugal have changed enormously in the past thirty years. By virtually all the indexes of development that we use, Iberia has moved into the modern age. Both countries are far more urban, literate, and economically developed than they were at the end of the 1950s. Industry and manufacturing have grown, and the per capita income has doubled. Their domestic communications and transportation grids have been impressively built up. There is more affluence, and the size of their middle classes—a key indicator of the existence of a stronger social base for democracy—is significantly larger. Psychologically as well, Spain and Portugal are now more solidly integrated into Europe, into the West, and into the community of modern Western democracies. These changes, it is argued, have provided a more solid base for democracy than ever before in Iberian history.[8]

While the changes have been impressive, they have not been as complete as is sometimes said—and hoped. Spain and Portugal send many mixed signals, and the traditional and the modern frequently overlap. The transitions to democracy have been impressive and at the same time not fully consolidated. Disturbing undercurrents remain, institutions in which the transition has been only partial. Though the period of the Spanish and Portuguese transitions in the 1970s were successful and prosperous, should things sour—as their economies have done in recent years—the "success democrats" who support representative government today because it has succeeded in delivering goods and services for them may begin to have second thoughts. In any case, after the extensive celebratory literature we have had to this point, a more cautious and skeptical view is warranted. Here an effort is made to provide that view while also remaining balanced in our final assessments.

Attitudes. Public opinion surveys taken in Spain and Portugal show an overwhelming preference for representative democratic government. Support for democracy is in the range of 70–80 percent, the highest level of support ever registered there, and it may signal the development of a solid base for democracy that had not existed before.[9]

Other attitudes, however, may also be found:

• Support for democracy is far stronger in Spain than in Portugal. In Portugal, while there is strong support for democracy in the abstract, when asked to identify the recent government in Portuguese history that they felt was the best, a solid majority chose that of Salazar-Caetano.[10] Such a response may be predictable given the instability and ineffectiveness of several of Portugal's more recent democratic governments, but it does not augur well for the future of democracy.

• There is widespread preference in both countries for "strong government." The opinion surveys that ask what types of government the people prefer usually miss this point because they do not ask the follow-up question: What do you mean by democracy? When that second question is asked, the response is often a preference for strong, authoritative government that really governs. The image that is conjured up is that of strong executive leadership as in the French Fifth Republic under DeGaulle. But "strong government" can easily verge toward Bonapartist rule, especially in times of crisis.

• While there is popular support for democracy in Spain and Portugal, there is little support for what we think of as democracy's necessary institutional foundations: political parties, labor unions, and the like. Support for these institutions is only in the 20–30 percent range. If such attitudes persist, they do not provide a very strong foundation on which to build a democracy.

5

- Although Iberia prefers democracy, it favors it in its Rousseauean rather than Lockean forms.[11] That is, it favors a democracy that is integral, organic, and unified. It wants strong central authority. It supports a corporate-organic conception of society as well as of the polity. In my writings I have supported attempts by various countries to develop their own focus of democracy, true to their own indigenous culture and institutions. But one also has the right to worry that democracy in its Rousseauean forms may have a tendency toward authoritarian corporate rule (or totalitarianism) with which most democrats would feel very uncomfortable.[12]
- Both Spain and Portugal remain very conservative on many issues. Portugal has gone steadily back toward the right since 1974 and in 1987 elected a moderately conservative government, the first democratic and parliamentary government—and conservative one—ever to enjoy majority support in Portugal. In Spain there is widespread disenchantment with Felipe González and the Socialist party, but so far the Right has not reorganized itself successfully after Franco and lacks a charismatic leader who could challenge González. In both countries the strength of the Communist and far-left parties has been progressively eroding. In Setúbal, what was long considered Portugal's "red belt," 70 percent of the youth want to grow up to be entrepreneurs. In both countries the signs of conservative and even rightist resurgence are widespread. Efforts are being made to rediscover what was valuable and perhaps worth saving or resurrecting from the Franco and Salazar eras, or to find a formula that would blend and reconcile the two nations' democratic with their more authoritarian currents. In its public policy (destatization, free markets, and the like) as well as in its constitutional revision Portugal has already embarked on this course; Spain seems likely to follow suit soon. The climate in both countries is toward greater conservatism, and some would argue that Spain and Portugal are *inherently* conservative in their political cultures.[13]

Institutions. While there has been considerable development of democratic institutions in Spain and Portugal in recent years, these institutions tend still to be weak, often disorganized, and ineffective. This is particularly true of political parties, which tend in both countries to be poorly organized, thin in leadership, and without strong grass-roots organizations (see chapter 8); but the same applies to other institutions as well. Labor unions, farmers' associations and cooperatives, business associations, and interest organizations of all types are woefully unorganized. In many areas there is still an institutional void, the "absence of associability" that Tocqueville talked about, the *falta de civilización* that the Hispanic countries have long lamented.

In the absence of a strong associational life, which characterizes not just the political area but all areas of society, the central state has once again become exceedingly powerful. There are numerous centralizing tendencies in both Spain and Portugal: the state has greatly increased its levels of intervention in the society and the economy, and the central government has kept a strong hand in local government. Part of this is due to a long tradition of statism in Iberia, part is due to pressing economic and political concerns that reinforce centralization. Spain and Portugal remain statist, *dirigiste,* Colbertian, or state-capitalist systems, despite the more recent pressures to destatize. Statism and centralization are of course signs of the relative weakness of the democratic system.[14] Moreover, such a powerful and all-encompassing state system, in both the economic and the political spheres, invites not only autarchy but also authoritarianism. Statism is one of those continuities with the past that has not changed much in the transition to democracy and may come to represent a threat to it.

The state system itself is not very efficient. It is one of the least-developed and least modern institutions (actually a myriad maze of institutions) in Spain or Portugal. It is shot through with graft, sinecures, nepotism, inefficiencies, patronage, and corruption. In both countries the state sector is vastly bloated in size. It lacks technical and decision-making abilities. It is not very effective. If the effective deliverance of goods and services is one of the hallmarks and requirements of modern democratic government, then the Portuguese and Spanish state systems are not delivering.[15] And if in the modern era of raised expectations such services must be delivered—or else—then it may be that these ineffective state systems, however democratic, may soon be in trouble.

The result in both countries has been growing disillusionment. The sentiment is widespread of "a pox on all your houses." It is becoming rather like the voting behavior of French peasants in earlier times who smeared excrement on the ballots or voted Communist or Fascist as a protest against the series of ineffective, Fourth-Republic governments in Paris in the 1940s and 1950s. Now such voting behavior is beginning to come to Spain and Portugal: more disillusionment, more blank ballots, and greater simmering antipathy and cynicism with regard to all changes of cabinet and prime ministers.[16] Politics is seen as a game played in the capital city by and for the politicians, but the bulk of the population receives few benefits and is increasingly cynical about the process. Such growing cynicism and disillusionment do not provide a strong grounding for democracy.

As yet, the people have not expressed a marked increase in preference for a strong military or fascistic regime. In both countries the traditional far right has been gaining in electoral strength only gradually. But of course numbers of electoral ballots have never been the right's sole or even most important source of power. We have not actually seen any precipitous swings to fascism or a Franco- or Salazar-like regime. It seems to me unlikely that such a far-right regime will soon come to power, although in both countries disillusionment with Socialist government has been growing. In Portugal, in 1987, a center-right party garnered over 50 percent of the popular vote for the first time, and in Spain unhappiness with Prime Minister Felipe González and the normal alternation among parties in a democratic polity will slowly bring the right into a challenging position.[17]

While we are all cheered by Iberia's democratic successes and may view with trepidation any stirrings on the far right, it is important to remember that not all institutions in Spain and Portugal have been democratized. The armed forces have been changing in both nations, but no one knows how much, how they would behave in a crisis, the degree to which the officers have accepted their role as subservient to civilian authority, or which of them harbor secret ambitions and are privately building political coalitions. There have been several coup attempts in both countries. The church remains conservative in Iberia, only weakly influenced by the currents of liberation theology and grass-roots participation that stir their Latin American brothers. The economic elites are powerful, especially in Spain, and have not lived long under democratic rule and are not sure that they like it. There are powerful conservative currents among the peasants, workers, and middle class, the last of which now dominates most Iberian institutions and will likely be a decisive swing element in any future crisis. Within both countries, in addition, there are strong institutions—the judiciary, the military, the bureaucracy—that have not been greatly affected by democratization, and whose loyalties may still lie with a regime of the older type.

Political Culture. The political culture of Spain and Portugal has shifted in a more democratic direction. There is widespread admiration for democratic government, and both countries now have a level of freedom they have not had in fifty years or more. The press is free, discussion is free, there is no censorship, and the pornography is explicit (yet most Spaniards and Portuguese, while liking the new-found freedom, do not care for some of the magazines and movies they are now able to see).

Spain and Portugal have moved away from a "subject" political culture toward democracy, but they have yet to develop a participatory and "civic" political culture.[18] The democratic political culture is still thin; it does not reach down deeply into the society. Spain and Portugal are still governed strongly by considerations of rank, hierarchy, and social status. The element of egalitarianism, of "all men created equal," that is so necessary for democracy remains only weakly established. Birth and other ascriptive criteria are often more important than merit or considerations of achievement. Many have disdain for those who fall below them in the social order. The historic Spanish haughtiness and exaggerated sense of station and self-importance, although attenuated in the new democratic era, are still present. Overall, though Spain and Portugal have developed the formal mechanisms and institutions of democracy, they have not yet established a deeply rooted democratic consciousness, civism, and egalitarianism.

A related phenomenon is the unevenness and incompleteness of the new democratic consciousness. Democracy has triumphed in the political realm but not in all others. When Franco was alive, for example, Spain's first and then virtually only polling firm conducted a survey that showed some surprising results. It demonstrated that while Spanish political attitudes and institutions tended to be conservative, its social institutions—the family, the church, interpersonal relations—were even *more conservative* than the Franco regime itself.[19] To the consternation of the pollsters, who were themselves quite liberal, Spanish society was revealed to be even more conservative than the Spanish regime. My own interviewing in Portugal in the early 1970s revealed many similar responses. In the late 1980s it is not entirely clear that the same results would apply, but there is little doubt that while politics have become more democratic, many of the social institutions—family, the firm, social relations—have remained quite conservative. Eventually these disparities and the unevenness of the democratic temper may spell trouble for Iberian democracy.

Political cultures can and do of course change; they are not fixed now and forever more. The economy and society change and with them the political culture, loyalties toward the political system, and identification with the national community may be altered, and—especially relevant for the Spanish and Portuguese cases—values may change from one generation to the next. Cultural change (including political culture) is a continuous process that is always under way.[20]

9

The question here, however, is not whether Spanish and Portuguese political culture is changing, but how thoroughly internalized the changes have been, and among which groups they have taken place.

I find Spain and Portugal more ambivalent about democracy now than five or ten years earlier, when most of the opinion surveys were done. Because democracy has not succeeded in solving many of their problems, attitudes toward it are mixed; much of the romance and enthusiasm for democracy has faded. Such attitudes may not soon result in large antidemocratic movements or in the people's wish to return to the predemocratic era. But there is greater criticism and discontent, a willingness to consider mixed political formulas, and a strong sense that what was good about the past ought to be blended with what is good in the democratic present. We are likely, therefore, to see continued questioning of current institutions and willingness to experiment with new forms.

Socioeconomic Factors. While the socioeconomic development of Spain and Portugal (especially of Spain) has been impressive in recent years, immense problems remain nonetheless. These include large and, in some areas, widening gaps between rich and poor, social and class cleavages that seem all but unbridgeable, an immense problem with agriculture and a rural sector that lags farther and farther behind, still large percentages of the population who are illiterate and without adequate housing or health care, cities that have swollen in size to the point where they are almost unmanageable, major unemployment and underemployment especially among youth, and a host of others. These problems often make some areas of Iberia today look like the third world area that it was not many years ago. Poverty and the third world in Iberia often loom just around the corner, away from the tourist centers. Major strides toward socioeconomic progress have been made in both countries, but the interlocking vicious circles of underdevelopment are likewise still present in both.

Related to the problems of underdevelopment are the political implications of socioeconomic change. A rich literature of development theory suggests that as social and economic modernization proceeds, political democratization is almost certain to follow.[21] Such certainty, inevitability, and even universality of these processes are enormously comforting to many within the Spanish government who have absorbed this same literature. But the experience of Latin America does not support the inevitability and universality of these development processes. There, post–World War II economic development gave rise not to a happy, liberal, bourgeois polity but, at least in the short run, to fragmentation, breakdown, and a new wave of bureaucratic authoritarianism in the 1960s and 1970s. The similarly expanding middle class in Latin America proved not to be a bastion of democracy and stability but a polarized and polarizing force that undermined and destroyed democracy for the sake of preserving the middle class's own newly won status. It is only now, in the longer term, that Latin America is returning to democracy and that the earlier development literature is starting to look better. The question for Spain and Portugal is whether they are in the first phase of post-authoritarian rule when socioeconomic change leads to breakdown and renewed dictatorship, or in the second phase when democracy appears somewhat more secure. The very uncertainty of our answers is, again, not very reassuring for Iberian democracy.

One also needs to remain aware of the immense differences between Spain and Portugal. Spain has a per capita income about twice that of Portugal (over $4,000 per year versus somewhat over $2,000 per year) and a middle class that is, correspondingly, roughly twice as large. Spain's literacy levels are higher, its industry is far more developed, and on virtually every other socioeconomic index Spain is in far better shape. Our predictions need to take these vast differences between the two Iberian nations into account. My own sense is that the affluence, the strength of the middle class, and the level of development of Spain make it unlikely that it will soon destabilize, or that democracy there could be undermined by either the left or the right.

For Portugal, where the living standard is far closer to that of Latin America—that is, to the third world—one cannot be so sure. It may be, with all the reservations offered earlier, that Spain has passed that threshold at which communism or fascism ("diseases of the transition," as developmental economist W. W. Rostow called them)[22] represents a threat. Portugal may be on the way but has not yet reached that threshold. In short, Spain may already have developed to the point that democracy is more or less ensured. But Portugal may still be in the first phase of its development, comparable to Latin America's position, when an authoritarian takeover, while not imminent, may still be possible.

International Pressures. In Portugal after the 1974 revolution and in Spain after Franco's death, the United States and its Western European allies were deeply involved in the internal political process. The goal in Portugal was to keep the Communists from gaining power and to support a transition to a stable democratic polity. To this end the United States funneled in a vast amount of aid, channeled some through our allies, and the allies also provided their own assistance to like-minded political parties, trade unions, and other groups. A similar policy was followed in Spain (though less dramatically or publicly) aimed at preserving a smooth transition, keeping the Communists from taking advantage of the instability that many foreign observers assumed would follow Franco's death, and supporting the non-Communist opposition.

Indeed it can safely be said that the whole effort to incorporate Spain and Portugal into the European Economic Community (EEC) was based less on economic grounds than on the political basis outlined above. The Western European nations wished to guarantee democratic political stability on their own and NATO's southern flanks and to prevent a Communist or renewed Fascist regime from coming to power. At the same time they wished to prevent the "Portuguese virus" (a romantic leftist, sometimes Communist-led revolution) from spreading into their own territories. Hence Western Europe, supported by the United States, sought to envelop Spain and Portugal in such a vast web of NATO, EEC, and European relations that the question still raging intellectually in Iberia as to whether they would be first, second, or third world would be moot. Spain and Portugal would become so much a part of Europe that politically a right- or left-wing takeover would be ruled out—in fact, would no longer even be a worthwhile question for discussion.[23]

This was a quite clever strategy on the part of the Western Europeans. The trouble is that it put the European support for Iberian democracy purely on a pragmatic basis, one that had everything to do with the domestic politics of the European countries and very little to do with Spain and Portugal. Moreover, the purely pragmatic considerations offered a relatively weak basis for supporting democracy. They represented not so much a philosophical commitment to democracy as to self-interest. And because the commitment was pragmatic and circumstantial, it could change over time.

The same kind of prudent and parochial considerations governed U.S. attitudes. The United States saw its support of democracy in Spain and Portugal as a way of getting the Congress, the public, the bureaucracy, and our allies on its side and of avoiding the grief that an alternative regime of either the far right or the far left would cause for NATO and for U.S. policy.[24] The U.S. support for Spanish democracy was prudent and measured, which in Iberia may not be sufficient. That is precisely why when democracy in Spain was threatened by a *coup d'état* in 1981 and Secretary of State Alexander Haig declared that it was a domestic matter for the Spaniards to decide, shock waves rippled throughout Spain. Democracy in Iberia is still a fragile reed, and anything less than *total* U.S. and European support for it—as distinct from "situational" support—might be enough to undermine it.

Moreover, even that level of support has dwindled over the years. Spain and Portugal are out of the headlines, and the threat of a Communist or right-wing takeover has slowly receded. Europe and the United States have lost interest.[25] The Europeans now also think that the threat of the "Portuguese virus" infecting their own countries has diminished. Spain and Portugal are presently thought to be "safe" for democracy and stability, in accord with the Lipset-Rostow developmentalist thesis. Hence the levels of aid and attention to Iberia are way down. But I am not as convinced of the "inevitability" of those developmentalist interrelationships. Nor am I certain that Spain and Portugal are quite as immunized from the left- and right-wing threats as the lack of attention abroad would seem to indicate. Indeed the very lack of attention from Western Europe and the United States— not-so-benign neglect, if you will—is precisely what might help trigger the success of some future antidemocratic movement.

One further international influence of immense importance merits attention, and that is the economy. In the past several years Europe has been going through a severe depression, which has had far worse consequences in Iberia than in the more developed countries. The economic downturn was more severe, unemployment rates were higher, and fewer social safety nets existed. The depression has been not only deeper in Iberia but longer. Moreover, Iberia's recovery has been slower than that of the rest of Europe. Nor does it show signs of ending soon.

The depressed economic conditions have begun to have a negative effect on the socioeconomic indicators that earlier seemed to provide such a solid new base for democracy. Furthermore, historically in Iberia, when the bottom drops out of the economy, the political system has usually followed shortly thereafter. It is easy to be a democratic leader when the economic pie is expanding and there are always new pieces of the pie to hand out to the clamoring new groups. But when the economy turns stagnant or the pie begins to contract, in a time of raised popular expectations, the problems for a democratic government not entirely secure to begin with can become severe. The increased economic ties to Europe through the EEC have now compounded the problem: when Europe flourishes it has positive multiplier effects in Iberia; but when Europe flounders economically that also is now reflected more strongly in a negative way than used to be the case before integration. The potential exists for Spain and, more likely, Portugal to be destabilized by the very European forces that once looked so hopeful.

A Summing Up—and a Beginning

It is very likely that Spain and Portugal will continue as democratic regimes into the future. It is not useful, however, to assume that this is a foregone and inevitable conclusion or to ignore the strong currents that point toward other possible conclusions or to wish them away. We need to base our assessments on hard realities, uncomfortable though we may be with some of these, to be coolly analytical and not just celebratory of the recent transitions to democracy in Iberia. In general, the prospects seem considerably better for Spain than for Portugal.

While democracy is likely to continue in both countries, one can envision conditions under which it could be threatened. If the economy remains stagnant for longer periods or goes into a tailspin, if there is high unemployment and hence rising discontent, if terrorism in the Basque country or elsewhere increases, if the military senses that the country is unraveling or that it can govern better than the civilians or that the far left might come to power, if austerity continues and the middle class (now the swing group) feels threatened or becomes disillusioned, if the United States and the Western Europeans lose interest—these are the classic conditions that have often in the past served as preludes to instability or extremism. Some of these conditions are already present or partially so in Spain and Portugal; others could develop into serious problems in the future.

Related is the question of change versus continuity in Iberia. Now that the early and somewhat exaggerated euphoria of the democratic transitions is wearing off, scholars are rediscovering how much Spain and Portugal remain the same. *Plus que ça change, plus que ça reste le même.* A centralized bureaucratic state, the corporate (albeit in new form) or sectoral organization of society (see chapter 1), authoritarian decision making, rock-hard conservatism, preeminent and often overriding considerations of rank and status, authoritarianism and traditionalism in many sociocultural and even political arenas—all these are carryovers from the past that remain strong in the present. Not only do these forces continue to represent a threat, or perhaps an alternative, to democratic rule, but they call into question how pervasive democracy is and how far down it reaches. For we have recently discovered, or begun to rediscover, that there are vast areas and institutions in Spain and Portugal that are nondemocratic and downright antidemocratic.

An additional worrisome point is the degree to which the changes that have occurred might just as easily undermine democracy as contribute to it. Socioeconomic change is heady stuff, and it does

14

not always or consistently correlate with democratization. In the Spanish and Portuguese cases, expectations have been raised, the population aroused, and social forces mobilized. These forces, once aroused, cannot be put back to sleep again. If the economy and the political system fail to deliver, however, frustration will certainly set in and destabilization may follow. As Samuel P. Huntington has argued, socioeconomic modernization may well upset political stability and democracy rather than bolster it.[26]

Although Spain and Portugal have come part of the distance to democracy, the transition is still incomplete. Yet in our enthusiasm for democracy, scholars, journalists, and public officials alike have tended to emphasize the democratizing currents and have too often ignored the nondemocratic ones. This book seeks to correct that imbalance by stressing the often nondemocratic side of the equation, while at the same time seeking to reach some balanced and judicious conclusions.

The message of the book is that our enthusiasm for Iberian democracy and its prospects may need to be tempered. The transition has been heartening, but it is still only partial. One's hopes for Spanish and Portuguese democracy should not be raised too high, for there are still major nondemocratic or antidemocratic forces in Iberia, and the process of democratization could still be reversed. Or, if not reversed, then democracy could be so redefined and reformulated (in its Rousseauean forms) as to leave genuine democrats very uncomfortable.

For despite the democratizing changes that have been so inspiring, there still exist the "other Spain" and "other Portugal" that are not very democratic and do not *want* to be democratic. In our rush to embrace the new and democratic Spain and Portugal, we have forgotten about the traditional Spain and Portugal. Perhaps the socioeconomic, cultural, and political changes of recent decades have transcended and superseded these historical differences. The book explores that issue in considerable detail. Certainly the democrats in power, especially the more ideologically oriented, would like to forget about and ignore, or wish away, these "other" countries.

But the historical record of these two nations is that the attempt by one Spain or one Portugal to govern entirely without the other—by ignoring the other and seeking to deny its legitimacy—is a formula for disaster. It produces discord, fragmentation, polarization and, in its most spectacular forms, bloody civil war. The last is certainly not my prediction for the future of Spain and Portugal. But discord, fragmentation, and a certain unraveling of the social and political fabric in these almost inherently "invertebrate" societies are possible and, in certain areas of the national life, may already be occurring.[27] True democrats need to take account of these renderings and to guard against allowing the process to proceed past the manageable point by taking due account of *all* the forces in Iberia; governing of, by, and for one group at the expense of the others is certain to produce polarization and possibly breakdowns.

These are, of course, strong statements; they are meant to be provocative and perhaps to set the reader's teeth on edge. For the fact is the transitions to democracy in Spain and Portugal, as well as some of the possibly disturbing themes set forth here, are controversial and deserve close attention from diverse perspectives.

I hope that this introduction will serve as a prelude and foretaste of some of the themes discussed in greater detail in the book.

The Book: A Look Ahead

Chapter 1 provides a statement of the main themes explored in the book—especially the idea of corporatism—and presents a model of corporatist development that for so long undergirded (and perhaps still today undergirds) the sociopolitical structure of Spain and Portugal as well as Latin America. The corporatist organization of society is one of the traditional institutions in Iberia that was supposed to collapse under the weight of modernization and rapid change but which—albeit in a new form—has proved to be remarkably durable.

Chapter 2 examines the historical background, origins, and continued presence of corporatism, authoritarianism, and nondemocratic attitudes and institutions in Iberia. Though the focus of the chapter is Portugal, much of the analysis is equally applicable to Spain.

Chapter 3 traces the development and actual practice of corporatism in Portugal under Salazar and Caetano and shows how the system did not work as intended. It also analyzes the revolution of 1974 that abolished the formal corporatist system but asks if corporatism might be continued in another form and if it is really possible for Portugal to transcend its historic institutions.

Chapter 4, on the Portuguese armed forces, examines the background and context of the Portuguese revolution of 1974. In contrast to some other interpretations, it suggests that the Portuguese Armed Forces Movement (MFA) that led the revolution emerged out of some very traditional concerns and that many of the policies it pursued were actually continuations of older ways of doing things.

Chapter 5 sums up the different forms corporatism has taken in Portugal: historically, under Salazar and Caetano, and in remodeled and often disguised form in the new democratic era.

Chapter 6 explores the question of whether Europe still stops at the Pyrenees, the degree to which Spain and Portugal wish to be integrated into Europe, and just how European, or democratic, their political institutions have become.

Chapter 7 focuses on political parties, exploring some parallel themes: to what extent have political parties, elections, and democracy now become institutionalized in Iberia or, alternatively, are there still other, nondemocratic routes to power?

Chapter 8 provides a wider focus—southern Europe. The chapter derives from a larger research project on the labor and industrial relations systems of Greece, Italy, Portugal, and Spain. The chapter presents the case for a distinctively southern European political process and for the continuity of corporatist, statist, and bureaucratic institutions, in different forms, regardless of the ideological label or self-identification of the particular government in power.

Chapter 9 examines the sociology of knowledge of corporatism: its origins and place in Iberia and Latin American political society as well as its recent shunting aside in favor of a democratic system and the resulting implications.

Chapter 10 similarly dissects Portuguese elections and democracy to assess the degree to which that country has been consolidated into the democratic camp.

In chapter 11 we look at Iberian-Latin American relations, the new thrusts of a more dynamic and democracy-oriented Spanish foreign policy, and the limits on Spain's playing a greater role in this area, as well as the future of Iberian-Latin American relations and the place of democracy in that relationship. A brief afterword summarizes the principal arguments of the book and recapitulates some of its implications, both regarding the prospects for Spanish and Portuguese democracy and for the social sciences of development as they seek to comprehend and come to grips with the dynamics of nations undergoing rapid and dramatic modernization. Some policy assessments and recommendations are also included in this final section.

Notes

1. See, among others, Victor Alba, *Transition in Spain: From Franco to Democracy* (New Brunswick, N.J.: Transaction Books, 1978); John F. Coverdale, *The Political Transformation of Spain after Franco* (New York: Praeger, 1979); Samuel D. Eaton, *The Forces of Freedom in Spain* (Stanford, Calif.: Hoover Institution, 1981); Enrique A. Baloyra, ed., *Comparing New Democracies: Transition and Consolidation in Mediterranean Europe and the Southern Cone* (Boulder, Colo.: Westview Press, 1987); Guillermo O'Donnell, Philippe C. Schmitter, and Lawrence Whitehead, eds., *Transitions from Authoritarian Rule: Prospects*

for Democracy (Baltimore: John Hopkins University Press, 1986); Juan Linz and Alfred Stepan, The Breakdown of Authoritarian Regimes (Baltimore: John Hopkins University Press, 1978); David Gilmour, The Transformation of Spain (New York: Quartet Books, 1985); José Amodia, Franco's Political Legacy: From Dictatorships to Facade Democracy (London: Lane, 1977); Ramón Arango, Spain: From Repression to Renewal (Boulder, Colo.: Westview Press, 1985); José María Maravall, Transition to Democracy in Spain (New York: St. Martin's Press, 1982); Geoffrey Pridlham, ed., The New Mediterranean Democracies: Spain, Greece, and Portugal (London: Totowa, 1984); Christopher Abel and Nissa Torrents, eds., Spain, Conditional Democracy (New York: St. Martin's Press, 1984); Thomas C. Bruneau, Politics and Nationhood: Post-Revolutionary Portugal (New York: Praeger, 1984); R. J. Morrison, Portugal: Revolutionary Change in an Open Economy (Boston: Auburn House, 1981); Beate Kohler, Political Forces in Spain, Greece and Portugal (London: Butterworth Scientific, 1982).

2. For a detailed discussion of this process and a conceptual framework see Howard J. Wiarda, "Toward a Framework for the Study of Socio-Political Change in the Iberic-Latin Tradition: The Corporative Model," World Politics, vol. XXV (January 1973), pp. 206–35; reprinted in Ikuo Kabashima and Lynn T. White, eds., Political Systems and Change (Princeton, N.J.: Princeton University Press, 1986). See also Wiarda, ed., Politics and Social Change in Latin America: The Distinct Tradition (Amherst: University of Massachusetts Press, 1982).

3. The history is detailed in chapter 2.

4. John Crow, Spain: The Root and the Flower (Berkeley: University of California Press, 1985).

5. Douglas Wheeler, The First Portuguese Republic (Madison: University of Wisconsin Press, 1978).

6. Howard J. Wiarda, Corporatism and Development: The Portuguese Experience (Amherst: University of Massachusetts Press, 1977).

7. Natalio Botana, "New Trends in Argentine Politics" (Paper presented at the Southern Cone Conference, Washington, D.C., June 5–6, 1983). Though focused on Argentina, the paper's concepts are also relevant to Spain.

8. Juan Linz, "Europe's Southern Frontier: Evolving toward What?" Daedalus, vol. 108 (Winter 1979), pp. 175–209; see also the multi-volume study edited by Larry Diamond, Linz, and Seymour Martin Lipset, Democracy in Developing Countries (Boulder, Colo.: Lynne Rienner Publishers, 1988).

9. See, for example, Richard Gunther, et al., Spain after Franco: The Making of a Competitive Party System (Berkeley: University of California Press, 1986).

10. Thomas Bruneau and Mario Bacalhao, Os Portugueses e a Política: Quatro Anos Depois do 25 de Abril (Lisbon: Meseta, 1978); and Mario Bacalhao, Inquérito à Situação Política (Lisbon: Heptagono, 1980).

11. The distinction is made by Richard Morse, "The Challenge of Ideologies in Latin America," Foreign Policy and Defense Review, vol. V, no. 3 (Winter 1985), pp. 14–23; see also Morse, "Latinoamerica: Hacía una Redefinición de la Ideología," Vuelta [Mexico], vol. XI (July and August 1987).

12. Karl Popper, The Open Society and Its Enemies (Princeton, N.J.: Princeton University Press, 1963).

13. Based on the author's field work in Spain and Portugal in 1987.

14. Manuel Lucena, "The Centralization of the State and of the Society in Portugal since the Revolution" (Instituto de Ciencias Sociais, University of Lisbon, 1985); see also Lawrence Graham, "Bureaucratic Politics and the Problem of Reform of the State Apparatus," in Graham and Douglas L. Wheeler, eds., *In Search of Modern Portugal* (Madison: University of Wisconsin Press, 1983), pp. 223–50.

15. Diamond, Linz, and Lipset, eds., *Democracy in Developing Countries.*

16. Thomas Bruneau, Howard Penniman, and Howard J. Wiarda, eds., *Portugal at the Polls* (Durham, N.C.: Duke University Press, 1988).

17. Based on the author's field work in Spain and Portugal in the summer of 1987.

18. The concepts are derived from Gabriel A. Almond and Sidney Verba, *The Civic Culture* (Princeton, N.J.: Princeton University Press, 1963).

19. See the Fundación FOESSA surveys carried out in the early 1970s and the data and studies done for FOESSA by DATA S.A. under the direction of Amando de Miguel.

20. Dennis Kavanagh, *Political Culture* (London: MacMillan, 1972).

21. W. W. Rostow, *The Stages of Economic Growth* (Cambridge: Cambridge University Press, 1960) and a host of other 1960s books.

22. Ibid.

23. See chapter 6.

24. Howard J. Wiarda, *The Democratic Revolution in Latin America* (New York: The Twentieth Century Fund, forthcoming).

25. See the special issue of the *Foreign Policy and Defense Review,* vol. VI, no. 2 (1986) devoted to southern Europe.

26. Samuel P. Huntington, *Political Order in Changing Societies* (New Haven, Conn.: Yale University Press, 1968).

27. The imagery is from José Ortega y Gasset, *Invertebrate Spain* (New York: Norton, 1937); it implies an institutional support structure or backbone that is extremely fragmented and prone to crumble.

1
The Question of Democracy in Iberia

This study is both a case analysis of corporatism and development in modern Portugal and an exploration with broader implications in the realms of comparative political theory and sociology. It grows out of a long-term scholarly interest in the comparative processes of national development, focused particularly on Latin America. It raises serious questions about the future of democracy in Iberia and Latin America.

Despite the obvious differences between a Paraguay, say, and a Peru, or between Spain and Portugal, there are also some remarkable similarities among the several Latin American and Iberian countries, particularly so as the values, assumptions, and sociopolitical underpinnings of Hispanic civilization, viewed as a culture area, are contrasted with those of North America. Whereas the North American context is thoroughly liberal and Lockean in assumptions, in Latin America and Iberia one is impressed by the continuity and persistence of organicist and corporatist conceptions of society and polity, of elitist, vertical, segmented, hierarchical, patrimonialist structures and practices. Not only has there been little discernible trend in the past toward liberalism patterned on the North American model, but, contrary to our usual social science assumptions, Latin America's and Iberia's own traditional institutions have shown remarkable adaptability to change and modernization.

The Latin American and Iberian systems and their development patterns conform imperfectly at best to the great social science paradigms with which North American students most frequently come in contact. Moreover, a closer examination of the Latin American and Iberian literature and development experience reveals not only that the cultural and political-sociological frameworks for dealing with modernization are distinct but that there is a whole body of political theory and sociological literature "out there" with which North Americans are almost wholly unacquainted. This literature and tradition stand as the Iberic-Latin alternative to the other major paradigms in history and the social sciences with which we are more familiar. What

20

I have termed "the corporative model" helps form the Iberic-Latin-Catholic world's response to the great twentieth-century issues of capitalism, industrialization, alienation, and mass society. It is, furthermore, a tradition of thought and institutions with which we must come to grips if we are to understand the nature of politics and social change in Iberia and Latin America, *and* to understand it on their terms rather than through the biased, often ethnocentric perspectives of North American sociology and political science—hence the idea for a research project in Iberia to get at the historical roots of these differences and the origins of the distinct Iberic-Latin tradition.

There are other currents and concerns running through the project. One involves the distinction between what might be called "natural corporatism" in the Iberic-Latin tradition and monolithic totalitarianism and fascism, as for example in Nazi Germany. Another, already hinted at, involves the appropriateness (or inappropriateness) of so much of what passes for "universal" social science in the study of Iberia and Latin America. A third concerns the degree to which "liberal" North America, and perhaps other modern industrial states, may have also come to approximate in several ways the highly centralized, bureaucratic-authoritarian, and corporatist systems of Iberia and Latin America. Fascinating also are topics such as the role and importance of intellectuals in the Portuguese system, the question of succession in a corporatist-authoritarian polity, and the decline-of-ideology theme as it relates to the discussion of corporatism in Iberia. Finally, there is the possible convergence between liberal, corporatist, and Socialist systems and the question of whether, in terms of regime performance, "systems" matter very much at all.

These are big and important issues; they cannot all be resolved here. The study is organized around the subject area of the theory and practice of Portuguese or Iberic-Latin corporatism, and surely a study of the Portuguese political system in its own right is long overdue. But the study's implications reach beyond Portugal to encompass parallel issues of corporatist development elsewhere in the Iberic-Latin world—and perhaps in our own and other modern nations as well. Though the case study materials here used are drawn from Portugal, the broader theme of corporatist development seen in historical and comparative perspective is of at least equal importance.

Having said what the study is about, we should mention what is left out. Although, like almost everyone living in Portugal at this time (1972–1973), the author was fascinated and preoccupied with the Portuguese colonial situation, this subject is not dealt with in any detail except as it became intertwined with domestic Portuguese politics and insofar as the effort was made to export the corporative

21

system to the "overseas." Nor does the book deal extensively with the politics of the Portuguese opposition groups during the long Salazar-Caetano era, except as their critiques of the corporatist system had implications for this study. Finally, although the author has followed closely the Portuguese Revolution since 1974 and has elsewhere written about it, in this chapter the revolution's chronology is not traced in detail. Instead, in keeping with the main focus of the study, the author has concentrated on showing how easy it was to dismantle the *formal apparatus* of the corporative state, yet how difficult it is to overcome or transcend the nation's historical, *natural* corporatist tradition, and how persistent corporatist forms and institutions are, even in the newer charged and revolutionary context.

This is a serious and scholarly study but it is also likely to be a provocative one. Portugal has become a modern nation over the course of the past several decades, but it became so on the basis of frankly authoritarian and corporatist institutions. Given our frequent assumptions of unilinear development toward democracy and pluralism, that a nation can modernize on an authoritarian-corporatist basis may be surprising to some, that it can do so without seeming to have, at that time, much desire for liberalism and democracy, North American style, may be more controversial. This book argues that corporatism, authoritarianism, and patrimonialism may be characteristic, even permanent features of the Portuguese and Iberic-Latin systems, not just transitory ones doomed to fade away or be superseded in the course of societal evolution. These contentions will doubtless provoke disagreement since they run contrary to popular beliefs and hopes and to many of the accepted "truths" growing out of the development literature and the great systemic models in the social sciences. They also challenge some of the prevailing interpretations of the revolution of 1974 by implicitly questioning just how "democratic" and "liberalizing" that revolution was. The study is purposely provocative in these regards: it was conceived and designed with the expectation of challenging prevailing orthodoxies, and it is hoped that the ideas presented will stimulate discussion of themes too often closed.

This study is hardly an apology for the Salazar regime, but it is not a blanket condemnation of the Estado Novo either. It seeks to strike a balance between the contending interpretations of the Portuguese regime, to be fair and impartial in analyzing both the successes and the failures of the Portuguese corporative experiment. The corporative system of Salazar and Caetano was far more oriented toward social justice than it is often portrayed, and use of the "Fascist" label serves more to perpetuate myths about the regime than to illuminate its actual assumptions and workings. Those long sympathetic to the Portuguese regime, however, will find the corporative system did not work at all in accord with the original theory; contrary to what many, especially Catholic and Latin American writers, thought in the 1930s, the future proved not to lie in Portugal.

Why Portugal, Why Iberia?

A number of the themes mentioned in the opening section demand further explanation. Some of the ideas expressed may be surprising, a few shocking. The main questions are, Why study Portugal at all, other than as a single, heretofore unimportant nation whose internal politics have suddenly become of interest to us; and what is there, if anything, that we can possibly learn from the Portuguese and, more broadly, Iberic-Latin development experience?[1]

These are good questions, and they merit serious consideration. We are used to thinking of Latin America along with the rest of the "emerging," "backward," or "developing" nations, and we think of Spain and Portugal (when we think of them at all) as the retrograde backwaters of Western Europe. It is not only our economic indexes that confine Spain, Portugal, and Latin America to an inferior place, however, but our social, political, and perhaps even moral measures as well. We have tended to consider these nations as twentieth-century anachronisms, countries whose traditional authoritarian, patrimonialist, and corporative political institutions are of another, earlier era, bound inevitably to give way or be transcended under the onslaught of modernizing pressures. Some of this sentiment stems from historical prejudices held by North Americans and northern Europeans ("Europe stops at the Pyrenees"), some undoubtedly originates in racial and ethnic prejudice, and some probably comes from a certain vague hostility that the Protestant and secular nations of the north still direct toward the Catholic cultures of the south. What gives these historical prejudices the cover of academic respectability is that vast body of development literature that, despite numerous individual differences in formulation, continues to posit a unilinear path to modernization. The "developed" society is seen as open, liberal, pluralist, secular, and democratic, a society in fact "just like us," or at least as we thought of ourselves up to the mid-1960s. Viewed in terms of these ostensibly "scientific" and "value-free" but actually heavily normative developmental characteristics, the Iberian and Latin American nations clearly do not measure up.[2]

Intervention in the Dominican Republic in 1965, Vietnam, the decline of U.S. power and influence in the 1970s, reassertive nationalism in other areas of the world, the structural weaknesses of the

23

American economy, Nixon, Watergate, the decline of many of our own institutions, the fact that other countries have surpassed us in both social services and per capita income—these things and others have disillusioned us and sapped our belief in the superiority of American institutions. They have also helped challenge our assumptions of the inevitability of progress, American style, and of the unilinear nature of the development process, with our own and perhaps a select group of Western European nations serving as the model toward which all other nations both aspired and inevitably developed. The recent crisis in American and "Western" institutions has also been influential in forcing social scientists to see more clearly what should have been perceived all along: that there are not one or two but several paths to development and that the particular North American and northern European one is not necessarily universal or inevitable.

By this time it is likely that we do not have the will or power to impose our particular model of society, economy, and polity on the rest of the world. Nor do the models based exclusively on the North American and North-West European development experience any longer carry such credibility as universally valid phenomena. Meanwhile, our own political institutions, which derive from the time of the English Tudors, have recently been challenged as being old-fashioned, outdated, and "underdeveloped."[3] It may surprise us to know that four and a half centuries ago Spanish and Portuguese intellectuals saw the fundamental flaws in the liberal-secular model that the "death of liberalism" scholars are now again bringing to our attention. The question merits more attention than can be given here, but we raise it nonetheless: who are we, after all, to assume that the often prevailing Thomistic-Suárezian-corporatist social and political institutions of Iberia and Latin America are any more dated or less developed than liberal-Lockean ones, any more corrupt or nefarious in an ethical sense, or any less functional or capable of adaptation, responsiveness, and modernization?[4]

The twentieth century, particularly the period between its two world wars, has been a time of intense interest in such "system" issues and of immense competition among contrasting ideologies. Organized Communist, Socialist, corporatist, Fascist, and a number of other major movements emerged. The ideas undergirding these movements had all been present before; what now gave them special importance was the mushrooming collapse of aristocratic society in Britain, Germany, and Austria, World War I and the changes it ushered in, the Russian Revolution, the world market crash, the intense political conflicts of the 1920s and 1930s, the rise of Hitler and

Mussolini, and the events leading to World War II. In this context new and challenging social and political forces grew while old ones struggled to survive, and various means of combining them were attempted. To moderates and Catholics, socialism, especially as practiced in Stalin's Russia, was totally unacceptable; the depression seemed to indicate that liberalism and capitalism were no longer viable; and the totalitarian excesses of National Socialism were also repugnant. To comprehend the impact of corporatism as an alternative "great ism," particularly in the Catholic southern European and Latin American context, one must try to place oneself in the collapsing, disintegrating context of the 1930s and to understand corporatism's popularity in the light of what seemed the unacceptability of the other alternatives.

Full-fledged corporatist regimes came to power not only in Portugal, Spain, Brazil, Argentina, and a number of other Latin American countries but also in Austria, Poland, and France. Corporative institutions or "mixed" corporative systems were also established in one form or another in *all* the other Iberian and Latin American nations and in countries as diverse as Belgium, Holland, Italy, Norway, Sweden, and the United States (such institutions as the Tennessee Valley Authority, the National Labor Relations Board, and the Works Progress Administration all derived in part from corporatist inspiration). The Nazi regime incorporated some corporative aspects, but these had been shunted aside by 1936 in favor of the totalitarian behemoth. Italian fascism was closer to the Iberic-Latin (perhaps Mediterranean) model, but corporatism in Italy was consistently a dependent variable, subordinate to Mussolini's personal ambitions, the concept of the all-powerful state, and Italian great-power pretensions. Aside from these two "deviant cases," there were numerous other corporatist institutions and systems that were not only humane and socially just but also oriented toward national modernization. Our understanding of these systems, however, has been neglected and frequently obscured by our mistakenly lumping all of them together under the "Fascist" label and by the common assumption that corporatism's time, historically, had already come—and passed.[5] But what did become of all those corporatist systems and institutions of the interwar period; were they viable, how were they formed, and how did they work; what are their ideological underpinnings and assumptions; how have they merged and perhaps converged with other institutions and ideologies; what are we to make of the 1960s and 1970s revival of corporatist systems in Brazil, Chile, Peru, and elsewhere and of the new wave of academic interest in them; and what are the implications of corporatism as an alternative model for national development? These are some of the questions probed in this analysis.

Corporatist Traditions

The corporative tradition of the late nineteenth and especially the twentieth centuries is one of which we are almost wholly ignorant, or we are so hostile toward it that we dismiss it without further consideration. The fact is, nonetheless, that corporatist theory and organization form the foundation on which virtually all the labor laws and social security systems of the Iberian and Latin American nations are based, through which labor and industrial relations are structured, and on which the majority of the Iberic-Latin social and political systems are grounded, either de jure or de facto.[6] Corporatism and the corporatist tradition are a "natural," almost inherent part of Iberic-Latin political culture. Although the constitutional forms are often liberal and republican, patterned after British parliamentarism or U.S. representative democracy, the operating realities in Iberia and Latin America continue to be influenced heavily by both formal corporatist structures and, more important, organicist, vertical, hierarchical, and patrimonialist conceptions that lie at the heart of a broader, deeper corporatist tradition.

There is abundant literature on corporatism in French, Italian, German, Spanish, and Portuguese, but almost none in English.[7] Corporatism is a very old concept of state and society, but as a theory it never gained much importance in North American political thought. This relates to the fact that corporatism lies outside the mainstreams of the Anglo-American tradition and the liberal-Lockean ethos. John Quincy Adams and John C. Calhoun have both been claimed for corporatism, but their concepts made little dent in the prevailing individualism and liberalism of North America.[8] In the Continental systems, however, and particularly in the southern, Catholic, Latin nations of Europe and America, with their powerful hierarchical and agrarian-feudal traditions, corporatism found a fertile, lasting, and perhaps permanent breeding ground.[9]

Corporatism and Fascism. It is important to distinguish between corporatism in the Iberic-Latin tradition and monolithic fascism as practiced in Nazi Germany. "Fascism" is one of those terms that through widespread common usage has lost almost all analytic meaning; it has become a label of disapproval rather than a precise term of analysis. Corporatism was so discredited by its sometime association with Nazism that we tend to forget that Brazil, Portugal, Belgium, and even Spain and Italy practiced a form of corporatism that was fundamentally different from that of Nazi Germany. In the Iberic-Latin context the "Fascist" label has served often to obscure rather than assist our understanding of these systems, especially as the term implies a blanket condemnation. Nor is it true, as the North American and northern European literature frequently emphasizes, that "the Latins just aren't up to it," that corporatism in such diverse nations as Mexico, Spain, Portugal, Argentina, Peru, or Brazil is merely a "backward" and "less-developed" version of German and Italian fascism. Of course there is some overlap between the two concepts, and clearly what such classic writers as Orwell, Burnham, Hemingway, and Ortega y Gasset had to say in the 1930s regarding the looming threat of corporate-fascist-technocratic organization must weigh heavily upon us. In this study, furthermore, we shall be showing how a regime born in a corporatist tradition of concern for social justice and limited government ("corporatism of association" rather than "state corporatism") became an increasingly Fascist one. But the distinction between the two forms must still be kept in mind, and there are some fundamental differences. The fact is that in Iberia and Latin America we are not dealing universally with Fascist (although they may be corporatist) systems or with retrograde versions of a single "Fascist" type. Rather, in the corporatist tradition we are treating a distinctive, alternative, and in many ways peculiarly Iberic-Latin way of coping with and managing the great modern issues of industrialization, mass society, and accelerated social change. This tradition deserves to be examined with care.[10]

Not only have significant development and modernization been achieved in Iberia and Latin America within the corporatist framework, but we should remember also that corporatism, like liberalism or socialism, may take a variety of forms, both as between nations and within a single nation over time. There are humane forms as well as bureaucratic-authoritarian ones, pluralistic types as well as autocratic ones. There are modern, progressive, Christian-Democratic examples as well as earlier Catholic-conservative ones. Corporatism may be fused with liberalism, as in Colombia, or it may take a more Socialist or syndicalist form, as in Bosch's Dominican Republic, Goulart's Brazil, Allende's Chile, and perhaps the revolutionary regime that came to power in Portugal in 1974. Although it adds somewhat to the terminological confusion, we must recognize that corporatism may exist in diverse forms and combinations. At the least, therefore, we must examine closely the several national corporatist variations and begin to evaluate them, not through liberal lenses or the biased perspectives of North American social science, but within their own

27

corporate contexts. We shall also be trying to show the factors that account for these variations, the evolution of corporative institutions within a single nation, the relations of corporatism and socioeconomic development, and the dynamic, societal processes by which a simple and traditionalist corporative system may become a modern and complex one.[11]

That is where the study of Portugal enters in. For Portugal was the "purest" of the Iberic-Latin corporative systems, the only one of the numerous corporative experiments of the 1920s and 1930s to have survived into the 1970s—and perhaps beyond. In Portugal a vast body of corporative literature was elaborated, and the structures and institutions of the corporative state were strongly institutionalized. For a time in the 1930s the Portuguese corporative system was *the* model to which many Latin American states looked for inspiration. Moreover, the Portuguese consciously cultivated corporatism as *the* Iberic-Latin alternative to liberalism and socialism. While they were willing to concede that liberal democracy was appropriate for the Anglo-Saxon countries, they saw their own history and institutions as attuned to a different tradition. In Argentina, Bolivia, Brazil, the Dominican Republic, Ecuador, Mexico, Panama, Spain, and elsewhere throughout Europe and the Western Hemisphere, similar sentiments often prevailed and various kinds of manifestly corporative experiments were tried. But these never became full-fledged corporative systems as Portugal did, and in the post-World War II period they exhibited increasingly mixed and overlapping patterns of corporatism, liberalism, and sometimes socialism or syndicalism. Portugal too has by now experienced the superimposition of these other philosophies onto its older corporatist tradition, and since the revolution of 1974 many of the formal corporative institutions associated with the former regime have been dismantled. But for a long time Portugal was the most complete and fully elaborated corporative system extant, and as such it remained a unique social and political laboratory for looking at the "ism" that Manoïlesco fifty years ago predicted would be the dominant one of the twentieth century.[12] Moreover, given the remarkable persistence of a broader corporatist-patrimonialist political culture and tradition in Iberia and Latin America where, despite the recent overlaps of other forms and even some revolutionary restructuring, the corporative assumptions and modes may still be dominant (although now altered fundamentally by pluralist or syndicalist conceptions), it is instructive to look at the Portuguese experience with corporatism not only because it is interesting and significant in its own right but also because of what it tells us about the workings of other corporatist-inspired political systems.[13]

The Meanings of 'Corporatism.' Implicit in the above discussion are two meanings of the word *corporatism*. This distinction is critical, but in common usage it is often blurred and has led to a great deal of misunderstanding regarding "the corporative model." The first meaning refers to the consciously and manifestly "corporative" ideology and institutions of the 1920s and 1930s. This is what most people have in mind when they think of corporatism. Corporatism in this sense derives from an ideology articulated in the last half of the nineteenth century, most often Catholic but sometimes secular in origin, which stressed an organicist-solidarist conception of the state and society (government is natural, not evil—it must be unified and harmonized, not checked and balanced), in which governing bodies are chosen not by the direct vote of individuals (as in liberalism) but by indirect election by professional, institutional, social, or economic groups, based on a system of functional representation. This meant the organization of all sectors of the economy, both capital and labor, into exclusive, monopolistic groups and the integration of these groups into a hierarchy of syndicates and representative bodies culminating at the top in a series of "corporations" (hence the term *corporatism*) for each of the nation's major social, political, and economic sectors (government, industry, armed forces, agriculture, religion, and so on).[14] If such structuring was carried out voluntarily and at the grassroots level, it was called corporatism of association; carried out under government control and direction, as fairly consistently proved to be the case, it meant authoritarian "state corporatism." Within this framework a great number of distinct national corporatist systems and representational schemes were possible.

In theory at least, the various corporative plans of the 1920s and 1930s were aimed at restoring unity to strife-torn nations, providing harmony rather than class conflict, guaranteeing representation to all sectors, providing for social justice, ensuring collective bargaining, ameliorating the alienation of modern mass man, and ensuring that the national public interest would be served instead of some narrower sectoral or partisan interest. In the context of the interwar period corporatism struck a tremendously responsive chord, particularly in the Latin-Catholic nations of southern Europe and America, and virtually every one established one or another corporatist-inspired agency or body (most often the labor and social assistance ministries but sometimes also legislatures and councils of state based in whole or in part on corporatist functional representation), often with elaborate accompanying legislation. With the war, the Nazi atrocities, Nuremberg, and the discrediting of all such "integralist," "corporatist," or "Fascist" experiments (the terms were used interchangeably), how-

29

ever, all these nations (with Spain and Portugal the sole exceptions) divested themselves of their corporatist philosophies, or at least changed the labels of the institutions operating under that name.

Here is where the second definition of corporatism enters in, however, for while in many formerly corporate nations the labels were changed, actual practice remained much the same. The system of corporate sectoral and functional representation, of bureaucratic-patrimonialist state authority, of hierarchy and centralization, of an elite-directed patron-client system, of a predominantly Catholic-organicist society and political culture, and of an essentially mercantilist and state capitalist economy was often retained, in whole or in part; but "for the English (or maybe the Americans or the world) to see," it was rebaptized under "progressive," "populist," "liberal," or "neo-democratic" ("justicialist" in Argentina) labels. Moreover, most of these same practices and institutions have a history reaching back not just to the 1920s or late nineteenth century but hundreds of years to the very origins of Iberian civil society and the state system. This tradition will not be altered overnight regardless of the labels used or the substitution of one ruling clique for another. Although other terms might also be appropriately used (the concept of the "organic state," for example), it is this dominant, historical set of values and institutions in Iberic-Latin society and polity that I have referred to by the shorthand terms "the corporative tradition" or "the corporative model."[15]

This tradition and the undergirding political culture of Catholic, patrimonialist, organicist, corporatist values and institutions remain far stronger than any ephemeral "ism." Indeed, as we shall argue, the consciously "corporative" experiments in Spain and Portugal beginning in the 1930s were not a sudden apparition but represented a logical, sequential, twentieth-century extension and elaboration of an older, deeper, "natural" corporatist tradition that had long governed the structure of political institutions and behavior and continues in important ways to do so today. This also helps explain why the corporative solution to "the social question," to the demands of an emerging labor movement, was so strongly favored throughout the Iberic-Latin world, for it was in accord both with prevailing traditions and with the preservation of elitist-patrimonialist hegemony. It also helps make Portugal an interesting case since it provides a veritable "living ideal type," to use Philippe Schmitter's phrase, for observing the overlap and fusion (as well as the later dysfunctional aspects) of the historical corporative tradition with the modern practice of "corporatism." In one form or another the effort to adapt the historical corporatist traditions to the newer institutional requisites of twentieth-century national organization, administration, public policy, rising social demands, and now democracy remains perhaps the most pressing problem with which all the Iberian and Latin American nations must cope.[16]

The two meanings of *corporatism* hence come together in the study of Portugal. We shall here be concerned not only with the workings and evolution of the Portuguese corporative state from the 1930s through the revolution of 1974 (and beyond) but also with showing how these twentieth-century corporative developments related to (or eventually proved out of accord with) Portugal's historical, *natural* corporatist traditions. We shall be concerned with how the two overlap and commingle and with how the Portuguese state and society have, under corporative auspices, modernized, failed at modernization, or modernized in a skewed pattern. In tracing these developments we shall be drawing out the differences between corporative theory, the ideal-typical corporative model, *and* the actual practice of Portuguese corporatism. This implies also that if corporatism and the Portuguese corporative system are to be criticized, such criticism must be on that model's and society's own terms and in their own context. Comparisons with other systems may also be made, but clearly Portuguese corporatism cannot be condemned (if that is our final conclusion) on the basis of some outside and foreign model bearing little relation to Portuguese culture and history, or by its "failure" to live up to liberal-democratic standards (never its intention until recently; on the contrary, Portugal had explicitly rejected the liberal model). Rather, the Portuguese corporative system can most appropriately be evaluated by considering what preceded it in Portugal's own history, by what succeeded it, and by the realistic choices open to it in the course of the corporative state's own evolution.

Dynamics of Corporatism

These comments imply further that there are dynamics of choice and change within authoritarian-corporative systems, that bureaucratic statism does not rule out the give-and-take of politics and the interest conflict that is part and parcel of it, that the "corporative model" of Iberia and Latin America may be far more flexible and adaptable in responding to political and social pressures than we ordinarily think, and that these systems may, on their terms, be as efficient, rational, and functional in dealing with modernization as the liberal-democratic polities of the North.[17] Such statements fly in the face of our common assumptions regarding Iberia and Latin America, but such assumptions are precisely what this study aims to challenge. For as stifling bureaucracy, centralization, privilege, a certain de facto corporatism, and officially sanctioned immoralism seen to have grown in our own society, we have, we hope, become a bit more modest in regard to our inherent moral and political superiority. These shortcomings have also served to stimulate a reexamination of the American model and of the assumption that liberal democracy U.S.-style occupies a higher, more "developed" plateau and that somehow we know what is right for the rest of the world. Is it in fact the case that the liberal-democratic or social-democratic model is appropriate for or even desired by other nations cast in a different political-cultural framework? Is it not arrogant for us to impose—as we did so often in the 1960s, justified by so much of the social science literature—a set of particularistic, liberal-Lockean or New Deal institutions on culture areas where they do not fit? If we are to cease being the policeman of the world, is it not time also for our social scientists to cease presuming to be its philosopher-kings? And as American society seems to be wracked by crime, conflict, crisis, and a certain national unraveling, would it not be interesting to examine a society that has undergone a parallel experience of modernization, but apparently without sacrificing the sense of community, personalism, moral values, and national purpose which we seem to have lost and whose passing we now lament?

The practice of corporatism in Portugal, as it turned out, proved inauspicious for demonstrating the effectiveness and humaneness of the distinct Iberic-Latin development process. Even Portugal had its advantages, however, and unconventional though it may seem to North Americans and northern Europeans, a case can be made that, in comparison with both the liberal and the Socialist alternatives, a number of the Iberic-Latin systems, founded upon corporatist principles, come out not altogether badly on a variety of indexes of participation, social justice, and the management of the twentieth-century change process. These indexes would of course have to be more precisely spelled out, and doubtless some of them would differ from those social scientists have most often used to measure "development." But perhaps terms like *participation* and even *democratization* mean different things in different cultural contexts, and maybe the indexes of electoral participation used by North American social scientists are themselves culture bound. Moreover, given the growing realization that the United States has not coped very well with, much less solved, its fundamental problems of poverty, racism, unemployment, alienation, inadequate human services, and the like, it may be that the Iberic-Latin model and practice of dealing with some of these same issues contain lessons from which we can learn. These comments are not meant to minimize Iberia's and Latin America's own problems—the poverty and the immense social gaps—but to say that their way of fusing the traditional and the modern through essentially corporative as opposed to liberal means, of accommodating to change while at the same time preserving what is considered valuable in the past, of adapting to modernization without being overwhelmed by it, may offer instruction concerning our own developmental dilemmas and institutional malaise.

A Convergence of the Corporative and the Liberal

These remarks lead to a related theme, the increasing convergence of the corporative and the liberal polities, and perhaps the Socialist ones as well. Spain, Portugal, and the nations of Latin America have increasingly taken on the characteristics of modern systems. This means not just smog, traffic jams, and pollution but also the large-scale organizational paraphernalia of complex, highly developed states: planning offices, regulatory agencies, technical offices, elaborate social welfare systems, price and wage commissions, agencies for worker-management consultation and corepresentation, and mass associations for nearly everyone: workers, elites, professionals, women, students, and farmers. They are no longer the simple "banana republics" of *New Yorker* cartoons and popular stereotypes but complex, highly differentiated and rationalized, *modern* systems. Although many of these more recent changes have come under corporative auspices, one could see in them certain "liberal," "pluralist," and, in their more advanced forms, syndicalist and Socialist features. But while Iberia and Latin America have in a sense been "liberalized," we have undoubtedly been "corporatized." Many Iberian and Latin American scholars familiar with their northern neighbors and looking at the trends there toward increased centralization and bureaucratization, the incorporations of officially sanctioned and monopolistic interest groups into the administrative state apparatus, price and wage commissions with government intervenors, compulsory collective bargaining, corepresentation, and functionally representative organs at all levels, make a cogent case that, despite the liberal and social-democratic labels, the nations of North America and northern Europe have since the war been practicing and evolving increasingly toward a disguised form of corporatism.[18] In the United States, although most liberals hailed the move, the regulation of wages, prices, and production administratively and from above, as in Phase 1 of Nixon's economic controls, instead of through direct bargaining from below, was unheard of previously in peacetime America. The government's setting of prices, wages, and production quotas had long been characteristic of the corporative systems of Iberia and Latin America, not of a liberal laissez-faire polity; and although his comment was an exaggeration, George Meany's cry of "Fascism!" when the Wage and Price Board was first announced was not altogether inaccurate. Canada and other modern industrial nations have recently experienced similar corporatizing trends.

If there is something to this convergence theory, if bigness, bureaucracy, and technocratic state administration of industrial and labor relations are the hallmarks of the modern systems rather than the political "isms" of the past, then we must ask ourselves whether ideology counts for much any more, whether "systems" matter, and if they do, how and in what sense. We know that there has been a certain decline of ideology in other modern nations, that liberalism and socialism may well have lost some of their appeal;[19] is there any reason to think that, as modernization goes forward in the Iberic-Latin countries, the same phenomenon will not occur regarding corporatism? Perhaps such a decline has already occurred. Or, in a related vein, is this the wrong question to ask? Is it true that the corporatist ideology and political culture determined the nature and structure of the Portuguese Estado Novo, or was it rather such structural variables as class and power that determined the direction Portuguese corporatism took? Is corporatism the dependent variable, and are the elite-bourgeois society and authoritarian state established by Salazar the independent ones? Or is it the case that both sets of factors were important and interrelated in shaping the direction of Portuguese corporative development? Answers to these questions are critical both for understanding the Portuguese regime and for looking at other systems similarly fashioned in the corporatist framework.[20]

Corporatism as a political tradition, ideology, and mode of sociopolitical organization must be taken seriously and examined with care. For just as we take liberalism and socialism seriously, we must also examine this other great "ism" in a serious way. Going further, we may say that corporatism is *not just* a part of some ideological superstructure or facade, a "confidence trick" played upon the workers (as was the case with corporatism in Italy), nor was it merely a smoke screen to disguise the power ambitions of the Portuguese elites and thus an instrument of class oppression (although, as we shall see, it became that also). The corporatist ideology and political structures, this study clearly shows, had some autonomy and existence of their own; in addition, in the broader political-cultural sense in which the term is also used, corporatism may have been among the most important determinants of how the system actually worked. Portuguese businessmen and workers took corporatism seriously indeed; the same was true for a whole generation of university students and government officials. An entire national system was erected on the corporatist edifice, and much of the corporative system was alive and functioning right to the end. Although certainly there were numerous gaps between theory and practice, the same could be said for liberalism and socialism, and in any case the gaps themselves tell us much about how the system worked or failed to work. It is also the case that corporatism was only tardily and partially implemented, that the "corporative complex" was gradually shunted aside until it was no longer at the base of the entire national system, and that some of the main centers of power in Portugal lay outside the corporative system. All that is also true in varying degree of the other great "isms," and again, the reasons for this and the processes by which these developments occurred are what interest us here. Had the corporatist experiment run its course by the 1960s, and, if so, why? And how did that parallel or diverge from the evolution of other types of systems? The study of the Portuguese corporative regime helps answer these questions—if at the same time we recognize that corporatism is but one part of a broader Iberic-Latin political culture and tradition and, similarly, that the corporatist institutions established in Portugal in the 1930s must be studied in the light of other institutions (secret police, armed forces, the instruments of dictatorship, state capitalism, and class rule) that gained equal, perhaps greater importance as explanatory variables.[21]

There are two other themes noted earlier that deserve brief mention. The first, not intrinsic to the main arguments of the book but intriguing nonetheless, concerns the role of intellectuals in power. Not only was the Portuguese corporative system designed by intellectuals, it was also staffed and run in large measure by them. Perhaps in few other nations have intellectuals and sheer intellectual brilliance (as long as it was within the corporatist tradition) been so rewarded by high-level government posts and decision-making influence as in the *catedrátocracia* of Portugal. The fact that the system was implemented by the same intellectuals who designed it makes the huge gap between theory and practice especially intriguing. It also suggests some interesting hypotheses as to why Portugal under a particular group of corporatist intellectuals remained locked into a discredited and increasingly dysfunctional form of corporatism at a time when similarly cast corporatist regimes under more pragmatic leadership (Brazil and Spain) cast off their corporatist ideological baggage or skillfully updated and modernized their systems while staying within the broadly corporatist tradition.[22]

A test of any system and ideology, furthermore, lies in its ability to adjust, survive, and persist in a changing national context and after the demise of its first-generation leadership. Hence our concern is also with the transfer of leadership following the end of the longest one-man rule of the twentieth century, with the post-Salazar regime of Marcello Caetano and his efforts to preserve and reinvigorate the corporative regime while at the same time loosening it somewhat and modernizing and updating it.[23] This subject takes on particular poignancy in the light of the revolution of 1974, the formal repudiation of "corporatism" as practiced by Salazar and Caetano, and the question of whether a new national "ism" will take its place or whether the corporatist tradition will be perpetuated in a new and different form.

The questions raised here for discussion are large, and they speak to some critical issues of social change, political development, and national modernization, not just in Portugal but throughout the Iberic-Latin world. By an interesting inversion of priorities, philosophies, and self-inspection in recent years, they have also come to have relevance to our own time and place.[24] The theme of the "Latin-Americanization" or "corporatization" of the United States no longer seems so farfetched.[25] But as the "purest" and most complete of corporative systems, the Portuguese experience offers abundant illustrative materials as to the special, distinctive character of corporatist development in Iberia and Latin America—and of its implications. Some of those implications may also carry lessons for us.

The Corporative Model

The nations of Iberia and Latin America have long been woefully misunderstood.[26] Although geographically a part of Europe, Spain and Portugal are often culturally and politically considered apart from it; Latin America is frequently lumped with the "non-Western areas." But in their Iberian origins these nations, including the so-called Indian countries of Bolivia, Guatemala, and Peru, are an integral part of a dominantly Western tradition, fragments of that tradition, perhaps, in Louis Hartz's terms, but still deeply and profoundly Western—and, many Iberians argue, with their powerful Roman and Christian traditions, perhaps more "Western" even than the rest of Europe and North America. Nor with their long histories as independent sovereignties do they fit the "new nations" syndrome. And despite the efforts of a few intellectuals to identify them with the cause of "third worldism," few Iberian or Latin American nations have very close ties with the nations of Asia and Africa, and when they do, they like to think of themselves not as equals but as leaders and teachers of the third world in accord with their more developed condition, as bridges between it and the West.[27]

It is not only the classificatory schemes that have proved problematic, however, but the models and paradigms used for explaining Iberic-Latin development as well. The Iberic-Latin systems fail to correspond very well to Rostow's "stages of growth" or to the developmental paradigm of Almond and Coleman on the one hand or the Marxian categories on the other. Socioeconomic "modernization" and political "development" have not gone forward hand in hand, one "stage" has sometimes stubbornly refused to be replaced by another, the usual developmental correlates do not correlate very well, and the pluralism, middle-class consensus, and inevitable democratization that supposedly lie at the higher reaches of the development process have not always necessarily taken shape. At the same time, the Marxian paradigm has not accounted very well for either the modernizing tendencies of the traditional elites or the continued conservativeness of labor, peasants, and even students; it does not help us understand much about the "class" behavior of such institutions as the army or the church; nor does it explain adequately why such commonly middle-sector-dominated nations as Brazil, Peru, Mexico, Portugal, or Spain should go in such distinct ideological directions. Class has not proved to be the mirror reflection of socioeconomic history, nor can the political, ideological, or organizational structures of the Iberic-Latin nations be neatly subordinated to some supposed class determinants. The fact that few of these systems correspond very well to the major categories and models used in the social sciences helps account for the many bad books written about them. For we only weakly perceive the Iberic-Latin development process, and when we have sought a better comprehension, we have usually applied to the area a model derived from our own developmental experience that fits poorly, if at all, in the Iberic-Latin ambience.[28]

This brief critique of some of the conventional wisdom regarding the nations of Iberia and Latin America serves as the main point of departure for this section: namely, that there are some unique aspects to the processes of sociopolitical change in the Iberic-Latin tradition. Because of their history and antecedents, the Iberic-Latin nations are subject to special imperatives of interpretation and require a model of sociopolitical change derived from the actual Iberic-Latin experience. The Iberic-Latin model, however, is one that seldom finds expression in our studies of the history of political thought or the literature of social and political change. It is one of the arguments of this study that the corporative model helps provide that needed framework, a distinctive, even *fourth* world of development that has not yet received the attention it merits.

Historical Influences on Iberia

The major historical influences on the Iberian mother countries of Spain and Portugal were probably the Roman system of law and governance, Christianity and the Thomistic tradition, feudalism and the medieval guild system, and the centuries-long reconquest of the peninsula from the Moors. Roman law gave Spain and Portugal their legal and political foundations; Christianity provided them not only a religious and moral base but also a lasting system of natural law and a powerfully unifying cultural ingredient; and feudalism, pa- trimonialism, and the guild system brought forth some characteristic forms of social and economic organization, while the crusade against the Moorish "infidels" gave religion a more militant outlook and shaped the Iberian pattern of walled-enclave cities, military orders and special privileges, and class-caste stratification that predominates today. These traditions came together and perhaps reached their apogee in the conquest of the Americas.[29]

We can better understand Iberic-Latin development if we view that culture area as founded upon traditional feudal, semifeudal, and patrimonial institutions rather than "modern" ones. In fifteenth- and sixteenth-century Spain and Portugal and in the colonies they estab- lished in the New World, the dominant institutions were an essen- tially feudal-patrimonial system of land ownership, power, and lord- peasant relations; an absolutist, hierarchical, and centralizing struc- ture of political authority; a similarly authoritarian and hierarchical church structure that buttressed and reinforced the state concept; a social order divided vertically in terms of its various corporate units (church, army, nobility, universities, municipalities, and the like) and horizontally according to a rigid system of estates, rank orders, sta- tuses, and supposedly natural or God-given inequalities; an economy based on monopoly, mercantilism, and privileged grants emanating from the highest authority; and an educational system and intellec- tual tradition based on absolute truth, deductive reasoning, and scho- lasticism. Forged and crystallized during and after the crusade against the Moors, these traditions had been firmly established in Spain and Portugal by the end of the fifteenth century, and beginning in 1492 they were transferred to the Americas, where they persisted and received a new lease on life.[30]

The isolation of Latin America from the outside world during the next four centuries, as well as the isolation of Spain and Portugal from the rest of Europe, helped to lock the Iberic-Latin nations into this historical pattern and made their development pattern distinctive. The Iberic-Latin nations were largely bypassed by the great revolutions associated with the making of the modern world. The Protestant Reformation, the rise of capitalism, the Enlightenment and the growth of science, the emergence of social pluralism and of a dominant middle class, the concept of separation of powers and of representative government, the Industrial Revolution and its many-faceted ramifications—all of these had little effect on the nations of Iberia and Latin America. They remained cut off and isolated from these modernizing currents, at the margin of the ideological trends and sociopolitical movements emerging elsewhere in Europe, fragments of an Iberic-European tradition dating from approximately 1500 with a political culture that was two-class, authoritarian, elitist, patrimonial, hierarchical, and Catholic to its core. Moreover, it was not just an accident that the Iberic-Latin nations were formed in this pattern and experienced only weakly those secular and liberalizing forces taking place to the north; rather, it often involved a conscious, careful filtering or rejection of that route to modernization, an opting instead for a path that was slower, to be sure, but that enabled the Iberic-Latin nations to adapt to change while preserving the traditions and institutions considered valuable from the past.[31]

Given the times and circumstances, it should not be surprising that the Iberic-Latin nations should be structured on these lines. What *is* remarkable is the durability and persistence of these patterns and structures to the present. For despite the recent accelerated onslaught of modernization, the traditional political culture and institutions have proved amazingly permeable and accommodative, bending to change rather than being overwhelmed by it, absorbing what was useful in modernization but rejecting the rest, and thus in many respects retaining their traditional essence even under the pressures of social forces set loose by twentieth-century changes.[32]

Main Currents of Iberic-Latin Corporatism

In chapter 2, we shall be tracing in more detail the sociopolitical underpinnings of the Portuguese corporative system, but it is useful here to outline some of the main currents of this tradition to set it in proper perspective. In the realm of political thought, for example, while modern political analysis beginning with Machiavelli was to lead to the glorification of the accomplished fact and of political pragmatism, secularism, and materialism, Iberic-Latin culture retained at its base a sense of moral idealism, of philosophical certainty, and of a Catholic-corporate-unified-organic view of state and society. The Iberic-Latin conception derived from Cicero and Seneca, from Augustine and Aquinas, and from the traditional legal precepts of medieval times.[33]

In pursuing paths other than those of Protestant or secular thought, the great Spanish thinkers of the sixteenth century such as Suárez laid the foundations for a modern theory of the Christian state and corporative society. In contrast to the separation of politics from morality, which dates from Machiavelli and which *we* usually take to be the beginning of modern political analysis, the Iberic-Latin ideal remained the organic integration of the ethical and sociopolitical spheres. Suárez was able to fuse the older Thomistic conception and the system of juridical estates derived from Spanish feudal and customary law with the newer concept of absolute, state-building, royal authority.[34]

Absolutism. Iberic-Latin political culture, therefore, continued to rest on a philosophy of absolutism, of a world governed by divine authority, of a hierarchy of laws and estates, and of a distrust of popular democratic rule. Government remained feudal, aristocratic, and patrimonial, dominated by "natural" elites, and with the rights and obligations of all groups defined in elaborate charters. The prevailing view of the state and society was organic and conservative and rejected liberal individualism and the materialistic and secular conceptions that accompanied development in northern Europe. Power remained centered in the crown, around which all national life swirled; there was no conception of separation of powers or of authority resting ultimately in the people. Rather, a unified, monistic structure was required to keep the peace and to maintain the natural order. The king could not rule as a tyrant, however, and he was obligated to respect the fundamental rights of the nation's component corporate groups. This fundamental sixteenth-century pattern remained dominant not only through the colonial and imperial periods of the seventeenth and eighteenth centuries but also, obviously restructured and updated in various ways, during the emergent republicanism of the nineteenth century and even in the accelerated industrialization of the twentieth. Indeed, it is the remarkable persistence of this dominant pattern even today, now further adapted to account for contemporary pressures and requirements, that makes the Iberic-Latin development experience so distinctive.[35]

Sociopolitical Structures. In the sociopolitical realm similar patterns prevail. A good starting point is to picture Iberic-Latin society as organized horizontally in terms of sharply defined hierarchies and a persistent and overriding two-class structure, and vertically in terms of a variety of sharply segmented corporate elites and *intereses* (interest associations). The crown—and, now, the central state apparatus—controls, manages, and regulates all these sectors and components. Each corporate unit as well as each "class" in the hierarchy has its own responsibilities, status, and special privileges, corresponding to natural law and God's just ordering of the universe. Men are expected to accept their station in life; there can thus be little questioning of the system and little social mobility. The crown (or premier or president) rests at the apex of the sociopolitical pyramid, employing its near monopoly of financial affairs as well as its supreme authority to grant or withhold legal recognition to regulate the corporate group life that swirls beneath it. These units, hence, tend to relate to each other bureaucratically through the central administration, rather than through direct negotiations. The Iberic-Latin model of sociopolitical organization is essentially a patrimonialist one where the wealth of the realm and the groups and individuals that make it up are all a part of the ruler's private domain.[36]

The nineteenth century brought on a severe legitimacy crisis in the political realm, through the influx of republican ideas and the breaking of the ties between colonies and metropoles. Few sharp changes occurred in the socioeconomic underpinnings or the dominant political culture, however. Indeed, in many ways the independence movements in Latin America were conservative movements, designed to preserve and perpetuate the system of corporate privilege against the democratizing currents then at work. Republicanism called for some new institutional arrangements, but in essence the hierarchical patterns of class and caste, the system of *fueros* ("rights," *foros* in Portuguese) and corporate privilege, the seigniorial system of patron-client relations, the dominant Catholic political culture, and the patrimonialist political structure were in the main unchanged in their fundamentals by nineteenth-century trends.[37]

Nineteenth- and Twentieth-Century Changes. Considerable change and some modernization could and did take place within this framework; however, these changes were accompanied by only limited shifts in the basic structure of power and society. Thus, in the late nineteenth and early twentieth centuries the rising merchant and business elements were co-opted into the prevailing elitist system, and the traditional *hacienda* began to give way to the capitalistic farm or plantation, but without the fundamental patron-client relations of the *hacienda* system being very much altered. From roughly 1910 on, the emerging middle sectors began to be assimilated in a similar

41

fashion; rather than forming a distinguishable "middle class" with an ideology and consciousness of its own, however, these middle elements aped upper-class ways, subscribed to the elitist values (such as disdain for manual labor), and thus helped preserve the dominant two-class system instead of paving the way for a more pluralist and multi-class one. By the 1930s—and this is largely what the manifestly corporative experiments of that time were all about—it had become the turn of the working class. They too were absorbed into the prevailing structure through the creation of corporatist-inspired, officially sponsored and directed syndicate organizations. By the 1960s it was the peasants' turn to be assimilated, largely through "agrarian reform" programs and the extension of the labor laws of the 1930s and 1940s to the rural areas. In this fashion all the rising social forces have been integrated, in varying degrees, into the prevailing pattern; new corporate and institutional pillars have been repeatedly added onto the original structure consisting of church, army, nobility, university, and the like. But with all these modifications, the basic order of society and polity remained intact.[38]

Change in the Iberic-Latin context has thus not often been "fundamental" in the Marxian or Weberian sense (that is, implying a revolutionary transformation of one class to another or the replacement of one form of authority by another) as it has been a gradual, mediating accommodation of the forms and labels of modern industrial civilization to a political tradition that is still in essence creole-feudal, patrimonialist, and Iberic-Catholic. Numerous adjustments have been made and some new social groups have been assimilated, but this has taken place under the guidance, tutelage, and containment of the older power brokers. The traditional structure of the Iberic-Latin nations, thus, far from having been rigid and impenetrable, has had sufficient flexibility for a good many of its component parts to be updated, but without a swift and radical process of "modernization."[39]

The contemporary change process is consonant with that older historic tradition. In keeping with the Catholic-Thomistic conception (although this conception has by now been largely secularized), society and the state in the Iberic-Latin context are still thought of as an organic whole with a profoundly moral purpose. Attempts are thus made, through personal and family ties, the *compadrazgo* (kinship), and personal identification with the leader, as well as an increasingly elaborate system of corporate associations, to construct various links so that a sense of belonging is engendered, alienation is reduced, and all are integrated into the prevailing structure. Branch associations and official syndicates now exist for all major groups in the society. The national system is, hence, conceived of in terms of the family metaphor, implying strong benevolent leadership, assigned and accepted duties, paternalism, a purpose greater than the sum of its individual parts. The state and its myriad agencies now serve as the agent of national integration, holding together the diverse groups, guilds, and *intereses* functioning in the national polity and serving as the filter and regulator through which the legitimacy of new social and political forces is recognized and through which they are admitted into the system.[40]

Power remains concentrated in the executive, more specifically in the *person* of the president, and in the bureaucratic-patrimonialist state machinery. The president is thus viewed as the personification of the nation with a direct identification with and knowledge of the "general will" of the people. The bureaucracy serves to dispense the available favors and privileges to the deserving. The traditional patron-client relationship remains strong, with the government and its many bureaus and local representatives replacing the *caudillos*, viceroys (literally "vice-kings," the crown's personal agents), and *hacendados* of the past.[41]

The historical hierarchical, elitist, corporative, and authoritarian system has been modified by twentieth-century changes but by no means destroyed by them.[42] Politics still centers around the old hierarchically organized and vertically compartmentalized structure of corporate interests, now expanded to include the newer social elements (middle-sector associations, trade unions, peasant leagues, and the like) but still authoritarianly controlled from the top and linked together through the governmental apparatus. The government controls and directs virtually all of associational life, holding power to grant or withhold not only recognition (the *sine qua non* for the group's very existence) but also access to official funds and favors without which no group is likely to succeed or even survive. Group rights hence have priority over individual rights; similarly, it is the "general will" and the power of the state that prevail over particular interests. The government not only regulates all associations and corporate bodies but also seeks to tie those that have earned their place in the existing system into a collaborative effort for integral, institutionalized national development. Obviously, such a system works best in a traditional context and within a framework of shared values, but what makes it so interesting is that it is not incompatible with a growing pluralism of ideologies and social forces.

Dynamics of the Corporative Polity

In the virtually inherently corporative and patrimonial systems of Iberia and Latin America, the effort is made to ameliorate social and political conflict, to deal with it bureaucratically rather than to provoke divisiveness, class conflict, and breakdown—hence, the strong controls imposed on capital, labor, and other types of interest associations and the loathing of competitive party politics, all of which are seen as divisive agencies subtracting from and perhaps threatening the unity and solidarity of the system. Administration supersedes politics in both theory and practice: society is represented functionally in terms of its component sectors and organized bureaucratically, with the government seeking to maintain the proper balance between the various interests and to coordinate them into the state apparatus.[43] Parties tend to be called national "movements" or "civic associations"; they are more likely to serve as patronage agencies and as mechanisms of the state apparatus than as agents of mass mobilization or electoral politics. Political issues in such a system are generally dealt with by co-opting new elites into the orbit of the patrimonial state through the granting of access and favors, spoils and privileges that accrue with acceptance into the system.[44] Effective program implementation is difficult for bureaucracies in systems where this was always at best a secondary function.

In the Iberic-Latin systems, the great need is felt to have social and political solidarity. There can be little room for divided loyalties, autonomous political organizations, or challenges to the system's fundamental structure. The personnel of government may shift, new groups and ideas may be assimilated, and the elites may circulate in power.[45] But the essentials of the sociopolitical order and the base on which it rests must remain steadfast. The newer groups may be co-opted and incorporated, but they cannot seek to topple the system itself. Those that try will likely be crushed—unless their goal is the limited one of trying to demonstrate a power capability and the right to be admitted as a participant in the larger system. This kind of controlled and usually carefully orchestrated violence (the student demonstration, the march on the National Palace, the general strike) may be tolerated, even accepted; a movement aimed at undermining the entire system, in contrast, can expect to and will probably be suppressed.[46] Rarely do full-fledged social revolutions succeed.

Considerable change can and does take place within a corporative system, but it usually comes from the top downward rather than as a result of grass-roots pressure from below. A culturally conditioned form of democracy may be established, as in Venezuela, Colombia, Costa Rica, or even Mexico, but its structure is that of a tutelary democracy directed from above. Moreover, one must be careful not to overstress the democratic aspects of these systems at the expense of their authoritarian, elitist, and corporative features. For government tends to remain dominated by elite interests and values, hierarchy and corporatism remain deeply ingrained, and the so-called democratic system is ordinarily founded on a structure of co-opted and *institutionalized* popular movements, rather than on independent and genuinely pluralist ones.[47]

Whether the system is authoritarian or democratic, the change process is dealt with in much the same way. An attempt is made to transfer the elitist values and political culture to the rising newer groups through education, co-optation, and example. First the business-commercial elements were "civilized" in this way, then the rising middle sectors, and now the lower or popular classes. This helps explain the persistent presence in the Iberic-Latin context of state-supported and controlled labor federations, peasant leagues, professional associations, and the like. Through these agencies, which like the parties often function as bureaucratic appendages of the state, the prevailing systems have sought to institutionalize and thus contain the rising social forces. Middle- and lower-class elements have been given certain benefits and a place in the system as a means of defusing discontent and of subordinating them to the bureaucratic-paternalistic direction of the state. Labor legislation and more recently agrarian reform have been used as instruments more of social control than of social change. In this way the dominant elites and the patrimonialist structure have managed the historical unfolding of the development process, channeling it in acceptable directions and either co-opting in or snuffing out new challenges to their power and way of life.[48] Through adaptation the traditional order, instead of being overwhelmed or discarded as development has gone forward, has profited, proving to be remarkably resilient and even strengthening itself in the process.

It is the duty of the state and its leader to organize public opinion and maintain the delicate equilibrium through the manipulation and balancing of these interests. Decisions are ordinarily made by a coterie of elite group representatives, linked by formal and informal ties to the administrative hierarchy and centering, ideally, in a single individual who personifies the national values, "knows" the general will, and is the most qualified leader. In much of Latin America during the 1960s (but not in Spain or Portugal), the U.S. ambassador and the various U.S. mission heads were at times also included in the decision-making machinery. Traditionally, patronage, status, favors, and special access to the centers of wealth and influence have served as the chief political currency with privileges, even whole programs and agencies, being doled out by the state to groups and individuals who might otherwise attempt organized opposition. These benefits are distributed in return for loyal support or acquiescence to official policies. It is also worth noting the reverse side of this coin that opposition to the regime in power in the Iberic-Latin context is not usually for the ideological and partisan reasons that American headlines often suggest but is simply a means by which the opposing group or individual will also in some fashion be included in the spoils system. Government thus becomes a kind of vast social security system, a haven for friends, relatives, clientele of various sorts, dissidents, and even a large part of the middle class and now, increasingly, the peasant and labor leaders who are, in effect, "bought off" by being placed on the public payroll.[49]

The corporative system thus helps maintain the traditional structure while concurrently providing for change through the incorporation of new social and political units into the state administration. Corporate structures reinforced by a political culture grounded on hierarchy, status, and patronage are what enable the prevailing system to hang on so tenaciously. The status quo is thus preserved, while provision is also made for the incremental accommodation to newer currents. The corporative system may thus respond to modernization and adopt those aspects that are useful and can be controlled; but in seeking to preserve stability and continuity, it may reject many of the social and political concomitants that accompanied development elsewhere. It should be reiterated that the corporative structures and values outlined here are not just a creation of the 1930s but have deep roots in the entire Iberic-Latin tradition. They have been reformulated, adjusted, and updated numerous times, but the fundamental nature of the corporative-patrimonial system has endured.[50]

In the Iberic-Latin political systems new social and political forces, ideas, and institutional arrangements may be added on in a continuous fusion-absorption process; but owing to the absence of genuinely revolutionary transformations in that tradition, old ones are seldom discarded.[51] Only in Mexico, Cuba, Nicaragua, and perhaps (and incompletely) Bolivia, Peru, Chile, and now Portugal have there been sharp breaks with the past that destroyed the power of the traditional elites. In the other countries, traditional structures remain strong. Furthermore, even in those nations that have had revolutions (and one thinks particularly of Mexico, Bolivia, Peru, Portugal, and Chile in this regard, although Cuba and Nicaragua may also qualify), the corporative-syndicalist-patrimonialist mentality and political culture remain exceedingly powerful, perhaps still predominant, even though the formal "corporatist" institutions established in the 1930s may have disappeared. The longevity and persistence of these traditional aspects, however updated to meet twentieth-century contingencies, remind one of Anderson's "living museum" idea.[52] Organizational forms and societal forces that have died off or been discarded elsewhere in the West continue in the Iberic-Latin context to exhibit a remarkable durability and viability; instead of being swept away, they have proceeded to adapt, persisting and continuing to coexist with and even absorb the newer currents spawned by industrialization and modernization.

As a result of the tenacity of these traditional sociopolitical institutions, there has been limited "development" in the Iberic-Latin nations in either a Marxian or an Almondian sense. The Iberic-Latin political process has usually involved not so much the transcendence of one "class" or "stage" over another, but the combination of diverse elements, rooted in distinct historical epochs, in a tentative working arrangement. The question has been not so much one of "development" or "modernization" as of reconciling the features of the older patrimonialist order with the imperatives of a twentieth-century urban and industrial one. The traditional order in these societies has not been so rigid as is usually pictured, but flexible, permeable, and capable of absorbing a variety of newer currents, without being undermined in the process. It has assimilated those features of modernity that were necessary and could be absorbed, but it has rejected the rest.

As the newer elites and social forces have been absorbed into the prevailing system, therefore, the number of participants and of institutionalized corporate groups has increased, but the system itself has changed little. Hence, in virtually all the Iberic-Latin nations there has grown up a series of layers of distinct social and political forms and world views, each superimposed upon the other, with new elements continuously being appended and adapted to an older tradition but without that older tradition being sloughed off or even undergoing many fundamental transformations. These distinct but overlapping layers originate in historical eras that range over the centuries from feudal to modern, combined and blended in the Iberic-Latin tradition. It is the genius and ongoing challenge of politics and politicians in these nations that they have been able to function and accomplish anything at all of a developmental sort, given the tentative, heterogeneous, frequently crazy-quilt political systems in which they must work.[53]

In seeking to explain these aspects of the Iberic-Latin change process, Richard N. Adams has fashioned a theory of what he calls "secondary development."[54] This refers to the course development takes when it enters an area previously isolated from the modern world. Hence, development in Iberia and Latin America does not *follow* the developmental patterns of northern Europe and North America but involves the *adaptation* of the newer forces to an older order. This is a process of assimilation and reorganization, not of innovation; it involves not the replacement of an already established sociopolitical order by a newer, more modern one but the adaptation of the newer wines to the older bottles.

In Anderson's terms, the key dilemma in the politics of these nations is to find a formula for reaching agreement among the various corporate groups and "power contenders," made difficult because their power is unequal and because their interests and world views are almost totally incompatible. Characteristically, the political process involves manipulation and constant negotiations among these several power contenders, since elections are tentative and but one legitimate means to power and do not carry the definitiveness of elections in the Anglo-American context.[55] The shuffling and reshuffling of the delicate power balance, the management of a diverse coalition, are necessary, almost everyday preoccupations. Anderson emphasizes that while new power contenders may be accommodated and admitted to the system, if they accept and conform to its rules, old ones are not eliminated. Because the several elites and special interests, including the army, the church, the oligarchy, the university, labor, the peasants, and so forth, emerged from distinct historical time periods with distinct expectations and uneven bases for their power and legitimacy, however, the attempt to fashion an accommodation among them is exceedingly difficult. The job of the president, who must juggle and reconcile these contending forces and maintain a working balance between them, is complex and uncertain.

Multiple currents of sociopolitical evolution may thus be operating within the framework of a given nation, institution, or even individual. Politics, Anderson says, involves the capacity to combine these heterogeneous and incompatible power contenders and capabilities in a conditional, continuously shifting arrangement. Frequently, these efforts involve what to North Americans appear to be incredible marriages of convenience—alliances that defy not only all "reason" but also our conception of ideological consistency—or the stretching or reinterpretation (or frequent rewriting) of the law and constitution so as to render them all but meaningless. Yet it is precisely these features—the application of a little "grease" here or a little "cement" there, a delicate compromise, accommodation, or favor—that help account for the distinctive flavor of the development process in these countries and that give them their dynamism and capacity to respond. Furthermore, if we wish to understand the Iberic-Latin development process, the focus of scholarly inquiry ought also to be in this direction. We must study, for example, how traditional institutions have been remolded and modified to meet the exigencies of modern times, as well as how such "modernizing" groups as trade unions have frequently used the traditional structure to further their own ends and have been incorporated into the classic system of hierarchy, corporatism, and authority.[56] These mechanisms, which lie at the heart of the Iberic-Latin change and development process, often bear little correspondence to the systems paradigms with which we are more familiar.

The late Kalman Silvert's analysis of what he termed the "Mediterranean ethos" or "syndicalism" closely parallels what is here called the "corporative framework."[57] This ethos is founded upon a value system and political culture dedicated to hierarchy, order, and absolutes. The urge toward corporatism is a powerful manifestation of this ethos, since the organization of men by functions is in accord with the historical tradition and actualizes the love of order and hierarchy, serves to contain divisive class conflict, and avoids the hated liberal and materialistic values. It also provides for the slow and at least partial adaptation of traditional, patrimonial society to urbanization, industrialization, and modernization. An effort is made through the prevailing system to bring into harmonious coexistence those characteristics venerated from the past and those considered valuable in modernity. The good society is still pictured as one in which each individual is rooted and secure in his life station, where representation is determined by function and status and not as the result of mere citizenship, where decision making is centered in the hands of corporate, sectoral elites who are harmonized and coordinated into an organic whole, and where the state exercises firm but benevolent authority over the entire system. The City of God still takes precedence in many respects over the City of Man, but since a modern society can no longer exist on this simple bi-institutional basis, the Iberic-Latin response has been to erect new institutional pillars to accommodate the changes taking place. Each vertical pillar or corporative sector in this hierarchical arrangement remains highly striated by social class with recruitment into the upper levels still largely a function of social position. As Silvert concludes, the major social purpose of the syndicalist or corporatist approach is to find a way of subsuming the new class complications of modernization to hierarchy and the ancient order, preserving the principle of authority, leaving inviolate the privileges and power of the traditional while at the same time adapting to the newer currents and thus achieving development while escaping the secularization and, to Latin eyes, immorality of liberalism and the modern era.

49

It is clear from the above that the Iberic-Latin model here termed "corporatist" conforms to neither the liberal-pluralist nor the "Fascist" or totalitarian model.[58] There is little evidence that the Iberic-Latin nations are moving inevitably or unilinearly in a liberal-pluralist direction—although their recent openings to democracy have been both inspiring and impressive. With their strong natural law traditions, the concepts of countervailing corporate group life, the competition of rival power contenders for power, and in the absence of any intense racial or ethnic persecution or of an all-powerful state or single party, the Iberic-Latin systems clearly do not fit Fascist and totalitarian molds either. Authoritarian and nascently democratic in certain respects, yes; but totalitarian, no.[59] Moreover, it bears reiterating that the corporative system provides for considerable change and modernization. The Iberic-Latin nations are not all wholly static and vegetative (Portugal almost became so) but have shown an almost incredible capacity to change, co-opt, and adapt, even within an authoritarian-corporatist context. They have accommodated themselves to the changed circumstances and the new social forces to which industrialization and modernization gave rise, but they have done so in a way that has enabled them to maintain many of their historical values and institutions. Fitting neither the liberal framework nor the Fascist-totalitarian one and far more dynamic and change oriented than is often thought, the Iberic-Latin model is a distinct type, with its own philosophic traditions, characteristics, and culturally conditioned behavior patterns and institutions. The Iberic-Latin tradition of corporatism merits examination on its own terms as "the other great ism."[60]

This is what the longer book from which this chapter is taken sought to do. It examined the Portuguese system through those historical traditions and institutions that have shaped its development. More important, it showed how the manifestly corporative state that grew up in the 1930s to deal with the phenomena of industrialization, rapid social change, and mass society was a reflection and modern-day extension of that earlier corporative tradition. It traced the evolution of the Portuguese corporative system and sought to assess its capacity to cope with the same great twentieth-century issues for which liberalism and socialism represent alternative responses. Finally, it tried to weigh the capabilities of the corporative system to continue to function and survive, its various alternative futures, and the implications of the overthrow of the system in April 1974.

For in many ways the corporative systems of Iberia and Latin America are now undergoing pressures never before experienced. The ancient fabric of natural law has been challenged from both within and without, some of the older power bases are in decline, new social forces have emerged organized around principles different from those previously considered the only right or legitimate ones, class-based and issue-oriented politics have grown up alongside the ancient patrimonialist system, the pace of change has accelerated and the number of interests to be satisified has grown, the older solidarity has been challenged, and a framework of change and democracy has increasingly replaced the older one of order and stability. Throughout the Iberic-Latin world these and other currents have posed an increasing challenge to the older tradition, raising the question of whether the corporative institutions will one day be fully submerged or swept away, or whether their contours will be so altered as to constitute a significant structural transformation. Or will the traditional order be able to weather and survive the contemporary challenge and crisis as it has weathered so many others in the past? These questions came to a dramatic head of course in the Portuguese Revolution of 1974.

Notes

1. Unlike the Department of State, the foundations, and many academic institutions, which segregate the world into rather rigid geographic divisions, the author here employs a culture area approach that sees Spain, Portugal, and the nations of Latin America as sharing many important characteristics. The differences among them are of course also important, but for now it is the common features that command our attention.

2. Among the more important early works in this tradition are Gabriel A. Almond and James S. Coleman, eds., *The Politics of the Developing Areas* (Princeton, N.J.: Princeton University Press, 1960); W. W. Rostow, *The Stages of Economic Growth* (Cambridge: Cambridge University Press, 1960); Karl W. Deutsch, "The Growth of Nations: Some Recurrent Patterns of Political and Social Integration," *World Politics,* vol. 5 (January 1953), pp. 168–95; and Seymour M. Lipset, "Some Social Requisites of Democracy: Economic Development and Political Legitimacy," *American Political Science Review,* vol. 53 (March 1959), pp. 69–105. These and other studies set the tone and ideological direction for an entire genre of literature dealing with national development written during the 1960s. The value assumptions inherent in this model are discussed in, among other places, Arthur Mitzman, *The Iron Cage: An Historical Interpretation of Max Weber* (New York: Knopf, 1970); Robert A. Nisbet, *Social Change and History: Aspects of the Western Theory of Development* (New York: Oxford University Press, 1969); and Howard J. Wiarda, *Dictatorship, Development, and Disintegration: Politics and Social Change in the Dominican Republic* (Ann Arbor, Mich.: Xerox University Microfilm Monograph Series, 1975), chap. 1.

3. Samuel P. Huntington, *Political Order in Changing Societies* (New Haven: Yale University Press, 1968), chap. 2.

4. See Richard M. Morse, "The Strange Career of Latin American Stud-

ies," *Annals of the American Academy of Political and Social Studies*, vol. 356 (November 1964), p. 11.

5. A good discussion of some of these procedures is Ellery Sedgewick, "Something New in Dictators: Salazar of Portugal," *Atlantic*, vol. 193 (January 1954), pp. 40–45.

6. See Howard J. Wiarda, *The Corporative Origins of the Iberian and Latin American Labor Relations Systems* (Amherst: Labor Relations and Research Center, University of Massachusetts, 1976).

7. Useful as starters are Matthew Elbow, *French Corporative Theory, 1789–1948: A Chapter in the History of Ideas* (New York: Columbia University Press, 1953); and Joaquin Azpiazu, *The Corporative State* (St. Louis: Herder, 1951). See also the useful bibliography compiled by Philippe C. Schmitter at the end of his "Still the Century of Corporatism?" *Review of Politics*, vol. 36 (January 1974), pp. 128–31.

8. Thomas Stritch, "Introduction," Fredrick B. Pike and Thomas Stritch, eds., *The New Corporatism: Social Political Structures in the Iberian World* (Notre Dame, Ind.: University of Notre Dame Press, 1974).

9. Corporatism is, of course, not confined to the southern European and Latin nations. In addition to the other European polities already noted, corporatist influences may be found in nations as diverse as Japan, India, Vietnam, Yugoslavia, Tanzania, and the Soviet Union. If corporatism is indeed so ubiquitous, present in so many culture areas, then its usefulness as a term of analysis becomes more limited. In this book we shall be concerned primarily with the particularly Roman, Catholic, and Iberic-Latin tradition of corporatism; but on this whole issue see Daviv B. H. Denoon, "The Corporate Model: How Relevant and for Which Countries?" (Paper, MIT, Dept. of Political Science, 1973).

10. See especially Charles W. Anderson, *The Political Economy of Modern Spain* (Madison: University of Wisconsin Press, 1970), chaps. 1–3 and 9; H. R. Trevor-Roper, "The Phenomenon of Fascism," in S. J. Woolf, ed., *European Fascism* (New York: Vintage, 1969), pp. 18–34; and João Manuel Cortez Pinto, *A Corporação: Subsidio para o seu estudo* (Coimbra: Coimbra Ed., 1955). An interesting statement by Catholic writer Marie R. Madden appears in the *New York Times*, August 7, 1941; see also the special reports in the *Times* (London), May 22, 1959, and November 16, 1961.

11. The best collection dealing with these themes is James Malloy, ed., *Authoritarianism and Corporatism in Latin America* (Pittsburgh: University of Pittsburgh Press, 1976).

12. Mihail Manoïlesco, *Le siècle du corporatisme* (Paris: Felix Alcan, 1934).

13. Brazil, for example, is less manifestly corporatist than Portugal in terms of its operating ideology, but it, Mexico, Argentina, Peru, and others are just as corporatist in their actual functioning. The comments offered here are not meant to imply that Portugal is in any sense the model for these others (although it was to a considerable degree in the 1930s) but that the whole framework of corporate theory and institutions, which was articulated more completely, institutionalized more fully and explicitly, and lasted longer in Portugal than in these other nations, still remains the dominant one

throughout the Iberic-Latin world. For a paper developed independently but that is concerned with some themes parallel to those explored in this study, see Philippe C. Schmitter, "Corporatist Interest Representation and Public Policy-Making in Portugal" (Paper presented at the Annual Meeting of the American Political Science Association, Washington, D.C., September 5–7, 1972).

14. The definition here used is derived from Elbow, *French Corporate Theory,* pp. 11–12; Schmitter, "Corporatist Interest Representation"; and Marcello Caetano, *Principios e definições* (Lisbon: Ed. Panorama, 1969), pp. 41–51. The European literature is rich but almost completely unknown in this country; in English, see Azpiazu, *Corporative State,* and Elbow, *French Corporative Theory.*

15. Howard J. Wiarda, "Toward a Framework for the Study of Political Change in the Iberic-Latin Tradition: The Corporative Model," *World Politics,* vol. 25 (January 1973), pp. 206–35.

16. See the special issue of the *Review of Politics,* vol. 36 (January 1974), dealing with corporatism in the Iberic-Latin world. A useful study that makes the link between corporatism in Iberia and in Latin America is Fredrick B. Pike, *Hispanismo 1898–1936: Spanish Conservatives and Liberals and Their Relations with Spanish America* (Notre Dame, Ind.: University of Notre Dame Press, 1971).

17. Perhaps the best statement of this view is Glen Dealy, *The Public Man: A Cultural Interpretation of Latin America and Other Catholic Countries* (Amherst: University of Massachusetts Press, 1977).

18. De Gaulle remained a corporatist in many ways. See also Samuel H. Beer, *British Politics in the Collectivist Age* (New York: Knopf, 1965); and Stein Rokkan, "Norway: Numerical Democracy and Corporate Pluralism," in R. Dahl, ed., *Political Opposition in Western Democracies* (New Haven: Yale University Press, 1966), pp. 70–115.

19. Daniel Bell, *The End of Ideology* (New York: Free Press, 1959). This is, of course, a controversial subject area on which there is by now a great deal of literature; further comment on this theme is reserved for later in the study.

20. This is another running debate about which we shall have more to say later; one discussion on this topic was the panel "Mediterranean Politics" of the 1973 American Political Science Association, New Orleans, September 4–8. Illustrative of the problems and issues in this debate are two of the papers presented at the panel discussion: Samuel H. Barnes and Giacomo Sani, "Mediterranean Political Culture and Italian Politics: An Interpretation"; and Alan Zuckerman, "On the Institutionalization of Political Clienteles: Party Factions and Cabinet Coalitions in Italy."

21. For some parallel arguments, see A. James Gregor, *The Ideology of Fascism* (New York: Free Press, 1969), introduction.

22. The intellectuals-in-power issue stems from, among other places, William Buckley's famous crack to the effect that he would rather be governed by the first 200 names in the Boston phone directory than by the whole of the Harvard faculty. In Portugal it was the Coimbra and University of Lisbon faculties (especially lawyers and economists) who played such a prominent role. On the corporatist-patrimonialist tradition in Brazil and its adaptations,

see Philippe C. Schmitter, *Interest Conflict and Political Change in Brazil* (Stanford, Calif.: Stanford University Press, 1971); and Riordan Roett, *Brazil: Politics in a Patrimonial Society* (Boston: Allyn and Bacon, 1972).

23. Arpad von Lazar, "Latin America and the Politics of Post-Authoritarianism," *Comparative Political Studies*, vol. 1 (October 1968). See also John H. Herz, "The Problem of Successorship in Dictatorial Regimes: A Study in Comparative Law and Institutions," *Journal of Politics*, vol. 14 (February 1952), pp. 19–40; and Keith Botsford, "Succession and Ideology in Spain and Portugal," *Journal of International Affairs*, vol. 18 (1964), pp. 76–85.

24. William F. Connolly, ed., *The Bias of Pluralism* (New York: Atherton, 1971); and Theodore Lowi, *The End of Liberalism* (New York: Norton, 1969). See also the recent critiques of Lockean liberalism, as well as the upcoming books dealing with Nixon, Watergate, and the like. A useful collection of these critiques from diverse perspectives is Jerome M. Mileur, *The Liberal Tradition in Crisis* (Lexington, Mass.: Heath, 1974).

25. Howard J. Wiarda, "The Latin Americanization of the United States," *The New Scholar*, vol. 7 (1979), pp. 51–85.

26. Some of the materials in this section were published previously in Wiarda, "Toward a Framework." For fuller elaborations see the author's "Corporatism and Development in the Iberic-Latin World," *Review of Politics*, vol. 36 (January 1974), pp. 3–33; "Law and Political Development in Latin America: Toward a Framework of Analysis," *American Journal of Comparative Law*, vol. 19 (Summer 1971), pp. 434–63; "The Latin American Development Process and the New Developmental Alternatives: Military 'Nasserism' and 'Dictatorship with Popular Support,'" *Western Political Quarterly*, vol. 25 (September 1972), pp. 464–90; and "Elites in Crisis: The Decline of the Old Order and the Fragmentation of the New in Latin America" (University of Massachusetts, Dept. of Political Science, 1972). For efforts at applying the model, see also the author's "The Catholic Labor Movement in Brazil: Corporatism, Populism, Paternalism, and Change," in William H. Tyler and H. Jon Rosenbaum, eds., *Contemporary Brazil* (New York: Praeger, 1972), pp. 323–47; and *Dictatorship, Development, and Disintegration*.

27. For an argument parallel to this one, that Latin America should be regarded "as something of a Fourth World, with characteristics of its own which entitle it to be studied in its own right and not forced to conform to whatever generalizations can be made about the Third," see J. D. B. Miller, *The Politics of the Third World* (London: Oxford University Press, 1967). See also John Martz, "The Place of Latin America in Comparative Politics," *Journal of Politics*, vol. 28 (February 1966), pp. 57–80.

28. Alfred Stepan, "Political Development: The Latin American Experience," *Journal of International Affairs*, vol. 20 (1966), pp. 223–34; Milton Vanger, "Politics and Class in Twentieth Century Latin America," *Hispanic America Historical Review*, vol. 49 (February 1969), pp. 80–83; Juan Marsal, *Cambio Social en America Latina: Crítica de algunas interpretaciones dominantes en las ciencias sociales* (Buenos Aires: Solar Hachette, 1967); and Wiarda, "Elites in Crisis."

29. Rafael Altamira, *A History of Spain*, trans. Muna Lee (New York: Van Nostrand, 1949); and Ronald Glassman, *A History of Latin America* (New York:

Funk & Wagnalls, 1969).

30. Irving A. Leonard, "Science, Technology, and Hispanic America: The Basis of Regional Characteristics," *Michigan Quarterly Review*, vol. 2 (October 1963), pp. 237–45. It should be noted that these descriptive classifications represent simplified "ideal types" in the Weberian sense, rather than precise mirrors of reality.

31. See Louis Hartz et al., *The Founding of New Societies* (New York: Harcourt, Brace, 1964), especially the essay, "The Heritage of Latin America," by Richard M. Morse, pp. 123–77.

32. Ibid.

33. See Mariano Picón-Salas, *A Cultural History of Spanish America* (Berkeley: University of California Press, 1968), pp. 39–40; and Richard M. Morse, "Recent Research on Latin American Urbanization: A Selective Survey with Commentary," *Latin American Research Review*, vol. 1 (Fall 1965), p. 41.

34. Picón-Salas, *Cultural History*; also Dealy, *Public Man*.

35. Bernice Hamilton, *Political Thought in Sixteenth-Century Spain* (Oxford: Oxford University Press, 1963); and Guenter Lewy, *Constitutionalism and Statescraft during the Golden Age of Spain: A Study of the Political Philosophy of Juan de Mariana, S.J.* (Geneva: E. Droz, 1960).

36. L. N. McAlister, "Social Structure and Social Change in New Spain," *Hispanic American Historical Review*, vol. 43 (August 1963), pp. 349–70; and Magali Sarfatti, *Spanish Bureaucratic-Patrimonialism in America* (Berkeley: Institute of International Studies, University of California, 1966). For the Portuguese-Brazilian tradition, see Raymundo Faoro, *Os donos do poder: Formação do patronato político brasileiro* (Pôrto Alegre: Ed Globo, 1958).

37. Glen Dealy, "Prolegomena on the Spanish American Political Tradition," *Hispanic American Historical Review*, vol. 48 (February 1968); and Charles A. Hale, *Mexican Liberalism in the Age of Mora, 1821–1853* (New Haven, Conn.: Yale University Press, 1968).

38. See Warren Dean, *The Industrialization of São Paulo, 1880–1945* (Austin: University of Texas Press, 1969); Jane-Lee Woolridge Yare, "Middle Sector Political Behavior in Latin America" (Paper, University of Massachusetts, Dept. of Political Science, 1971); and Kenneth P. Erickson, *The Brazilian Corporative State and Working Class Politics* (Berkeley: University of California Press, 1977).

39. Morse, "Recent Research"; and Economic Commission for Latin America, *Social Development in Latin America in the Post-War Period* (New York: UNESCO, 1964), introduction.

40. Lewy, *Constitutionalism and Statescraft*; and Ronald C. Newton, "On 'Functional Groups,' 'Fragmentation,' and 'Pluralism' in Spanish American Political Society," *Hispanic American Historical Review*, vol. 50 (February 1970), pp. 1–27.

41. Claudio Veliz, "Centralism and Nationalism in Latin America," *Foreign Affairs*, vol. 47 (October 1968), pp. 68–83; and John D. Powell, "Peasant Society and Clientelist Politics," *American Political Science Review*, vol. 64 (June 1970), pp. 411–25.

42. The discussion here draws heavily from James Petras, *Political and Social*

Forces in Chilean Development (Stanford, Calif.: Stanford University Press, 1969); and the introduction by the editor in John J. Johnson, ed., *Continuity and Change in Latin America* (Stanford, Calif.: Stanford University Press, 1964).

43. Michel Crozier, *The Bureaucratic Phenomenon* (Chicago: University of Chicago Press, 1964).

44. An illustrative case study of this process is Roett, *Brazil.*

45. The concepts derive from the Italian sociologists Mosca and Pareto. For an application see Orlando Fals Borda, "Marginality and Revolution in Latin America, 1809–1969," *Studies in Comparative International Development*, vol. 6 (1970/71), pp. 63–89.

46. See James L. Payne, *Labor and Politics in Peru* (New Haven, Conn.: Yale University Press, 1965).

47. For the countries mentioned, see Frank Bonilla, *The Failure of Elites*, vol. 2; and José A. Silva Michelana, *The Illusion of Democracy in Dependent Nations*, vol. 3, of *The Politics of Change in Venezuela* (Cambridge: MIT Press, 1970); James L. Payne, *Patterns of Conflict in Colombia* (New Haven: Yale University Press, 1968); Susan Kaufman Purcell, "Decision-Making in an Authoritarian Regime: Mexico" (Paper presented at the Annual Meeting of American Political Science Association, Chicago, September 7–11, 1971); and Charles F. Denton, *Patterns of Costa Rican Politics* (Boston: Allyn and Bacon, 1971).

48. Petras, *Political and Social Forces.*

49. Erickson, *The Brazilian Corporative State;* Lawrence S. Graham, *Civil Service Reform in Brazil: Principles versus Practice* (Austin: University of Texas Press, 1968); and Robert E. Scott, "The Government Bureaucrats and Political Change in Latin America," *Journal of International Affairs*, vol. 20 (1966), pp. 289–308.

50. Erickson, *The Brazilian Corporative State;* and Faoro, *Os donos do poder.*

51. The argument here is derived from Morse, "Heritage"; ECLA, *Social Development;* and especially Charles W. Anderson, "Toward a Theory of Latin American Politics" (Occasional paper no. 2, Graduate Center for Latin American Studies, Vanderbilt University, February 1964), incorporated as chap. 4 in his *Politics and Economic Change in Latin America* (Princeton, N.J.: Van Nostrand, 1967).

52. Anderson, "Toward a Theory of Latin American Politics."

53. Anderson, *Political Economy.*

54. Richard N. Adams, *The Second Sowing: Power and Secondary Development in Latin America* (San Francisco: Chandler, 1967).

55. Anderson, *Political Economy.*

56. This is the special merit of the Erickson case study of Brazil and of Schmitter, *Interest Conflict.*

57. Kalman H. Silvert, *The Conflict Society: Reaction and Revolution in Latin America* (New York: American Universities Field Staff, 1966).

58. Roett, *Brazil.*

59. Juan Linz, "An Authoritarian Regime: Spain," in Erik Allardt and Yrjö Littunen, eds., *Cleavages, Ideologies, and Party Systems* (Helsinki: Transactions of the Westermack Society, 1964), vol. 10, pp. 291–342.

60. A collection of essays that emphasizes this point and also brings together some of the leading sources cited here is Howard J. Wiarda, ed., *Politics and Social Change in Latin America: The Distinct Tradition* (Amherst: University of Massachusetts, 1982).

2
Iberian Background and Political Culture

From the time Portugal emerged as the first unified nation-state in Europe in the twelfth century, it was cast in the Catholic-authoritarian-corporatist-patrimonialist mold. This dominant tradition in Portuguese history, society, and political culture has been obscured because the history books that discuss the country and with which we are most familiar have been in the main written by English and American historians who share the common Anglo-American liberal biases and whose studies are often directed toward looking for a *cortes* that never played (and was never intended to play) the role of the British Parliament; institutions of popular, representative self-government that in Portugal never existed; and a liberal and democratic tradition that never received majority support. Of necessity, these accounts have branded Portuguese history a "failure," for it has not lived up to the ideals the Anglo-American writers ethnocentrically assumed to be common to all men. And in explaining the causes of this "failure," the historians have consistently painted the presumed foes of democracy, such as the church, the monarchy, strong government, Pombal, *caciquismo* ("bossism"), the Estado Novo, and much of Portuguese political culture in the vilest of terms, instead of examining them in an unbiased manner and in terms of their role or position in the Portuguese context. The works in English on Portuguese history are rather consistently condescending, written from the point of view of a "superior" political culture, and aimed at discovering in Portugal a liberal-democratic tradition that at best exists as a distinct minority viewpoint.[1]

This chapter looks at Portuguese history and the development of its society and political culture on their own terms rather than through an Anglo-American frame of reference. It seeks to understand that history in the light of Portuguese political institutions, values, and traditions, rather than branding it a "failure." This effort must perforce be incomplete, because of the inadequacies of the historical record and the limitations of space. And yet this way of looking at Portuguese history must be attempted if we are to escape the prejudices of our Anglo-American interpretations and if we are to understand the workings of the modern Portuguese system. Although there is a dominant tradition in Portuguese history, that tradition (or at least its major historical current) was and is not entirely democratic, and it is misleading and self-defeating to try to assert that it is or that it should be so.

Portugal before the Twelfth Century

Although Portugal emerged as a distinct national entity in the twelfth century, its characteristic political culture and form of political organization had begun to emerge long before that time.[2]

We know relatively little about the primitive peoples who first inhabited Lusitania. As was the case with other areas on the Iberian coast, it was visited by the Phoenicians and probably the ancient Greeks, and in the third century B.C. its southern region came under the domination of the Carthaginians. But it was not until Roman times, beginning in the first century B.C., that the region of Lusitania was stamped with a dominant and lasting imprint and its characteristic form of political organization and culture began to take shape.

The Romans constructed numerous bridges, highways, aqueducts, and buildings. The bridges and road network, to say nothing of the establishment of a central administration, helped link Lusitania's diverse and distant regions and provided a sense of unity they had lacked before. Unity and a certain cultural coherence were also forged gradually through a common language and law and eventually through Christianity. Roman law, administration, and politico-military (the two were inseparable) organization were imposed and indelibly imprinted on the area, in a form that later reached definitive shape in the growth of an administrative or bureaucratic state apparatus. In addition, the Romans gave to Portugal its particular conception of citizenship, its stoic conception of rights and obligations, its juridical structure of group rights and charters, its sense of hierarchy and class, and indeed much of its characteristic sociopolitical organization. And if later corporative theorists are correct, in its structuring of military orders, the religious caste, and a hierarchy of professional associations, Rome also laid the basis for the future establishment of a corporative state and society.[3]

During the five centuries of Roman rule, the foundations were laid on which future Iberian civilization developed. Spain and Portugal remain products of Rome in a way they are not of earlier or subsequent cultures.[4] The collapse of the empire paved the way for a

Visigothic conquest, which resulted more in an overlay on the earlier Roman tradition than a submerging of it. From the fifth to the seventh century A.D. the Visigoths helped spread Christianity and Catholic culture through the institutionalization of a state church. Visigothic rule also led to a certain hardening of absolutism and of authoritarian, centralized rule. Moorish rule, always softer and less complete in Lusitania than in Spain, was similarly an overlay on the dominant Roman tradition, since the Moors ruled as overlords and did not impose their culture and religion on the native Iberians. The centuries-long Moorish domination beginning in 714–716 left its influence on the language, in architecture, and—some historians would have us believe—in the inferior status of women in peninsular society. But the Moorish influence never reached as far and as deep into society, polity, and culture as did the Roman, and when the Moors were eventually driven from the peninsula, it was the Roman tradition that remained dominant.

The disorder and intermittent warfare occasioned by the long, drawn out reconquest of the peninsula from the Moors retarded the growth of feudalism in Iberia, in contrast to its development in France. Nevertheless, some further characteristic forms of social and political organization were now grafted onto the Roman base. During the reconquest the church became more than ever an arm of the civil authority. And as the reconquest proceeded, the power of the nobility and of the fighting lords became territorial as well as political and military, usually as a result of grants to them of the lands and peoples they had helped reconquer. Each lord was sovereign in his own territory, and an elaborate network of vassalage and of patron-dependent relations eventually began to grow up. The system of special *foros*, or "rights" and obligations, which defined the relationship of the citizen individually and of the community collectively to its overlord, who could be the monarch, noble, church, military order, or even municipality, thus became the means by which society and polity were defined. Organized hierarchically, the forms of authority were arranged so that the wealth and lands of the area, as well as the persons living in it, were considered a part of the overlord's private preserve. No separation existed between the public and the private domains. A strongly institutionalized patrimonialist social and political structure emerged, which only later took on its agrarian-feudal aspects.[5]

The Development of Portugal's National Identity

Present-day Portugal emerged out of the north or Trás-os-Montes area, an isolated, mountainous, obscure territory where the Spanish provinces of León and Galicia meet and still overlap in language, trade, and culture with the provinces of Portugal beyond the Rio Douro. Early in the twelfth century a separate kingdom of Portugal began to develop, independent of León, although it was not until 1139 with the victory of Afonso Henriques over the Moors near Santarém that a separate Portuguese national unit was founded. During the next three centuries, as the Portuguese conquered south, wresting more and more territory from the Moors, while also fending off León and Spain to the east, the consolidation of Portugal as a separate nation went forward, and its distinct characteristics began to emerge.

The traditions and institutions developed during the period of nation building and consolidation from the twelfth to the fourteenth centuries are crucial for understanding latter-day developments, for they were the foundation on which the modern Portuguese state was built.[6] Their origins lay in the Roman system of civil law, politics, and administration, in the spreading Thomistic philosophy of hierarchy and natural law, and in the emerging semifeudal pattern of land and conquest as the basis of wealth with payment in goods, services, and loyalty. The barons, the nobility, and the new landed aristocrats derived their positions from the king, surrounding him like a "college of influentials," owing allegiance to him and receiving in turn his favors. The church, the military, and the advisers of the king all became a part of the same centralizing, bureaucratic, state apparatus. Governance came to be exercised through a number of consulting organs or councils and directly through the king's ministers who served as his personal agents. The system was one of rule from above, of elite protection of those below them in the hierarchy in return for fealty and service. This was a reciprocal arrangement between "the people" and their "betters" in a classic patrimonialist structure.[7]

The Role of the Church. These arrangements were rationalized and reinforced in the Thomistic conceptions of the proper ordering of state and society. For the Catholic church was intimately involved in the founding and historical development of the Portuguese state and society. Catholicism helped provide the cultural, social, and religious base on which the nation was grounded. Society was organized hierarchically, on Christian principles, in accordance with natural law and God's just ordering of the universe. The "natural" inequalities among men meant that one was bound to accept the station in life to which he had been born. The social order was viewed as fixed and immutable. The state conception was similarly hierarchical, authoritarian and governed by natural law. Political authority flowed from God and was absolute in character; dissent and the right to rebellion were extremely circumscribed. Society and the state were viewed as "natural"

61

rather than as originating in a contract between government and governed, and this organic conception was (and remains) almost inherently traditionalist and absolutist. In the grounding of the philosophical foundations of political authority and civil society in Catholic theology, in the establishment of Catholicism as the official state religion, in the close harmony and overlap between the civil and the religious hierarchies, in the foundation of art and education in Catholic teachings and ceremony, and in a host of other ways, the Portuguese church and the Portuguese state were one and indivisible. The church, like the fighting barons and nobility, was more than a mere "interest group" in the American sense; it was the backbone, indispensable prop, and very essence of the state itself.[8]

Patrimonialism and the Rise of the Class System. Among the corporate groups, military orders, and municipalities existent in the emerging Portuguese system by the end of the fourteenth century, the monarchy and the central state apparatus had become overwhelmingly preeminent, regulating both social structure and economic life. The privileges and monopolies granted by the crown to favored groups and individuals helped develop and unify Portugal. It was a system based on status, hierarchy, and royal favor. No group or individual could challenge or reject the "proper" place in society to which it or he had been assigned. Eventually, a commercial elite grew up in Portugal alongside its barons and landed oligarchy—and it was the commercial elements who, with royal support and under royal auspices, in the fifteenth century launched the conquest of the vast Portuguese overseas empire. Despite this gradual change from feudalism to mercantilism, however, it was the patrimonialist state apparatus that remained constant, continuing to regulate the entire economy and to strengthen itself in the process.

Thus, as a class system began to emerge in Portugal in the early modern period, the structure of state patrimonialism continued to coexist along with it. Commerce, war, exploration, and colonization were all a part of the same extension of royal authority, at a time when the system of agrarian feudalism was also being consolidated under royal patronage. Further, in the promotion of trade and colonization, Portugal never developed a full-fledged system of capitalism. State capitalism or mercantilism, yes, but individual entrepreneurship and *laissez faire*, no. Hence, while commercialism and capitalism of a sort grew up parallel to the feudal landholding system, the former never replaced the latter but instead was fused with it. Meanwhile, the one constant remained the patrimonialist state apparatus and a social and political structure depending on and deriving its legitimacy from royal favors and patronage. As Herminio Martins, one of Portugal's leading political sociologists, has written: "Portuguese social stability stems in part from the circumstance that the formation of the state and the definition of national identity took place centuries ago, long before the social crises brought on by industrialization, urbanization, and other phases of modernization."[9]

Because this tradition is so strong and so omnipresent, it merits further elaboration. One can say, thus, that the Portuguese state was modeled after that of the imperial Roman caesars, now updated and given a Christian base. It was absolutist and administrative. The king exercised power in the name of the general interest, *res publica*. He required all powers and prerogatives for his superior mission of governance. Society remained dominated by the idea and presence of the state. The land of the kingdom and its individual members belonged to the monarch as part of his private domain. And the kings could name their own successors.[10]

The crown might grant part of its patrimony to certain individuals, sometimes in perpetuity, in return for their support and service. The concessions of land, favors, or a special monopoly were alienated in return for a formal oath of loyalty, a *juramento a fidelidade*. The system was highly personal and paternal. A vassal might abandon his contract with the king only if he received injury from him—and vice versa. The relations of lord or king to vassal, or to a corporate body, were thus not wholly one way but were governed by reciprocal relations, in a classic patron-client pattern.[11]

The crown was limited in other ways. Natural and divine law provided a set of guidelines beyond which the crown could go only at the risk of provoking rebellion. The crown was also limited by the traditional rights of the emerging orders and municipalities. Further, during the thirteenth and fourteenth centuries the first corporations of *artes e oficios* (artisans and laborers) were founded; the Casa de Vinte e Quatro (a corporately organized assembly of notables based on functional representation) was born, and certain other corporations and some artisans' groups came to be recognized by the king. These bodies too served as a check on royal absolutism. When the king overstepped his authority, he was likely to face a revolt on the part of the nobility, whose bloody uprisings continued throughout this period.[12] Custom, tradition, and the family also served as constraints on royal prerogatives.

The king had the supreme "fiscalizing" power to regulate and pass on all contracts and agreements. He also exercised his sovereignty by confirming the acts of the *senhor* (gentry)—for example, his military service, his land and vassals, or his right to a place in the

63

cortes. Thus, the king was not only theoretically supreme, but his effective power was enhanced by his ability almost literally to hand-pick those who sat in his parliament. The same individual who received a grant of land or monopoly from the crown would frequently serve as the king's royal agent in that territory. The political evolution of Portugal during this period served to reconstitute and unify the state and establish national sovereignty through the leadership of the king.[13]

The rediscovery of Roman law had given special impetus to these trends. The *corpus juris civis* provided a model of a powerful state, hierarchical and authoritarian in character, in which a strong central administration ensured order and justice. The Roman law favored the consolidation of the state by the crown against feudal rights, excesses, and violence. It contributed to the growth of royal power and also made it absolutist. The monarch became the focus of the *direito positivo* (positive law). He assumed the position of defender of "the public interest" in return for which the nation granted him virtually all power. This tradition evolved as the Iberic concept of popular sovereignty, and it found powerful echoes in the rules of Franco and Salazar.[14]

The Growth of Absolutism. The development of royal power resulted in the weakening of the legislative power, in the growth of general as opposed to localized taxes, in limits on seignorial power, in the gradual affirmation of secular power over the church, in the development of central administrative organs, in the fiscalization and intervention of the crown in political and economic life, and in the delegation of certain powers and privileges in return for fealty. Eventually, the doctrine of the illegality of usurping royal authority emerged, the idea that the king was not only superior in relation to other authorities but that he or his delegated agents had a true monopoly. The doctrine asserted that the rights of the various societal and corporate units came only through concessions from the king and not through any inherent or natural rights. In the sixteenth century the extension of this idea and the full consolidation of the crown's power led to royal absolutism.[15]

In opposition to the emerging absolutist doctrines and practices, the nobles continued to assert the crown's obligation to defend their traditional rights, to guard good customs, and to protect the rights of the people. This gave rise to the idea that the relations between the crown and "the classes" were governed by a kind of pact and maintained by mutual accords. Later, this same conception would serve as the Portuguese definition of "democracy." The inviolability of these rights was always invoked in conflicts with the king. The various "colleges," orders, brotherhoods, guilds, municipalities, and corporations all claimed to be governed by these norms. At the same time the king reserved the right not to respect these privileges when he had just cause.[16] Throughout Portuguese history, indeed, this conflict between the centralizing, absolutist forces and tendencies, on the one hand, and the defenders of corporate privilege and group rights, on the other, remained dominant. At no time in this long history of conflict between the crown and the various component units of the nation, until the past several years, was there a strong force arguing for genuine popular sovereignty, real grass-roots participation, and democratization in the Anglo-American mold.

Implied in this arrangement is the fact that the Portuguese *cortes* would never become an effective agent for popular representation. The *cortes* originated in the royal curia or council of the king. Its chief functions were consultative and administrative; it did not legislate. Although the *cortes* at several points accumulated some modicum of authority, no real separation of powers emerged, and it existed largely at the king's pleasure. Represented in it were the nobles and those allied with the king or owing him fealty; the church was also represented along with the masters of the major military orders, the heads of the major corporative bodies, and the *procuradores* (advocates) of the principal cities. The *cortes* could be called into session only by the king, and its members were required to heed this call as an obligation of their vassalage.[17]

The ordinary curia, or royal council, remained an administrative arm of the king; the extraordinary curia, however, comprising the greater nobles and church prelates, gradually acquired greater economic and legislative functions and was involved in some of the great political questions of the thirteenth and fourteenth centuries. But as the *cortes* sought to expand its powers, it was called less and less frequently. The three chief estates—clerical, noble, and military—were all represented, as were the municipalities, the heads of the major corporative bodies, and some persons of elevated position. But the franchise was always severely limited: the people were represented by their "betters"; municipalities also tended to choose local notables who went along with the governmental team. What vote existed was ordinarily for an assigned list of the "better" people, and the king would often suggest for whom one should vote—those who enjoyed his *confiança*.[18]

The Cortes met, irregularly and briefly, by separate functional estates, each jealous of its own privileges. It nonetheless gradually acquired some power over the purse, was sometimes consulted by the

65

king in the event of war, gained some limited power over law making, and could exercise some choice in the succession in cases where the dynasty had died out. It remained limited, however, never employing the supremacist doctrine that some few of its members occasionally voiced, and the king most often legislated without the *cortes* through decree-law. The power of the people thus remained nil, and the crown reserved the right to revoke the rights and liberties even of the major corporate groups and privileged elites. It was the popular sectors, day laborers and peasants, beginning to emerge in the fifteenth century though without anything approaching the power of the nobility or clergy, who probably had the most interest in the meeting of the Cortes, but they were the weakest of society's sectors and had virtually no representation. Only the elites enjoyed representation, and they had no more interest in genuinely popular and democratic government than the king. Hence, in the great conflicts between royal authority and the nobles of the realm, whose relative power varied over time depending on the force of each and the vicissitudes of politics, the people never had any voice at all.[19]

Was the Cortes ever representative of society or of the nation? Emphatically not, at least in the modern Anglo-American sense of popular representation. In the Portuguese sense the Cortes *was* representative, however; for when a Spaniard or Portuguese speaks of society or the nation, he tends to think of it in its component units: the religious institutions, the municipalities, the *gremios* (employer groups) and *sindicatos* (unions), the entrepreneurial interests, military orders, grand foundations, and the like—in other words, the major social and corporate groups. Not included in this conception is the general public or public opinion. Hence, the Cortes was at best occasionally an imperfect representative only of "the classes." Its membership was limited to certain privileged clergy, nobles, cities, military orders, *homens bons* (community leaders), and so forth, and it was their rights that were protected. The general public was not represented, and individual rights were protected only insofar as they corresponded to those of the major interests. The Cortes, however, did represent at least the major elites and corporate bodies, and, more than that, it sometimes presumed to speak in defense of the common interests. But the king also claimed that power, and eventually he won out. The Cortes met less and less frequently, the last time (at least in the pre-Republican period) in 1696–1698. Then divine right monarchy triumphed absolutely, and the Cortes came to be replaced by nonelective secretaries of state and superior tribunals. The Cortes never acquired the power of the British Parliament; the idea of popular sovereignty (and all its accompanying paraphernalia—elections, party government, separation of powers, popular rights, and so on) was never secured, nor did it become even a principle of public law.[20]

The Colonial Expansion of the Sixteenth Century

The themes developed above are important for several reasons. First, it is clear that the evolution of the Portuguese system up to this point has shown a close correspondence to the model of authoritarian and corporative society and of the patrimonialist political order outlined in chapter 1. Second, this structure served as the base on which the *modern* Portuguese state system was erected from the fifteenth century on. These ideas were probably most clearly articulated by the Infante Dom Pedro, brother of Henry the Navigator and a shrewd political analyst and royal adviser; by Alvaro Pais, the Franciscan bishop of Elvas; and later by Francisco Suárez, the great Spanish jurist (who also taught at Coimbra), who laid the basis for the modern Iberic conception of the Christian (Thomistic) state and authority. In their rationalizations of the emerging power relationships, political power derived from God and was both natural and immutable. The king was obliged to exercise power for the common good; he was a tutor whose power must be used to promote the general well-being of his people. The true king was thus distinguished from a tyrant in that his authority rested on a popular base through his knowledge of the general will. Power stemmed, therefore, not only from God but also through a pact of subjection by which the people agreed to submit to the authority of the prince and he in turn was obligated to rule justly. The king thus governed as a king, not as a tyrant, and in so doing he was obligated to take the corporate interests into account. In Suárez (though not in Dom Pedro) this contract was viewed as superior to the king himself, so that if the king acted as a tyrant, the contract could be revoked. In Portugal, especially with the election of the new Avis dynasty in 1385, this doctrine had particular significance, and it was also used to justify the ending of Spain's sixty-year domination of Portugal in 1640. With the era of Louis XIV, the doctrine of limited, tutelary monarchy disappeared, and that of divine right triumphed, but until then—and indeed virtually continuously in the Portuguese tradition—it was the conception of royal authority governing in an enlightened way and respecting the traditional rights that predominated. It was Dom Pedro who put all this political theory together, who showed the king how to grasp and exercise all the levers of power and patronage, and who erected an artfully fashioned model of the national patrimonialist state and society. It is no accident that the king he instructed, João II, is recognized by virtually all historians as the best ruler Portugal ever had.[21]

Third, one cannot help but be impressed with the parallels between this fifteenth-century conception and the Estado Novo of Salazar and Caetano. In terms of the authoritarian but tutelary role of the state, the limited role of the assembly (actually referred to as the "general *cortes* of the regime"), the treatment of opposition, the respect for the traditional interests, the concept of social structure as fixed and immutable, the erection of a corporative system of social and political organization, functional representation, the low place of public opinion and popular sovereignty, the emphasis on group rights rather than individual rights, the patrimonialist state apparatus, and so on, the parallels are remarkable. In part, of course, this is so because Salazar consciously tried to resurrect in his corporate state a model patterned in some respects on the older tradition. But one suspects it also represents the continuity of a dominant historical pattern and tradition, the logical extension in twentieth-century form of a historical form and order always characteristic of Portuguese society and polity.

The patrimonialist state apparatus, put together so painstakingly and with so much struggle from the twelfth to the fifteenth century, remained the dominant form of Portuguese political organization. Portugal's early consolidation as a nation and the development of its political institutions help explain the incredible, almost inconceivable Portuguese world explorations and conquests—in Africa, Asia, and Latin America—during the fifteenth and sixteenth centuries. This far-flung empire may be viewed as a worldwide extension of continental Portugal itself, a bureaucratic empire reflecting the dominant institutions of the metropole and carried over to the new worlds. It was not an empire of separate units but rather was integrated as a whole into the patrimonialist state apparatus and reflected the sociopolitical structure of the homeland.[22]

The sixteenth century saw the further elaboration and refinement of the prevailing system. Spanish and Portuguese jurists and political philosophers, especially Suárez, helped rationalize the emerging system, reconciled the older Thomistic and feudal order with the newer requirements of centralized, expansionist, state-building royal rule, and fashioned a system of power and society that proved remarkably durable.[23] The bureaucratic structure grew, chiefly through the creation of a variety of royal councils to help govern the newly acquired empire and through the grant of land and authority to Portuguese colonists, especially in Brazil. Through the royal charters and other imperial institutions, the colonies were similarly organized in a hierarchical and patrimonialist fashion, coming to represent smaller-scale extensions of society and polity in the mother country. The church, the military, the civil administration, and so on were all a part of the bureaucratic state apparatus with all the lines, however tenuously and ambiguously at times, reaching back to the crown.[24]

Politics and economic life, in the mother country and in her colonies, remained intimately linked. For the Portuguese patrimonialist state, from ancient times, was formed with the concept that the king would be not only the ultimate political authority but also the major merchant, landholder, and industrialist. Hence, the preoccupation with securing economic monopolies as well as political ones, with the minute regulation of the economy and the various economic interests and with the extraction of a royal percentage from virtually all economic transactions. One cannot but be impressed, for example, with the remarkable consistency with which the monarch was able to collect his royal due and revenue from all those who owed to him their grants of lands, mines, monopolies, and other favors. In this connection also, it should be emphasized that the Portuguese state and empire were organized not so much on a capitalistic basis, at least as capitalism came to be known in northern Europe, but rather on a monopolistic, tributary, mercantilist basis. The roots of this system lay more in the Roman and feudal patterns of allegiance, tribute, and vassalage than in the entrepreneurial, *laissez-faire*, or capitalist, order. The *estamento burocrático* (bureacratic state) meant not free enterprise à la Adam Smith, but an economy of privileges and special favors derived from the king.[25]

Not only had Portugal rejected, and in a sense been bypassed by, the philosophy of *laissez-faire* capitalism and thus never experienced until much later its own form of industrial revolution, but it also remained marginal to the other great social and political currents that we associate with the making of the modern world. In part this was due to conscious choices, in part to the force of circumstances. Portugal never experienced the Protestant Reformation; indeed, it repudiated Protestantism and took vigorous steps to root it out. Retaining its intensely Catholic culture and identity, Portugal was thus never challenged by the pluralism of beliefs and value systems to which the Reformation helped give rise, nor did the this-worldly concerns that linked Protestantism to the growth of capitalism gain widespread acceptance. In part because its industrialization was postponed, Portugal's middle class grew but slowly, and society remained fixed in the two-class pattern of lord and vassal, patron and client, elite and mass.

Education and intellectual life likewise remained dominated by the church. At the base of its art and method of reasoning continued a Christian tradition of moral certainty, and Portugal thus rejected, or only weakly received, the influences of the Renaissance, the scientific revolution of Newton and Galileo, and the Enlightenment. Nor did Portugal experience, or want much to do with, the trend toward limited, representative government, as in England. Instead, by the end of the sixteenth century Portugal developed in an even more absolutist direction. When there was political dispute at all, it revolved around the issue of this new absolutist conception as opposed to the efforts of other interests of the realm to retain or restore their traditional rights. The issue was never one of popular or democratic government; instead, the political process focused almost entirely on competing elites and their relations with the crown or central state apparatus.

As in the reconquest, the church, the nobility, the king, and the cavalry remained at the center of state power. The patrimonialist state continued, molded into a more efficient form of mercantilism. Elitist rule was perpetuated, exercised through the imperial state apparatus by means of royal patronage and military and church control. In this way the state remained largely autonomous, exercising control over the social classes and regulating through them the entire nation. Under the system of absolute monarchy, the king exercised unlimited authority, and the traditional rights were submerged. The prince and the state became one; the *res publica* became identified with the will of the monarch. There was no participation of the nation in the government. The king could still grant privileges, but they were no longer inviolate; he had "free administration" over all. This seventeenth- and eighteenth-century concept of an "organic monarchy" represented a further elaboration and more absolutist form of the earlier model. The authoritarian, hierarchical, corporate, patrimonialist state and society fashioned by the fifteenth and sixteenth centuries remained the operating reality, and even in the era of Portugal's decline in succeeding periods, it was this older and historical model that the Portuguese harked back to and sought to resurrect, not a more democratic one.[26]

The Decline of the Portuguese Empire

From its high point in the early sixteenth century, the Portuguese empire went into a centuries-long process of decay and eventual fragmentation. Portugal was a small country, which lacked the resources to manage such a far-flung empire in competition with the more powerful Dutch, British, and French. Moreover, as the royal family degenerated, its kings lost the skills necessary for the management of this complex, worldwide patrimonialist order. In retrospect, what seems important is not so much the Portuguese decline of the seventeenth and eighteenth centuries but the ability of such a small nation to explore, conquer, and hold as much as it did for as long as it did. In no small part, this was due to the strength and viability of the political institutions Portugal had developed, which, however, as we have repeatedly stressed, remained fundamentally different from those emerging in England and elsewhere in northern Europe.

The era of Pombal's reforms, 1750–1777, is important to this discussion in two major ways. First, Pombal sharply curtailed the influence of some of the major corporate units in Portugal, the church (especially the Order of Jesus) and the guilds. This was not so much the end of "feudalism" in Portugal and the ushering in of a new Enlightenment, however, as it was an effort to reassert the power of the centralizing authority, in the classic fashion, against the newest decentralizing tendencies that had been under way for some decades under a succession of weak and incompetent monarchs. Pombal's efforts at reform were aimed not so much at bringing Portugal abreast of the rest of Europe as at expanding the ruling elite loyal to absolutism. Viewed as the historic struggle between the central authority on the one hand and the influence of the nobility and the powers and rights of special interests on the other, this was really not a step toward "modernization" but, in fact, the reassertion of the classic Portuguese political struggle going back for hundreds of years. The second aspect of the Pombalian era that requires comment is the question of whether Pombal was a dictator. History provides a clue, for in essence what Pombal did, in an era of crisis comparable to that in Portugal in the 1920s, was to gather more of the strings of power in his hands than any ruler of Portugal in roughly two-and-a-half centuries. Pombal was in a sense a precursor of the modern-day dictatorship of Salazar, but he was also a particularly adept manipulator of the patrimonialist state apparatus, a late eighteenth-century practitioner of an ancient system that was and remained the dominant form of exercising political authority.[27] In this sense, too, there are parallels with Salazar and Caetano.

Following Pombal's demise, Portugal floundered again. The threads holding together society and polity unraveled further. The monarchy was again ineffectual. The unraveling reached the point of almost complete disintegration under the onslaught of French revolutionary ideas, the Napoleonic occupation, the popular uprising and expulsion of Napoleon's forces, and finally the loss of Brazil. In the meantime a fledgling middle class had grown up, principally in Porto and Lisbon, liberal and rationalist ideas had become fashionable among some urban elements, and Masonic and other movements had challenged the hegemony of church and crown.

Previously, the operational code of the Portuguese system had always been that while elite rule was necessary and that the dominant institutions would be perpetuated, the bases of elite rule could be broadened through patronage, sinecures, and accommodation to new social groups. Now, however, with the ruling elites failing to accommodate themselves to this code, the aspiring liberal republican forces had no choice but to go outside the system and seek to overthrow it. This occurred in the liberal revolutions of 1820 and 1836; it would occur again in the republican revolts of 1891 and 1910 and in the revolution of 1974.

The old order cracked, but it did not crumble. Although the constitution of 1822 and the abolition of the guilds in 1834 represented liberal triumphs, the ancient system of privilege and aristocratic rule survived. The new elites aped and adopted the old aristocratic ways. The laws changed, the persons in power changed, but the system endured. The landholding pattern remained intact, and the church maintained its near monopoly on educational and cultural life. Nor was the political structure altered very much in its operating realities. Indeed, in the person of the crown, now limited somewhat by "constitutional" restrictions, and in the administrative machinery, much of the structure of the patrimonialist state also remained intact.[28]

Nineteenth-Century Reforms

The theory of absolute monarchy of the seventeenth and eighteenth centuries had not been notably popular in Portugal because of the Portuguese tradition of countervailing corporate privilege and group rights; in the early nineteenth century the traditional ties with and admiration for Great Britain, the newer rationalist writings and liberal philosophy, and the growing popularity of French revolutionary doctrines made the old absolutism even less acceptable. Monarchy remained the ideal, but in the Portuguese tradition this would be a "tempered monarchy." The monarch would still hold the reins, but more loosely, and he would be restricted in his powers. This ideal, however, was now combined in a confused way with only half-digested Enlightenment ideas, with the model of the French Revolution, and with British parliamentarianism, party politics, and loyal opposition, which the Portuguese never fully comprehended and which were at variance with their own history and national values. Legal theorist and *político* Ribeiro dos Santos, for example, was a staunch admirer of the British ideas of contract between ruler and ruled, supremacy of laws, inviolable rights, popular sovereignty, and all the classic nineteenth-century liberal values. At the formal and constitutional level, indeed, these ideas triumphed in the nineteenth century, as reflected in the imitation of British institutional forms. In the idea of a constitutional monarchy in 1808, the liberal constitution of 1822, and finally the establishment of a republic in 1910, one sees the effort to solve Portugal's manifest and centuries-long problems through the imitation of a foreign, especially the British, model.[29]

Although the forms were constitutional and republican, the operating realities were quite different. It proved impossible to establish a system of self-government in a country where such traditions were wholly absent. The two "parties" that emerged, Regenerators and Progressives, were in fact coteries of politicians and local notables without solid backing from the people.[30] Elections were chiefly efforts by these two rival factions to buy the votes of the public. As in Spain, *caciquismo* flourished, with local and regional notables and "bosses" delivering the vote in their areas in return for certain favors and patronage. Rather than implying much genuine "democratization," politics became the way for the new urban bourgeoisie to rise to positions of power and wealth.[31] It was a means of expanding the elite somewhat to accommodate to nineteenth-century pressures, while maintaining the elitist system intact. No one, neither elites nor bourgeoisie, took the ideas of popular sovereignty and participation seriously. And although the remnants of feudal privilege had been legally abolished, the power of the church, the oligarchy, and other historical corporate groups remained intact. These sectors, and the *homens bons*, continued to dominate Portuguese society and politics as they had always done in the past. Moreover, in the more authoritarian constitution of 1824, which became the rallying cry of conservative elements opposed to the liberal document of 1822, the old ideas remained powerful, and the concept of the traditional monarchy with representation in the Cortes by the three traditional estates was resurrected. Indeed, these competing ideas and forces, the struggles and frequent civil wars between those who defended unequivocally the traditional authority structures of the old regime and those who would modify them somewhat to provide for the admission of several new elites to the system, furnish the background for much of nineteenth-century Portuguese history. Real democracy, however, was out of the question; indeed, it was seldom mentioned.

It is tempting to dismiss the entire century of earlier Portuguese "liberalism" and "republicanism" from 1822 until 1926 as an aberration, a temporary break in what was a far longer and stronger au-

73

thoritarian tradition, a set of institutions solely "for the English to see" and without basis in Portuguese history. This is what the New State propagandists attempted to do in their repudiation of the republican and liberal ideologies, painting this era in the vilest of terms, emphasizing its negative attributes and downgrading its accomplishments. While this interpretation is certainly too strong, the opposite and liberal one is certainly wrong as well. As exemplified especially in the writings of the liberal historian A. H. de Oliveira Marques,[32] the nineteenth century is pictured as a period of great progress, characterized by the gradual opening and democratization of the political system and hence demonstrating an *inevitable evolution* toward liberalism and republicanism, which culminated in the final overthrow of the monarchy and the establishment of the republic in 1910. This interpretation not only overstates and hence distorts nineteenth-century Portuguese history but also biases our perspective of the twentieth by lending support to the myth that the military revolution of 1926 that brought Salazar and the corporatist regime to power were of necessity unpopular and reactionary developments, a turning back from what had seemed the inevitable progression of liberalism and pluralism.

First, it should be said that Oliveira Marques is himself a partisan and a liberal and thus has a strong interest in marshaling the facts that support his interpretation. Second, it is clear that he has overstressed the "liberalizing" and "democratizing" influences of this period, for we have already seen that Portugal in the nineteenth century was still an elitist and patrimonialist system with only weakly articulated notions of genuine popular rule and where the historical corporatist and authoritarian patterns remained dominant despite the facade of constitutionalism and parliamentarism. The elites were expanded, to be sure, and some new elements managed to circulate in power, but the historical *system* remained.[33]

Third, the progress of the "liberal" period can easily be exaggerated. True, Portugal began a modest economic takeoff in the nineteenth century, and some other of its institutions were reformed, but one can also argue that, given the times, economic progress was virtually inevitable no matter who was in power and in fact would have been far greater had the country not been plagued by the partisan conflict and civil strife that passed for "democracy" during this period. Fourth, it is significant that even the so-called republican regimes and institutions in Portugal exhibit authoritarian, elitist, and patrimonialist features and in reality are not altogether different from those regimes and institutions that were manifestly authoritarian. One need only look, for example, at the so-called Magna Charta of

Portuguese associational life—the decree-law of May 9, 1891, governing the organization of class associations—to see that even in this "liberal" document group and associational life was about as carefully regulated and controlled from above as it had been under absolutism and would continue to be under the Estado Novo. The so-called republican era in Portugal was, in fact, far less republican and liberal and far more authoritarian and elitist than its proponents would admit. Indeed, as Oliveira Marques's own research has shown, the only time that the parliamentary regime functioned at all effectively was when it was least parliamentary—namely, when it was governed by a strong monarch.[34]

Even so, it must also be admitted that some new currents and social forces had emerged in Portugal during the nineteenth century and that alongside the traditional pyramid of power and only partially integrated with it there had, as in Spain, grown up a new and parallel structure, a "second Portugal," nascently liberal in character and challenging the traditional assumptions and institutions. Although it remained a minority strain, still secondary to the dominant elitist, authoritarian, and patrimonialist tradition, it was strong enough that it could not be dismissed out of hand. When Salazar later made an attempt to put it down, he found that to do so would require a full-fledged dictatorship and widespread repression—all ingredients that contributed to the ultimate failure of his corporative experiments. This liberal and democratizing current culminated in the establishment of a republic from 1910 to 1926;[35] it would later reemerge in the 1974 revolt.

The First Portuguese Republic

The first Portuguese republic, initiated in 1910, was characterized by disorder, chaos, and a long-term trend toward fragmentation, polarization, and anarchy. The litany of the Portuguese republic is the oft-repeated history of a futile effort to erect an inorganic, liberal parliamentary system in a country where organicism, centralism, and unity had always been the dominant characteristics. Its parties were personalistic and so fractionalized that no one of them was able to command anything like a majority. The country and its politicians lacked previous experience with effective self-government; excesses abounded and the usual machinery of government tended to break down. Radical reforms were initiated but seldom implemented; they nevertheless served to provoke the hostility of the traditional forces. A rising middle class in the cities was eager to inherit the wealth and privileges previously reserved for the elites, and a nascent trade

75

union movement was similarly organizing to challenge the traditional order. But the newer social and political forces were still inchoate and disorganized. During the sixteen years of the republic, Portugal experienced twenty-one revolutions and forty-four cabinet reorganizations. There were numerous assassinations, strikes, and bombings. The web of traditional society began to become unraveled; the historical way of managing change seemed to be getting out of hand.[36]

There were continuities as well. Patronage and spoils continued to serve as the grease that kept the wheels moving; only now the rewards and support system were managed in new ways and for the benefit of a somewhat expanded constituency. Even at the height of this republican period, Portugal remained an oligarchic system governed by the *homens bons*. The system remained authoritarian, tutelary, and paternalistic; government programs were carried out occasionally for the benefit of the popular classes, but these programs emanated from the top, and in no sense did the lower classes *participate* in their formulation or implementation. The administrative state continued to stand, although it was now manned by a new political elite that created new public positions and sinecures filled by its own friends and supporters. All in all, the republic did not represent such a sharp break with the past as is often imagined. Moreover, under the dictatorship of Sidonio Pais in 1917–1918, judged by many historians to be the best government Portugal had during this so-called republican period, some of the earliest experimentation with a revived structure of corporatist state organization and interest representation went forward.

To the political problems of the republic were added the economic crises of 1918–1919, the bank-note scandal of 1924–1925,[37] and a virtually continuous history of economic mismanagement and corruption. Meanwhile, right-wing and traditionalist forces of both integralist and monarchist orientation launched a number of abortive coups, which came close to toppling the government on at least three occasions.[38] The army was also restless. It had come out of World War I discredited; poorly trained and equipped, its recruits became to their humiliation the "trench diggers of Europe." Following the war the army was more and more determined to restore both its own and the nation's prestige.[39]

Public sentiment began to swing away from the republic. Significantly, this shift encompassed both the university students and the trade union leaders, as well as the bulk of the middle class who were made increasingly impatient by the disorder and accelerating chaos.[40] A whole generation of young intellectuals had grown up convinced of the bankruptcy of liberal parliamentarianism and of the unacceptability of socialism. To them, a third alternative, corporatism, seemed the wave of the future. Other integralist and Catholic political movements, Integralismo Lusitano and the Centro Académico de Democracia Cristã, were similarly gaining strength.[41] In the army, too, the same corporative, integralist, and nationalist ideas were widespread. Although the details had not been worked out, as early as 1922 it was clear that there would soon be a military solution and that the solution would be corporatist, authoritarian, and nationalist in character.[42]

The coup that toppled the republic in 1926 was thus not just the response of a handful of military officers and reactionaries but a reflection of widespread public dissatisfaction and general erosion of support for republican ideas. Certainly no one rose up to defend the republic; there were few laments for its passing and many cheers. Nor was the coup of 1926 the entirely reactionary movement often pictured. It was not the most right-wing Integralists, Monarchists, and Fascists who came to power but the more moderate elements, who sought to restore a system of order and social peace. Nor did they necessarily want to roll back the reforms that had occurred under republican rule. In keeping with its nationalist character, the new regime sought to restore Portugal to its previous national prestige. It sought to create indigenous institutions to replace the British imports that in the Portuguese context had proved inappropriate. In other words, the new government sought not to turn the clock back but to ratify the social and political changes that had taken place (the emergence of new elites and bourgeoisie and of an urban labor movement) and to do so within a framework of order, discipline, and authority.

Other than these vague general ideas, however, characteristic of so many military coups in the Iberic-Latin context, the generals who seized power in 1926 lacked a concrete program. Hence, the government muddled along through 1927 and 1928, when Salazar first became finance minister, and even until 1930, by which time he had more strongly consolidated his influence.[43] For Salazar and his supporters *did* have a specific plan and program, a "third way" that called for the corporatization of the entire Portuguese system. In the early 1930s Salazar began to put his corporative and traditionalist ideology into practice.

Portuguese Political Culture:
An Overview of Social and Economic Structures

In 1926 Portugal was, as it remained until 1974, at the outer margins of Europe, a distant country far from the centers of "civilization," as measured not only in kilometers but also in time. Portugal was *in*

Europe geographically but not *of* Europe socially, politically, or psychologically.[44] That ambiguity continued up until the last few years.

Continental Portugal lies at the westernmost point of Europe, bounded on the west and south by the Atlantic Ocean and on the north and east by Spain. It is shaped somewhat like an upright rectangle running approximately 350 miles from the northern border with Spanish Galicia along the Minho River to the southern coast of the Algarve on the Gulf of Cadiz. Across, it is approximately 140 miles from the Atlantic to the Spanish border. Including the Azores and Madeira islands, Portugal contains about 35,000 square miles, roughly the size of the state of Indiana.

Geographically, mainland Portugal is divided into three distinct regions.[45] The north is hilly and mountainous, characterized by small plots and farms carved out of the valleys and hillsides. The land is harsh and cruel, the temperatures extreme, and for six months of the year (October through March) there is no rainfall. One need only look at this rocky countryside to understand why Portugal was never able to develop the agricultural surplus on which a more advanced economy might have been based. Over the centuries strong, resilient smallholders, through backbreaking hand labor, have cut steps into this mountainous terrain and carefully conserved and tilled the meager soil, and it is in the weather-beaten but enduring faces of these people that many Portuguese still see the true virtues and original character, Catholic and conservative, of their people and their nation.

Southern Portugal, the Alentejo, is flat and gently rolling, dominated by large estates and a lord-peasant pattern that, until recently, had not changed greatly since feudal times. The land here is also generally infertile, suitable for grazing but probably not for intensive agriculture. That Portugal could solve its rural and agricultural problems by dividing up these estates and giving the land to the peasants, a recurrent theme in reformist and revolutionary programs, may be no more than a dream. The issue is politically charged, but economically it is clear that land redistribution by itself will not be sufficient to make the Alentejo prosperous and viable.

Central Portugal is more varied in the size of the landholdings, social relations, and economic conditions. There are numerous medium-sized and family farms, something of a rural middle class, and agriculture oriented toward internal consumption. This area includes the country's major city, Lisbon, most of the industry, and hence an urban-industrial class system as well as a rural-agricultural one. The three regions of Portugal thus support quite different life styles, and their social structures often reflect their varied patterns of man-to-land and man-to-man relations. To integrate these diverse regions, to link them by roads and other grids, and to centralize authority in a diverse and difficult land have been among the historical tasks of all Portuguese governments.

The population of continental Portugal is just under nine million, and in recent decades it has been declining because of falling birth rates and heavy emigration, chiefly to the other Western European nations where wages are higher. Emigration, the drafting of a generation of young men to fight in Africa, and the steady flow of rural elements to the big cities like Porto and Lisbon have drained the farm areas of their ablest workers, at the same time adding to the slums and concomitant social problems of the cities. As a reflection of its agricultural and traditional character and the incipient nature of its industry, Portugal remains 30 to 40 percent rural, but the rural-urban ratio is changing rapidly. Porto now has a population of approximately 400,000 while that of Lisbon is around 1,000,000; numerous smaller towns and provincial capitals have populations ranging from 20,000 to 100,000.[46]

Portugal's Class System. Socially, Portugal has retained, even in modern times, a hierarchical and rigidly stratified system with immense gaps between classes.[47] Its elites, we have seen, have been expanded somewhat, but the system is still an elitist one, and the elites themselves constituted no more than 1 or 2 percent of the total population. While these elites have often been exceedingly wealthy and influential, the urban and rural masses remain powerless and shockingly poor by European standards, while the middle class was comparatively small, constituting perhaps 15 to 20 percent of the population. Illiteracy was officially given at about 20 percent of the population, but the percentage of actual and functional illiteracy was surely far higher. In housing, medical care, social services, and the like, Portugal has also lagged far behind the rest of Europe. Family, neighborhood, kinship, and patronal ties have remained exceedingly important at all levels of society, often more important than the impersonal ties of professional associations, political organizations, and government social programs.

Since Portugal (before 1974) had never had a full-scale social revolution, its ancient ruling classes remained largely intact. The nobility and the older aristocratic families were still powerful, and there remained a strong monarchist movement. The elite was not monolithic, however; its members could be found in a number of political movements. The elite's wealth to a considerable extent was concentrated in land and agriculture and in the picturesque *quintas* (ranches) and *latifundia* (estates) that dot the Portuguese countryside.

But in recent decades commerce, industry, shipping, banking, and manufacturing had grown immensely. There emerged not one but several elites, both old rich and new rich, though often intermarried and interrelated, an older rural aristocracy and several newer urban ones. Well-connected, wealthy, arrogant, and socially "superior," closely bound up with the state and its various political and economic activities, able generally to protect their interests no matter which faction controlled the government, the powerful elites were all-pervasive, although they were not always of a single mind.

The growing middle sector developed little consciousness as a class, tending to ape upper-class ways. Although this group is expanding in numbers there was—up until recently—no such thing as a "middle-class society" emerging in Portugal in the Anglo-American mold. The line between those who work with their hands and those who do not has remained a rigid, almost impenetrable, barrier, perpetuating the fundamental two-class nature of society. Social mobility existed for some lower-class elements, but only up to a certain point, when the ascriptive criteria of wealth, family, prestige, social background, and the right access and connections became all-important.[48]

The Portuguese lower classes are diverse, but they are all exceedingly deprived by any one of a host of social and economic measures. The ranks of the "popular" classes include the smallholders and tenant farmers of the north, the day laborers and peasant farmers of the Alentejo, the flood of recent arrivals in the cities' teeming shanytowns, and the slightly better-off industrial workers and low-level government employees. Except for the latter groups, the bulk of the lower classes had received few benefits from recent government social programs and had not yet begun to share in the new affluence of modern Europe. It is among these elements that illiteracy, malnutrition, and malnutrition-related diseases were most pronounced; frustration and despair were also widespread. Largely disfranchised, uninvolved in national social and political life, without any say in the government programs that affect them most intimately, the Portuguese lower classes, who constitute the overwhelming majority of the population, remained only marginally part of the nation; they constituted the "clients" of the upper- and upper-middle-class "patrons," third- and fourth-class citizens looked down upon and kept in place by the other two.

Class lines in Portugal were, if anything, even more tightly drawn than in Latin America. Portugal was not only a Latin society organized in the historical hierarchical fashion but also decidedly Old World—and Old World in a pre-World War I sense.[49] It is as though a whole half-century (or more) had passed Portugal by, and in a sense it had. There were probably few societies left in the world—and certainly not in Europe—where breeding, dress, family, speech, bearing, and the proper credentials remained as important in determining where an individual fit in the social order. The sense of place, status, and hierarchy was all-important. The system provided for little social mobility across class lines, except perhaps through education and through government itself (a theme particularly important for our study since Salazar, Caetano, and many others of the Estado Novo were of comparatively humble, middle-class origins and earned their elevated positions in the society through intellectual brilliance and achievement and then through government service). One's turn in line, how and when one gets waited on by service people, access to government officials or to the patron, when one's papers are processed, the treatment one receives in a store, business, or governmental agency—all of these are determined by where one fits in the system, what rank one holds.

Portugal's Economic Structure. Historically, Portugal has been a poor country, the poorest in Western Europe, an economic "embarrassment" to the West, just as Albania is to the East. Portuguese workers are the lowest paid in Western Europe, and in the rural areas the bulk of the population ekes out a meager subsistence. More recently, however, Portugal, too (particularly its upper and middle classes), has begun to benefit from the new economic affluence that characterizes so much of Western Europe. GNP has increased in recent years at a steady rate of 5 to 6 percent per year, and since the 1940s per capita income has doubled, tripled, and was in 1972 close to $1,000 per person per year. Although one still is shocked at the poverty, wretched living conditions, and disease endemic in both rural and urban slums, it is clear that Portugal had begun to "take off" economically to the extent that it was difficult any longer to classify Portugal with the rest of the underdeveloped world. Though the economy is often still weak, the income curve skewed, and the standard of living low by the criteria of the rest of Western Europe, Portugal has clearly passed an economic threshold; its society has accelerated the process toward modernity and even a certain *embourgeoisement*. All this has had important implications for our study of corporative ideology and institutions and their relation to Portuguese development.[50]

Until the 1930s Portugal remained overwhelmingly an agricultural economy and country, and even today in many outlying areas and villages social and economic arrangements are still largely tied to the ownership of land and the traditional relations of patron and peasant.[51] In the early 1970s agriculture contributed only about 15 percent of GNP, but it still employed some 30 percent of the labor force in arrangements generally hampered by a lack of modern production techniques. Since the 1930s, manufacturing and industry have constituted a steadily increasing share of GNP (now up to 35 percent), creating a large urban work force, raising living standards and expectations, and hence hastening the flood of migrants to the cities. Tourism has also become a major Portuguese industry in recent years, with both its positive and negative consequences. Portugal is moderately rich in mineral resources, with significant deposits of wolfram (especially profitable during World War II), tin, iron ore, coal, and copper. The fishing industry is of special importance, tied as it is to Portugal's historical preoccupation with the sea. Principal exports include wine and other alcoholic beverages, wood and wood products, textiles, chemical products, both common and precious metals, and electrical equipment. Imports include chiefly the mineral and vegetable products that Portugal does not produce, chemical products, clothing, machinery, trucks, and transport equipment.

There are three further points about the Portuguese economy that should be emphasized. First, although Portugal was in a sense a capitalist system, it remained dominated in so many ways by a tradition of monopoly, mercantilism, and state ownership that some distinct interpretations of political economy are required to understand how the system worked.[52] The Portuguese were not so much Schumpeterian entrepreneurs but rather a nation of small merchants, family enterprises, and established or aspiring burghers, tied together at the top by class, family, and political relationships and dependent on government for contracts, access, and special privileges. It is more an etatist system, or system of state capitalism, than one of *laissez faire* and free enterprise.

The second point that needs emphasis is the close relationship that existed between the state-capitalist economy of metropolitan Portugal and that of her former overseas possessions, principally Angola and Mozambique. The two were bound together through a powerful conglomerate of banks, shipping companies, import-export concerns, landholding and mining interests, and so forth—to say nothing of the governmental structure of a bureaucratic empire.[53] And, third, we should mention the increasing importance of Portugal's economic relations with Europe and the Common Market with its future implications for Portuguese trade, internal industrial development, and international alignments.[54]

Conclusions

In the first part of this chapter we emphasized the pervasive influences of elites and elitism in Portuguese history, of authoritarian-

corporatist social and political structures, and of the expanding patrimonialist state apparatus in the Portuguese system. These structures and behavior patterns encompass not only the civil bureaucracy
but also the army, the church (although in present-day Portugal
church and state are officially separated and the Catholic church
seems less important as a political force), and virtually all groups and
institutions. Elitist, authoritarian, corporatist, and patrimonialist social and political patterns are so strongly a part of the Portuguese
political culture that they remained intact even in the face of significant economic growth, industrialization, and accelerated social
change. Indeed, the persistence of these traditional institutions, the
way they have adapted to modernization, is one of the main themes of
this study.

One cannot but be struck by the conservative and traditionalist
character of the entire Portuguese nation, socially, politically, economically, and psychologically. The importance of history, place, tradition,
formality, hierarchy, and the past is the main theme running through
the travel accounts as well as the more scholarly literature.[55] Portugal
remained a nation of melancholy, frequently of lethargy and social
stagnation. Its people were peaceful, patient, acquiescent, and conservative. Theirs was a culture and character molded by detachment
from the outside world, by centuries of struggle against sea and
infertile hillside, by resignation, and by hard labor and few opportunities for advancement. Although their condition was improving
and most Portuguese by the early 1970s had come to feel more
optimistic about the future, life had always been difficult for them.
Even in an era of rising economic prosperity, they continued to cling
to the older and simpler values and to reject the untried, the uncertain, and the new. In many respects, therefore, theirs remained a
subject political culture rather than a *participatory* one.[56] Clearly the
Portuguese revolution will force a reinterpretation of some of these
stereotypes, but just what has changed and how much Portugal
remains the same in the wake of the revolution are still open questions.

In short, Portugal had, at least until the 1974 revolution and
perhaps beyond, both a corporate state, formally instituted in the
1930s, and a corporate society, culture, and tradition. The emphasis
throughout Portuguese history, reaching back to the origins of
Lusitania, in virtually all areas of national life and among all social
sectors, had been on hierarchy, authority, patrimonialism, and a kind
of inherent, ingrained, almost natural corporatism. These factors
weigh heavily in Portuguese history, where neither the political
culture nor the society or economy nor the historical tradition itself

provided a strong basis for democracy. Indeed, one is struck in this survey by how weak and infrequent democracy has been in Portugal. The history and political culture surveyed here may serve to indicate how precarious the opening toward democracy that began in Iberia in the mid-1970s may still be—and how strong the non- and anti-democratic institutions most likely still are.

Notes

1. A good example of this tendency is vol. 10 of Will Durant's epochal *The Story of Civilization*, entitled *Rousseau and the Revolution* (New York: Simon and Schuster, 1967), chap. 10; also, Marcus Chique, *Dictator of Portugal: A Life of the Marques of Pombal* (London: Sedwig and Jacobson, 1938).

2. Useful surveys in English include William C. Atkinson, *A History of Spain and Portugal* (Baltimore: Penguin, 1960); W. J. Barnes, *Portugal: Gateway to Greatness* (London: Stanford, 1950); H. V. Livermore, *A New History of Portugal* (Cambridge: Cambridge University Press, 1969); Charles E. Nowell, *A History of Portugal* (Princeton, N.J.: Van Nostrand, 1952); and Stanley Payne, *A History of Spain and Portugal* (Madison: University of Wisconsin Press, 1973).

3. Roman rule in Iberia is summarized in Rafael Altamira, *A History of Spain* (New York: Van Nostrand, 1949), chap. 3. For the corporative link, see Marcello Caetano, *O sistema corporativo* (Lisbon: Oficinas Graficas de O Jornal do Comercio e das Colonias, 1938).

4. Atkinson, *History*.

5. Patrimonialism, of course, was one of Weber's forms of traditional authority. See the discussion in Reinhard Bendix, *Max Weber: An Intellectual Portrait* (Garden City, N.Y.: Anchor-Doubleday, 1960), pp. 329–81. For an application to Latin America, see Richard Morse, in Louis Hartz et al., *The Founding of New Societies* (New York: Harcourt Brace, 1964), published also in Howard J. Wiarda ed., *Politics and Social Change in Latin America* (Amherst: University of Massachusetts Press, 1982).

6. The discussion here is derived chiefly from Manuel Paulo Merêa, *O poder real e as cortes* (Coimbra: Coimbra Ed., 1923); Raymundo Faoro, *Os donos do poder* (Pôrto Alegre: Ed Globo, 1958); and Henrique de Gama Barros, *Historia da administração pública em Portugal nos séculos XII–XV* (Lisbon: Liv. Sa da Costa, 1945).

7. Faoro, *Os donos do poder*. For a contemporary extension, see Lawrence S. Graham, "Portugal: The Bureaucracy of Empire" (Paper presented at the Workshop on Modern Portugal, University of New Hampshire, Durham, October 10–14, 1973).

8. Guenter Lewy, *Constitutionalism and Statescraft during the Golden Age of Spain* (Geneva: E. Droz, 1960). The critical importance of Catholicism and the church in Portuguese history and political culture is stressed by Thomas C. Bruneau, "The Politics of Religion in an Authoritarian Regime: The Case of Portugal" (MS, McGill University, Dept. of Political Science, April 1974).

9. Martins, "Portugal," in Archer and Giner eds., *Contemporary Europe: Class, Status, and Power* (London: Weidenfeld and Nicolson, 1971).

10. The concept of the administrative state is elaborated in Graham, "Portugal." See also Magali Sarfatti, *Spanish Bureaucratic-Patrimonialism in America* (Berkeley: Institute of International Studies, University of California, 1966); and Faoro, *Os donos do poder.*

11. See Arnold Strickon and Sidney M. Greenfield, eds., *Structure and Process in Latin America: Patronage, Clientage, and Power Systems* (Albuquerque: University of New Mexico Press, 1972).

12. Later corporatist theorists, in harking back to the order, stability, and unity of this era, largely ignored its violence, terror, conflict, and misery. In fact, the medieval era and the guild system, which the corporatists so romanticized, were not always efficient, happy, or pleasant. See Barros, *Historia,* vol. 4, pp. 113–72.

13. Faoro, *Os donos do poder;* Merêa, *O poder real.*

14. Merêa, *O poder real,* p. 9.

15. Ibid. See also Morse, in Hartz, *Founding of New Societies,* pp. 123–77.

16. Merêa, *O poder real.*

17. Ibid.

18. Ibid.

19. Barros, *Historia,* vol. 3, pp. 104, 129ff; also Vitorino Magalhães Godinho, *A estructura na antiga sociedade portuguesa* (Lisbon: Ed. Arcadia, 1971).

20. Merêa, *O poder real.*

21. The importance of Dom Pedro in articulating the model of a national patronage system has been stressed by Sidney Greenfield, "The Patrimonial State and Patron-Client Systems in the Fifteenth Century Writings of the Infante D. Pedro of Portugal" (Occasional Paper Series, Program in Latin American Studies, University of Massachusetts, 1976). For the importance of Suárez, see Morse, in Hartz, *Founding of New Societies;* and Ronald C. Newton, "On 'Functional Groups,' 'Fragmentation,' and 'Pluralism' in Spanish American Political Society," *Hispanic American Historical Review,* vol. 50 (February 1970), pp. 1–27. Both the Morse and Newton essays are reprinted in Wiarda, *Politics and Social Change.*

22. Stuart Schwartz, *Sovereignty and Society of Colonial Brazil* (Berkeley: University of California Press, 1973). See also Graham, "Portugal."

23. Bernice Hamilton, *Political Thought in Sixteenth-Century Spain* (Oxford: Oxford University Press, 1963).

24. Faoro, *Os donos do poder;* and Schwartz, *Sovereignty and Society.*

25. Ibid.; and José Calvet de Magalhães, *Historia do pensamento economico em Portugal: Da idade média ao mercantilismo* (Coimbra: Coimbra Ed., 1967).

26. An excellent discussion is Francisco Sarsfield Cabral, *Una perspectiva sobre Portugal* (Lisbon: Morães, 1973).

27. This interpretation derives from the preliminary research findings of two University of Massachusetts colleagues, Susan Schneider and Robert White.

28. Cabral, *Una perspectiva sobre Portugal.*

29. Merêa, *O poder real.*

30. Nowell, *History,* p. 209.

31. See Joel Serrão, " 'Decadence' and 'Regeneration' in Contemporary

Portugal" (Paper presented at the Workshop on Modern Portugal, University of New Hampshire, Durham, October 10–14, 1973).

32. Marques, *History of Portugal* (New York: Columbia University Press, 1972), vol. 2, p. 48.

33. An interesting historical interpretation of how Portuguese elites have been broadened without this implying much fundamental change in the nature of elitist rule is Henry Keith, "Point, Counterpoint in Reforming Portuguese Education, 1750–1973" (Paper presented at the Workshop on Moden Portugal, University of New Hampshire, Durham, October 10–14, 1973); see also Godinho, *A estructura.*

34. Marques, *History of Portugal,* vol. 2, p. 48.

35. A balanced treatment is Douglas L. Wheeler, "The Portuguese Revolution of 1910," *Journal of Modern History,* vol. 44 (June 1972), pp. 172–94.

36. Douglas L. Wheeler has written a book on this period; my own interpretation relies on his thorough historical investigations.

37. See the entertaining account by Murray Teigh Bloom, *The Man Who Stole Portugal* (London: Secker and Warburg, 1966).

38. See the three-volume study by Carlos Ferrão, *O integralismo e a República* (Lisbon: vols. 1 and 2, Inquérito.; vol. 3, O Século, 1964–1965).

39. This comes out clearly in the memoirs of Salazar's first secretary and military aide, Assis Gonçalves, *Intimidades de Salazar: O homem e a sua epoca* (Lisbon: Liv. Bertrand, 1972).

40. See A. H. de Oliveira Marques, "The Portuguese 1920s: A General Survey," *Iberian Studies,* vol. 2 (Spring 1973), pp. 32–40.

41. Richard A. H. Robinson, "The Religious Question and the Catholic Revival in Portugal, circa 1900–1930" (Paper presented at the Workshop on Modern Portugal, University of New Hampshire, Durham, October 10–14, 1973).

42. Based on Wheeler's oral account to the author of some of his research findings.

43. Marques, *History of Portugal,* vol. 2, pp. 139–40; and H. Martins, "Portugal," in S. J. Woolf, ed., *European Fascism* (New York: Vintage, 1969), pp. 312ff.

44. The material in this section is based upon the statistical materials available, as well as my own investigations, interviewing, and participant observation. Among the usual descriptive works are Nowell, *History,* chap. 1.

45. This division is the classic one in the geography books. For a study that discusses the distinct social patterns implied in these regional differences, see Martins, "Portugal" in Archer and Giner, eds., in *Contemporary Europe.*

46. Massimo Livi Bacci, *A Century of Portuguese Fertility* (Princeton: Princeton University Press, 1971).

47. An interesting historical interpretation is Cabral, *Una perspectiva sobre Portugal;* the best sociological discussion is that of Martins, "Portugal."

48. João Baptista Nunes Pereira Neto, "Social Evolution in Portugal since 1945," in Raymond S. Sayers, ed., *Portugal and Brazil in Transition* (Minneapolis: University of Minnesota Press, 1968), pp. 212–27.

49. Portugal in many respects still reminds one of Barbara Tuchman's

description of Europe on the eve of the twentieth century; see *The Proud Tower* (New York: Macmillan, 1962). See also Godinho, *A estructura.*

50. A useful survey compiled by the Bureau of International Commerce of the U.S. Department of Commerce is "Basic Data on the Economy of Portugal," *Overseas Business Reports,* October 1971; official Portuguese data are summarized in the *Sinopse de dados estatísticos.*

51. See the excellent work by José Cutileiro, *A Portuguese Rural Society* (Oxford: Clarendon, 1971).

52. Cabral, *Una perspectiva sobre Portugal;* Magalhães, *Historia do pensamento económico;* and Martins, "Portugal." For a general discussion, see also Andrew Schonfield, *Modern Capitalism: The Changing Balance of Public and Private Power* (London: Oxford University Press, 1965).

53. Graham, "Portugal."

54. Francisco Pereira da Moura, "Por onde vai a economia portuguesa?" (Paper presented at the Workshop on Modern Portugal, University of New Hampshire, Durham, October 10–14, 1973).

55. See, for example, the useful books by Hugh Kay, *Salazar and Modern Portugal* (London: Eyrie and Spottiswoode, 1970); and Peter Fryer and Patricia McGowan-Pinheiro, *Oldest Ally: A Portrait of Salazar's Portugal* (London: Dobson, 1961). It is significant that it is not just conservatives who point to the seemingly inherent conservative character of Portugal but liberals and leftists as well.

56. The reference is to the significant book by Gabriel Almond and Sidney Verba, *The Civic Culture* (Boston: Little, Brown, 1963). The most thorough comparable study of Portuguese political and social attitudes is Instituto Português de Opinião Pública e da Estudos de Mercado (IPOPE), *Os Portugueses e a política—1973* (Lisbon: Moraes, 1973).

3
Can Portugal Transcend Its Corporatist Tradition?

Not long ago both Portugal and Spain were widely viewed as examples of stable, modern, authoritarian-corporatist regimes. In scholarly papers and academic conferences, the Iberian cases were often cited as distinctive polities whose authoritarian-corporatist structures, rather than being swept away or transcended by the onslaught of industrialization and modernization, had proved to be remarkably stable, permeable, and long-lasting. Instead of temporary discontinuities on some unilinear path to modernity and democracy, the Spanish and Portuguese corporatist systems were viewed as constituting a third alternative route to development that was neither liberal nor Socialist, having particular dynamics and permanent sociopolitical structures of its own.[1]

The apparent about-face that Portugal has executed during the 1974–1975 revolution, however, has clearly rendered obsolete the argument for the permanence and stability of that particular authoritarian-corporatist regime. Although there remain important institutional continuities, Portugal has probably irrevocably abandoned the older corporative institutions of the Salazar era, and in the process it has increased considerably the pressures on neighboring Spain. What then is the precise nature of the new regime ushered in by the Portuguese revolution? What links does it have with the past, and how radical are its departures from earlier traditions? What possibilities exist for evolution toward liberal democracy, revolutionary socialism, or, alternatively, a more advanced and restructured form of corporatism? These are the principal questions that lie at the heart of this study.

Those who knew Portugal before the revolution of 1974 often find it difficult to believe that country could emerge from being a "sleepy," often backward, traditional, almost feudal and underdeveloped nation to become, in a few months perhaps, the cutting edge of a radical sociopolitical transformation (as it seemed in 1974–1975) in Western Europe. Portugal is usually remembered as a clean, whitewashed, and profoundly conservative country. Locked into a nineteenth-century, Catholic-corporatist form of society and polity on the model of Vatican I (1870) or at best *Rerum Novarum* (1889) or *Quadragesimo Anno* (1931), it was a place where peasants along rural roadways still doffed their hats to their "betters" and where "the proud tower" of a pre-World War I social hierarchy remained solidly in place.[2] That such a traditionalist country should suddenly emerge at the forefront of European social and political change, striving to achieve full and genuine participation and manifesting a pluralism that encompasses and accepts the most widely divergent views, seems almost inconceivable.

Few would quarrel with the argument that the older, "dinosauric" Portuguese system needed a thorough restructuring, and the coup of April 1974 was thus warmly welcomed by liberals and social democrats everywhere as opening the way to a new period of democracy and social justice. But liberals too were astounded at the pace and comprehensiveness of the changes taking place. For the Portuguese seemed already to have considered liberalism and European-style multiparty government, however briefly, and to have rejected or transcended them in favor of more radical solutions. In 1975 it was the only country in Western Europe with Communists in the cabinet; the Communists also moved rapidly to gain a virtual monopoly in the trade union structure and to dominate much of the media and local administration. Moreover, both the government and an important segment of the armed forces seemed inclined to support an opening to the left. Social and political institutions throughout the country were overturned and their leadership replaced by radical and revolutionary elements; and on the Portuguese best-seller lists in late 1974 books by Marx, Engels, and Lenin occupied seven of the top ten places.[3]

It was clear that a revolution had begun in Portugal, not just another palace coup; a profound restructuring was going forward, not just the usual circulation of elites or modest "renovation" so common in Iberian and Latin American history. From numerous indications, and apart from the April 1975 election results, Portugal appeared in some of the literature of the time to be veritably leaping across stages, bypassing liberalism and "bourgeois" democracy, and perhaps proceeding directly and rapidly to a stage of revolutionary syndicalism or socialism. In terms of U.S. national security preoccupations, furthermore, Portugal was beginning to look like the leading (and tilting?)

member in a new domino theory that envisioned the entire northern rim of the Mediterranean possibly turning red in the not-too-distant future.

We now know that corporatism and authoritarianism, at least in the Salazar-Caetano mold, are not necessarily stable, much less permanent, systems. New options are being considered and acted upon, new routes are being explored, and new developmental avenues are being opened up. As the dust and smoke begin to settle in Portugal we need to ask ourselves to what degree this revolution is authentic. Can Portugal really transcend its corporatist-authoritarian past so completely and so quickly, or is it more likely in the final reckoning to initiate more limited changes, to renovate and adjust, to update its older historical practices and institutions, and to form a newer, modernized, and more pluralist system that may eventually evolve toward a more typically European polity of the type that Lijphart calls "consociational democracy" or that Lorwin refers to as "segmented pluralism" and Rokkan labels "corporate pluralism"?[4] Is it reasonable to expect that Portugal may now represent a certain wave of the future, an example of "advanced" European politics and social change, a nation proceeding directly from one of the most backward and retrograde capitalist systems into a fully Socialist or syndicalist type? If so, how and in what sense? How also do these changes affect our interpretations of the Iberic-Latin development process? Do they challenge some of the dominant paradigms of society and polity found in the literature? Finally, what do these developments imply not only for Portugal, but for Spain, Western Europe, NATO, and the United States as well?[5]

Corporatism and Political Change: Beyond "Criollo" Politics

Peruvian President Juan Velasco Alvarado (1968–1975) once contrasted his revolutionary regime with the previous "democratic" system, which, he declared, had little meaning for the average citizen. Formal democracy, he asserted, "represented nothing more than the interplay of political interests, for which the people and its great problems were always secondary matters." Because it ignored "the authentic interests of the people," and rested on "respect for the rules of a politically decadent game which only benefited the privileged groups of the country," Alvarado rejected its legitimacy. "Our objectives," he declared, "have nothing to do with the traditional forms of *criollo* politics."[6]

American scholars have focused on the "*criollo* politics" pattern as typical of the Iberian and Latin American countries. The most influential analytic model for explaining that pattern, as indicated in chapter 1, was elaborated by Charles W. Anderson.[7] In his view, the focus of politics in Iberia and Latin America is constant negotiations among competing groups to balance and adjust their power position. While newer and more modern groups and institutions have gradually been grafted on in a more or less continuous process of fusion and absorption, the Iberian and Latin American political systems have retained a mausoleum-like appearance. Few genuine revolutions have occurred to overturn the social class structure of these societies from the fifteenth century to the present. Hence, political ideologies and social institutions such as Thomistic political doctrines and world views, landed oligarchies, the plantation system, and other feudal structures, which have largely disappeared or been superseded in northern Europe and North America, still survive in Iberia and Latin America. Alongside them, newer societal interests and political currents such as an emergent middle class, trade unions, and the class-based parties and ideologies to which industrialization and modernization often give rise, now coexist.

Change has occurred, but it has seldom been democratic, let alone revolutionary. In Iberia and Latin America one stage or epoch, instead of transcending or replacing another, has characteristically been fused with it. Similarly, development has taken the form not so much of a fundamental transformation in social structure as of a gradual accommodation of an Ibero-Catholic, patrimonialist social order to the pressures of modern industrial civilization. Change has come to Iberia and Latin America, but most often under the auspices of an authoritarian and paternalistic elite, which directed it from above; it has been nonrevolutionary in character and has not necessarily implied any automatic movement toward liberalism and democracy.

More recently, the Anderson framework for analyzing politics and sociopolitical change in Iberia and Latin America has been given a broader, deeper historical and political-cultural interpretation. What Anderson describes as the "power contenders" syndrome, Silvert referred to as the Mediterranean-style "syndicalism" and I have termed the "corporative tradition" or "corporative framework."[8] Under this rubric, the prevailing characteristics of the Iberic-Latin political process described by Anderson have been traced far back into Iberian history to their origins in Roman law and institutions, the Thomistic tradition of medieval Christianity, the reconquest of the peninsula from the Moors, and the resulting system of feudalism. These formed the foundations of the modern authoritarian-corporate Spanish and Portuguese states in the twelfth, thirteenth, and fourteenth centuries and influenced those definitive, characteristic forms, institutions, and modes of political behavior that emerged during the "Golden Era" of Spanish and Portuguese power in the fifteenth and sixteenth centuries—the "Hapsburgian model."

The argument advanced by these scholars is that the features described by Anderson as distinctive to an essentially corporatist, authoritarian, elitist, hierarchical, Catholic, segmented, clientelist, and patrimonialist society and polity are not temporary or ephemeral phenomena. They have their origins deep in the past and may be inherently, permanently characteristic of all the Iberic-Latin systems, whether the formal labels used are "monarchist," "republican," "liberal-democratic," or perhaps even "Socialist." These profound continuities in the Iberic-Latin tradition may be as strong or stronger than any particular regime of the moment; hence the argument has been advanced that there is a distinctive corporative-patrimonialist, Iberic-Latin political culture that shapes the process of political change. Moreover, it is a process that is not accurately described either by the systems analysis models elaborated in the 1960s developmentalist literature by Easton, Almond, Rostow, and Lipset or by the unrefined categories of the Marxian class conflict model. Iberia and Latin America have thus been pictured as constituting almost a "fourth world of development," distinct from the other three and with a long, particular tradition and special dynamics of its own.

Although the Anderson framework and the complementary models of Silvert and others have been widely accepted and may perhaps represent a dominant interpretation in the study of Iberian and Latin American politics, more recently this approach has been subjected to some searching questioning and criticism. Both the Anderson framework and the recent questioning of it bear directly on how one interprets current changes in Portugal.

First, the Anderson framework has been criticized as a political-cultural explanation that may no longer have validity or that has been superseded by the march of industrialization, dependency relations, and class- and interest-based politics.[9] This criticism seems a misrepresentation of Anderson's argument and a straw man set up for easy attack. No one, and certainly not Anderson, would deny the explanatory power of class analysis, economic variables, and institutional structures. But at the same time, these factors should not be emphasized to the exclusion of all others. The Anderson thesis, particularly the elaborations of that thesis and the "corporative" explanation that followed, was formulated in reaction to the general disillusionment with systems theory and the development literature of the late 1960s, but it was also a response to what many scholars saw as an exaggerated emphasis on class-based, structural explanations. In seeking to make a case for the continued importance of historical and political-cultural variables in the understanding of Iberic-Latin civilization, the thesis supporting that view was undoubtedly overstated; but there was never any intention to inflate this model into a single-cause explanation excluding all others. It seems obvious that political-cultural, structural, institutional, and class-based explanations, and doubtless others as well, are useful in enabling us to understand Iberia and Latin America better. What is interesting is not the sterile arguments between the dogmatic advocates of each view but the particular mixture and overlap between political-cultural and structural factors over time and in different circumstances, and their relations to degrees of national development. Efforts to describe the Anderson and corporatist explanations as wholly political-cultural explanations run the risk of being accused of purposeful misrepresentation.

A second criticism of the power contenders approach or the corporatist framework is that they provide essentially static models, tied to one time and place, and are useful in describing only a single kind of tradition, that is, tradition-dominated regimes such as the Estado Novo of Salazar and Caetano. But as shown in this chapter, corporatist regimes can also change over time. They evolve as do other kinds of regimes from one type to another. One must also keep in mind that distinction made earlier between "natural corporatism"[10] with its roots lying deep in Iberic-Latin history and the more manifestly corporatist systems of which Salazar's was one example. This distinction is critical, for while the corporatist regimes and formal institutions fashioned in the 1920s and 1930s may have proved to be ephemeral phenomena of only passing historical interest, the corporative tradition or "natural corporatism" may be more fundamental and of lasting importance. In addition we must recognize that there are various corporative forms and that they are by no means all reactionary. They include populist forms as in Vargas's Brazil, *Rerum Novarum* and bureaucratic-authoritarian forms as in Salazar's Portugal, Christian-Democratic types as in Frei's Chile, pluralist-participatory types as in Norway, and perhaps even syndicalist-Socialist ones as in Allende's Chile. One of our purposes here will be to show the evolution from one form to another and the reasons for it, to relate particular corporatist types to levels of sociopolitical development and thus to show the dynamic aspects of the model as well as the continuities between one form and the next, particularly as this relates to the change process in contemporary Portugal.[11]

Third, the Anderson scheme and the corporatist framework have been criticized as essentially conservative interpretations of political change. By examining, rationalizing, and explaining the functional aspects of many of the existing Latin American and Iberian systems, the Anderson model serves, in a sense, to justify those systems. However inadvertently, the Anderson analysis, with its emphasis on competing power contenders and gradual change within the framework of an authoritarian, corporatist, and paternalistic state, serves to legitimize both these features *and* the status quo. The Anderson scheme, therefore, has been viewed not as a neutral model for analysis, but as a form of ideology. The Anderson scheme and the corporatist structure have been depicted, particularly among those radical critics of existing institutions in Iberia and Latin America, as a standpat ideology to be refuted and as a part of "the system" to be overcome.

Finally, the Anderson framework and the corporative model have been seen as ultimately leading to particularly deleterious and perhaps even disastrous consequences. If pushed to its logical conclusion, the Anderson scheme of rival power contenders seems to lead not to a stable, middle-class, pluralist system like that of the United States or northern Europe but to fragmentation, stagnation, and seemingly perpetual conflict similar to what is presently occurring in Argentina, Chile, and Uruguay.[12] The latter are among the most modern and "developed" nations in Latin America, but it is precisely because they are so modern, so complex, and so highly differentiated that they are the most divided and prone to recurrent political breakdowns. The number of corporate pillars and power contenders, to say nothing of the divisive factions within each pillar, has multiplied, and the differences between them have become so intense that it has proved impossible for government—any government—to keep the various centrifugal forces from pulling the nation apart.

From this perspective, therefore, the future of Latin America may lie not in Bolivia (as students in the 1960s used to say when Che Guevara was active there) or even in Cuba, but more likely in Chile or Argentina with their spiraling discord, "invertebrate society," and "war of all against all."[13] But if in Anderson's interpretation, society-wide praetorianism and immobility seem to be the end products of the Iberic-Latin American mode of development, increasing numbers of Latin Americans and Iberians have begun to see this outcome as undesirable and have reacted against it. Hence, they have recently attempted to reverse the slide toward "Argentinization," to devise new, often revolutionary developmental strategies, and, by implication, to avoid the consequences predicted by the Anderson model.

In Cuba, Peru, Chile under Allende, and now in Portugal, we have seen, or are seeing, varied attempts to experiment with new formulas and to break out of the vicious circles both of underdevelopment *and* of the traditional game of *criollo* or system politics. Renewed efforts are being made, with varying degrees of success, to overcome the historical pattern, to find new substitutes for authoritarian-elitist-corporatist politics and society, and to surmount the impasse of stagnation and immobility by going outside the accepted rules of the power contenders game and by abandoning the dominant corporative framework in favor of genuinely revolutionary and often Socialist solutions and transformations. Closely related to this has been the effort to break out of the dependency pattern strongly associated with this model and identified in the Portuguese case by the NATO and the Azores Base agreements. The question we must ask is whether such a sharp break is conceivable, given the heavy hand of history in Iberia and Latin America, and, if so, what its precise forms and characteristics will be.

The Portuguese Corporative State: An Interpretation

The Portuguese corporative system was ushered in by the nationalist and vaguely "integralist"[14] military coup of 1926, and it gained more definitive form in the constitution, Labor Statute, and the series of decree-laws of 1933. It was seen, both by its architects and by many others throughout the Iberic-Latin world, as a "third way," an alternative to liberalism and socialism: a particularly Portuguese way of facing up to the great twentieth-century issues of industrialization, accelerated social change, and modern mass society. After the chaotic debacle of the Portuguese Republic (1910–1926) and the nearly hundred years of ineffective parliamentary rule patterned on an inappropriate British model, both the coup of 1926 and the initial phase of corporative implementation were warmly welcomed by a wide spectrum of Portuguese opinion, including not only rightists, but centrists, many liberals and social democrats, and Catholics of all shades. Initially the Estado Novo, with its programs for restoring financial and political stability and stimulating economic growth, social reform, and national modernization, enjoyed widespread popular support, and it was by no means the repressive and reactionary, even "fascistic," state that it later became. It is important to bear in mind the context of those years, 1929–1933, when the Estado Novo was constituted. Liberalism seemed to be bankrupt, capitalism appeared to be collapsing in the great depression, and socialism à la Stalin's Russia, with its bloody purges and repression, was wholly unacceptable. Corporatism seemed to offer the only way out of the crises and conflict of those turbulent years. It seemed a viable alternative for solving Portugal's age-old problems of social disorganization and the lack of an effective state capable of confronting the nation's manifest ills.[15]

Early Phases of the Corporative State. At the outset, four key points should be made concerning the Portuguese corporative state in its early phases. First, of all the various corporative regimes and experiments attempted in the 1930s (not just in Brazil, Argentina, Italy, and Spain but also in Holland, France, Scandinavia, Britain, and even the United States), the Portuguese was undoubtedly the most elaborate, ambitious, and comprehensive, at least in a formal-legal sense. The very thoroughness and completeness of the Portuguese corporative structures rendered them much more difficult to reform, update, or scrap altogether once their usefulness was ended.

Second, the corporative institutions established in Portugal in the 1930s both represented an updated, modernized, twentieth-century extension of an earlier Portuguese political-cultural tradition and reflected the type of society that still existed in Portugal in the 1920s and 1930s. For Portugal at this time was still in many respects a rural, traditionalistic, paternalistic, hierarchical, and small-town society where only the earliest stirrings of industrialization had occurred, and the corporative political structure closely approximated the nature of that society. Later, however, the pace of industrialization accelerated, social change went forward, and large urban middle and laboring classes came into being. But because the corporative structure remained locked in its original form, serious questions began to be asked as to whether "the system" had kept pace with social modernization, and eventually the pressures for change began to build.[16]

Third, the Portuguese corporative structure was never quite the artificial façade for totalitarian dictatorship that corporatism was in Italy, nor was it merely a "confidence trick" played upon the lower classes. It *became* an autocratic system, and the corporative structure was employed as part of the web of authoritarian controls. It also *became* a system of state capitalism where the lower classes bore an inordinate share of the burden. But at the beginning (and to some extent throughout) it was a form of corporatism based upon *both* an authoritarian concept *and* a Catholic one, which implied a natural law tradition with *limits* upon authoritarian rule.

Finally, the strong concern with social justice inherent in the Portuguese concept of corporatism needs emphasis. The Estado Novo was not merely a reactionary throwback to some *status quo ante;* within the Catholic-corporatist framework it was a movement aimed at raising social and economic living conditions and relieving the misery and alienation of the lower classes.[17] What happened to that social justice orientation and whether it was realistic given Portuguese political realities and class structure are questions we must try to answer.

Evolution of the Corporative System. The evolution of the Portuguese corporative system is a history of wrenching contradictions and tragic ironies, of high initial hopes and bitter final disappointments. It began with a burst of energy in the 1930s and a flurry of organizational activity: *sindicatos* (unions), *gremios* (employer groups), *casas do povo* (people's houses), *casas dos pescadores* ("fishermen's" houses), and the like; by the end of World War II the system had become discredited, stagnant, immobile, and virtually dead. Although the Portuguese corporate system was based initially on the assumption of the coequal representation of labor and capital through the corporative system, by the 1950s and 1960s Portugal had become one of the most rapacious and exploitative of capitalist systems, in which the owners and manipulators of land and capital overwhelmingly dominated while the working classes remained by far the worst off in Western Europe, with no say whatsoever in the decisions that affected them most closely. Founded upon a principle of class harmony, Portugal instead became a nation of intense class hatred and bitterness, which ultimately spilled over into violence and revolution and threatened civil war. Instead of guaranteeing participation by all groups through the corporative system, the Salazar regime became a severe dictatorship relying on repressive controls and terror tactics. As the gaps between theory and practice widened and as the Portuguese state became increasingly divorced from the realities of Portuguese society and change, the contradictions and dysfunctional aspects of the system became more apparent.

Despite the often noble and undoubtedly sincere social justice motives of its originators, the corporative system was soon co-opted and then literally captured by wealthy business and economic interests. The corporative regime was gradually perverted into one of the most authoritarian and plutocratic forms of state capitalism where the few profited enormously and the corporative agencies were converted into instruments to control and dominate the working classes, regulate their activities, and guarantee that wages and social benefits were maintained at low levels while the trade unions were kept small, weak, and powerless. Casting off its Christian-Catholic-corporatist social justice orientation, the regime increasingly fell into a rigid, unyielding, exploitative, bureaucratic-dictatorial, fascistic mold. The questions we must ask are how and why?

It is tempting to answer these questions by using an easy, con-spiratorial, class-based "power elite" mode of analysis. Such an analy-sis would discount as a mere smokescreen the social justice orienta-tion of the early corporatists, seeing it as a part of the "confidence trick" played upon the workers by a "Fascist" regime dominated by an upper-bourgeois elite that employed the corporative structure to freeze the lower classes in place while reaping advantages for itself and the emerging middle classes, by controlling government posi-tions and economic wealth.[18] Such an interpretation is easy because a power elite did in fact emerge under the Estado Novo who did employ the corporative system as a control mechanism and whose own eco-nomic wealth and ability to manipulate political outcomes and to take advantage of the system were considerable. While these factors were certainly significant in shaping the evolution of the corporative state in Portugal, their importance should not be exaggerated, nor should other factors be excluded. The actual situation was in fact more com-plicated than the unrefined class analysis and "power elite" interpre-tation prevalent in the literature.[19]

In-depth research on the beginnings of the Estado Novo during the early 1930s reveals a very powerful concern with bettering lower-class living standards and shows that the corporatists' emphasis on social justice was not just a ruse. How then can one explain that the system was so quickly captured and controlled by wealthy elements with good connections and by the newer men on the make who turned it into a regime of capitalist exploitation? How does one recon-cile the social justice orientation of those in authority with the equally demonstrable class and power biases that came to exert so strong an influence upon the system?

Catholic Assumptions behind the Corporative State. In addition to the explanations already alluded to, part of the answer lies in the very Catholic assumptions on which the corporative state was based and in the intensely Catholic, Thomist background, training, and thought processes of its founders. In classic Thomistic thought, the great social and political tasks have always been to discover the common good, to correct the evil in men, to fashion the Christian community, to achieve an ordered universe, to overcome original sin through injunc-tions to live a better life, to raise men's consciousness of their individ-ual shortcomings, and to show them the way to salvation. These concerns were intensely felt by the young Salazar—ex-seminarian and founder and chief driving force of the Centro Académico de Democracia Cristã of Coimbra and of the more political Centro Político—and by the

Catholic corporatists and integralists he brought with him into the government.

Although their sincerity in seeking to bring social justice to the masses through Catholic corporatist means cannot be doubted, it was precisely this emphasis on fashioning better men, as Kenneth Sharpe has persuasively shown, that blinded the Catholic corporatist thinkers to the realities of existing power structures and who controls them. Catholic corporatist ideology, defined as the search for the common good and as a means of correcting the evil in men, acted as a set of blinders that masked existing power relations and obscured the way institutions and structures determined outcomes. No doubt Salazar, Caetano, Pereira, and other early founders really believed they could carry out their contemplated reforms through the new corporative system by educating both workers and employers to their responsibilities of Christian charity and brotherhood without tampering with the structure of society. But it was this very way of thinking that kept them from recognizing the powerful impact of institutions, money, land, and elemental self-interest. These same blinders prevented them from seeing that the old institutions would inevitably lead to dominance by the old elites and the newer men-on-the-make and to the frustration of the new regime's reform efforts. The very Catholic-corporatist framework in which Salazar operated hindered an adequate understanding of that system's failure to achieve his desired goals. Indeed, as we shall see in a moment, the corporatist ideology actually encouraged further control and corruption by creating a set of institutions that allowed the rising entrepreneurial and capitalist elements to regulate and manipulate the lower classes more effectively.[20]

Corruption of the Corporative Ideal. Almost from the beginning, therefore, those with wealth, status, and connections dominated and profited from the corporative system, while the lower classes were forced to bear the brunt of the system's costs. The co-optation and eventual takeover of the corporative agencies by big business, industrial, and commercial elements paralleled the phenomenon described in American society by Ralph Nader and others,[21] namely, the increasing dominance of the regulatory agencies by those enterprises whom they were designed to regulate. Playing upon the fears born of the economic crisis of the 1930s, the Portuguese business elites were able to persuade Salazar of the overriding need to maintain economic stability and to avoid possibly disruptive social experimentation. In this way they were able to extract preferential treatment from the corporative regime (while the unions were tightly regulated) and to postpone indefinitely the effective implementation of corporative programs. Meanwhile, business and industrial interests moved quickly to dominate the *juntas*, commissions, and institutes charged with regulating prices and fixing production. Those agencies gained more importance and power than any of the other corporative institutions, and through them the elites were able to monopolize control over much of the national economic life. Ultimately, they became the instruments for the growth of a powerful and all-pervasive system of state capitalism. Hence, the biases of corporatism led to developments that were remarkably similar to those produced by the "biases of liberalism."[22]

In hindsight, it is easy to say that such outcomes were probably the inevitable result of the class biases of the system, given the Portuguese social structures and the corporatist regime's reluctance to tamper with them. That was less clear at the time, however. The motives of the leaders were mixed and ambiguous, and the corporatist ideology itself blinded the Estado Novo's architects to those underlying realities. Nevertheless, by the end of the 1930s, the basic structures of the corporatist system had been set in place: it was an authoritarian, bureaucratic state, with a system of state-supported capitalism and an autocratic regime that carefully controlled and regulated the country. The vision of achieving social justice through the action of corporative agencies had been indefinitely postponed; the corporative complex, instead of inspiring the entire national system, had been shunted aside and confined to a narrow range of activities, chiefly in the areas of social assistance and labor relations.

Postwar Corporatism in Portugal. During World War II the corporative agencies deviated farther from the original intention. They were given the unpopular task of administering wartime controls, rationing, production quotas, wage stabilizations or reductions, and the like. In addition, the war, the Nazi experience, and the revelations at the Nuremberg trials discredited further all corporative experiments. Hence, in the postwar period the system stagnated, despite some feeble efforts at revival. After years of having been mocked as a "corporative system without corporations," the Salazar regime began setting up the long-awaited corporations—the nominal capstones of the system—in 1956. By that time, however, the functions of the corporative system had become extremely circumscribed. It administered limited social assistance, medical care, family allowance, and retirement programs; it supervised day-to-day labor relations (aimed chiefly at locking the trade unions in place and keeping them weak and docile); and it had some very limited consultative and representational functions. But clearly the corporatist agencies established in the 1930s were no longer at the center of the Portuguese political system, and corporatist ideology was increasingly ignored even by Salazar.[23]

Meanwhile, other agencies and institutional pillars of the regime had grown to fill the vacuum. The secret police—the dreaded PIDE—had become an instrument of increasingly systematic terror and repression, replacing the unsystematic authoritarian controls of the prewar period. The control mechanisms of the bureaucratic state had been greatly enlarged. The regulatory agencies, now thoroughly monopolized by industrial and commercial interests, had been given greater power in the everyday management of the economy and served as the means through which profitable monopolies were granted and inefficient businesses shielded from competition. The censorship was strict, and the unions, people's houses, and other corporative bodies, rather than serving the original social justice functions, had more and more assumed the responsibilities for controlling the lower classes, keeping them fragmented and powerless, squeezing ever-greater sacrifices out of them, preventing strikes and slowdowns, and keeping popular discontents from getting out of hand. The structure of state capitalism enabled a dozen or so major elite and family-based conglomerates, through their control and manipulation of Salazar and the administrative apparatus of the state, to monopolize the most important areas of national economic life, including the wealth of Portugal's African possessions as well as that of continental Portugal. In this labyrinth of interrelated power, the corporative agencies had become one more instrument of both class rule and state power. Like the censorship and the secret police, they operated primarily to keep the masses under control.[24]

Tensions in the System. By the 1960s, however, some cracks had begun to appear in the Portuguese monolith. Internal opposition grew, and external pressures on the regime intensified. Reflecting the industrialization and economic growth of the preceding decades, a sizable middle class and an increasingly vocal proletariat had grown up, impatient with the rigidities and arbitrariness of the regime and seeking greater freedom and the removal of the barriers to social mobility that Salazar's corporative state placed in their way. These groups demanded a larger share of the affluence being generated and the consumer goods available, and they were impatient to catch up with European living standards and social benefits, as well as to gain acceptance into that community. Rebellions in Portuguese Africa shattered the myth of Portuguese uniqueness among colonial powers and

101

the claim that Portugal was succeeding in building a genuinely multi-racial society in Africa. In addition, during the 1960s Salazar and his followers became increasingly out of touch with domestic conditions. Rather than widening the base of the regime to reflect the new social realities, they became increasingly aloof.[25] Instead of opening new avenues for upward advancement, Salazar closed them off, thereby creating a simmering cauldron that finally boiled over in the 1974 revolution.

The Caetano Regime. The Caetano regime was dedicated to bringing about precisely such an evolution toward a more modern, pluralistic, participatory corporative system aimed at greater social justice. Where Salazar had attempted to limit participation, Caetano sought to expand the circle of groups loyal to the regime. His was not an effort to "liberalize" the polity, as the foreign press accounts often described it, for Caetano remained an authoritarian, and he shared Salazar's corporatist conviction that liberalism and parliamentary democracy were unworkable and dysfunctional in the Portuguese context—a view that, in the light of the immediate post-1974 disintegration, seemed not altogether misapplied. In his effort to revitalize Portugal after the lethargy and stagnation of the Salazar years, Caetano set out to make the corporative structure really work for the first time by broadening elite participation and providing new opportunities for controlled social advancement. To that end, he instigated educational reforms aimed at expanding the elite loyal to the government, thereby widening the political appeal and the social base of the official party but without allowing any real competition between parties. He also sought to curb the power of the secret police while still maintaining authoritarian control and to implement more fully the corporative ideology of coequal representation of business and labor, but without endorsing the idea of economic liberalism. In this way, Caetano sought to stimulate economic development and to give greater benefits, wage increases, and social programs to the working classes but without permitting the formation of genuinely *independent* workers' and peasants' associations.

Caetano's ultimate goals were to adjust the corporatist regime to the realities of the 1970s by restoring confidence in Portugal's economy and the public service and by reinvigorating a political structure that had gone to sleep under Salazar. In the hope that he could revive a set of corporative institutions that had become almost moribund, Caetano made political accommodations at home and in Africa to satisfy the legitimate demands of the lower classes for improved living conditions and to recognize the rising strength of a number of new middle- and urban working-class power contenders. "Liberalization" is clearly the wrong term to describe these changes. Rather, Caetano aimed to restore the older Portuguese system of corporatism built on rival power contenders that was part of the Iberic-Latin tradition of *criollo* politics described by Anderson. During his later years Salazar had ridden roughshod over that system and eventually had lost the popularity and base of support he once enjoyed. Caetano attempted a renovation that would recoup that support, but his efforts remained within the structure of the paradigm of *criollo* politics.

In short, the Caetano regime operated within an authoritarian-corporatist framework and ushered in some significant changes.[26] But Caetano proved inept and ineffectual as a manager and manipulator of the new emerging system. Unable to control the complex forces he had helped to set loose, he pursued policies that repeatedly led to stalemate, as, for example, in the case of the African colonies, thereby alienating more and more of his supporters. From the time he assumed power in 1968 until his demise in 1974, Caetano engaged in a complicated series of maneuvers to solidify his regime. He sought initially to staff the party and the civil service with new men loyal to himself, but he soon abandoned that policy and removed or silenced most of the new *técnicos* (nonpolitical technicians). On a host of issues, he seemed at first to encourage change and reform, only to reverse himself when he came under pressure from those groups most closely identified with Salazar. These reversals were so numerous they gave rise to popular jokes about how Caetano signaled left and turned right. Finally, it became apparent that Caetano's policies were tentative, ambiguous, weak, uncertain, and reversible. In this respect, they reflected the tenuous and precarious political position he occupied. Caetano had been given the reins of government, but he held them so weakly and uncertainly that he eventually lost control of the powerful interests he was trying to direct. Caetano had opportunities to increase his own power base, to dismiss the *Salazaristas* who were a constant threat to him, to reform the economy, even to seek a way out of the African imbroglio, but he let those opportunities slip by without decisive action. He was not a forceful autocrat, as Salazar had been, and he lacked the personal qualities necessary to walk the tightrope of political leadership between the hurly-burly of contending power groups that made up the game of *criollo* or *sistema* politics.

The coup that toppled Caetano and the corporative Estado Novo was not the result of a widespread mass movement or of a series of revolutionary upheavals. True, there were ample reasons to criticize the regime, and discontent was contagious. Most Portuguese wanted

103

a somewhat greater relaxation of controls, an end to the colonial wars in Africa, greater affluence and more consumer goods, and broader integration and acceptance into Europe. But in early 1974, real per capita income was about double what it had been only a decade earlier, more Portuguese were enjoying a higher standard of living than ever before, and public opinion surveys showed a stronger feeling of optimism, hope, and sense of personal advancement among the population than at any time previously.[27] To many the pace of change still seemed too slow, and the young, in particular, considered it to be in the wrong direction. Nevertheless, at that time Portugal did not appear to be a churning volcano ready to explode.

Beneath the apparent calm, however, lay other major discontents: the desire for a settlement in Africa, the hope for somewhat greater social freedom, for international acceptance, and the demand for a reorganization of the equilibrium among power contenders. These were the disagreements that moved General Antonio Spínola to lead a military coup d'état. His action was not so much a social revolutionary upheaval as it was a classic struggle among rival elites and factions for control of the system. The coup of April 25, 1974, implied some new openings and accommodations, but it was by no means the sharp break with the past that is sometimes imagined. Instead, it involved a reordering of the power contenders' game, with a new "juggler" (Spínola) in command and with the several military and civilian elites engaged in a renewed scramble for power and influence. What happened next, however, is particularly interesting. In the process of change and renovation the possibility arose for a genuinely revolutionary transformation. The question then became not so much one of merely reshuffling old elites in the manner described by Anderson but of actually transcending the *criollo* system by proceeding from a more pluralistic form of authoritarian-corporatism under Caetano to a genuinely revolutionary system with a Socialist or syndicalist orientation.

The Revolution of 1974: Overcoming the System

The Portuguese coup of April 1974 began as a typical barracks revolt. The private political ambitions of men like Spínola, as well as the professional concerns of the younger military officers who desired salary raises, promotions, and an end to Caetano's often high-handed treatment of them (treated in detail in chapter 4), were as important as motivating factors as any popular demands for liberation and democratization. But the public justification for the coup was based on liberal ideas, and in Portugal and abroad it was generally accepted and welcomed as such. Liberalization implied a relaxation of censorship, the familiar call for new elections, a further curbing of the secret police, and a new policy of federation for the African territories. Spínola himself, with his monocle, his authoritarian bearing, and previous Nazi sympathies, was looked on as a curious and improbable liberal but a liberal nonetheless. He was welcomed by most Portuguese as a man who would usher in desired changes but who would not let the change process go uncontrolled.[28] In the first two weeks following the coup (which included the May Day celebration) orderly euphoria reigned. A million carnations bloomed as the joyful population celebrated in the streets and put flowers in the rifle barrels of their liberators.

In the aftermath of the April coup, the control mechanisms of the old dictatorship were among the first institutions to be sacrificed. The secret police, the censorship, the *Legião*, and the apparatus of authoritarian rule were abolished almost literally overnight, either by decree-laws or by spontaneous actions in the streets. That was the liberalizing and indeed liberating phase of the revolution.

It remains something of a mystery how that repressive apparatus, which foreigners and Portuguese alike assumed to be so strong and all pervasive, could be overturned so quickly and so easily.[29] But more than merely the apparatus of the old dictatorship came apart. The April revolt set loose a variety of conflicts and disintegrative forces, both in Portuguese Africa and in continental Portugal, whose stirrings had been under way for some years. The revolt released the pent-up frustrations of the later Salazar decades and freed the fragmented, fragile social forces that made up Portuguese society itself. As Ortega y Gasset argues with regard to Spain in the 1930s, once freed from the strong unifying force of a powerful central state apparatus and leader, the centrifugal forces and distinct corporate pillars that composed Portuguese society began to separate.[30] The armed forces, the church, economic elites, organized labor, and the middle sectors began to pull in different directions, and the divisions within each of their ranks became accentuated. At the same time, the horizontal, hierarchical class structure also began to give way. The "mass," in Ortega's words, refused any longer to accept its assigned station in life; it became impatient with traditional paternalistic leadership by its "betters" and began to revolt against the old authority structures. One must be careful to qualify such statements, since the pace and degree of these changes were uneven, and urban areas like Lisbon were affected far more than the rural areas. Nevertheless, the key point is incontestable: what had begun as a conventional barracks revolt—a circulation of elites, with modest liberalizing and renovative inclina-

105

tions—quickly led to both a wrenching fragmentation of Portuguese society *and* to stirrings of deeper class and social conflict.

The April coup was followed by mini-coups in hundreds of industries, plants, government offices, educational institutions, and professional associations throughout the country.[31] There were innumerable confrontations between workers and employers, students and teachers, faculties and administrations, servants and patrons, civil servants and the state, masses and elites, the functionaries of the Gulbenkian Foundation (almost a shadow government in Portugal) and its director-general. In scores of offices and agencies signs were placed in the windows announcing "liberation" from the old "Fascist" leadership. Few would deny that many such actions were justified or that, after Salazar, Portugal could have used a dose of disorder. But along with the old leadership and authority structure, the social hierarchy, which gave unity, stability, and a sense of purpose to the community, was also challenged and, in many cases, overturned. As the older social and political institutions gave way, there was frequently little to replace them. The result was disorder and fragmentation. Many of these confrontations, it should be noted, were carried out with the blessing or acquiescence of the MFA (Armed Forces Movement), and frequently over the objections of Spínola and the civilian moderates in the government. Thus, the revolution had entered a second phase, which was capped off in July by the resignation of moderate, centrist Premier Adelino da Palma Carlos and the appointment, over Spínola's objection, of leftist MFA ideologue Vasco dos Santos Gonçalves.

The Rise of the Left. The entire formal web of corporate controls, regulations, and institutions was also eliminated. The old *sindicato* system was abolished, and many of the most important unions began passing into the hands of Communist leadership. The Corporations Ministry, whose chief functions were in the complex realm of labor relations and social assistance, was also initially given over to the Communists, who could thus use their official position to facilitate and legitimate the party's emerging dominance of the trade unions. Later, the renamed Labor Ministry was run directly by young, inexperienced, vaguely Marxist members of the MFA. The old corporative Labor Statute was declared inoperative before a new one had been drawn up to replace it. The whole vast panoply of labor tribunals, arbitration commissions, and collective contracts, which under Salazar had largely protected employers but under Caetano were increasingly being used to benefit workers, was abolished. Also overturned were the networks of economic regulatory commissions, bureaus, and agencies, which were part of the Portuguese corporative system but are essential for the functioning of any modern state and economy. Social services, including health care, pensions, and social security, had also been administered through the corporative system, and these too were severely disrupted. The abolition or disruption of a host of public services and government agencies together with purges in the civil services was accompanied by strikes, confrontations, and constant political maneuvering that resulted in the interruption of many needed social programs. In less than a year the economy was in a shambles, social tensions and conflicts flared, and the political system drew increasingly closer to collapse. Portugal was threatened with civil war.

Faced with pressure from the left and what he perceived as a growing disorder, Spínola tried to rally moderate liberal and middle-of-the-road forces. He and his *junta* were, after all, establishment figures, upper middle class, moderate to conservative in their views; they might lean to the left, as the Portuguese put it, but they were men of the right. They favored change but only within carefully controlled (Anderson's model of *criollo* politics) bounds and certainly not under Socialist-Communist hegemony. The Spínola government thus began to warn against anarchy. It called for a halt to the purges, broke up some leftist demonstrations, and warned public employees to stop seeking to remove their superiors. A few people were jailed, and the government took over full control of the state-run news media. It urged a halt to disruptive strikes and promised that the military would intervene where necessary to preserve order and discipline. A series of decrees was issued imposing new restrictions on political party and labor union activity as the government returned to some of the careful regulative methods of managing change used by the old Portuguese regime. Spínola sought to rally his "silent majority," while the left saw in some of these moves the possibility for a rightist countercoup. Throughout the summer and early fall of 1974 these developments provoked considerable internal strains within the government and between it and some of its earlier supporters. In a showdown at the end of September, Spínola lost and abruptly resigned, warning that the country was headed toward chaos and "new forms of slavery."[32] Spínola was replaced by General Francisco da Costa Gomes, also a moderate but a more acceptable figure to the left than Spínola. The real control of the Portuguese revolution, however, now rested with the young leftist officers of the MFA. This was the beginning of the third phase of the revolution, which carried the country further to the left.

The Radical Tilt of the Revolution. With the departure of Spínola (once referred to as the savior or the de Gaulle of Portugal but now as its possible Kerensky), Portugal passed from a regime of military-civilian elements with a centrist outlook into one which was clearly controlled by men committed to "socialism," although still divided over the meaning of their commitment. This realignment of political forces in late September was even more fundamental than that which resulted from the original April coup. Gone now were most of the moderate and liberal elements that had come in with Spínola, their places being taken by men of a left and even revolutionary persuasion. The officers and military units loyal to Spínola were purged, and the possibilities for a rightist countercoup were closed off by the arrest of many civilian and military leaders associated with the Salazar and Caetano regimes. The Communists further cemented their control over local government, educational institutions, and the press and publishing. In this they were supported by the left wing of the MFA, which was increasingly self-conscious regarding its role as the nation's chief guiding force but at the same time was growing increasingly sensitive to criticism and, therefore, moved to cut off the expression of opinion by opposition groups. It also took action against a number of leading members of the old economic elite, as if to indicate that neither they nor the old-style oligopoly capitalism was assured of continuing in their privileged position. These and other signs all pointed to the radicalization of the regime and to the conclusion that the turn left might have proceeded so far as to be irreversible.[33]

As the leftward trend continued, tensions mounted, and fear increased within the government and among the population at large. There were new warnings of anarchy and a possible leftist dictatorship. Charges of "subversion" were used to curb and in some cases eliminate political competition. The cabinet was split over a campaign directed against "monopoly capitalism" launched precisely when the government was beginning its own economic emergency plan to stimulate production and rebuild confidence. The climate of fear, suspicion, and mutual intolerance spread, and no one seemed certain where Portugal was heading. There were dark mutterings of coups and countercoups, warnings of possible civil war, discussions of foreign interventions, calculations of barracks' reliability, and worried speculations about the intentions of this or that man or group. The Communists' strength seemed to grow, based upon the party's discipline and organization, its history of martyrdom and heroic survival under Salazar, and its no-nonsense approach to the existing circumstances, as reflected in the attempt to mobilize the rural peasantry. The MFA meanwhile began deprecating the civilian politicians and parties and raised doubts about whether and to what degree it would respect the electoral results. The Socialists and social demo-crats (organized in the Popular Democratic party) talked of "anti-democratic escalations" that might lead to civil war, of Communist "assaults" on the centers of power, of an increasingly radicalized military, and of the potential for "disorder, chaos, and blood."[34]

The Communists and Labor. Perhaps the most critical question of phase three of the Portuguese revolution involved the formation of a single unified labor confederation. The Communists, who had a long head start in the trade union field, controlled the largest and most powerful unions and were also dominant within the loose con-federation called the Intersindical. Understandably, they favored the measure, which had the practical effect of cementing their dominance and giving them a virtual monopoly over the labor movement. They rationalized this reach for power by arguing that a strong united labor front was necessary to bargain more effectively on behalf of workers. The Socialists and Popular Democrats, who had been late getting started and who had little solid labor support, saw this measure as permanently freezing them out of the labor field; therefore, they opposed it. They argued for a more "pluralist" structure and reasoned that a decentralized labor movement would not necessarily be an ineffective one. The proposal split the cabinet and again threatened its breakup. There was also a split within the MFA, but a majority of the military favored the plan for a single labor organization; hence, it was decreed as law. The Portuguese Communist party (PCP) victory gave it hegemony over the labor movement, and set the stage for a new and even more strongly leftist fourth phase in the Portuguese revolution.[35]

During January and February of 1975, the Communists moved to consolidate their gains. Meanwhile, the MFA began to consider a series of proposals that would further deepen the revolutionary pro-cess by nationalizations and land reform. These moves also implied an extension of armed forces' rule beyond the scheduled April elec-tions. At the same time, the United States pressured the Portuguese to limit Communist influence, while the Soviet Union attempted to press its advantage by requesting base and port facilities at Figueira da Foz in continental Portugal and, later, on the island of Madeira in the Atlantic. Throughout this period there were renewed rumblings of military discontent, divisions within the MFA, and rumors of centrist and rightist challenges to the prevailing leftward trend. Meanwhile, public opinion surveys began showing that the Communist party had nothing like the electoral support that its position of dominance within the regime implied and that, if the elections were held as scheduled and the ballots honestly counted, the more moderate center, Social Democratic (PPD), and Socialist parties were closer to the mainstreams of Portuguese public opinion.

Before the first year of the revolution had run its course, there was a fifth stage in Portugal's leftward turn. In early March 1975, an abortive, almost comic-opera coup attempt was launched against the regime apparently aimed at restoring General Spínola to power. Although the details remain obscure, the attempt was so badly planned and executed as to raise doubt whether it was a serious effort at overthrowing the regime or whether it might not have been provoked as a means of discrediting Spínola and the United States. The upshot was that the more moderate elements within the MFA, which had been gaining ascendancy in the weeks preceding the coup attempt, were purged, and General Spínola fled into exile in Brazil. The United States was severely criticized and leading members of the MFA issued statements saying that they could no longer guarantee the safety of American Ambassador Frank Carlucci, who was alleged to have had a hand in the conspiracy. Some of the more rightist and centrist parties (along with the Maoists on the far left) were declared illegal and thus prohibited from participating in the elections, while the PCP was given an even stronger hand. The cabinet was reorganized so as to restrict further the influence of the democratic left and to award additional portfolios to the PCP and its allies. A wave of nationalizations followed in which banks, insurance companies, and all major industries were expropriated. Premier Vasco Gonçalves announced that Portugal had definitively embarked on the path to socialism and that there would be no turning back; the prevailing sentiment within the MFA now also seemed to favor revolutionary socialism. As Portugal swung more radically to the left, serious talk began to be heard of a full-scale Communist takeover, of a repetition of the Prague *putsch* of 1948, of a new Soviet satellite in Western Europe, of the threat to NATO that this implied, and of an American-inspired "destabilization" to head it off.[36]

As the leftward trend proceeded and tensions mounted, the scheduled elections grew closer. Spínola and the MFA had promised, when they took power in April 1974, to hold elections within a year. Now the year was nearly up, and the three main factions were jockeying for position.

The Weakness of the Communist Party. The Communists, who at that point seemed to be riding high, sought to postpone the elections, perhaps indefinitely. They recognized that their popular support was weak and felt that elections could only damage their position. They preferred to maintain the working alliance with the military, which had given them so many advantages; hence, they followed a strategy of "unity with the MFA." In contrast, the other parties, particularly the Socialists and the Popular Democrats who had been increasingly ignored by the MFA in the successive turns to the left, looked upon the elections as a means to regain some of the stature they had lost and to demonstrate their popular support. They insisted the elections be held as scheduled, that the results be respected, and that the military live up to its earlier promise to return to the barracks and allow a civilian regime to take office.

The MFA, the third faction in this complex, was caught in the middle. On the one hand, although it did postpone the elections to the last possible date—April 25, the first anniversary of the revolution—it could not cancel them entirely without risking its legitimacy, which was based on the claim that the MFA knew and reflected the popular will. On the other hand, there was mounting evidence that the MFA had begun to enjoy its leading and heroic role and wished to perpetuate its supervisory position and to expand its powers. By this point the military had built an elaborate set of political and administrative state agencies parallel to and often bypassing the civilian ones. It had become the nation's strongest "political party," more coordinated, better organized, and, at least in its own eyes, more popular and with a stronger sense of national aspirations than the divisive civilian parties. Its leading officers had come to believe that further institutionalization of the MFA was necessary and that it should continue to play a dominant role even after the scheduled elections for the Constituent Assembly.

To this end the MFA began an effort to shape the outcome of the elections or, failing that, to downgrade the importance of the results. In addition, the MFA began hinting that it intended to continue to play a leading role in the drafting of the new fundamental laws of the nation. Further, the military moved to establish a new set of rules and institutions, essentially corporative in character, that gave a specially privileged place to the armed forces and would enable them to continue to serve as the "guarantors" of the revolution. Among other things, the MFA insisted on a system of representation in the Constituent Assembly that would ensure a dominant voice for the military itself. It also demanded for the armed forces a "right" (like the traditional military *foro*) to reserve to itself the selection of the defense and economics ministers, and it insisted on the right to approve beforehand (and presumably to reject) any presidential candidate. The Council of State, which the MFA officers already controlled, was to be converted into a "superior" upper chamber, thereby enabling the military to remain in power indefinitely and to guarantee that the MFA's program would be carried out faithfully.

These plans were formalized in an accord, which the civilian parties were forced to sign only two weeks before the election, giving the military the power to handpick the president, to veto legislation, and to continue to rule for at least three to five years. This accord considerably diminished the importance of the elections by tying the hands of the Constituent Assembly to a large degree even before its members had been chosen and eliminating the possibility for an effective opposition or an alternative to the MFA. The civilian parties, however, had no choice but to sign it or to risk their own legality and continued ability to function, as well as the possibility the elections might be canceled entirely.[37] Holding the elections themselves and interpreting their meaning had become critical issues in the spring of 1975, and some fundamental interests as well as the future course of the regime depended on their resolution.

The results of the election on April 25, 1975, considered in more detail in chapter 10, have been widely interpreted as a significant victory for the moderate elements. Thirty-eight percent of the voters supported the Socialists, and 26 percent chose the Popular Democrats, while the Communists, with 12.5 percent, were said to have received a severe setback. Nevertheless, one should not read too many implications into these results. The elections were, in effect, a referendum or plebiscite on the revolution and, to a degree, an indication of the current balance of political forces. They did not offer a full range of choices, and their importance had previously been undermined by the military. They provided a set of signals, like a public opinion poll, which did not convey definitive legitimacy to any group or faction. Hence, the elections were part of an ongoing political process that afforded new opportunities to some groups and implied a new defensiveness for others.

The non-Communist left was clearly buoyed by the results, as were the moderates in the MFA. The U.S. embassy was granted a second chance to aid and align itself with a more moderate, social democratic revolution in Portugal, rather than having to face the option of military intervention or a feared Communist takeover. At the same time, the Communist party was put on the defensive and so, in a sense, was the MFA. The elections, however, provided only some tentative indications rather than a clear-cut choice as to who should rule. Their implications for the PCP, which fared badly, should not be exaggerated. Some members of the MFA quickly indicated that the direction of the Portuguese revolution would not be altered by the elections, but other military officers clearly saw the situation in a different light. The real question, therefore, may not be the election results themselves but how the signals they provided will be read and whether those parties and groups that did well will be able to exploit their advantage and how those who did poorly go about rationalizing the results and recovering their losses. The election marked the end of the first year of the Portuguese revolution, but it was only a tentative ending that left most of the big issues undecided and the political struggle certain to continue.

Conclusions and Implications: Has Corporatism Been Transcended?

To many, it still seems almost inconceivable that Portugal, with all its old rigidities and seemingly inherent conservatism, should be one of a handful of Western and Iberic-Latin nations to break out of the traditional pattern of competition among rival power contenders and to move in a revolutionary direction. Those who knew this quiet and tradition-dominated country before 1974 were certain to find many aspects of the contemporary Portuguese scene both unbelievable and unrecognizable. Some profound transformations were then under way in Portugal, the first steps in a fundamental social restructuring, not the mere circulation of elites and modest renewal that most observers expected. It would have been ironic if a nation so backward and so eager to catch up with and be accepted by the West had suddenly rejected the Western model in favor of a more "advanced" social and political form. Such a move, given the strategic importance of Portugal and its Atlantic islands within NATO, would have carried immense implications, not only for Portugal, Spain, Western Europe, the Atlantic Alliance, and the United States but also for our interpretation and analysis of the Iberic-Latin change process.

Although we have stressed the revolutionary restructuring and successive turns to the left ushered in initially by the coup of April 1974, it is important to emphasize the continuities and moderating forces as well. The image of constant upheaval and accelerating chaos portrayed by the U.S. news media does not always accurately reflect the discipline, calm, and order that most often continued to reign in Portugal. Although it pursued some profoundly revolutionary policies and though some of the leadership occasionally said or did some unfortunate things, surely one would also have to be impressed by the pragmatism and common sense of the MFA, by its mainly moderate and piecemeal programs, by the absence of grandiose schemes of a dogmatic sort, and by its generally eclectic and careful approach. In most respects it has lived up to its promises to dismantle the "Fascist" regime, provide for social and economic reconstruction, and help construct, in its own terms, a "free and pluralist society." At the same time, the strong, disciplined, Moscow-oriented Communist party also sought to restrain its members and the more radical Maoist groups, to discipline labor, to keep the peace, and to prevent social and political breakdown, in order to retain the support of the MFA. The flexibility and adaptability of many Portuguese bureaucrats, professionals, and others, under the changed and often charged circumstances of that time, similarly helped provide stability and even some continuity.

There remained some remarkable parallels between the old and the new regime. The Portuguese government was, after all, a military-dominated regime. It was authoritarian, ruling from above. It presumed to govern for and in the name of the people, but it showed little enthusiasm for initiating a genuinely participatory democracy or for sharing power, through the parties or the interest-group structure, with the people's representatives. Even the election of April 1975 was rather like the elections under the old regime: plebiscitary in form, providing an opportunity to ratify the government in power, but offering only a few limited choices and conveying no definitive legitimacy. The leading members of the MFA implied that they already knew the collective "general will" regardless of any electoral outcomes. The Portuguese state remained largely the administrative and technocratic state that it was before: dominated by the middle class, although representing different elements of that middle class than under Salazar and Caetano, and based upon a shifting, still uncertain and tentative alliance between military and civilian managers and technicians. It also remained a heavily bureaucratic system, still carefully regulated and controlled, with elaborate legal-administrative procedures, still organized hierarchically and governed by decree-law without much genuine grass-roots involvement. The economy remained a mixed form, blending private and public, but all of it under strict state direction, control, and monopoly. Finally, our attention must be called to the new institutional arrangements the MFA inaugurated, with its functionally representative bodies, its essentially corporative and syndicalist structures, and the special place within the system given to the military.

Thus, there are some remarkable continuities with the older corporative regime, as well as some sharp departures from it. A consideration of these parallels and continuities is critical, regarding both an understanding of political trends in present-day Portugal and a final assessment of the changes that have taken place since April 1974.

Has Portugal, therefore, overcome its corporate past and abandoned the type of accommodative politics described by Charles Anderson? The answer is both yes and no, and at the same time the question itself may have been rendered at least partially irrelevant. There is no doubt that Portugal has repudiated its earlier *Rerum Novarum* and *Quadragesimo Anno* forms of corporatism and has overturned many of the authoritarian controls of the Salazar *Estado Novo*. It may well have also rejected—at least for a time—the Andersonian *sistema* of nonrevolutionary but "renovative" pluralist power-contenders politics. Whether it can succeed in transcending the historical, bureaucratic, authoritarian-corporatist tradition that is so much a part of Portugal's past, however, is still an open question. The continuities noted earlier that link Portuguese politics before and after the 1974 coup are important. But like Mexico, Bolivia, Peru, and other Hispanic countries, Portugal has begun the process of weakening some of the major corporate groups associated with the old regime including the old landholding class, the church, the oligarchy, and the plutocratic elite.

Nevertheless, many of its more enduring political institutions and culture are still strongly corporatist. Portugal remains a technocratic, authoritarian-bureaucratic state. Its economic system is still based on state-directed enterprise and monopoly, now redirected but still cast essentially in a statist mold. The use of top-down decree-laws rather than genuinely democratic participation is prevalent. Representation still depends in part on functional roles with the balance between the several corporate groups now readjusted but with the rights and obligations of each major sector still carefully defined in law and special charter and with the military's own privileged place in the system explicitly guaranteed.

Hence one might look for a regime that continues to try to blend and reconcile the nation's historical corporative and statist traditions and control mechanisms with the newer demands and complexities of political and economic modernization, greater democratization, and a changed social structure. Such a regime would attempt to ratify the changes that have taken place and perhaps to usher in other ones, but without letting the process of modernization get completely out of hand. Although the possibility for an abrupt shift is always present, it is more reasonable to expect that the regime will continue to develop a blend of more participatory and democratic forms to go along with the corporatist, authoritarian, and statist forms still present.

These comments also suggest that corporatism in the Portuguese tradition is not necessarily incompatible with change and that corporatism in the broader political-cultural sense used here may take left

115

and centrist directions as well as a right-authoritarian one. Hence, corporatism may be embodied in a dynamic and change-oriented regime as well as in a static one, and the particular form corporatism may take is intimately related to levels of economic development and political modernization. The real question for Portugal may not be whether to have corporatism but the particular blend and dynamics of the nation's evolving but persistent corporative forms. The Salazar regime was one type, while the present government, although obviously of a quite different orientation, is another type that is still strikingly within a distinctly Portuguese and corporatist tradition. The regime that came to power in Lisbon in 1974 reflects genuine structural transformations as well as some powerful continuties with the past. The more complex, multiclass, pluralistic Portuguese society of the 1970s demanded a more complex, renovated, pluralist, possibly syndicalist-corporatist political structure. The issue hence is not so much one of rejecting corporatism in this traditional sense but of replacing an older, discredited, narrowly based, and excessively authoritarian form of corporatism with a newer, modernized, more participatory and representative one.

That transformation, however, may imply such a mammoth change that the Anderson rival power-contenders framework and the corporative model would have only partial utility. They remain useful perspectives and helpful in explaining some aspects of recent Portuguese developments but not all of them. They provide a partial picture rather than a finished one. They imply that we could understand the Cuban revolution by concentrating on its Hispanic aspects alone and not its Socialist character or that a portrait of the Peruvian regime (pre-1975) would be complete, which dealt only with its corporatist features and ignored its revolutionary ones. Portugal is now undergoing a similar restructuring. The country's new social, economic, and political institutions combine in many ways to reflect the historical corporatist heritage that Portugal shares with other Iberian and Latin American countries,[38] but the extent of the changes taking place is so far-reaching that they can no longer be fully explained by analytic models like the one offered by Anderson. Hence the Portuguese experience assumes added significance for students of Iberia and Latin America since it implies not just the end of an older political regime but also perhaps the partial eclipse and transcendence of the prevailing conceptual frameworks used for analyzing this area. As societies and polities change and come to incorporate new forms and systems, so must scholars and political analysts devise new models for interpreting such changes.

Notes

1. Juan Linz, "An Authoritarian Regime: Spain," in Erik Allardt and Yrjo Littunen, *Cleavages, Ideologies and Party Systems* (Helsinki: Westermarck Society, 1964), pp. 251–83; Philippe C. Schmitter, "Paths to Political Development in Latin America," in Douglas A. Chalmers, ed., *Changing Latin America* (New York: Columbia University, Academy of Political Science, 1972), pp. 83–105; Schmitter, "Corporatist Interest Representation and Public Policy in Portugal" (Paper presented at the Workshop on Modern Portugal, University of New Hampshire, Durham, October 10–14, 1973); Howard J. Wiarda, "The Portuguese Corporative System: Basic Structures and Current Functions," *Iberian Studies*, vol. 2 (1973), pp. 73–80; Wiarda, *Corporatism and Development: The Portuguese Experience* (Amherst: University of Massachusetts Press, 1977); and the essays collected in Fredrick Pike and Thomas Stritch, eds., *The New Corporatism: Social and Political Structures in the Iberian World* (Notre Dame, Indiana: University of Notre Dame Press, 1974).

2. The image is Barbara Tuchman's in *The Proud Tower* (New York: MacMillan, 1962). The papal encyclicals *Rerum Novarum* and *Quadragesimo Anno* represent church efforts to come to grips with modern capitalism and society, but to do so without sacrificing the orderly, hierarchical, Thomistic traditions of the past.

3. They are: by Marx, *Capital, The Poverty of Philosophy,* and *A Critique of Political Economy;* by Engels, *The Origins of the Family;* and by Lenin, *State and Revolution, Left-Wing Communism: An Infantile Disorder,* and *What Is to be Done?*

4. For a discussion of the European polity model, see Martin O. Heisler, ed., *Politics in Europe* (New York: McKay, 1974). See also Arend Lijphart, "Consociational Democracy," *World Politics,* vol. 20 (1969), pp. 207–25; Val Lorwin, "Segmented Pluralism: Ideological Cleavages and Political Cohesion in the Smaller European Democracies," *Comparative Politics,* vol. 3 (1971), pp. 141–75; and Stein Rokkan, "Norway: Numerical Democracy and Corporate Pluralism," in Robert Dahl, ed., *Political Opposition in Western Democracies* (New Haven, Conn.: Yale University Press, 1966), chap. 3.

5. The strategic implications of the Portuguese revolution are dealt with more explicitly in a subsequent paper, "Can We Learn to Live with a Socialist World? Foreign Policy Implications Stemming from the Portuguese Revolution and Other 'New Forces'" (Paper presented at the conference "Iberia and the Defense of the Western Alliance," Institute for the Study of Conflict, London, May 29–31, 1975).

6. Quoted in David Scott Palmer, *"Revolution from Above": Military Government and Popular Participation in Peru, 1968–1972* (Ithaca, N.Y.: Latin American Studies Dissertation Program, Cornell University, 1973), p. 53.

7. Charles W. Anderson, "Toward a Theory of Latin American Politics," Occasional paper no. 2, The Graduate Center for Latin American Studies, Vanderbilt University, February 1964, reprinted in Howard J. Wiarda, *Politics and Social Change in Latin America: The Distinct Tradition* (Amherst: University of Massachusetts Press, 1982); see also Anderson, *The Political Economy of*

Modern Spain: Policy-Making in an Authoritarian System (Madison: University of Wisconsin Press, 1970).

8. For Kalman Silvert's argument, see especially, *Man's Power* (New York: Viking, 1970), pp. 59–64 and 136–38; see also Howard J. Wiarda, "Toward a Framework for the Study of Political Change in the Iberic-Latin Tradition: The Corporative Model," *World Politics,* vol. 25 (1973), pp. 206–35; and Wiarda, "Corporatism and Development in the Iberic-Latin World: Persistent Strains and New Variations," *Review of Politics,* vol. 36 (1974), pp. 3–33, as well as the references cited in these works.

9. See the comments in Philippe C. Schmitter, "Still the Century of Corporatism?" *Review of Politics,* vol. 36 (1974), pp. 85–131.

10. Ronald C. Newton, "Natural Corporatism and the Passing of Populism in Spanish America," *Review of Politics,* vol. 36 (1974), pp. 34–51.

11. See James Malloy, ed., *Authoritarianism and Corporatism in Latin America* (Pittsburgh, Penn.: University of Pittsburgh Press, 1977), which makes these points; see also Robert R. Kaufman, "Transitions to Stable Authoritarian-Corporatist Regimes: The Chilean Case?" (Paper presented to the Inter-University Seminar on the Armed Forces and Society at the Annual Meeting of the American Political Science Association, Chicago, August 29–September 2, 1974).

12. See, for example, Kalman Silvert, *The Conflict Society* (New York: American Universities Field Staff, 1966); Kenneth L. Johnson, *Argentina's Mosaic of Discord* (Washington, D.C.: Institute for the Comparative Study of Political Systems, 1969); and Kaufman, "Transitions to Stable Authoritarian-Corporatist Regimes."

13. This point was made previously in Wiarda, "Toward a Framework for the Study of Political Change," pp. 234–5; see also José Ortega y Gasset, *Invertebrate Spain* (New York: Norton, 1937).

14. The Integralists were militant Catholics, monarchists, and corporatists, comparable to Maurras's *Action Française.* The Salazar *Estado Novo* derived some of its precepts and personnel from this faction.

15. The analysis in this section derives from the author's recently completed book-length study *Corporatism and Development.*

16. João Baptista Nunes Pereira Neto, "Social Evolution in Portugal since 1945," in Raymond Sayers, ed., *Portugal and Brazil in Transition* (Minneapolis: University of Minnesota Press, 1968), pp. 212–27; and Herminio Martins, "Portugal," in Archer and Giner, eds., *Contemporary Europe: Class, Status, and Power* (London: Weidenfeld and Nicolson, 1971), pp. 60–89.

17. The strong social justice orientation of the *Estado Novo* comes through clearly in all the literature of the period. See the writings of Salazar, Caetano, João Pinto da Costa Leite, Pedro Teotonio Pereira, Augusto da Costa, and numerous others.

18. A particularly stimulating presentation of this argument is Schmitter's "Corporatist Interest Representation." Compare Wiarda, *Corporatism and Development.*

19. In fact the principal leaders of the *Estado Novo* were of middle-class social origins rather than from the upper oligarchic and capitalist classes. The

middle-class origins of those in power had important implications for the direction of Portuguese corporatism, but these implications, as we shall show later on, did not stem wholly from their membership in an alleged "power elite." My quarrel here is not with the several power elite and class-based interpretations, so long as they are properly qualified, but with the unrefined and unqualified forms such analyses have frequently taken.

20. The argument follows that of Kenneth Sharpe, "In-Corporation through Agrarian Reform: The Consequences of Catholic *Accion Social*," in Malloy, ed., *Authoritarianism and Corporatism*.

21. See Theodore Lowi, *The End of Liberalism* (New York: Norton, 1969); and Grant McConnell, *Private Power and American Democracy* (New York: Knopf, 1966).

22. The theme derives from the title of the book by William E. Connolly, *The Bias of Pluralism* (New York: Atherton, 1971); see also Howard J. Wiarda, "The Latin Americanization of the United States," *The New Scholar*, vol. 7 (1979), pp. 51–85.

23. These developments are discussed in detail in Wiarda, *Corporatism and Development*.

24. For this conclusion see Schmitter, "Corporatist Interest Representation." For the structure of the administrative state, see Lawrence S. Graham, "Portugal: The Bureaucracy of Empire" (Paper presented at the Workshop on Modern Portugal, University of New Hampshire, Durham, October 10–14, 1973). For the major economic groups and their links with the state, see Maria Belmira Martins, *Sociedades e grupos em Portugal* (Lisbon: Estampa, 1973).

25. The term derives from a thinly disguised parody of the Salazar regime by one of the country's leading writers, José Cardoso Pires, *Dinossauro Excelentissimo* (Lisbon: Arcadia, 1972).

26. See chapter 9 of Wiarda, *Corporatism and Development*.

27. See especially the IPOPE surveys *Os Portugues e a Politica—1973* (Lisbon: Moraes, 1973).

28. For Spínola's views see his *Portugal e o Futuro* (Lisbon: Arcadia, 1974), a book that was more a political launching pad for Spínola's private political ambitions than a great liberating document, as the non-Portuguese press has often presented it.

29. Some of the materials in this section were previously discussed in Howard J. Wiarda, "Prospects for Portugal" (Paper prepared for the Office of External Research, Department of State, October 16, 1974).

30. See Ortega's classic *Invertebrate Spain*. For a parallel case and fuller discussion, see Howard J. Wiarda, "From Fragmentation to Disintegration: The Social and Political Effects of the Dominican Revolution," *America Latina*, vol. 10 (1967), pp. 55–71, reprinted in Eugenia Chang-Rodriguez, ed., *The Lingering Crisis* (New York: Las Americas, 1969) and in Richard Fagen and Wayne Cornelius, *Political Power in Latin America* (New York: Prentice-Hall, 1970).

31. These events may be followed in the newspapers, especially *Expresso, Diario de Noticias,* and *Vida Mundial.*

32. Ibid. Spínola comments are quoted in *New York Times*, October 1, 1974.

33. An especially useful account written during this period and on which the present analysis relies is Lawrence S. Graham, "The Current Political Situation in Portugal: The Collapse of the Center and the Shift Leftward" (Paper prepared for the Office of External Research, Department of State, October 16, 1974).

34. The reports of Henry Giniger in the *New York Times* have traced these issues; see especially his dispatches of December 27, 1974, and February 10, 1975.

35. The positions of the several parties, the labor law itself, and the positions within the MFA may be followed in *Expresso* (January–February 1975).

36. See Howard J. Wiarda, "Can We Learn to Live with a Socialist World?"

37. The discussion here is derived from various accounts in *Expresso* and *Le Monde* during this period; from the perceptive articles of Douglas Wheeler and Takashi Oka in the *Christian Science Monitor,* February 21 and 25, 1965; and from newspaper accounts leading up to the elections of April 25. The formal accord between the MFA and the political parties was published in the Portuguese newspapers of April 11 and 12, 1975.

38. See Richard M. Morse, "The Heritage of Latin America," in Wiarda, ed., *Politics and Social Change.*

4
Change and Continuity in the Portuguese Armed Forces Movement

The Portuguese revolution that began in 1974 was one of Europe's great dramatic events, certainly of that decade and maybe of the century. It began as a reaction against the old, tired, outdated regime of Antonio Salazar and Marcello Caetano, as a response to the backwardness and isolation of the country and its debilitating efforts to hang onto its colonies in Africa. What began as a limited revolution (a *renovação*, in Portuguese terms) to change the character and direction of the existing regime, however, soon spilled over into widespread street demonstrations and, by some groups, an effort at social revolution. But as the Portuguese revolution gradually turned back toward the center and eventually became quite conservative, its more traditional origins also became clearer. In this chapter we look at the motives and social forces operating on that group of young military officers that led the revolution, the Portuguese Armed Forces Movement, as a way of demonstrating the quite limited, traditionalist, and often conservative currents at work even in this most "radical" of events in Iberia in recent decades.

Although Portugal and its revolution were much in the news during the 1970s, the early literature did not satisfactorily answer the most important question of why the Portuguese revolution took the direction it did. There are few scholars with the research background in Portugal to speak authoritatively on contemporary Portuguese events (during the long Salazar era social science research on and in Portugal was virtually nonexistent). Moreover the popular and journalistic accounts have been generally characterized by an ahistoricism that necessarily stems from being assigned to this trouble spot without the necessary background to comprehend it fully. Therefore, a concentration on the surface political and ideological conflicts that, in the absence of a deeper understanding of the country's traditions and society, is perhaps about all that the popular media can be expected to impart.[1]

A full understanding of the Portuguese revolution, however, requires more in the way of analysis and explanation than the accounts provided so far. Rather than superficial explanations or, worse, sheer stupefaction at the fact that this—the most conservative, traditional, and underdeveloped of Western countries—should suddenly emerge as the most radical, at the forefront of rapid social change and mobilization and perhaps on the cutting edge of "advanced" European politics, what is required is careful analysis of the Portuguese revolution in the light of that country's national psychology, culture, and character and its historical pattern of sociopolitical relations.[2] It is toward such an analysis that this chapter is directed, focusing particularly on the psychosocial background of the Armed Forces Movement (MFA), which was from the beginning the most critical force in Portugal's revolutionary transformation. The thesis argued here is that the direction of the Portuguese revolution can be best understood by employing such a focus; at the same time it must be remembered that the information presented is still incomplete, that the hypotheses offered are still often suggestive and tentative rather than definitive, and that much additional research in these areas is still required.

Social Background

The members of the MFA, numbering some 240 men, whose assembly served as the chief guiding force and final decision-making body of the Portuguese revolution, were bourgeois and petit bourgeois almost to a man. Although Americans especially, because of their own history and traditions, are often reluctant to use class-based interpretations of political events, in the Portuguese case class explanations are crucial to an understanding of the armed forces' political behavior.[3]

The Portuguese army is no longer, as it was traditionally, a haven and training ground for upper- and upper-middle-class youths. Up through World War I the armed forces officer corps, particularly at the highest levels, had remained largely an aristocratic preserve. That army was so woefully ill-equipped and trained for fighting in the Great War that, while the officers sipped cognac and played politics in Lisbon, the enlisted men were humiliated by their sobriquet, "trench-diggers of Europe." The entire army was disgraced, and it hence began efforts to restore its pride and power.[4]

In the 1920s under Salazar the army was considerably modernized, and the officer corps became the preserve more of middle- and upper-middle-class men on the make, displacing the older aristocrats. But this new, rising middle sector aped and imitated the traditional elites, assumed the same haughty attitudes as the older upper class, and used the military hierarchy as a means to rise to wealth and power on a grander scale. By its coup of 1926 the military sought to recover its pride and save the country from the chaos and corruption of republicanism. Salazar was clever in playing on these sentiments: he provided pay raises, new equipment, new uniforms, and promotions, and he was also careful to give the army full credit for protecting and saving the nation. It must be remembered that the presidents under Salazar and Caetano were from the ranks of this new high military elite; at the same time virtually all officers from colonels on up served simultaneously on the boards of directors of the large conglomerates intimately linked to the government in the Portuguese form of monopolistic state capitalism and through which these officers were able to increase their personal incomes.

So long as Portugal remained peaceful and stable, with its economy growing and new opportunities continually opening for rising middle-class officers to benefit from this same system, the Estado Novo survived, even thrived. But in the 1960s several things began to happen, presented here in summary form, that profoundly affected the attitudes and orientation of the officer corps.

• The military loss of the Portuguese enclaves of Goa, Damão, and Diu on the Indian subcontinent and the subsequent cashiering of the officers involved served as an immediate and lurid example of what happens to Portuguese soldiers who lose wars.

• The revolt in Angola in 1961 and subsequent black African uprisings in Guinea and Mozambique shattered the myth of the special nature of Portugal as a colonial nation and of the "civilizing" role of its armed forces.

• By the 1970s the wars in Africa had begun to go badly, with the prospect of another defeat and humiliation for the army.

• Those officers comfortably ensconced in their elevated and profitable positions in Lisbon hung on to them even more tenaciously. Middle-level officers grew impatient with the barriers to wealth and promotions that a top-heavy (and ancient—Admiral Thomaz, the president, was eighty; other high regime and military figures were similarly elderly) officer corps placed in their way.

• As a result of these professional and career discontents, as well as rising civilian opposition to the Salazar regime, the army's own growing embarrassment about serving as the bulwark of such a regime, and the frustrations of being isolated and outcast from Europe and the world, a number of military revolts were launched, which were put down successfully by the government but which nonetheless served as indicators of growing military opposition, both to the Estado Novo and to the military's own most senior officers.

• As the threat developed that long stints (five years and more) in the African wars might ruin one's opportunities to "make it" in Lisbon society and business or, worse, result in death or maiming, the officer corps became less attractive to middle- and upper-middle-class youths as an avenue for upward mobility. As the economy expanded, these elements turned to business, industry, the professions, and other more profitable occupations.

• Hence the officer corps came to be recruited increasingly from lower-middle-class ranks. The provision of salaries to the cadets and free tuition made the military life attractive to a new social class when the academies were opened to those of humbler origins. These were the sons of shopkeepers and low-level officials in rural areas and provincial towns who could not afford the high school and university education for their sons that the upper-middle and middle classes could. For those who qualified, entering the military academy and receiving a smart uniform, pay, promotions, status, and regular officer's commission remained the only means of obtaining further education, escaping the confines and lack of opportunities in Portugal's small towns, and advancing their and their family's social position.

• These newest upwardly mobile recruits saw their recently acquired positions and future careers threatened when, in 1973, in order to increase the number of officers, the Caetano government began granting regular commissions to conscript officers (many of whom were already high school and university graduates and thus of a higher social class than the academy graduates), who up till then had received separate militia commissions. The academy graduates saw this as an insult to their own professional training and a threat to opportunities for further advancement up the ranks.

No claim is here made that these social and professional considerations regarding pay, promotions, opportunities for advancement, and the resentment of lower-middle-class officers against upper-middle-class and elitist officers who at one level blocked and at another cut short the path to the top were alone responsible for the formation of the MFA and for the coup against Caetano. Dissension within the officer corps, as Professor Kenneth Maxwell has shown, was a reflection of a deeper malaise having to do with the frustrations of the wars in Africa, the corruption and heavy-handedness of the Lisbon regime, and Portugal's own underdevelopment and backwardness.[5] Nevertheless, it was the professional concerns and the social resentments that helped galvanize these other discontents and that remain of paramount importance even today, a fact that is ignored in our emphasis on political and ideological differences. The truth is that the social and political resentments became entwined with and inseparable from the officers' later efforts to fashion a revolution in Portugal, and our difficulty in understanding the course of Portuguese events stems in large measure from our inability to comprehend these connections.

By early 1974 there was a widening chasm within the officer corps that was not only generational but class based as well. The division was sharp between those above the rank of lieutenant colonel (largely upper-middle class and elitist in attitudes) and those below (lower middle), who formed the ranks of the MFA. Because this class basis of the MFA is so crucial, it deserves detailed treatment. The now extensive literature on the political behavior of these elements within the Iberian and Latin American middle class, both civilian and military, helps us understand this same sector in Portugal, particularly in the MFA.[6]

• Socially and culturally the middle sectors place a central emphasis on personalism, on leadership built upon intimate personal relationships. Family, patronage, and kinship ties tend to be more important than impersonal party and group affiliations and hence the continuing organizational weakness of most political parties in Portugal. Values centering on hierarchy and authority rather than on equality remain the rule, with political bonds still based largely on paternalistic patron-client relationships. While emphasizing higher transcendental or ideological values, materialism and status considerations are exceedingly important.

• The middle sectors are deeply divided politically and ideologically. While often verbally advocating liberal or radical solutions, they frequently remain tied to traditionalist, particularist, and paternalistic conceptions. The divisions and conflicting pulls within the MFA reflect the divisions within Portuguese society, particularly the emerging middle class.

• The military officer corps, however, by training and inclination is in some ways set apart from other middle-sector groups. On the one hand, it is suspicious of and hostile toward civilian parties and politicians and is particularly resentful of those superior to itself in class and educational background, such as the "elevated" upper bourgeoisie in the Socialist and Popular Democratic parties. On the other hand, it is particularly jealous of the military's own special and elevated place in the system; its corporate rights and privileges; its higher sense of patriotism, verity, and the national interest, which stands above the divisive partisan squabbles; and its higher-order role and responsibility as the heroic savior and guardian of the nation.

• Perhaps above all else the middle sectors, including their military representatives, are intensely socially conscious and ambitious. In a society where place and rank are virtually all important, the middle class is particularly preoccupied with preserving its newly won position, feels constantly threatened because it knows that position is precarious, and hence reacts strongly against any perceived challenge.

The middle class shares few of the so-called middle-class virtues, nor has it acquired the values presumed to undergird the functioning of Anglo-American democracy. In fact, the Iberic-Latin middle classes tend to ape, aspire to, and imitate their vision of upper-class ways. Specifically regarding the MFA, it wanted to enjoy the fruits of its revolution and to live in a comfortable fashion. Beneath the revolutionary rhetoric, undoubtedly sincere, these were also ambitious, self- and status-seeking men on the make. They enjoyed the prestige and perquisites of newly won wealth, power, and influence: the women; the limousines; the popular respect; the plush palaces and offices; the private homes; and the glory, trappings, and symbols of power. The repeated purges that occurred after April 1974 were not just for political and ideological reasons but to make room for the younger officers to occupy the positions previously held by their ousted seniors. Whatever the ideological orientation the Portuguese regime eventually takes, it would also be illuminating to see how many of the majors and captains who formed the MFA had since become colonels and generals (starting with such leading members as Vasco Gonçalves and Otelo Carvalho); how many had enhanced their military salaries with lucrative civilian positions in the ministries, agencies, and newly nationalized government industries; and how many new opportunities for wealth and advancement had opened up through the advantages and access that go with a high military officership.

These comments are not meant to cast aspersions upon the sincerity or honesty of the MFA or its officers. The intent is simply to place the actions taken in a broader social and cultural framework of Portuguese middle-class political behavior. For the fact is the MFA in many respects (obviously not all) behaved in classic middle- and lower-middle-class patterns, reflecting its own social origins. The revolution of 1974 provided the officer corps with an opportunity simultaneously to serve itself while also serving the nation. It basked in the new prestige and admiration that accrued to those who made the revolution, and it served as a popular national symbol against all those cruel (usually Brazilian) jokes about the Portuguese lack of intelligence and stature. It erased the image of the Portuguese army as corrupt, incompetent, antipopular, and inefficient. Members of the army were no longer considered the "trench diggers of Europe" but had forced Europe, America, and the world to pay Portugal serious attention, even to beat a path to its door.

Educational Background

The educational background of the new officer corps reflects the social origins from which its members emerged. These are not, as some have claimed, illiterate peasants with guns (although there were some of these within the MFA and particularly in the ranks) but the middle- and lower-middle-class sons of small-town shopkeepers and government workers whose educational opportunities were usually limited to the local grade school. Few MFA members (except the more recent militiamen) had been educated outside the military system, although some had attended the military high school in addition to the academy. Few MFA officers had a university education or its equivalent.[7]

Moreover, the test scores for entrance to the military academy, resulting from the difficulties of recruiting sufficient candidates and the changed social composition of the cadet corps, had been declining for the past dozen years. As a result of the unattractiveness of being sent to fight and perhaps die in Africa, fewer upper-middle-class or even middle-class youths, presumably somewhat better educated and with broader preparation, were seeking entrance to the academy; hence it was forced to change its requirements and accept those scoring lower on the exams, which meant the less well-educated sons of the lower-middle class. If one examines the government's own figures published in the *Anuario,* the curve of the test scores of those in command positions pointed precipitously downward.[8]

Once in the academy the young officers received little in the way of training that would prepare them to manage and govern the complex economy and nation that the Portuguese had become. Luigi Einaudi has shown that the Peruvian officers who ushered in a revolution in 1968, and to whom the Portuguese officers were often compared, had been well trained for their role in the military general command school and that what they carried in their briefcases was not lunch or a pistol but national development plans and homework.[9] In contrast, the Portuguese academies provided little such training. So far as may be ascertained, there was almost nothing in the way of development planning, administration, international economics, or modern management; there was no sociology or political science; and economics remained largely pre-Keynesian. Up until the last years of Caetano, by which time it was too late to effect much change, these subjects were not viewed as a useful or necessary part of military training (university offerings in these areas were also only beginning to develop). The last thing Salazar wanted was an economic and political training that might offer alternatives to his own or a military with administrative skills and the ability to govern. Nor under Salazar's system of enforced isolation did the young Portuguese officers have much contact with their better-trained colleagues in other NATO nations. All such "modernizing" training and "corrupting" contact were avoided; the country is now paying the price.

Few of the MFA officers had thus ever been outside Portugal and its territories; only a handful had traveled to the United States or Western Europe. Many were narrow, parochial, and unsophisticated. The centers of instruction and consciousness raising established by the MFA after the 1974 coup functioned irregularly, as indoctrination centers rather than open agencies of learning, and still with only a limited effect since the constant tussles within the officer corps left little time for serious education. Hence the young officers remained not at all well read in economics, sociology, or political science; what had been digested in these disciplines was often superficial, unquestioned, half understood, and often without the necessary factual background to understand how alternative systems actually do function. The MFA's vision of capitalism was the monopolistic state capitalism of Salazar benefiting a narrow elite and not the many; its vision of liberalism was the failed regime of Marcello Caetano or the earlier (1910–1926) republic with its "café liberals"; democratic socialism was represented by the disorganized, divisive, carefully manicured and coiffed upper bourgeoisie of the Socialist party (PS) and the Popular Democratic party (PPD). Without any detailed knowledge of economics or political sociology, the MFA had become convinced— helped by a clever and vociferous left, a distorted and nearly officially orthodox media, as well as a strong and influential extreme left element within its own ranks—that only socialism could provide the road for social justice and economic betterment in Portugal. But even this was a heavily idealized conception and had not been grounded in concrete programs and realities. One cannot help thinking that for a group of men who overthrew what they considered a Fascist regime, it then became necessary to adopt what they considered its precise opposite, which was socialism.[10]

Numerous commentators, while trying not to demean the Portuguese, have nonetheless remarked about the seeming incompetence of the military regime, its economic mismanagement, its hodgepodge and often confused ideological formulations, and its political and administrative fumbling. If one looks at the educational background, training, and experience of those now governing Portugal, the explanation would seem to be clearer.

Familism, Personalism, Caudilhismo, and Their Implications

It requires almost literally a lifetime of living in a country to appreciate fully all the family interconnections and personal slights and relationships that often undergird political behavior and give it meaning. Lacking this background, journalists and foreign service personnel are necessarily often inclined to employ easier, more familiar, and more visible criteria, such as ideological orientation and the left-right continuum.

Explanations derived from these manifestly political and ideological indicators are, of course, important in helping us understand the behavior of the MFA. But these are certainly not the only criteria; and particularly in a society as small, as interpersonal, as family based, and as socially interlocked as the Portuguese, they may not even be the most important. Elevation of the political and ideological variables to an explanatory importance they do not have, particularly at the expense of ignoring these others, is certain to result in misleading and false conclusions.

Unfortunately we almost entirely lack systematic information on these other variables, particularly as they relate to an understanding of the behavior of the MFA. There has been little research concentrated on these areas; yet most careful observers of the Portuguese scene sense impressionistically that knowledge of personal and family relations, clean and dirty business deals, social slights and favors (and who received them from whom), patron-client relations, and class attitudes and interactions are as important as the political-ideological variables in understanding the attitudes and actions of the Portuguese regime, and maybe more so.[11]

We know, for example, that General Spínola was of the high bourgeoisie, with all the haughtiness and sense of superiority that this implies in Portugal, and that part of the resentment against him on the part of the more radical (now) General Carvalho, who came from lower-middle-class ranks and was born almost completely outside of Portuguese society in Mozambique, was due to never-forgotten social slights when both served in Guinea and Spínola excluded the brash, ambitious young captain from his inner circle. Carvalho got his revenge by playing a key role in the later ousting of Spínola. We know also that regional differences are important politically in Portugal, with the north (from whose small towns many MFA members came) more Catholic, traditionalist, and conservative, for instance; but so far we lack systematic information on how region of origin helped shape the attitudes of individuals and factions within the MFA. We know that cousins and political kinship-related officers have sometimes received special treatment within the military, but we lack basic research on family patterns and interrelationships.

We know too that where officers served in Africa (Angola, Guinea, or Mozambique) helped shape the orientation they carried back to Lisbon, but again we lack systematic data on how precisely this influenced their subsequent behavior in groups and as individuals. We know also that many of the bonds, friendships, factions, and *panelinhas* (interpersonal networks) that existed in the MFA were first cemented in Africa, but we lack knowledge as to the precise nature of these groups, who was in them, and how strong the personalistic connections were. To offer one illustration, General Carlos Fabião, army chief of staff and one of the leaders of the MFA, was part of the Spínola *panelinha* in Guinea, but his loyalty to Spínola was not sufficient to ensure his continued support of the general in the abortive *Spínolista* coup attempt of March 11, 1975. In the article cited earlier, Maxwell rightly points out that virtually all the leading military actors in the revolution during the first year worked with Spínola in Guinea and that their subsequent political positions were shaped by either hero worship or profound distrust of him. It should be remembered, however, that there were other, rival *panelinhas* operating under General Kaulza de Arriaga in Mozambique, others in Angola, still others headquartered at various posts in continental Portugal, and that the rivalries of these various personalistic factions were reflected in the successive purges and military jockeying for position after the April coup. The fact is, however, that we lack information on almost all these social, family, regional, and interpersonal relations and, short of a long-time immersion in Portuguese society, most foreign observers would be ill equipped to interpret these data even if they could be obtained.

Reliance on political and ideological differences alone to explain MFA behavior, which of necessity dominates in the media and diplomatic assessments, provides a superficial, incomplete, and hence inaccurate means of interpreting Portuguese politics. What is required is to begin to come to grips with the intensely personal and strong social class orientation of Portuguese political behavior, together with the pattern of social slights and favors that goes with such relationships. These aspects frequently underlie the political and ideological differences. We need to sort out all these family patterns, the patterns of spoils and favors that tie junior officers to their superiors and the loyalty that is expected in return, the social slights and social advancements, the patterns of nepotism and graft and who gets what from whom, as well as the interactions and bonds of men thrown closely together in far-off battlegrounds. Only then will we begin to understand Portugal—not on some unidimensional basis but in all its multifaceted complexities.

Ideology, World View, and the National Inferiority Complex

It is not only the north European who frequently (and ethnocentrically) expresses the sentiment that Europe stops at the Pyrenees; the Portuguese is also often uncertain of his culture, political and otherwise. Stemming from the parochialism of the Portuguese small towns and rural areas, the distance of the country from the main centers of Europe, exposure on the Atlantic and centuries-long colonizing ventures in Africa, the Far East and South America, and finally the poverty and backwardness of Portugal as compared with the rest of Western Europe, the Portuguese, including the military officers, have tended not to feel fully European, even though they may strongly aspire to be so considered. The question of whether Portugal is fully European and hence "Western" or whether its destiny lies in some South Atlantic Luso-tropicalism has always loomed large in Portuguese history. It wants to be treated as a European equal, yet its repeated rejection by or unacceptability to the rest of Europe has bred in the Portuguese a gigantic national inferiority complex that itself often results in contradictory postures. On the one hand it breeds retreat into isolationism, a go-it-alone attitude, the shunning of Europe, and the ideology of Luso-tropicalism (or, as during the revolution, third worldism), and on the other (and frequently at one and the same time), it calls for dramatic explosions into the forefront of Europe, as a way of showing that Portugal is not really a second-rate country.

As Portugal has done historically, it continues to look concurrently north and south. Instead of its "special vocation" for dealing with blacks and the persistent myth of the multiracial society, Portugal during the revolution sought to be in the vanguard of change and decolonization, talked vaguely of serving as a bridge between Europe and the third world, and, in the pronouncements of some of its more radical leaders, identified itself with third worldism. Much of this was done to gain European recognition and acceptance ("for the English [or Americans or NATO] to see"). But if the forlorn hope of full acceptance as a European equal failed, the Portuguese had already erected a set of defense mechanisms so that they could once more, as they have periodically done, retreat into their own house of isolation, thumb their noses at an Atlantic Community that continued to reject them, and go their own way regardless, out of a combined sense of spite and injured pride and in reaction to their sense of inferiority.

It has been alleged, most notably by Kenneth Maxwell in two significant articles in the *New York Review of Books*,[12] that the MFA learned the ideology of socialism, third worldism, and revolutionary liberation from long years of fighting against—and eventually acquiring admiration for and identification with—the liberation movements in Portugal's African territories. Hence, it is argued, the unusual tolerance, in a Western military organization, of far-left political thought, socialism, and third worldism. The case has rested largely on the brief political tracts that some of the leading MFA members have published since the 1974 revolt and on their public statements of position.[13]

Although there was considerable knowledge of the structure and ideology of the African liberation movements on the part of the Portuguese, and probably some grudging admiration of them, this explanation is probably not a sufficient one. Before the April 1974 revolt one was not apt to find in Portugal much admiration for the African guerrillas; in fact what was more common was the stereotypical racial and ethnic slurs concerning blacks. The situation was perhaps comparable to the American troops' attitude toward the "gooks" in Vietnam. Hence another reader reviewing the same statements that Maxwell apparently took at face value might interpret them less as expressions of admiration for the African guerrillas than as *post hoc* rationalizations for the seizure of power. They were written after the fact to justify actions already decided upon for other, subtler, sometimes baser reasons. In the Portuguese case as in others, motives that were in considerable measure self-serving were subsequently covered over and camouflaged with grandiloquent arguments over the national destiny; what particularly benefits one group (in this case the MFA) was wrapped in the language of a truly national and patriotic act that was for the good of all.[14] The learned-from-the Africans argument is not entirely convincing.

What seems at least equally plausible in explaining the MFA's actions and appears to be supported by the evidence, admittedly incomplete, here put forth, is both the social advancement and the reactions from the national inferiority complex arguments. This is, of course, not to say the MFA officers were wholly cynical or that they lacked genuine motives of patriotism and social justice; indeed, some have been known literally to weep at the backward plight of their country. But there can be no doubt that powerful self-serving motives, as well as more selfless ones in many cases, were at work in the coup that toppled the Caetano government and in the political struggles that followed. That these particularistic interests often overlapped with and, at least during the first year of the revolution, paralleled to a major degree popular sentiment and the national interest (the struggle for democracy and greater pluralism, wage increases, social justice, and decolonization) should not be surprising. Few national leaderships, after all, instigate programs designed to serve the national interest that do not also simultaneously work to the narrower advantage of themselves, their associates, their party, or their class. For the young Portuguese officers the "revolution of carnations" provided an opportunity to achieve a place in the sun, both for themselves and their nation.

But why should the revolution initially turn so far to the left? In addition to the answers given by Maxwell and others, it may be suggested that one important reason derives from that same current of national inferiority that runs so strong in Portugal. Because the country is last in Europe on most indexes of development and modernization, it has sought to be the most advanced on others. Portugal's incredible feats of exploration and conquest in the fifteenth and sixteenth centuries can in part be explained in this manner. So can the advanced (and largely unworkable) constitutional documents of the nineteenth century, and the same applies to Salazar's Estado Novo. Rather than selectively choosing the aspects of the corporatist philosophies then current that could be usefully applied, as other European nations did (for example, councils of state, partially functionalist representative bodies, joint workers-employers' councils, and the like), the Portuguese embraced corporatism *in toto* as the ideology of the future. The Portuguese saw corporatism, in its most advanced manifestation, as a way of vaulting from a backward, disorganized state into what it thought would be Europe's leading form of sociopolitical organization.[15] So, in a sense, it was with socialism in the 1970s. It may thus be hypothesized that the radical direction of the Portuguese revolution stemmed not so much from a weighing of what was pragmatically useful and workable in the Socialist vision but, in strong

133

measure, from a deeper, national psychological desire to leap across stages, to proceed directly from a retrograde corporatism to the most advanced forms of socialism, to bypass a Europe that continued to reject Portugal or to place impossible demands upon it, and in this way to overcome that historical sense of inferiority by catapulting to the forefront of radical social and political transformation—to become again a leader of Europe instead of a second-rate camp follower.

Such an explanation also helps us understand why the Portuguese brand of socialism was at once so radical and so romantic and chaotic. The plans and programs drawn up by the MFA were abstract, highly theoretical, grandly stated. Like so many such documents in Portuguese history, they represented a kind of constitutional and social engineering, on an elevated plane but typically far divorced from practical reality and with no possibility of being implemented. Marxism, socialism, and third worldism had become the latest great visions, replacing the great visions of Thomism, republicanism, and corporatism of the past. They were more for the foreigner to see and admire and for the Portuguese to hold up as a national goal than they were meant to be effectively carried out. Although the more realistic politicians within the MFA understood this and the impossibility that the flaming rhetoric concerning full democracy and social justice could be realized, one of the difficulties was that many Portuguese, as well as many foreigners, took the rhetoric seriously at face value. During the first fifteen months of the new regime, hence, the country experienced an incredible outpouring of revolutionary pronouncements, with each group seemingly vying to outdo the others in the degree of its radical commitments to socialism. Although this orgy of long-pent-up ideological argument acquired a political dynamic of its own and was not entirely irrelevant to the main political realities, it also remained true that the real crunch came as the euphoria of the revolution wore off, as the political and economic reserves on which the revolution had luxuriated were exhausted, and as politico-economic decisions, not necessarily ideological ones, had to be made.

Since the early nineteenth century at least, the Portuguese have been in search of a formula that would solve their age-old problems of underdevelopment and lack of national organization. Usually the formula arrived at—constitutionalism, republicanism, corporatism— was derived from the outside; it was imperfectly understood, and ultimately it failed to solve Portugal's problems. In the circumstances of the mid-1970s, other than a rather romantic and often naive conception of socialism, most MFA members had only a limited notion of what that meant and how to go about implementing it. They took some revolutionary steps, nationalized major concerns, and wanted to redistribute wealth, but they did not really know how to go about the redistribution or how to proceed from nationalization to genuine socialism. Here, to informed observers, is where the potential Communist threat to Portugal came in: not from some supposed 'Prague model' (who, after all, could possibly lead such a *putsch* against a well-equipped army and without the assistance of Soviet troops?) but from the real possibility that in the absence of any concrete programs of their own, young, inexperienced, proud, and bitter military officers might turn to the one group that does have a blueprint for implementing socialism, has the dedication and heroism that the military also admires, and appears to know how to get things done: the Portuguese Communist party.[16] After all, in similar circumstances in 1928, another well-meaning but inexperienced military government turned to the one element that then also claimed to have a formula—Salazar and the corporatists.

Political Attitudes

Much has been written about the politics of the military regime; here it seems useful to emphasize five major points.

1. Although most observers tended to treat the MFA as a single unit, any prediction of the armed forces' political behavior must employ a more refined analysis than that. In addition to the personalistic, class-based, and other factions and *panelinhas* noted earlier, careful study must be made of the differences between the services, the political attitudes of the officers at various levels in the chain of command, and divisional and regimental differences, among others. Is it really true that the navy is the most radical of the services and why; does the proposition hold that those higher up in the hierarchy tend to be more conservative; what are the differences between those regiments stationed in the north and those in Lisbon; and what are the reasons for those differences? To all these questions some impressionistic answers can be given, but clearly sound policy requires a far more systematic analysis.

2. Above and beyond the factions and military rivalries, it must be recognized that the armed forces also share a common *esprit de corps*, revolving around the accomplishments of the revolution, a certain unity of purpose, and a powerful corporate self-interest. Attempts to divide the Armed Forces Movement and play off one faction against another have up to now frequently had the opposite effect of strengthening its unity and solidarity.

3. In keeping with the above, the MFA continued to see itself and

135

the revolution as heroic and fundamentally apolitical. Its action in toppling the Estado Novo was viewed as a patriotic and nationalistic gesture, above mere partisan political squabbles. For this reason it was also surprised, even mystified, by the opposition that has grown to what it perceives as its selfless actions.

4. Because of this perception, the MFA had a common hostility to *all* political parties, which it saw as divisive and as detracting from the truly national interest, which it alone represents. It was particularly hostile to the Socialists and the Popular Democrats whom it viewed as compromised and forming part of the upper-middle class, who had not suffered and struggled as had both the MFA members and the Communists and who could not govern effectively without the usual partisan bickering and corruption. In addition, the MFA resented that these parties had been critical of the military, again in contrast to the Communists, and the fact that their whole *raison d'être* implied a civilian democracy, which would necessarily exclude the armed forces from its great self-appointed role.

5. Whatever final ideological formula is developed, the MFA will almost certainly insist on an administrative state structure that is authoritarian and fundamentally apolitical (meaning that it will not be party based but above the partisan struggle), with its own corporate self-interest securely protected and with the armed forces continuing to serve as guarantors of the revolution and ultimate arbiters of national affairs. That was essentially the implication of the MFA's creation of an entire hierarchy of new military institutions (the MFA Assembly, Council, Triumvirate, and the like) parallel to the civilian agencies but in all cases superior to them.[17]

Pride, Nationalism, and Paranoia

In the so-called "revolution of flowers" of 1974 the Portuguese military ended a dictatorship dating from 1926. It changed the direction of Portuguese history and did so without bloodshed. It terminated those exhausting, debilitating, ruinous colonial wars and moved to give independence to Portugal's former colonies. It brought a new freedom to Portugal and a new respect among the community of nations. Of these accomplishments the MFA was extraordinarily proud.[18]

From the start, however, the MFA officers felt Western Europe and America failed to acknowledge adequately the magnitude of their accomplishment and their altruistic motivations. They had destroyed a "Fascist" regime and made a revolution, catching the world's attention and imagination. In this they showed themselves to be six feet tall instead of only five, just as good as anyone else.

But the MFA felt the applause and support it deserved from abroad was not forthcoming. Moreover, as the Portuguese applause also died away, the criticism mounted, and the foreign pressures applied, their response was not to accept the criticism and correct the problems mentioned but, in a reaction formation similar to the way the Portuguese have long responded to foreign criticism, to get their backs up, to retreat again into isolation and an attitude of "the whole world be damned," and frequently to go in precisely the opposite direction from what their foreign critics have suggested. An understanding of this aspect of the Portuguese psychology helps us see why President Ford's or Secretary Kissinger's warnings to the effect that Portugal was "going Communist," instead of serving to reverse that process, in fact helped accelerate it and thus seemed to take on the character of self-fulfilling prophecies. The same reverse psychology operated against the initial efforts of the Common Market nations to pressure the Portuguese in more democratic directions and to withhold economic assistance until such changes were forthcoming. To what they saw as carping criticism, foreign interference in their internal affairs, and nonrecognition of their heroic acts, the MFA reacted by rejecting all such criticism and repeatedly lurching even further toward a left-authoritarianism. Given this form of national reaction, one might speculate what might happen if the reverse psychology were applied, that is, praise of the Portuguese regime and the showering on it of economic assistance with no strings attached.

Under Salazar, particularly as the criticism of Portugal's actions in Africa was mobilized and the ostracism from Europe because of the internal character of the regime continued, the government's response was to harden its shell even more and play heavily on the theme of "little Portugal alone against the world." The new revolutionary regime did the same. This reaction too derived from the national inferiority complex, a certain bitterness, and a desire to "show you." The MFA's pride and inferiority were tinged with a resentment directed not only against outside Western critics who failed to understand Portuguese culture and realities, but also against the Western-oriented parties within their own country who articulated the same criticism as the foreigners and did not follow the Communist strategy of publicly siding with the MFA on all issues. Given the MFA's conception of its patriotic and unselfish role, it became understandable why the parties and opposition press were frequently denounced as antinational, subversive, and unpatriotic.

Highly resentful and suspicious, thus, of U.S. and NATO criticism of their actions, the MFA alleged the existence of an economic boycott by the West to strangle the revolution. They were almost paranoiac about the CIA and plots they assumed were directed against them from both outside and inside the country. The Portuguese press was full of warnings about "another Chile." Convinced of the hostility of the West, they retreated even further into their shell of isolation and defensiveness. Indeed the great fear among the Portuguese, whatever its foundations in fact, that the CIA was about to destroy the revolution, proved one of the few effective levers the U.S. embassy in Lisbon was able to employ.

A familiar theme running through the speeches and statements of the MFA was the need for *Portuguese* solutions. This was an intensely nationalistic revolution, almost paranoiacally so if the discussion above is correct, one that insisted it would not duplicate any other form of government and that it would seek the best from all systems and adapt them to Portuguese traditions. That claim was similarly made by the earlier corporatists, who also played upon this same intense Portuguese nationalism (and itself, in its strident paranoiac forms, a product of the self-same national inferiority complex). In part this attitude is a matter of pride, in part an effort to establish for the country a position between the world's great power blocs, in part an attempt to achieve parity with or even leadership among the advanced nations, in part a reflection of a lack of understanding of how other societies function. Whatever the complex of psychosocial causes, however, it remains clear that this was a fiercely nationalistic regime and that foreign criticism, by challenging the "rightness" of the MFA's ideals, which it considered purely patriotic and hence unassailable, in effect challenged the very legitimacy of the revolution. Such criticism was likely to have the effect, not of reversing the course of the revolution, but of fostering greater paranoia and even more precipitous turns to socialism.

Much the same holds true about the internal threat from the ousted Portuguese right. Foreigners belittled the counterrevolutionary activities of those associated with the old regime, but the Portuguese took them very seriously indeed. Having lived through forty-eight years of what is now universally referred to in Portugal as "fascism," the Portuguese and particularly the MFA considered a rightist countermovement as a life-and-death matter. To a certain extent, of course, the threat was manufactured to generate public support for the government, and rightist conspiracies were frequently used as red herrings to purge those found unacceptable by the regime. But one should not underestimate the extent to which the right and its army of former Legionnaires, *Guardas,* secret police, and others constituted a real fear in the men who risked their careers and perhaps even their lives in rising up against the old regime. Nor can one neglect a newly remobilized church and other conservative elements who see themselves as the last bastions of Portuguese values, betrayed by the MFA and the Communists. On the highest level, a rightist coup would imply a repudiation of the cherished ideals that a proud military, already suffering from a profound inferiority complex, had staked its entire self and soul upon; on another, it would have meant the end of all the power, prestige, promotions, government positions, and other perquisites that had gone with the achievement of power. Neither of these reasons for the MFA to defend vigorously its revolution against all attacks should have been taken lightly.

Concluding Remarks

Since the early nineteenth century the Portuguese armed forces have always been at or close to the surface of power. There is no reason for us to expect that to change now. Indeed, one of the more interesting aspects of the revolution in Portugal was the effort of the military to cement its power further, to subordinate civilian politics to the military authority, and to erect institutional structures to safeguard the military's continuance as the final voice on national affairs.[19]

In these circumstances it remained chiefly the military arena that was critical in Portugal, not so much the civilian one. The political party struggles were significant, particularly as they overlapped with and reflected the divisions within the armed forces, and the changing balances of public opinion and among civilian cabinet members and administrators were also important. But one should not, as most visiting journalists and foreign observers often do, read their own preferred political arrangements into their interpretations of Portuguese events and thus see this as a civil *versus* military struggle or elevate the parties and party struggle into an importance they do not have. The fact is the military could abolish *all* parties tomorrow and few Portuguese would lament their passing. The most strategic political arena thus remained the military arena, especially the relative strength and maneuvering of the several military factions, including the ways these are altered by the changing balance among civilian groups.

Given these conditions, we need to know far more than we now do about the social-psychological values, assumptions, and background of the armed forces and their political-behavioral attitudes, reactions, and orientation. Other factors relating to Africa, economic issues, international pressures, and the like are also important, of course, but it is the psychosocial ones that are the most neglected, and that command our attention here. Without questioning the inten-

139

tions and motives of the MFA officers, without engaging in the simplifications of national character studies, and without casting slurs upon the Portuguese or their nation, we need to go below the surface aspects of political and ideological differences that, because of the nature of journalistic coverage, received exaggerated attention in the public media. This essay has attempted to delve beneath these often superficial interpretations by probing more deeply into the class, background, and psychological determinants of Portuguese, particularly MFA, behavior.

As we did so, we discovered some quite traditional, quite historical, quite conservative forces operating within what has been portrayed as a profoundly revolutionary regime. Subsequent developments in Portugal tended to confirm the persistence and continuity even during this revolutionary phase of a country and institutions that remained quite conservative in character.

Notes

1. I have in mind particularly the coverage of the Portuguese revolution in the *New York Times,* which, based upon my own experience in Portugal, I often found to be incomplete, misleading, and inaccurate. The broad indictment here stated also holds true for other journalistic accounts and the broadcast media, however. Some of the better coverage was in *Time* magazine and *Le Monde;* among Portuguese sources *Expresso* provides a gold mine of information.

2. Broadly speaking, this study belongs in the tradition of psychosocial investigations, such as Ruth Benedict's account of the underlying cultural currents of Japanese behavior in *The Chrysanthemum and the Sword* (Boston: Houghton-Mifflin, 1946); and Nathan Leites's investigations of Bolshevik behavior in *A Study of Bolshevism* (Glencoe, Ill.: The Free Press, 1954). Closer to home, see Howard J. Wiarda, ed., *Politics and Social Change in Latin America: The Distinct Tradition* (Amherst: University of Massachusetts Press, 1982); and, specifically on Portugal, Wiarda, *Corporatism and Development: The Portuguese Experience* (Amherst: University of Massachusetts Press, 1977).

3. The social class background of the MFA was emphasized more by European than American writers; see especially Kenneth M. Maxwell, "The Hidden Revolution in Portugal," *New York Review,* vol. 22 (April 17, 1975), pp. 29–35; Jane Bergerol, "Defining the Left in Portugal Is Not Simple," *New York Times,* July 27, 1975; and Henry Giniger, "Lisbon Military, Roots Middle Class, Disproving Rhetoric of Revolution," *New York Times,* August 18, 1975.

4. See the revealing memoirs of Salazar's military aide and secretary Assis Gonçalves, *Intimidades de Salazar: O Homem e a sua Epoca* (Lisbon: Liv. Bertrand, 1967).

5. Maxwell, "The Hidden Revolution," p. 30.

6. See, in general, Richard Adams, *The Second Sowing: Power and Secondary Development in Latin America* (San Francisco, Calif.: Chandler, 1967), chap. 3;

Charles Wagley, *The Latin American Tradition* (New York: Columbia University Press, 1968), chap. 7; John P. Gillin, "The Middle Segments and Their Values," in John Martz, ed., *The Dynamics of Change in Latin American Politics* (Englewood Cliffs, N.J.: Prentice-Hall, 1971), pp. 86–99; José Nun, "The Middle Class Military Coup," in Claudio Veliz, ed., *The Politics of Conformity in Latin America* (London: Oxford University Press, 1967), pp. 66–118; Luís Ratinoff, "The New Urban Groups: The Middle Classes," in Seymour M. Lipset and Aldo Solari, eds., *Elites in Latin America* (New York: Oxford University Press, 1967), pp. 61–93; and Jane-Lee Woolridge Yare, "Middle Sector Political Behavior in Latin America" (Amherst: University of Massachusetts, Dept. of Political Science, 1971).

7. The analysis here is based upon interviews with Portuguese scholars, journalists, American embassy personnel, and other informed foreign observers. The interviews were conducted in May–June, 1975, on a not-for-direct-attribution basis.

8. See the figures in the *Anuario* from roughly 1960 on.

9. Luigi Einaudi, "Revolution from Within? Military Rule in Peru Since 1968" (Paper presented at the Annual Meeting of the American Political Science Assn., Chicago, September 7–11, 1971).

10. Based in part on the interviews cited above; also *New York Times*, August 18, 1975.

11. Neil Bruce is one of the principal students of the military *panelinhas* (literally, a "little saucepan," here defined as a relatively closed but completely informal primary group held together in common interest by personal ties) particularly as they relate to the Portuguese forces in Africa; see his *Portugal: The Last Empire* (New York: Wiley, 1975).

12. Maxwell; the second article was published under the title "Portugal under Fire" in the issue of May 29, 1975.

13. See, for instance, General Galvão de Melo, *MFA: Movimento Revolucionario* (Lisbon: Portugália Ed., 1975); Cap. Vasco Lourenço, *MFA: Rosto do Povo* (Lisbon: Portugália Ed., 1975); Lourenço, *No Regresso Vinham Todos* (Lisbon: Portugália Ed., 1975); Otelo Saraiva de Carvalho, *Cinco Meses Mudaram Portugal* (Lisbon: Portugália Ed., 1975). See also Avelino Rodrigues, Cesario Borga, and Mário Cardoso, *O Movimento dos Capitães e o 25 de Abril* (Lisbon: Moraes, 1974).

14. The best example is Spínola's *Portugal e o Futuro* (Lisbon: Arcadia, 1974), a tract that stimulated the great debate over Portugal's future and its African colonies and thus helped to launch the revolution and that was also a launching pad for Spínola's private political ambitions.

15. On the ideology of the Portuguese corporative state and the influence of that doctrine, see Wiarda, *Corporatism and Development*.

16. These aspects are explored at more length in Howard J. Wiarda, "Can We Learn to Live with a Socialist World? Foreign Policy Implications Stemming from the Portuguese Revolution and Other 'New Forces,' " to be published in a forthcoming volume dealing with political change in the Iberian Peninsula, edited by Brian Crozier and issued by the Institute for the Study of Conflict, London.

17. On the organization and functioning of the administrative state structure, see Lawrence S. Graham, *Portugal: The Bureaucracy of Empire* (Beverly Hills, Calif.: 1975).

18. Based in part on the interviews cited above.

19. See the text of the pact between the MFA and the political parties signed prior to the 1975 Constituent Assembly elections, which guaranteed the military's specially privileged place in the Portuguese system and its control over the domains of civilian politics and administrative affairs.

5

The Corporatist Tradition and the Corporative System in Portugal

Structured, Evolving, Transcended, Persistent

The term "corporatism" is exceedingly ambiguous and often loosely employed. Enjoying a certain resurgence and new-found popularity of late,[1] among both political analysts and certain political elites, it nonetheless remains a frequently confusing and misleading term and framework. Moreover, it is often a highly emotive term, conjuring up past images of Nazi atrocities and Fascist dictatorships. At one time so-called corporatist regimes, with Portugal and Spain the major exceptions, seemed to be safely confined to the ashcans of history. Now, however, the term has gained a new credence and respectability, and regimes calling themselves "corporatist" have reemerged in what are, from a policy and ideological perspective, such distinct nations as Chile, Mexico, and Peru. We are also discovering that regimes we are used to thinking of as liberal and social-democratic—such as Costa Rica, Venezuela, and even Sweden and Austria—often exhibit numerous, though frequently disguised, corporative features.[2] Moreover, even those long-term and manifestly "corporatist" regimes, such as the Portuguese, remained for a long period almost wholly unstudied and covered over by myth and misunderstanding. The time to begin clarifying both the meaning of the term corporatism and our understanding of how such corporatist regimes as the Portuguese actually function is long overdue.[3]

Corporatism as Tradition

The model for "the system" implemented during his regency (1439–1447) . . . and which was to become the standard system in the Portuguese kingdom for several centuries was that developed by Dom Pedro in his *Livro da Virtuosa Bem-*

143

feitoria. Moreover the model developed by this Portuguese prince in the early fifteenth century is almost a prototype of what political scientists and others refer to as the corporate, patrimonial state.[4]

Iberic-Latin history, in this case specifically Portuguese history, is often analyzed as a presumed unilinear and universal evolution toward liberalism and democracy. This viewpoint is not surprising when it emanates from British and North American writers; occasionally, though, it finds its way into Portuguese writers as well. This perspective uses the British Parliament for its model of the Portuguese Cortes, the Bill of Rights as its model of civil liberties, the New England town meeting as its model of participatory democracy, and the liberal-Lockean tradition as its model for the ideal political system.[5]

The process of development in Portugal, however, has proved to be far from that unilinear model, and what is frequently presented as a universal framework is in fact quite particularistic. The liberal model may thus be appropriate in tracing the patterns of development of the Anglo-American democracies, but it seems to have little relevance for Hispanic and Portuguese traditions. The fact is that in Portugal the Cortes never had, nor was it ever intended to have, the independent, coequal, or even supreme position enjoyed by the British Parliament. And while a long list of human and civil rights was usually included in a succession of Portuguese constitutions, these rights, in law and practice, have consistently been subordinated to a higher end and duty. Participatory rule has also come to be a fundamental principle of Portuguese governance, but what the Portuguese mean by participation is quite different from the unstructured and individualistic concept of Lockean liberalism. Finally, as for democracy, the Portuguese have not historically been convinced of its efficacy or ultimate legitimacy, and, even when they have, their meaning has implied some quite different understandings than are implied in the Anglo-American conception.[6]

The narrow and ethnocentric interpretation of Portuguese history, which sees liberal democracy Anglo-American style as the inevitable outcome of a long-term societal evolution, not only clouds and obscures our understanding but also positively distorts our comprehension of key Portuguese institutions and developments. It not only paints the presumed enemies of democracy, such as the church, the monarchy, Pombal, and Salazar, in the vilest of terms, but also generally exaggerates the accomplishments of "liberal" regimes (from 1822 to 1926) the better to discredit and paint as wholly "reactionary" and "fascistic" the one that followed.[7]

A focus on Portugal's "corporative tradition" helps avoid some of these distortions and pitfalls. Rather than seeing Portugal's history and institutions as some presumed, hoped-for, foreign, and nonindigenous tradition or through the sometimes equally ethnocentric biases of the "developmentalist" literature,[8] this newer perspective seeks to examine Portugal on its own terms and in its own context. Because corporatism seems to be so much at the heart of the Portuguese tradition, because a kind of "natural," organic, and homegrown corporatism seems so deeply imbedded historically in the Portuguese psyche and institutions,[9] this approach has been termed the "corporative model" or the "corporative framework."

It is at this juncture that some conceptual confusion arises, for "corporatism" is now plainly being used in two different senses. One widely cited definition is that employed by Philippe C. Schmitter:

> Corporatism can be defined as a system of interest representation in which the constituent units are organized into a limited number of singular, compulsory, noncompetitive, hierarchically ordered and functionally differentiated categories recognized or licensed (if not created) by the state and granted a deliberate representational monopoly within their respective categories in exchange for observing certain controls on their selection of leaders and articulation of demands and supports.[10]

Professor Schmitter goes on to contrast this kind of corporatism with pluralism, which he defines largely in terms of laissez faire; with "free" associability that is the reverse of his corporatism definition; with a "monist" model à la the Soviet Union; and with "syndicalism," which implies an autonomous and less-structured pattern of interest aggregation.

Although the definition of corporatism offered above is useful as a description of the Salazar system at one time, it provides more a static model than a dynamic one, gives a too-restrictive meaning to the term corporatism, and is thus not altogether useful for purposes of this analysis. Let us therefore recognize its utility with regard to some aspects of the Salazar regime, while also introducing the following qualifications and reservations, the first two of which have implications for our discussion later on and the third of which is of immediate concern.

1. The definition offered makes no provision for the dynamics of change within a single corporative regime, that is, from the dynamic corporatism, often oriented toward social justice, of the early Salazar regime, to the repressive state corporatism of the middle years, to the

145

moribund, "dinosauric" system of the 1960s, to the revitalized Estado Social of Caetano. It fails to convey adequately the possibility of evolution from a closed system of state corporatism to a more open and pluralist corporatism of association; indeed, by defining corporatism and pluralism in such a way that they constitute polar opposites, it negates the possibility of pluralism within a corporate society and policy as well as within a liberal one.[11]

2. The definition makes no allowance for an even more fundamental transformation from corporatism to syndicalism, nor does it entertain the possibility that the latter is a more developed, more "advanced," more socially differentiated form of the former. Later, we shall make precisely this argument, that while the revolution of 1974 marked a significant turning point, there were some continuities as well, and that while the establishment of a form of syndicalism and socialism in the wake of the 1974 revolt implied a major reordering (or *regeneração*, in Portuguese terms), that restructuring could also be interpreted in the light of a broader corporatist tradition, now updated with syndicalist and Socialist aspects.

3. The definition is too narrow and restrictive to serve our historical purposes. It focuses exclusively on the system of interest representation during one phase of the Salazar regime. But clearly the "corporatist tradition" as here used implies some broader phenomena. Obviously the system of interest representation is one particularly critical part of the historical corporative model; but it is not the only part. To describe the tradition of natural corporatism, we prefer a broader, more encompassing definition than that.

What, then, is meant by the corporative model or the corporative framework in Portugal? Let us recognize, first, however, that to pin a single all-encompassing label on a varied national and, more broadly, cultural tradition in itself represents a series of oversimplifications. Second, let us recognize that other key words—"organicist," "patrimonialist"—should also be employed along with "corporatist" to describe this system and tradition.[12] Third, let us accept the fact that, in speaking of the corporatist model, we are employing a streamlined, paradigmatic, ideal type, only the main outlines of which are spelled out. The "corporative tradition" is used here to describe only some of the more salient features of Iberic-Latin development, particularly as that model stands in contrast to the liberal-Lockean tradition and to other social science paradigms.

The corporative tradition implies a value system based upon widespread acceptance of hierarchy, elitism, organicism, and authority. It means a pattern of corporate sectoral and functional representation with authority vested in the crown or central state apparatus and with the various corporate units (nobility, church, military orders, universities, municipalities) incorporated into a single, organic whole for purposes of integral national development. It implies a system of bureaucratic-patrimonialist state authority and a social order based similarly on patron-client interdependence. It means, in its Iberian forms, a predominantly Catholic society and political culture based upon Thomistic principles. It implies an etatist and mercantilist economic system. And it implies a political system based on patrimonialism, authority, and hierarchy, with a centralized, vertical, pyramidal structure of power and decision making.

The terms "corporatist tradition" or "corporatist model," in brief, are shorthand terms used to describe some fairly distinctive features of Portuguese and Iberic-Latin history, political culture, and the development process. For example, in keeping with the Catholic conception, the Portuguese state has historically been based on the reciprocity of a patron-client system—a state that was natural, moral, and just and therefore did not have to be limited by institutional checks and balances. Stratification and differentiation in the social and political sphere not only exist but also were presumed to be right, necessary, and not to be challenged. Society consisted of functionally diverse, hierarchically ordered corporate groups, each of which made its distinct contribution to the political society and was guaranteed representation in it. The nobility, the church and the fighting knights stood near the apex, directly below the crown, in this vertically segmented, hierarchically ordered scheme. They constituted the higher order "corporations"; their function was to govern, to harmonize the human social order with a higher responsibility, and to be responsible not just for themselves but for the good of all. The king (or, later, prime minister or president) remained unencumbered by a coequal parliament or judiciary, as in the Anglo-American conception; but he too was obligated to rule in accord with a higher natural law, to govern for the common good, to respect the rights of the constituent corporate groups, and not to overstep the bounds that separated authoritarianism (legitimate) from tyranny (which justified rebellion). Politics usually centered on the competition among rival elites and corporate groups to capture the patrimonialist state apparatus, from which wealth and position flowed, and on the dynamic, changing relations between these constituent units and the central authority.[13]

Although this brief description does not begin to do justice to the complexities and subtleties in law, theory, and practice of the workings of the Portuguese corporative system historically, it does at least provide a hint as to some of the main directions. Further, it makes clear how far removed this dominant Portuguese tradition is from the dominant liberal-Lockean one of the Anglo-American nations. Although no claim is made that all of Portuguese history can be interpreted in this light and although as with all ideal constructs a greater understanding of the Portuguese *Weltanschauung* is obtained at the cost of a certain definitional precision, still an understanding of the corporative tradition or of "natural" corporatism helps illuminate some areas of Portuguese development that were unexamined before or examined only in the light of Anglo-American referents. It provides a needed, valuable corrective to this other approach. Moreover, this model applies not just to the centuries of national organization and then consolidation in premodern times but, in reconstructed and updated form, to the "liberal" and "republican" periods of the nineteenth and early twentieth centuries, as well. For despite the constitutional façade, Portugal remained more a corporatist than a republican regime; the power of the major corporate units (church, army, bureaucracy, nobility) remained undiminished and even enhanced; and the parliamentary regime worked best when it was least democratic and when the organic-corporatist conceptions prevailed. The corporative pattern of sociopolitical relations not only was thus deeply imbedded but also proved to be remarkably long lasting. It remains as a major, persistent tradition even today. "Corporatism" as a shorthand term to describe this Portuguese tradition is comparable to the use of "liberalism" to describe the dominant American tradition and also serves further to distinguish these two national and political-cultural traditions.[14]

Some Portuguese corporatist theorists would of course go even further and dismiss all of nineteenth-century republicanism as mere façade, a temporary interruption in an otherwise dominant corporatist tradition.[15] This perspective, however, seems as inaccurate as the earlier interpretation from the liberal perspective. The "liberal" and "liberalizing" perspective of Portuguese history produced one set of distortions, but an equally unrefined corporatist perspective implies a distortion of another kind, for beginning in the eighteenth century a fissure had begun to appear in the Portuguese culture and society. On the one hand stood the dominant, inward-looking, Catholic-corporatist-traditionalist-patrimonialist conception; on the other, a European-oriented, early-liberal, rationalist, urban, middle-class, secular one. No one viewpoint could enjoy absolute legitimacy; no one dominated entirely. Much of Portuguese history during the period 1822–1926 can be interpreted as the conflict and virtually constant civil war between the two. As in Spain during this same period, two distinct Portugals had evolved, and there was little basis for compromise between them.

This development has two major implications for our study: first, in the context of Portuguese history, it implies that neither the liberal nor the corporatist interpretation can any longer be used exclusively to the neglect of the other. From this point Portuguese politics and society can be understood, even on their own terms, only in the light of both models and of what each tells us about two distinct, separate Portugals. It is here, where these two models and the once-parallel structures they represent sometimes meet and overlap, that perhaps some of the most fruitful areas of research lie. Second, on a more practical level, it implies that no regime coming to power in Portugal can afford to govern wholly for and in the name of one tradition and its attendant sociopolitical forces while entirely ignoring the other. When the monarchy tried in the late nineteenth century, it faced a series of republican revolts that eventually toppled the monarchy itself. When the republicans disfranchised the church and sought to rule without the traditionalist elements, they faced a series of revolts that eventually succeeded in toppling the republic in 1926. And, when Salazar sought subsequently to reestablish the corporatist tradition as the sole national tradition, he found he could do so only with the use of widespread repression and police-state methods; his regime and system were repudiated in 1974.

Whether the new regime that comes to power in the wake of the 1974 revolution can transcend or overcome these historic divisions, or whether the revolution marks the superimposition of a third layer—Marxist and Socialist—over preexisting corporatist and liberal ones, thus introducing further discord and fragmentation, are questions we shall have to weigh. But of the existence historically of a powerful, perhaps dominant, corporative tradition and model of sociopolitical organization, there can be little doubt.

Corporatism as Manifest System

> In seeking to avoid imitation of United States liberalism and of Marxian approaches in finding models for government, social relations, and economic development, much of the Iberian World has been turning increasingly to . . . corporatism.[16]

The 1926 revolution that toppled the Portuguese republic was carried out by the armed forces with strong backing from a variety of civilian parties and movements. The chaos, disorder, and corruption of the republic and the apparent bankruptcy of liberalism as practiced in Portugal had led to their general discrediting. When the coup finally came, it was warmly welcomed. It had the support of a variety of monarchist, integralist, nationalist, Catholic, and center elements, together with the bulk of the middle class and many politicians and republicans who sought to break the patronage and sinecure monopoly of the Democratic party. Although the military was itself vaguely integralist, corporatist, and nationalist in character, it lacked a clear-cut program. Once it had restored order, banished some of the republican political groups and politicians, rooted out corruption, and restored a degree of economic solvency—the usual practices of military regimes—it floundered for several years in search of a national formula. It was precisely such a formula that Salazar and the corporatists provided and that helps explain their ascendance to power within the context of a military regime.[17]

The Corporatist System of Salazar. The corporatist system that was gradually institutionalized in Portugal over the course of the 1930s can be explained in terms of at least seven dimensions.

1. The corporatist regime represented a reaction against the chaos and disorder of liberalism and the republic. By restoring order, stability, and national solvency, Salazar enjoyed widespread initial support. The early strength and popularity of the corporatist regime can only be understood in the light of the disorder and national humiliation that went before.

2. The corporatist regime was a strongly nationalist regime. It was nationalist in three senses. First, it was in part the heir of the Catholic, conservative Nationalist party. Second, it represented a nationalistic repudiation of the influence of foreign institutions, chiefly British parliamentarism, which had governed the country, often with ruinous results, intermittently from 1822 to 1926. Third, it was nationalist in its efforts to fashion a new political model upon indigenous Portuguese sources: the family, the local community, the fishermen's centers, such "natural" corporations as the church, the army, the employers' groups, the university, and so forth.

3. The corporatist regime was a middle-class regime. It marked the replacement of the older elitist and oligarchic order with a new middle-class one. That process was begun under the republic and completed under the Estado Novo. Obscured by our attention to the political aspects of the Salazar regime is the gradual class shift that occurred; by the end of the Salazar-Caetano era, virtually every institution in the country had become thoroughly middle-class domi-

nated: army officer corps, church hierarchy, bureaucracy, universities, high civil service, political parties, and even the trade union structure.

4. The original corporatist scheme, as envisioned by Salazar, was a fairly close reflection of the kind of society Portugal still had in the 1930s: predominantly rural and small town, Catholic, traditionalist, hierarchically structured, governed by a nationwide system of patronage, static. To the extent that Portugal had urbanized, modernized, and become oriented to change, and with its historical hierarchies breaking down, corporatism in the original sense under Salazar became less and less viable with, as we shall see, wrenching social and political consequences.

5. The corporatist regime initially had a strong reformist, even progressive orientation. My own investigations of the early period of the corporatist system have led me to conclude that this concern was genuine and real. It can, I think, be explained along two dimensions. First, it seems clear that the strongly Catholic orientation of Salazar and his collaborators led them to be concerned with the welfare of the poor, to feel a powerful obligation to Catholic charity, and to initiate a series of social programs, paternalistic to be sure and undoubtedly insufficient but still no less genuine, to relieve the miserable plight of the poor and to speak to the problem of alienation in the emerging mass society that Portugal was in the early stages of becoming. Second, it seems clear the new social justice measures were related to the efforts of the emerging middle-class system to consolidate its power and to forge an alliance with some working-class elements so as better to wrest control away from the oligarchy and the traditional governing elites. Once middle-class domination had been consolidated, the old alliance with the working class could be—and was—conveniently forgotten: but for a time the middle class needed labor support, and that was accomplished by instigating a large number of programs of social justice.[18]

6. The corporatist system was designed, in Schmitter's words, to fill a certain organizational space.[19] The early 1930s were a period not only of economic depression in Portugal but also of potentially threatening revolutionary movements from below. The corporative system was designed, therefore, not, as is often alleged, as a reactionary throwback to some *status quo ante*, but as a way of structuring, channeling, and hence controlling the emergence of new groups, principally labor, who might otherwise threaten the entire edifice. Corporative principles of social solidarity and class harmony were emphasized as a way of discouraging class conflict, and corporative syndicates and structures of participation were introduced and made obligatory, filling the organizational space once occupied by the now

151

illegalized Socialist, Communist, and anarcho-syndicalist groups. Through the corporative restructuring, a middle-class–dominated change process was initiated from the top down as a way of holding in check and heading off in advance the possibility of more mass-based and revolutionary solutions.

7. The corporatist regime must also be understood in the light of the foreign inspirations and influences of the time. The Portuguese corporatists not only built on their own indigenous history and institutions but also drew heavily upon Mussolini's *Carta del Lavoro* (1927) and the encyclical *Quadragesimo Anno* (1931). More than that, however, corporatist regimes or corporatist institutions seemed to be the wave of the future, not just in Fascist Italy and Nazi Germany but seemingly everywhere: Austria, Poland, Hungary, France, Belgium, Holland, even the Scandinavian countries, Britain, and, perhaps in the form of the National Recovery Administration, Works Progress Administration, and the National Labor Relations Board, the United States. Mihail Manoïlesco proclaimed in a famous book of the time that, whereas the nineteenth century had been the century of liberalism, the twentieth would be the century of corporatism.[20] Corporatism's impact on Portugal must be understood in the context of a period when in the Western world corporatist solutions seemed to be becoming universal.

Implementing the Corporatist System. Once the corporatist formula had been decided upon, Salazar and the regime sought rapidly to institutionalize it. Although some of the first corporative decrees had been promulgated earlier, 1933 marked the real beginning of the corporative restructuring. In that year a new constitution was adopted proclaiming Portugal a "unitary and corporative republic" and establishing both a superior Corporative Council and a functionally representative Corporative Chamber; a labor law was handed down that detailed the new benefits the workers were to receive as well as restructuring their participation in the political process under strong state control; and a series of decree-laws was promulgated governing virtually all areas of Portuguese associational life. These encompassed the creation of a nationwide system of *casas do povo* (people's centers) for rural workers, *casas dos pescadores* (fishermen's centers) for fishing communities, *sindicatos* (syndicates) for industrial workers, and *grémios* (guilds) for business, commercial, and industrial employer interests. In the meantime a Subsecretariat of State (subministry) of Corporations and Social Welfare and the Instituto Nacional do Trabalho e Previdência were established to administer the corporative system.

This flurry of corporative legislation in Portugal in 1933 was comparable to the changes ushered in by Roosevelt in his first ninety days and probably just as far-reaching in its implications. By 1937, with the designation of the *casas do povo* as the representative agents of rural workers and hence the creation of separate *grémios da lavoura* for landed interests, the corporative restructuring had been all but completed. Although the creation of the corporations themselves, nominally the capstones of the entire system, had been scheduled for late 1939, the outbreak of war that year forced a postponement, and it was not until 1956 that the regime finally got around to creating the first six corporations. For twenty-three years, hence, Portugal remained a corporative state without corporations.

Between 1933 and 1935 the regime moved quickly toward implementation. The trade unions were reorganized under the syndicate system; by 1935, 191 had been duly recognized by the state, and by the end of that same year, 141 had been granted charters. The first guilds and fishermen's centers were also organized. A nationwide system of social welfare funds was in the process of being established; the first elections under the corporative constitution of 1933 were scheduled; the organizational scheme for the Corporative Chamber was promulgated; and the detailed provisions concerning workers' rights and obligations contained in the Labor Statute of 1933 began to be fleshed out.

The period 1933–1935 was a heady, exciting period for the Portuguese corporativists; the corporative revolution was already moving; the system was being implemented. But it was precisely at this point in the mid-1930s that the first biases began to appear in the corporative structure, and the main lines of corporative development were fundamentally altered. Rather than a corporatism of free associability, reform, and social justice, the Portuguese system became a corporatism of the state, of controls and repression, and of favoritism toward one social group at the expense of the others.

Corporatism as Controls

Traditionally corporatism has been a means of providing social solidarity, avoiding class conflict, and discouraging individualism among the masses, while at the same time providing opportunities for participation by the masses in local, regional, and functional groups. In its new guise in the Iberian world, corporatism also aims at replacing an entrenched oligarchy with a more nationalistic elite whose members hope to mobilize popular support for development and greater economic independence. *Above all, it is the objec-*

tive of the new corporatism to prevent a revolution from below by initiating one from above [emphasis added].[21]

By 1935 the first biases had become clearly visible in the Portuguese corporative system. Corporatism as originally conceived, it will be recalled, had been posited on the coequal representation of capital and labor. Moreover, the corporatist solution had been proffered as a "third way," which repudiated both capitalism and socialism. In actual practice, however, corporatism in Portugal became one of the most oppressively monopolistic of state capitalist systems, and it came to favor employer interests at the expense of labor to the point where industrialization was achieved by imposing its costs primarily on the industrial working class (which thus corresponds to A. F. K. Organski's definition of "fascism").[22]

The promulgation of the corporative decrees had been greeted in early 1934 by one of the most massive strikes Portugal had ever experienced. The brutal repression of the strike made it clear that, if the syndicates refused to accept corporatization peacefully, it would be forced upon them. No such repression was ever practiced against employer groups (although over a long period the regime used strong leverage to subordinate capital as well as labor to state direction). Moreover, the business and fledgling industrial elements were able to make the case to Salazar that, if corporatization was to be enforced upon them as it was upon labor, it would lead to a lack of investment and the ruination of the economy. Particularly in the depression years of the 1930s, and then as the regime moved to stimulate economic development, these arguments of the business community were persuasive.

A second bias in the system may be found in the decree-laws themselves. For workers, membership in a syndicate was made obligatory; furthermore, the syndicates could gain no benefits for their members until their charters had been granted by the state and they had been reorganized along corporative principles. Business groups, however, had two major "outs." First, the government had allowed the old "class associations" (chambers of commerce, merchants' associations) to continue without forcing them, as was the case with the syndicates, to reorganize along corporative lines. Second, on the employer side the regime provided for voluntary guilds as well as compulsory ones, while on the labor side such a possibility had been specifically ruled out.

A third bias had to do with the enforcement of the corporatist decrees, and it soon became clear that the government was enforcing the corporative restructuring more on the labor than on the employer

154

side. The corporative system increasingly meant a web of controls for those on the bottom while providing for little accountability for those on top. In the urban industrial areas this implied favoritism to business and commercial interests and industrialists increasingly at the expense of labor, and in the rural countryside it implied a perpetuation of the traditional patron-client system through both benign governmental neglect and domination by wealthy landed elements of both the landowners' associations and the poor people's houses.

Probably a fourth bias had to do with the growing security and consolidation of the Salazar regime itself by the mid-1930s, due to its institutionalization and the absence of major internal threats. No longer so threatened, both the regime and the broader middle class on which it rested felt no need to coddle labor. Hence, the strong orientation toward social justice and reform legislation of the early corporative regime was increasingly shunted aside.

Moving toward State Corporatism. Biases in the regime were one thing, and perhaps to be expected given the structure of wealth and power in Portugal and the corporatists' belief that they could educate the rich and the middle class to their obligations to Christian charity without wrenching social revolution; but the next step involved the development of a full-fledged system of authoritarian state corporatism, replacing the "corporatism of association" of the original conception. The move toward an authoritarian, state-directed corporatism was dictated by the fact that corporative consciousness in Portugal was still inchoate, the corporative agencies that had been created enjoyed meager support, and Salazar became convinced that something else had to be created to fill the institutional void. The continued depressed economic conditions, the perceived need for a stronger set of economic controls, the outbreak of civil war in Spain, a new series of internal conspiracies and assassination efforts launched against Salazar and the regime in 1936–1937, and, I am convinced, the publication of Manoïlesco's book and its dissemination in Portugal all contributed to the growth of an increasingly centralized and bureaucratic system of state corporatism.

In 1936 the regime moved to create a variety of Organizations of Economic Coordination—commissions, juntas, and institutes—which were to serve as "precorporative" intermediaries between the state and the nascent corporative complex. These agencies came to serve as the Portuguese equivalents for the plethora of regulatory bureaus that have grown up in other modernizing systems for the coordination and regulation of national economic life. But in Portugal the process went further. The Organizations of Economic Coordination helped set wages, fix prices, and regulate production, imports, and exports. They served as the means by which state power was extended to virtually all areas of the national economy, including control over those elusive business groups that had to this point evaded full corporatization. The Organizations of Economic Coordination were the prime instruments for the growth of etatism and state corporatism.

The relations between the Organizations of Economic Coordination and the business community were more subtle than this, however, for while, on the one hand, these agencies were used to subordinate the business elements to state control, on the other, these same business elements were moving to infiltrate and eventually capture the entire regulatory complex. There were very close interrelations between the Portuguese corporative state system and the industrial elite; individual career patterns showed an almost constant coming and going between private firms and the government regulatory agencies—including the frequent holding of private and public positions simultaneously. Salazar had brought some of the major economic satrapies—the wine industry, fishing, canning, cork—under state direction, but they had also learned to manipulate him, chiefly through the argument that all his hopes for continued political stability and economic prosperity would be sabotaged if he really moved to divest this powerful, emerging bourgeoisie of its power and wealth. These arguments were even more persuasive because of the constant crises the regime faced: depression, opposition, the Spanish conflict, then World War II. The result was a sellout to private economic interests, a vast expansion of state power, and the end of the vision of a free system of corporative associability and social justice.[23] It was at this point that the Portuguese system corresponded most closely to the narrower definition of corporatism propounded by Schmitter.[24]

Economic Statism. To the system of corporate structures and controls, Salazar now added a series of economic laws and regulations that served both to reinforce the corporative structures and, eventually, to supplant them. These laws have generally been ignored by students of the Salazar regime, but they are essential to an understanding of it and the evolution of the Estado Novo toward an increasingly state capitalist or, essentially, mercantilist form. Briefly, these laws prohibited the creation of a new economic enterprise or the expansion of an old one without government permission and gave the government virtually all power to set wages, prices, production quotas, exports, and imports. They vested enormous, heretofore unprecedented economic power in the state (political and associational life had already been concentrated in the state through the new constitution and the corporative system) and gave it the power to oversee, regulate, and command virtually all national economic life.

Although these laws were "neutral," that is, adaptable to virtually any economic goal, under Salazar the purpose was concentration and consolidation of the economy under state direction. Where monopolies already existed, they were protected; in industries where they did not exist, new monopolies and oligopolies were created through the use of these laws. By the time World War II broke out, the nation's major economic sectors had all been reorganized on the basis of a great, interconnected complex of conglomerate monopolies, intimately tied to and inseparable from the government structure, linking both continental Portugal and its colonies through the same monopolistic companies, and protected against competition from local businesses or from abroad. The result was enormous economic power concentrated in the hands of the state. In this sense Portugal came ironically, given the regime's strongly anti-Communist ideology, to resemble more the centralized, state-run economies of Eastern Europe than the planned but still in large measure laissez-faire systems of the West. In addition, extraordinary economic wealth was concentrated in the hands of a few rich and powerful families and of a new plutocracy—precisely those same elements who, we have just seen, had come to dominate the state regulatory agencies. A system of state capitalism thus grew up alongside, and eventually supplanted, the corporative structure as one of the main institutional pillars of the regime.[25]

Corporatism's original principles came to be abandoned more and more all across the board, and the role of the corporative complex was increasingly circumscribed, confined chiefly to some limited representational functions, the regulation of labor relations, and the administration of woefully inadequate social security. As this occurred, other agencies moved to fill the vacuum. The police apparatus, whose controls had previously been sporadic and unsystematic, became increasingly brutal, total, and systematic; in so doing it developed into yet another of the prime pillars on which the Estado Novo had come to rest. The power of the state regulatory agencies, already extensive, grew even more. With the end of World War II and the general discrediting of all such "fascistic" schemes, the corporative system was still further shunted aside, circumvented, and ignored. All but completely moribund, its functions and activities dwindled almost to nothing. Moreover, the sclerotic character of the corporative system was reflected in the regime itself, which seemed to have lost all purpose and direction. As liberal and social-democratic opposition mounted in the postwar period, the police state apparatus continued to expand, and repressive, dictatorial measures were increasingly employed.

Nonetheless, a brief flurry of corporativist activity did ensue during the 1950s and 1960s, and new concepts of social welfare were attempted. The old Subsecretariat of Corporations was made a full ministry. The first corporations were established, and a Plan for Social and Corporative Formulation was initiated. Some new functions were also found for the corporative agencies to administer, chiefly in the areas of social security, but this implied a still further circumscription of the range of activities assigned to the corporative complex. These developments were probably related to the new economic prosperity in which Portugal shared from the mid-1950s on and to the regime's conviction that, since its first-order priorities of maintaining political stability and providing for economic solvency were now accomplished, it could again move ahead with further corporative implementation.

But by this point it had become clear that corporatism and the corporative complex were no longer (if indeed they had ever been) at the base of the system, constituting, as the early ideology had proclaimed, the focus around which national life swirled. The gaps between corporative theory and corporative practice were distressingly vast, plain for all to see; and even the new social security legislation existed more on the paper of the *Diário de Governo* than in actual fact. Corporatism as a manifest system and ideology was hence increasingly ignored, both by the regime and by the Portuguese people. It had ceased to have meaning, and in fact the entire national system came to function almost as though corporatism and the corporative complex were not there.

By the late 1960s it was not just the corporative system that had increasingly gone to sleep, however, but the entire national system. Salazar was old and tired, some say senile. The fighting in Africa dragged on, by now on three fronts. The ship of state seemed rudderless, directionless. Needed decisions were not being made. Corruption had become widespread. The secret police constituted almost a separate state-within-a-state. The opposition grew and so did the terror tactics used to repress it. Both the regime and the corporative system seemed to be locked in a deep freeze. In the historic pattern the demands began to mount that something be done, not only because the regime had become "dinosauric" but also because it seemed to have overstepped the bounds between permissible authoritarianism, which was both at the heart of the historic Portuguese tradition and its most recent manifestation in the corporative regime, and outright tyranny, which therefore legitimized the right to rebellion. By the late 1960s the demand was clear: either renovation from within or revolution from without.[26]

Corporatism Revitalized

The corporative spirit lives and is practiced. . . . The Government, in remaining faithful to the Political Constitution, of necessity remains faithful to the corporative ideals.[27]

The regime of Marcello Caetano, it is true, was quite different from that of his predecessor, Salazar, but it did not correspond very well to the picture of it portrayed in foreign press accounts. Those accounts described Caetano as a would-be but frustrated "liberal," seeking to preside over a process of "democratization" and constantly thwarted in these efforts by powerful rightists and forces loyal to Salazar. The evidence, however, points to the conclusion that, while Caetano sought to update, loosen, and modernize the main pillars of authoritarian-corporate rule, he remained an authoritarian and a corporatist, and it is within that context that his rule must be judged and not in the context of some supposed desires for "liberalization" and "democratization."[28]

Caetano's Changes. Caetano had inherited a government that, as one account put it, was sluggish to the point of torpor. Government, administration, decision making, public policy, the corporative structure—indeed the entire national system—had all but come to a standstill during the last years of the Salazar regime, and it would be Caetano's job to invigorate, activate, rejuvenate, and revitalize it—to evolve from "the dinosaur," to "thaw out" from the "deep freeze." Note that nowhere in this list of purposes and popular metaphors do the words "liberalize" or "democratize" appear. It is unlikely that Caetano's intentions were ever to liberalize or democratize; that idea probably represents mere wishful thinking on the part of journalists and the American embassy, and it may hence be inappropriate to criticize him for not moving faster toward democracy when that was never his intention. Caetano aimed at broadening the directing elites somewhat but by no means at democratization; he tried to widen the base and appeal of the official party but not to provide for real choice between parties; he sought to rein in and control somewhat such "uncontrollable forces" as the secret police but not by sacrificing authoritarian control; he aimed at better implementation of the corporative system but did not intend to turn to liberalism.

159

Caetano changed the style of the regime more than its essence, presided over a far more open, more pluralist, more socially just system than did his predecessor, but that was done within the limits of the corporative system and not some presumed movement toward liberalism. Caetano's goals were to adjust the system to new realities; to recognize and accommodate the new social forces that had grown up rather than turning his back on or repressing them as Salazar had done; to restore confidence in the economy and the public service that had almost disappeared under his predecessor; to wake up and invigorate a nation and system that had gone to sleep under Salazar; and to revive a slumbering, almost stagnant set of corporative institutions long neglected through disuse. It is on these criteria, not according to some imagined "liberal" ones, that his regime must be judged; and I think both the revolution of 1974 and the judgment of history indicate that by these criteria the regime failed.

While Caetano remained a corporatist, as a leader he proved weak, uncertain, vacillating, not able to manage very well the complex divisive currents that modernization, in the face of institutional paralysis, had set loose. Although the pattern was similar in other policy areas—educational reform, governmental remodeling, African affairs, and so on—for the purposes of this study the arena of labor relations is central. Caetano's strategies may be summarized as follows: first, a tenuous opening up, then a crackdown, followed by uncertainty, vacillation, new openings, more indecision, and an ultimately disastrous temporizing. The breakthrough for labor came in June 1969 in a decree that gave the syndicates the right to select their own leadership without government approval. Under Salazar the labor leadership had ordinarily been imposed by the regime. Another decree provided that, on the three-man arbitration commissions used for settling wage disputes, one member would be chosen by the syndicate, one by the guild, and the third by the other two. Under the old system the third member had been selected by the government and had almost invariably sided with employer interests in enforcing austerity and wage controls. Another provision shortened the time limits given the guilds to respond to syndicate demands and made it impossible for the guilds simply to ignore these demands, which had usually been the case in the past.[29]

Within months the syndicates, which for decades had been trade unions in name only, began to be transformed from amorphous government agencies into genuine instruments of the workers. For the first time opposition elements, including Communists in the case of some syndicates, swept the union elections, and the elections were allowed to stand. Under the old regime, whenever an oppositionist had somehow managed to win a union election, the election was immediately canceled, and new leaders were found who were more amenable to government direction. At the same time, the new arbitration commissions were in numerous cases deciding in labor's favor. This was due both to a general political and generational shift that had begun to take place within the state ministries (in this case the Corporations Ministry) and to explicit directions given out by Caetano's office. As the trade unions started to gather strength and some independent bargaining power, the government for the first time began enforcing the corporative laws obligating the guilds to respond and calling for coequal bargaining power between workers and employers. Strikes, slowdowns, and protest demonstrations, although legally banned, increased with government acquiescence. A number of new collective bargaining agreements were signed between 1969 and 1971 that provided for major wage increases. With government approval, the syndicates had begun to acquire some teeth. Meanwhile, under Caetano's Estado Social, a vast range of new social programs was introduced, programs that no longer existed just on paper or for foreign consumption but were actually being implemented. The corporative system was revitalized and for perhaps the first time started to live up to some of its original ideals.

These changes were of course related to broader Portuguese social and political developments. Accelerating industrialization had by now created a far larger and more militant work force and a real laboring *class* in such centers as Lisbon and Setúbal, as distinct from the earlier, "sleepier," deferential "servant" element of the past, on which Salazar's earlier, Rerum novarum-based conception of corporatism had been founded. Large-scale emigration and declining population had produced some severe labor shortages, thereby strengthening the syndicates' bargaining position. The government's commitment to expanded production, continuous economic growth, and broadened social programs also gave it a strong interest in avoiding ruinous strikes by acceding to labor's demands. Expanded tourism and contact with the outside world, the push for entry into the Common Market, and the emigration of Portuguese workers to other freer and more industrialized nations also helped break down the Salazar walls of isolation and open up the system. The freer climate, in turn, and the 1969 legislative elections gave the opposition a new impetus and stimulated it to greater organizational efforts among the workers.

Then came the clampdown. In the fall of 1970 the metallurgists, one of the most politicized of the syndicates, had rejected a proffered labor contract, demanded higher wages, and called a meeting in the soccer stadium to rally support. The government banned the rally and accused the metallurgists of "fomenting class struggle." Meanwhile, other militant unions had begun following the metallurgists' lead. Employers appealed to the government to do something to halt the ferment, and it responded with two new decrees: the first giving the right to appoint the third member of the arbitration commissions back to the government and the second restoring the government's right to suspend elected syndicate officials for activities "contrary to social discipline." The decrees opened the way to renewed state control of the syndicates, and armed with this power the government moved against the metallurgists and the other militant oppositionists.

Growing Challenges to the System. These actions failed to restore labor peace. Once the door had been opened, it proved difficult to slam it shut again. Other unions increased their demands. Since strikes had been outlawed in corporative Portugal, it was left to the government to decide whether a work "slowdown" or "stoppage" was really a strike. Although it sounds scholastic and far removed from reality, a whole new politics grew up around the question of when a work stoppage was a strike and therefore required suppression and when it was not and could therefore be allowed to go forward. The government vacillated: it broke up a demonstration by the clerks with police brutality, but it acceded to other union demands. New restrictions were enforced, but new openings were allowed also. The government gave local authorities the right to approve candidates for syndicate elections, and, according to personal interviews conducted by the author with local labor leaders, "these petty bureaucrats used their powers unmercifully." Candidates for union elections had to meet endless qualifications, and local authorities—if they wished—could always find one that would disqualify a particular candidate. Whether the labor laws and restrictions were enforced or not depended on the play of forces at particular moments and frequently on whim. One week the government would approve an important wage increase for one sector; the next it would reject it for another. The syndicates were bitter about the indecision and uncertainty, but they kept up the pressure. The regime also continued to face in two directions at once, sometimes paternal, at others brutal.

Meanwhile, as the challenges from inside the system from the corporative regime's own syndicates mounted, a new and perhaps equally ominous threat loomed from without, as workers in sizable numbers began reorganizing in unsanctioned factory committees. These clandestine, nongovernment unions were organized into a broad umbrella organization called the Intersindical and had appeared in all the nation's major industrial firms. As part of its strategy to keep labor in check, the Salazar regime had consistently disallowed the creation of a strong and independent national labor confederation, but now Caetano, believing he could contain it, tolerated precisely such an interunion group, which came to represent some fifteen to twenty of the largest syndicates with a membership variously put at between 150,000 and 200,000. Intersindical, however, was not content with the wage increases Caetano had secured and began making stronger demands for full freedom of association and the right to strike. By mid-1971, after Intersindical had sought recognition from the International Labor Organization (ILO), Caetano moved to outlaw the organization and to purge its affiliated unions.[30]

But now the union movement could not be suppressed so easily, and Intersindical, having gained a strong foothold and widespread worker support, simply moved underground, where it provided a ready vehicle for infiltration by the similarly clandestine Portuguese Communist party. The government now had to deal with both a restless official syndicate structure and the powerful but subsurface Intersindical. Intersindical moved to organize "unity committees" in numerous factories, industries, and even government offices where it could convert worker dissatisfaction into crippling strikes. The government responded by arranging wage increases, which it hoped would increase its popularity and undercut Intersindical's appeal, but it was unwilling to give the unions independent bargaining power. In this way, too, it sought to preserve the essential paternalistic and authoritarian structure of the system while at the same time staving off discontent. When that tactic failed, however, it continued to use riot and secret police to break up demonstrations, arrest strike leaders, and curb the clandestine unity committees. But these tactics seemed only to lead to still larger strikes. The tendency of foreign and domestic firms to respond differently to worker demands and pay different wage scales added to the inequalities and the bitterness. The foreign firms paid more and were more responsive; domestic firms sought to resist negotiations and relied on the state for support against the unions.

By 1973, while the government continued to provide for some major wage increases, industrial unrest had become so rampant that forty major strikes occurred. These strikes almost literally closed down the economy in some cases. They undermined both the African war effort and Caetano's plans for social reform and thus led to further paralysis. They also stimulated discontent among center and rightist elements to such a point that they now began to plot in earnest the regime's overthrow. As pressures from labor center and forces loyal to Salazar increased and as the question was more frequently asked whether the regime could continue to manage and cope with these conflicting currents, the government lost all public confidence; the plotting grew more intense; and several aborted coup attempts were launched before the final one succeeded in April 1974. Caetano had proved incapable of managing the divergent forces now loose. The regime fell; his efforts at presiding over a revitalized corporatism had ended in failure.

Corporatism Dismantled, Transcended, Persistent

Corporatism is far from dead. Many continuities exist in the present regime. Corporatism may reassert itself, not just in a fascist form but in more subtle manifestations.[31]

The 1961 *Programa para a democratização da república,*[32] drafted by the Portuguese opposition movement, urged that the following action be taken with regard to the corporative structure:

1. The corporations were to be abolished and replaced by institutions of a "democratic nature."
2. The various agencies and institutions of the corporative state were to be dissolved, transformed, or integrated into a new democratic order.
3. The functions of the Organizations of Economic Coordination would be integrated into the normal services of public administration.
4. The workers' associations, orders, and syndicates connected with the corporate structure would be converted into genuine class associations and complete sovereignty would be granted their general assemblies.
5. The guilds would be converted into class associations whose leaders would be elected by the membership.
6. The rural workers' and fishermen's associations might continue as reorganized agencies without prejudice against the rights of labor associations also to organize their members.

In the wake of the 1974 revolution, this program, in only slightly modified form, did in fact serve as the basis for dismantling the Portuguese corporative system. Not only were the control mechanisms of the Salazar regime—secret police, censorship, and the like—quickly overturned, but also the entire web of corporative agencies, the corporations, and the corporative complex were eliminated. The dismantling of the corporative system took place initially at the popular and street level and then was ratified by official decree. The old official syndicate system broke down as the underground factory unity committees emerged, as workers seized factories, as plant managers and directors were driven out, and as strikes multiplied and direct action became the means for solving disputes. The Corporations Ministry became the Labor Ministry; it was given over initially to the Communists, who used their control of the power structure of the labor organization to gain advantages for themselves while keeping the basic structure intact. The Labor Statute of 1933 was declared inoperative before a new one had been drawn up to replace it. The whole vast panoply of labor tribunals, arbitration commissions, and collective contracts was abolished; also overturned were the networks of economic regulatory commissions, institutes, and juntas. The leadership of the *ordens* and guilds was soon replaced, and the Communist-dominated Intersindical gained an overwhelmingly preponderant position in the trade union movement.[33]

Direct action in the streets was followed quickly (and occasionally anticipated) by action at the official level. Although in our attention to other, perhaps more dramatic events it has been neglected, the process by which the corporative system was dismantled in the aftermath of the April revolution merits more detailed study, particularly in the light of other, comparable experiences with post-authoritarian "decompression." Although space considerations rule out a detailed treatment here, some of the major decrees may be noted as a means of illustrating the thoroughness, flavor, and completeness of the changeovers. On May 2, 1974, it was decreed that harbor masters (generally state appointees or the servants of employer interests) would no longer serve as the presidents of the fishermen's associations. On May 9 the Junta of National Salvation (the Spínola government) gave itself the power to suspend all employees of the corporative agencies and Organizations of Economic Coordination and to name all replacements. On May 27 a decree overturned the old syndicate structure and opened the way to the "just satisfaction of worker demands." On June 3 the Junta Central of the fishermen's associations was relieved of its duties. On August 17 the corporations were dissolved. On September 9 the Junta da Acção Social of the Ministry of Corporations was "extinguished." On September 12 all corporative agencies "dependent" upon the old Corporations Ministry were dissolved and their responsibilities transferred to the Organizations of Economic Coordination. On September 25 the landowners' associations were similarly abolished; on October 23 the Fundação Nacional para a Alegria no Trabalho was "sanitized" and "restructured." On December 5 "patronal interests" were given the right to form associations in defense of their own interests. On December 23 the Federação das Casas do Povo was scuttled; in January 1975 some guilds were eliminated; others were to be "investigated." The "obligatory guilds" were replaced by a new confederation of industry, while the "voluntary guilds" were reorganized as private-interest associations. And so it went. Thus, by the end of the first year of the revolution, virtually the entire formal structure of the corporative state had been dismantled or restructured.[34]

Reorganization, Not Elimination. But the process was not nearly so thorough, and the changeovers not nearly so complete, as the analysis of the "street" action and the formal decrees implies. There was no "180° turnabout," as some of the accounts have alleged. The fact is that, while many agencies of the corporative system were abolished, a good many others (guilds, syndicates, rural workers' associations, and fishermen's associations) remained in existence. They were reorganized, often renamed, and their leaders were changed; but a good part of the structure continued intact, and, while the leadership was often turned over at the top, at lower levels the same personnel largely continued in the same old agencies. We can see this particularly in the syndicate structure and the Labor Ministry and at the local and municipal government levels, where a new leadership moved in but where the hierarchical, pyramidal structure was often preserved intact. The new private associations continued to act in most respects as had the old guilds; the rural workers' associations and fishermen's associations remained almost identical to what they had been under the old regime. Obviously, this is not to discount the clearly revolutionary transformations that occurred in some agencies and some policy areas, but it is to say that there were important continuities as well. Some of the corporative agencies continued largely intact; in others the names and faces changed, but the same functions continued to be performed. A close examination of the unfolding of the revolution through both street politics and the formal decrees indicates that it may have been far less abrupt, more gradual and accommodative, more deliberate and less radical or chaotic than the U.S. press accounts conveyed. While no one would deny the fundamental transformations and regeneration that the revolution implied, it is perhaps equally important to understand the sheer persistence of some earlier forms and practices.

Not only were some of the older corporative agencies often slow in being confined to the ashcans of history, but also the new regime moved to resurrect a new set of corporative institutions. They were, of course, called by other names, but they were essentially corporative in character. There emerged an ideology and structure of class collaboration rather than conflict, a feature that may be correctly identified as one of the essential features of corporatism. The movement toward an increasingly strong and authoritarian state structure, toward an increasingly state-directed economy, and toward a carefully structured and state-directed system of interest associations and representational bodies is similarly characteristic of corporate state systems. The Portuguese government and its constituent agencies are still heavily military dominated, infused with hierarchical and authoritarian structures. Although the regime presumes to govern for and in the name of the "common good," it showed little enthusiasm for democracy and genuine grass-roots participation on the liberal model, and elections carry but tentative, not definitive, legitimacy. The Portuguese state is still a bureaucratic state, still carefully regulated and controlled, with elaborate legal-administrative procedures left over from the old regime, still organized from the top down and governed by decree-law. Increasingly, the control mechanisms of the historical tradition have been resurrected as a way of preventing the spontaneity and joy of the early street demonstrations from getting out of hand and of channeling them, again, in preferred directions. Finally, our attention must be called to the new institutional arrangements inaugurated by the MFA and then reorganized by succeeding regimes, with their functionally representative bodies, their corporative and syndicalist tendencies, and the special place within the system given the military and other corporate groups. Thus, in this respect, too, there are some remarkable continuities with the older corporative regime, as well as some sharp departures from it.[35]

Dynamic Corporation. Another consideration in weighing the corporative state and the corporative tradition in Portugal has to do with the models we have used to interpret the changes under way both before and after 1974. So many of these models, implicit in the popular accounts but finding their way into more scholarly analyses as well, paint the older corporative system in rigid and entirely static terms, hence portray the post-1974 regime in generously liberal and liberating terms, and see the entire political process in Portugal in the light of a dichotomous struggle between dictatorship and democracy. Now, surely, if it is fair to call the later Salazar regime rigid and static, there were indeed some liberalizing and liberating aspects to the 1974 revolution, and there is clearly something of a struggle between dictatorship and democracy. But that is not the entire picture.

From this analysis it becomes clear that there are various dynamic aspects to corporatism and not just static ones, that the corporatism of Caetano was of a quite different sort from that of Salazar, that corporatism is not entirely rigid and impermeable but may change and

167

evolve depending on societal conditions and developmental transformations, and that instead of being perceived wholly through "liberal" or "liberating" frameworks the postrevolutionary regime might also be examined in the light of revolutionary, more complex, perhaps "higher" forms of corporatism. The dictatorship-versus-democracy dichotomy is too confining, too restrictive, too culture bound to provide a very useful model. It represents a false and artificial choice, a too limited set of possibilities. It fails to recognize, for instance, that corporatism may take populist, leftist, and revolutionary directions as well as conservative and rightist ones, or that even within a single country various corporative forms may be related to broader societal transformations. Where the dictatorship-versus-democracy framework is useful and bears some relation to actual Portuguese events, by all means let us use it. But let us keep open the possibility that from Salazar through Caetano to the present regime we have witnessed some remarkable changes in—as well as the persistence of—an essentially corporative system, from the conservative, rigid, unyielding Rerum novarum–Quadragesimo Anno form of Salazar to the more open, pluralist, and socially just form of Caetano to the more populist, revolutionary, Socialist, syndicalist forms of the 1970s. This is a paradigm that also carries considerable explanatory power.

Finally, we return to the two senses, the two meanings, of the term "corporatism" with which we began. Corporatism has been discussed here in two ways: a political-cultural sense that implies a long tradition of what has been called "natural corporatism," and a more manifest and explicit ideology and structure of "corporatism" that found expression in the Estado Novo of the 1930s. It has proved rather easy to dismantle the corporative institutions associated with the Salazar regime since they were often ephemeral, surface agencies that lacked deep roots, were but weakly institutionalized, and enjoyed but limited legitimacy. Whether Portugal can as easily escape the yoke of its entire corporatist tradition and political culture and transcend them may be quite a different matter. From the analysis presented here, it seems clear that the continuities with and persistent features of that historical tradition remain strong even in the wake of the revolution of 1974. Portugal may evolve toward a "higher," more "developed," more pluralist, participatory, revolutionary, Socialist, or syndicalist form, but of the fact that those forms will continue to exhibit important corporatist characteristics there would seem to be little doubt. For Portugal to depart from this broader corporatist tradition would also involve shucking off some 800 years of history, and that seems more problematic than simply ridding itself of the corporative institutions fashioned by Salazar.

Final Considerations

The formal corporative system in Portugal from 1933 to 1974 was an incredibly mixed bag of successes and failures. Corporatism was successful in the 1930s in providing Portugal with a new national mythos badly needed after the chaos and failure of republicanism, with a new sense of national purpose and destiny, with restoration of order and stability and a set of institutions based upon national and indigenous sources, with help to restore rationality and probity to the national accounts, with provision for economic growth and development, and with help to fill the organizational void of a country whose historical, long-term problems had always included a lack of organization and a vacuum in its associational life. The reestablishment of a stable, functioning regime and the strengthening of the economy, closely related to the creation of the corporative system from 1933 on, were among the more notable and fundamental accomplishments of the Salazar regime. But after 1945, as the regime became more brutal, repressive, and fascistic, as corporatism in the earlier 1930s sense was discredited and became increasingly dysfunctional, as corporatism served more to retard national growth and modernization than to stimulate it, the failures of the system came to outweigh its earlier successes. The efforts of Caetano to revitalize the corporative system were again a mixture of successes and, ultimately, failure.

But perhaps "success" or "failure" is the wrong way to assess the situation. Perhaps we should simply take the Portuguese regime on its own terms and in its own context. In that sense the regime neither "succeeded" nor "failed"; it was rather the product of a historical period whose time had simply passed. The 1930s were probably the high point of corporatism in the global context, and the conservative Rerum novarum form of corporatism as propounded by Salazar still fitted fairly well the rural, conservative structure of Portuguese society. By the postwar period this was no longer the case. Portugal had changed and so had the international context. What was required was no longer a corporatism of control, demobilization, and selective repression but a corporatism of change and development. Corporatism in the earlier 1930s (or 1890s?) form was an idea and mode of organization whose epoch had been superseded. Time had passed the Portuguese regime by, while Salazar continued to cling to and enforce a system that had become anachronistic, even on its own corporative terms.

Here then lay the real difficulty for the Portuguese regime. It was not that it refused to move toward liberalism or socialism (neither apparently strongly favored nor enjoying the support of a majority of the Portuguese population) but that it failed to modernize even the corporative structures that it did have. The regime instead went to sleep, stagnated, lost touch. While other countries—Spain, Argentina, Brazil, Mexico, Peru—gradually evolved away from older Rerum Novarum forms of corporatism and toward more dynamic, participatory, change-and-development-oriented, even revolutionary forms, Portugal remained locked in the older conception, in the outdated bourgeois ideal of an ordered, hierarchical, Catholic, paternalistic state and society. It failed to take account of the emerging social forces or sought simply to repress them. Caetano made some frantic and too feeble efforts to rescue and dynamize the system at the last minute, but these came too late. Portugal's chief problem was, thus, that it failed to update and restructure its ideas, programs, and ideology even within the corporative framework it had set for itself.

By the same token—and at least until the revolution of 1974—it was not necessarily corporatism per se that was increasingly rejected by the Portuguese population in the postwar period but the particular direction it had taken under Salazar. If Salazar had proved more adaptable, if he had modernized the nation instead of allowing it to drift, if his had not become a repressive dictatorship, and if he had been willing to recognize the changing nature of Portuguese society and the just demands of the middle and lower classes (all big *ifs*, obviously, but *ifs* that in considerable measure came to pass in the warp and woof of postwar change in other Iberian and Latin nations similarly cast in the earlier corporative mold), the corporative system might well have lasted. It became instead a symbol of dictatorship and backwardness, a thing to be despised. The outdated, discredited corporative conception of Salazar was thus repudiated, as it deserved to be. Had that conception and its accompanying institutional arrangements proved more flexible, accommodative, and adaptable, however, it is likely that Portugal would still be a corporative system, not in the old-fashioned and now thoroughly discredited sense but in a newer, more modern sense, providing for the development of the Portuguese nation and its people. That is how development has usually gone forward elsewhere in the Iberic-Latin world; unfortunately, it did not take place in Portugal.

All this augurs ill for the future of the Portuguese system and for the possibilities of the establishment of any stable, democratic, functioning, development-oriented regime. For if it is in fact the case that corporatism in its natural, historical forms lies at the heart of Portuguese political culture and may even today still be the dominant tradition, then we should recognize the possibility that the particular Salazar practice and variant may have so thoroughly discredited corporatism that no new government will be able to build upon that heritage.[36] At the same time we must recognize that corporatism is no longer the only tradition in Portugal, that alongside it has grown up a liberal and republican tradition and, more recently, a nascent Socialist one. But these latter traditions are still so new and so weakly institutionalized that they may not have sufficient support or legitimacy to serve as the basis for the establishment of a new regime either. With these three concepts and world views continuing to coexist uneasily side by side, representing wholly different ways of life and modes of organizing society and polity, with little connection between them and with no one enjoying absolute legitimacy or even majority support, it may well be that Portugal will remain invertebrate, ineffective, and inefficient, chaotic, fragmented and disintegrated, subject to recurrent breakdowns, a kind of permanently crippled nation unable to establish any functioning system, be it liberalism, an updated form of corporate pluralism, or a newer variant of socialism or syndicalism, to replace the older form of corporatism that the new regime has dismantled.

Notes

1. Howard J. Wiarda, "Toward a Framework for the Study of Political Change in the Iberic-Latin Tradition: The Corporative Model," *World Politics*, vol. 25 (January 1973), pp. 206–35; Wiarda, ed., *Politics and Social Change in Latin America* (Amherst: University of Massachusetts Press, 1982); Fredrick Pike and Thomas Stritch, eds., *The New Corporatism: Social-Political Structures in the Iberian World* (Notre Dame, Ind.: University of Notre Dame Press, 1974); and James Malloy, ed., *Authoritarianism and Corporatism in Latin America* (Pittsburgh, Penn.: University of Pittsburgh Press, 1976).

2. Martin O. Heisler, "Patterns of European Politics: The 'European Polity' Model," in Martin O. Heisler, ed., *Politics in Europe: Structures and Processes in Some Post-industrial Democracies* (New York: McKay, 1974), chap. 2; and Leo Panitch, "The Development of Corporatism in Liberal Democracies" (Paper presented at the 1976 Annual Meeting of the American Political Science Association, Chicago, September 2–5).

3. The longer, more detailed case study from which much of this discussion and subsequent analysis derives is Howard J. Wiarda, *Corporatism and Development: The Portuguese Experience* (Amherst: University of Massachusetts Press, 1977).

4. Sidney M. Greenfield, "The Patrimonial State and Patron-Client Relations in Iberia and Latin America," Occasional paper, University of Massachusetts Program in Latin American Studies, 1976.

5. An example is A. H. de Oliveira Marques, *History of Portugal*, 2 vols. (New York: Columbia University Press, 1972).

6. I am now preparing for publication a paper defining what precisely the Iberic-Latin conception of "democracy," "representation," "participation,"

"pluralism," and the like implies; a preliminary statement is Howard J. Wiarda, "The Transition to Democracy in Portugal: Real or Wishful?" (Paper presented to the Joint Seminar on Political Development (JOSPOD), Center for International Studies, Massachusetts Institute of Technology, Cambridge, December 8, 1976, and published in summary form in the minutes of the JOSPOD Seminar).

7. Marques, *History of Portugal*, provides perhaps the clearest example.

8. One thinks particularly of the influential volume edited by Gabriel A. Almond and James S. Coleman, *The Politics of the Developing Areas* (Princeton, N.J.: Princeton University Press, 1960); but much of the writings of Karl Deutsch, S. M. Lipset, W. W. Rostow, and others during this same period exhibited much the same ethnocentric and culture-bound perspectives.

9. Ronald Newton, "Natural Corporatism and the Passing of Populism in Spanish America," in Pike and Stritch, eds., *The New Corporatism*.

10. Philippe C. Schmitter, "Still the Century of Corporatism?" in Pike and Stritch, eds., *The New Corporatism*, pp. 93–94.

11. "Pluralism" is another of those terms, like "democracy" or "representation," that mean something different in the Portuguese context from its meaning in the Anglo-American one; still the possibilities for corporate pluralism should not be ruled out or defined away. Indeed, in the absence of a strong liberal-democratic tradition in Portugal, a degree of corporate pluralism represents a hopeful evolution.

12. Patrimonialism is of course one of Weber's categories of traditional authority and was applied to Latin America, among other places, in Magali Sarfatti, *Spanish Bureaucratic-Patrimonialism in America* (Berkeley: Institute of International Studies, University of California, 1966); on organic-statism see Alfred Stepan, *State and Society* (Princeton, N.J.: Princeton University Press, 1978).

13. For further elaboration see Henrique de Gama Barros, *História da Adminstração Pública em Portugal nos Séculos XI–XII* (Lisbon: Liv. Sa da Costa, 1945); Raymundo Faoro, *Os donos do poder: Formação do patronato político brasileiro* (Porto Alegre: Ed. Globo, 1958); Manuel Paulo Merea, *O Poder Real e as Cortes* (Coimbra: Coimbra Ed., 1923); and Sidney M. Greenfield, *The Patrimonial State and Patron-Client Relations in Iberia and Latin America: Origins of "The System" in the Fifteenth Century Writings of the Infante D. Pedro of Portugal*, (Occasional paper no. 1, Program in Latin American Studies (Amherst: University of Massachusetts, 1976)).

14. For the contrasting traditions see Louis Hartz, *The Liberal Tradition in America* (New York: Harcourt, Brace, and World, 1955); and Richard M. Morse, "The Heritage of Latin America," in Wiarda, ed., *Politics and Social Change in Latin America*.

15. Such Estado Novo propagandists as Augusto da Costa argued this case; so did Salazar.

16. Fredrick Pike and Thomas Stritch, eds., *The New Corporatism* (Notre Dame, Ind.: University of Notre Dame Press, 1974).

17. It should be said that Salazar was also very clever in his relations with the military. Although he had incorporated many of the integralist, monar-

chist, nationalist, and Catholic principles into his own corporatist formula, he had not accepted one of their chief goals—the restoration of the monarchy. Instead, Salazar elevated the armed forces to the role of the "moderating power" historically reserved for the crown, thereby securing the loyalty and support of the military while at the same time retaining the backing of all but the most fervent of the monarchists, integralists, and Catholic traditionalists.

18 This analysis is clearly related to the question of the Latin American middle class and whether it is progressive or reactionary. The answer is, a bit of both, depending on the pragmatic circumstances. For the debate, see John J. Johnson, *Political Change in Latin America: The Emergence of the Middle Sectors* (Stanford, Calif.: Stanford University Press, 1958); and James Petras, "The Latin American Middle Class," *New Politics*, vol. 4 (Winter 1965), pp. 74–85.

19. Philippe C. Schmitter, *Corporatism and Public Policy in Authoritarian Portugal* (Beverly Hills, Calif.: Sage, 1975).

20. Mihail Manoïlesco, *Le Siècle du corporatisme* (Paris: Lib. Felix Alcan, 1934).

21. Pike and Stritch, *The New Corporatism.*

22. Fascism, according to Organski, is a model of development based on a partnership between agricultural and industrial elements to carry out industrialization but to impose its costs primarily on the industrial working class (A. F. K. Organski, "Fascism and Modernization," in S. J. Woolf, ed., *The Nature of Fascism* (New York: Vintage-Random, 1969), pp. 19–41).

23. See especially Theodore Lowi, *The End of Liberalism* (New York: Norton, 1969).

24. See Schmitter, "Still the Century of Corporatism?" pp. 93–94.

25. Freppel Cotta, *Economic Planning in Corporative Portugal* (Westminster: King and Staples, 1937); Maria Belmira Martins, *Sociedades e grupos em Portugal* (Lisbon: Ed. Estampa, 1973); and George McGovern, *Revolution into Democracy: Portugal after the Coup* (Washington, D.C.: 1976), which contains important information collected by the Department of State and the Senate Foreign Relations Committee staff.

26. Implied in these paragraphs are two ideas that need to be developed at greater length. First, it seems clear that the biases that developed in the Estado Novo and the particular directions that the regime took were not necessarily inherent in corporatism per se but had to do more with the nature of power and influence in the broader Portuguese system; the priorities that Salazar and the army had established, which relegated corporative implementation to a third-order priority; and the particular choices that Salazar opted for at especially critical junctures. Corporatism in Portugal might just as well have taken a more populist, developmentalist, and pluralist direction, as it did in other nations organized initially on some similar corporatist bases. Corporatism per se seems not to be the independent villain variable on which Portugal's retarded growth could be blamed; a more likely candidate is Salazar himself. For further discussion, see Wiarda, *Corporatism and Development*, chap. 11.

Second, it seems worth considering in more detail that the regime was eventually repudiated and overthrown, not because it was corporatist and authoritarian, or because it refused to go toward liberalism or social-democracy, but because it had become oppressive, had ridden roughshod over corporate group rights, had violated the natural rights of its people, and had become a full-fledged tyranny—all of which constitute grounds for revolt, both in Portuguese practice and in legal theory. In short, the regime both developed and was eventually repudiated, not in terms of the liberal and democratic paradigm, but in terms of the very *Portuguese* institutions and practices on which it was based. For some orienting concepts, see Lawrence E. Rothstein, "Aquinas and Revolution" (Paper presented at the 1976 Annual Meeting of the American Political Science Association, Chicago, September 2–5).

27. Marcello Caetano, *O Corporativismo* (Lisbon: National Secretariat of Information, 1973).

28. A more detailed analysis is in Wiarda, *Corporatism and Development*, chap. 10. The assessment presented here, it should be said, is based upon considerable field research in Portugal during this period and on a series of interviews in the prime minister's office, with the Corporations Ministry, with labor elements, and with oppositionists.

29. The decrees are published in the *Boletim do INTP* for this period; see also Henrique Nascimento Rodrigues, *Regime Jurídico das Relações Colectivas de Trabalho* (Coimbra: Atlantida, 1971).

30. Based upon the field work in Portugal in 1972–1973 and especially the return visits in March–April 1974 and May–June 1975. By the latter postrevolutionary date, many of the clandestine activities of the Intersindical had been described in the numerous new journals and newspapers of the leftist parties; a useful summary may be found in the report appearing under Senator McGovern's name, *Revolution into Democracy*.

31. Manuel de Lucena, *A Evolução do Sistema Corporativo Português* (Lisbon: Perspectives e Realidades, 1976).

32. *Programa para a democratização da república* (Porto: Tip. J. R. Gonçalves, 1961).

33. For a more detailed treatment of these events, see Howard J. Wiarda, *Transcending Corporatism? The Portuguese Corporative System and the Revolution of 1974* (Columbia: Institute of International Studies, University of South Carolina, 1976); chapter 3 in this book.

34. Based on the field work and interviews in Portugal in May–June 1975. The decree laws are published in the *Boletim do Instituto Nacional do Trabalho e Previdência* for this period.

35. Most analysts feel the Spínola government sought not a complete break with the past but to turn the economy and the existing corporative system away from its close ties to the colonies and toward a new relationship with the European Common Market (that was also clear, if unspoken, Caetano policy).

36. Kenneth P. Erickson has suggested some of these points to me.

6
Iberia, Latin America, and the Second Enlargement of the European Community

The petition of Spain and Portugal for entry into the European Economic Community (EEC) came at precisely the time the community itself had developed increasing doubts as to whether there were such an entity. These doubts were neatly captured in a stimulating contribution by Stanley Hoffmann, entitled "Fragments Floating in the Here and Now: Is There a Europe, Was There a Past, and Will There Be a Future," in a special edition of *Daedalus*, "Looking for Europe."[1]

Examined closely from within the community, Hoffmann argues, "Europe" is a great idea that has been tamed, leashed, and co-opted. It no longer evokes great hopes, expectations, or prospects of unitary integration. The postwar economic boom seems to have ended, and there is a sense of foreboding that future events might spin out of control. But for the Spanish and the Portuguese, the very distance and historical isolation from Europe of their two countries make Europe look larger and more singular than is in fact the case; for them, Europe remains very much a reality, a model, and a symbol both of economic modernity and of "civilization." "Europe" and the "European Community" in this understanding obviously mean something more than commodity agreements and lowered tariff barriers; to the Iberians "Europe" implies cultural, political, social, and psychological interconnections as well as economic ones.

From the time Talleyrand proclaimed that "Europe stops at the Pyrenees," and doubtlessly much earlier in the myths and prejudices northern Europeans often carry around as part of their cultural and intellectual baggage,[2] the notion has been widespread that Iberia is both "different" and inferior. This idea was widely shared not just by the rest of Europe but by the Spaniards and Portuguese themselves. The roots of these prejudices, which take the form often of an air of superiority in northern Europe and of national inferiority complexes

175

in Iberia, have complicated historical, cultural, religious, racial, political, and economic origins. The condition of comparative economic underdevelopment was so pronounced as recently as twenty-five years ago that, looking at the statistics for per capita income, Bruce M. Russett and his collaborators in the *World Handbook of Political and Social Indicators* were tempted to add a new twist to the "Europe stops at the Pyrenees" adage by proclaiming that in reality Latin America and the third world began there.[3]

These economic conditions of underdevelopment have changed dramatically in the past two decades—less so in Portugal than Spain but significantly there also.[4] Quite some time ago both countries passed the threshold that separates the "developing" from the "developed," and in Spain especially the changes have been so great as to take on almost "miracle" (like Japan, West Germany, or Brazil) dimensions. The political transformations have been no less dramatic: a sudden transformation by means of revolution from authoritarianism to democracy in Portugal and a more gradual, though perhaps no less significant, transformation to democracy in Spain following Franco's death.

In the past twenty years, then, not only have Spain and Portugal been more integrated into Europe economically and the gaps between the developed northern countries and the underdeveloped southern ones lessened or blurred to an appreciable degree, but the political reasons for excluding Spain and Portugal from Europe—their authoritarian and "Fascist" regimes—have disappeared as well.[5] Indeed, many Spanish and Portuguese government officials look on entry into the European Community rather as a reward that they richly deserve (and that helps explain their bitterness and resentment at every rebuff prior to their actual joining) for their success in evolving from authoritarianism to democracy, a prize that ought automatically to have come to them for their political accomplishments and not as a subject for further, from their point of view humiliating, negotiations over complex, arcane, and degrading issues like tomatoes or cucumbers. Iberia's sense of social and psychological entry into Europe has of course been hastened by the recent onslaught of northern European culture, with the accompanying tourists, fashion, and life styles, as well as by the equally important flow of hundreds of thousands of its own workers toward the north. And all these changes have come at a time of major, worldwide economic crisis and "stagflation," and within a context of shifting international power balances in the Mediterranean, Europe, NATO, and the Middle East and between the superpowers. These changes, involving fundamental debates about the area's destiny and future, also make Iberia's ties to the rest of

Europe far more complex than would be the case if they merely involved economic, trade, and tariff considerations.[6]

This chapter explores these themes in the light of Spain's and Portugal's entry into the EEC.[7] But it seeks to go beyond what seem to be comparatively simple and easy economic issues to explore the broader political, sociocultural, and strategic position and relations of Iberia to Europe as well and the implications for Latin America. It presents an overview of Spain and Portugal: their historical isolation, the social and economic transformations of recent decades, and the political transformations since the mid-1970s and the role of both the European Community and the United States in these. It examines the degree to which Iberia remains suspended between two worlds, its own or perhaps an "Atlanticist," "Lusitanian," or "Hispanic" vision as opposed to that of Europe and the "hidden agendas" (often more politico-strategic than economic) of Spain's and Portugal's entry into the European Community. The essay thus examines some of the complex dimensions, in a macrocultural and political-sociological sense, of the relations between Iberia, the EEC, and Latin America. It concludes by returning to the issue of whether Europe still, in fact, ends at the Pyrenees and whether Latin America begins there.

Spain and Portugal: An Overview

A Part of Europe or Apart from It? Iberia has been, historically, both a part of Europe, and apart from it. This conflict, this paradox, lies at the heart of Spain's and Portugal's complex, often wrenching and conflict-prone relations with their European neighbors and with the larger outside world. A glance at the map provides one indication of the roots of this trauma: Iberia occupies a peninsula, cut off from Europe except for steep and often treacherous mountain passes through the Pyrenees. At the same time, Spain has a long south- and eastward-facing Mediterranean coast; commands the Straits of Gibraltar and, with it, both the entryway to the Mediterranean and considerable portions of North Africa, while its port of Barcelona, once Spain's chief city, has long been important in Mediterranean trade and commerce. Portugal, on the western-most promontory of the continent, has, since Henry the Navigator, believed that its destiny lies at least as much south and with the Atlantic as with Europe, pointing toward Brazil, the Atlantic islands, the coast of West Africa, and beyond. These historic and geographic Mediterranean and Atlantic connections and loyalties help explain the ambivalence many Iberians still have toward joining Europe and their strong third world, Arabic, African, and Hispanic or Lusophonic ties.[8]

We have stressed that it is not just distance and geography that have separated Iberia from Europe, however. The gaps are social, cultural, psychological, and racial as well. Rather like Italians from the south and the islands, the Iberians are often presumed to have been tainted by the long occupation of the peninsula by the Moors. Notwithstanding that Moorish Spain represented perhaps the highest of European cultures during the otherwise "dark" ages, the Iberians are often thought to be less civilized than their north European counterparts, more African, darker and "swarthier"; and the legacies of such manifest racial and cultural prejudices are still felt strongly in Spain and Portugal. The Iberians have long been considered second-class citizens, in the European view perhaps a notch above the Turks and Algerians, but certainly not up to the fair-haired, less "excitable" northerners. Although Spaniards and Portuguese may now be acceptable, they still have to prove themselves in ways that north Europeans do not.[9]

The social, cultural, and psychological gaps stem from the widespread sense that Iberia has been bypassed by the great transformations we associate with the modern, Western world. These include the Protestant Reformation and the ensuing religious pluralism and tolerance, the Industrial Revolution and its accompanying sociopolitical effects, representative and democratic government, the Enlightenment and the revolution of science, and the growth of a more participatory, multiclass, and pluralist society. In the realm of ideas, for instance, Spain is thought to have been shackled by its neo-Thomistic and scholastic philosophy, which insisted on a link between morality and politics. By other indexes of what the northern Europeans (and most social scientists) called modernity—secularization, democratization, untrammeled social pluralism, and the like—Iberia simply did not measure up.[10]

The sense of isolation and separateness prevailing in the cultural, social, and political attitudes of other Europeans toward Iberia and in the sense of distinctiveness, not untinged with inferiority, felt by the Spaniards and Portuguese themselves was also reflected in the international arena. Here again the attitudes that need to be studied are both those of their northern and central European neighbors and those of Spain and Portugal toward the rest of Europe. The attitudes were consistently ambivalent, and they seemed to fluctuate over time, depending among other things on the waxing and waning of the power of the two Iberian nations, their development as compared with Europe, and their domestic political, social, and economic conditions. Northern Europe continued to recognize that Iberia was a part of the continent; yet it was always perceived as unique or distinctive.

For their part, the Spaniards and Portuguese have consistently wished to be included as part of "Western," European, "advanced" civilization; but they have always been cognizant too of their "exceptionalism," of their Atlantic, Latin American, and African ties as well as their European ones.[11]

Hence when Europe accepts them as part of the European community, Iberia too tends to look in a European direction. But when, as during the Franco and Salazar eras, Europe seems to reject them on political or other grounds, the Iberians also tend to get their backs up, to look elsewhere, to reemphasize their separateness, to strengthen their Luso-Hispanic, American, or African and third world ties, to thumb their noses at a Europe that has given them the cold shoulder, and to pursue quite independent policies, domestic and foreign. Leaders like Franco and Salazar, in fact, recognizing these ambivalent feelings, were masters at manipulating these psychological elements and nationalistic and isolationist sentiments to maximum political advantage.

Portugal had been unified as a nation-state by the fourteenth century and Spain was unified in the fifteenth through the marriage of Isabella of Castile and Ferdinand of Aragon. In the sixteenth century both nations reached the height of their international power. The crowning at that time of Hapsburg Charles I as king of Spain and later as Holy Roman Emperor, together with Spain's attempt to maintain Catholic orthodoxy and unity in the face of the Protestant Reformation, thrust Spain into the forefront of Europe. Its infantry was considered the finest of its time. Under Charles's successor Philip II, Spain was probably the most modernized and bureaucratized state in Europe, and its culture and literature flourished during this "golden century." At the same time both Spain and Portugal had acquired far-flung empires, in the Americas, Africa, and the Far East.[12]

Then began a three-centuries-long decline (some would argue nearly four). The economic, social, political, and dynastic causes of that decline are perhaps familiar and need not concern us here. As Iberia declined, it also turned inward, defensive, isolationist. It remained cut off from those great movements mentioned earlier— religious, intellectual, economic, sociological, political—that the West associates with the making of the modern age. As Spain and Portugal lagged even farther behind the rest of Europe on various indexes of modernization, their sense of separateness, withdrawal, and self-centeredness grew. It was during this period that the notion that "Europe stops at the Pyrenees" was born and gained widespread acceptance.

Iberia's active participation in European affairs essentially ended with the termination of the Napoleonic wars. Both Spain and Portugal were subsequently torn by domestic upheaval, civil wars, and repeated military coups. They had lost most of their American colonies to independence by 1824, the rest to the United States in 1898. The great economic expansion experienced by the central and northern European countries in the nineteenth century did not occur in Iberia.[13] Hence when the economic drive to maturity did finally begin in Spain and Portugal in the twentieth century, it came in a different historical context and therefore not necessarily with all the same social and political concomitants of modernization that had accompanied the urban-industrialization process elsewhere in Europe.[14]

The establishment of a republic in Portugal, 1910–1926, and in Spain, 1930–1936, seemed to offer hope that Iberia might yet come abreast of the rest of Europe. But the two republics were rather quickly replaced by authoritarian-corporatist regimes, under Salazar and Franco respectively. In the 1930s corporatism seemed to be the wave of the future; and one reason Salazar and Franco embraced it so emphatically, at least for a time, was that it seemed to offer a way for Iberia to argue that it too was part of this future, was in the forefront of change. But the defeat of the Axis powers led to a general discrediting of all such "Fascist" systems and, with them, the discrediting and isolation of the Salazar and Franco regimes. Their entry into the United Nations was questioned and delayed for a time, NATO eventually agreed unenthusiastically to accept Portugal but not Spain, neither was considered for membership in the EEC in its early decades, and both were labeled as pariah states and kept on the fringes of Europe.[15]

Once again it was this very isolation from Europe that prompted Spain and Portugal to look first inward and then elsewhere for friends and support. Portugal endeavored domestically to maintain and resurrect its past in the form of almost nineteenth century institutional forms and traditions, meanwhile seeking to hang onto its African colonies (Angola, Cape Verde, Guinea, and Mozambique) and the last vestiges of its Asian empire (Macão, East Timor, Goa, Diu, and Damão), while also trying to co-opt its giant former colony Brazil into a vast Lusitanian alliance. Spain sought a conquest in North Africa and the recovery of some of its lost influence in its former colonies in the Americas through *Hispanidad*, a concept implying the expansion and extension of Spain's perceived distinct Hispanic, Latin, Christian culture to the Latin American countries of "Hispanic-Iberian soul and language." The efforts of both Iberian countries were grandiose, haughty, and rather pathetic at the same time: the last dying gasps of fading imperial powers seeking unrealistically to reassert their grand-mastership over former colonies that had since grown more powerful than the mother countries.[16]

With the overthrow of the Salazar-Caetano regime in Portugal (1974) and the death of Franco in Spain (1975), Iberia again embarked on some new courses, both domestically and internationally. Democracy, of a particular Iberian sort, was restored, which made Portugal and Spain again acceptable in the European community of nations, no longer pariahs. It now seemed as though Spain's entry into NATO and both Portugal's and Spain's entry into the EEC and European councils more generally would be welcomed. At the same time, acceptable once again, Spain and Portugal seemed inclined to abandon their fiercely independent attitudes, overcome their complexes, jettison the largely romantic notions of a Lusitanian federation or of Spanish-led *Hispanismo*, and identify once more closely with Europe—not just economically but also politically, socially, culturally, and psychologically.[17]

Iberia's relations with the rest of Europe historically have thus gone through a series of ups and downs, periodic oscillations, and some violent, pendulum-like swings. Especially interesting from the point of view of this study are the preeminently political and cultural-psychological factors causing such oscillations; the close interrelations between the nature of the reigns in Spain and Portugal and the Europeans' attitudes toward them; the nationalistic sentiments, phobias, and complexes these attitudes engender in Iberia; and the way Spanish and Portuguese foreign policy, at times oriented toward Europe and at times elsewhere, is also related to these same attitudes, or the Iberian perception of them. These considerations will have major implications as we explore further the forces shaping Spain's and Portugal's entry into the EEC, the underlying political motives governing these relations, the changed socioeconomic conditions now altering the assumptions about the situation, and the implications of these changed conditions for Latin America and for Iberian-Latin American relations.

Socioeconomic Transformation in Spain and Portugal: Have the Givens of Their Historic Relations Also Been Altered? Although historically Iberia has long been somewhat isolated from the rest of Europe, and Spain and Portugal still sometimes voice sentiments, largely nostalgic and unrealistic, about third worldism or "going it alone," in fact the social and economic realities are such that they no longer have that choice. Spain and Portugal are now preeminently European, indeed so closely tied in with European markets, tourism, trade patterns, and, yes, even culture that the choice of independence or interdependence is no longer a realistic one. A brief look at some of the statistics shows why this is so.

The socioeconomic changes that have been occurring in the peninsula, more so in Spain than in Portugal, are little short of astounding and are insufficiently recognized elsewhere in the West. Spanish economic growth during the 1960s and 1970s has significantly reduced the previous gap in living standards between Spain and the rest of Europe. In fact along a wide range of socioeconomic measures, Spain is no longer "different"; it is unequivocally European.[18]

Per capita income in Spain in 1977 was, according to World Bank figures, above $3,000 per year (see table 6–1). (It is now above $4,000.) That places Spain ahead of European Community member Ireland and only a few dollars behind Italy. Spain ranks as the twenty-fourth richest country in the world per capita and twelfth among the world's some 150 nations in total gross domestic product. Spain's per capita income is only about 25 percent less than the United Kingdom's, which it may well surpass eventually, and it is wealthier per capita than Greece, Hungary, or Yugoslavia. It is virtually tied with Poland and the Soviet Union. The figures for Portugal still lag behind, at about three-fifths the per capita income of Spain; but in the 1960s and early 1970s Portugal also experienced such rapid growth that some time ago it passed over that magic but arbitrary dividing line separating the developed from the undeveloped nations. In short, the image we have of Spain and Portugal as extremely poor and unalterably underdeveloped countries, more akin to the third world than to the world of advanced industrial nations, is no longer accurate.

The economic growth of Spain and Portugal has been fueled by the general world prosperity, especially European, of the past three decades and has also had the crucially important side effect of tying the Iberian economies into the European economies to a degree unprecedented in the past. One aspect of this is of course the enormous labor supply that Spain and Portugal have provided to Europe. Paris now is, for example, the city with the world's third largest Portuguese population; it is frequently remarked that without their Spanish and Portuguese "guest workers," a number of French, German, Swiss, and Dutch industries and services would likely collapse. A second factor is tourism. Tourism is now the second or third most important sector in the Spanish and Portuguese economies, critical for foreign exchange earnings and the balance of payments. Fully 70 percent of these tourists come from Europe. All this requires the free movement of people across Iberia's frontiers. Excess Spanish and Portuguese labor must be placed abroad at wages and under conditions that permit remittances back to the home countries, while in the

TABLE 6–1

Comparison of Spain and Portugal with Selected Other
Countries in Population, Gross National Product, Gross
National Product per Capita, and Average Annual Growth,
1979

Country	Population (thousands)	Gross National Product (U.S.$)	Gross National Product per Capita (U.S.$)	Average Annual Growth Rate, 1970–1977
Sweden	8,263	77,200	9,340	1.2
United States	216,729	1,896,550	8,750	2.0
Germany (Federal Republic of)	61,418	529,380	8,620	2.2
France	53,051	397,670	7,500	3.1
Austria	7,506	48,390	6,450	3.8
United Kingdom	55,932	254,100	4,540	1.6
Israel	3,604	13,570	3,760	2.0
Italy	56,468	199,270	3,530	2.0
USSR	258,932	861,210	3,330	4.4
Poland	34,724	114,280	3,290	6.3
Spain	36,298	118,170	3,260	3.6
Hungary	10,628	32,940	3,100	5.1
Ireland	3,198	9,770	3,060	2.1
Greece	9,231	27,200	2,950	4.0
Yugoslavia	21,738	45,600	2,100	5.1
Argentina	26,036	48,710	1,870	1.8
Portugal	9,577	17,580	1,840	3.1
Romania	21,648	33,030	1,530	9.9
Brazil	116,100	163,880	1,410	6.7
Chile	10,553	13,160	1,250	−1.8

Source: 1979 World Bank Atlas.

opposite direction policies encouraging tourism must also be followed.[19]

The pattern of Spanish exports, imports, and investment flows similarly shows a far greater interdependence vis-à-vis Europe than was ever the case before. In 1977 fully 56 percent of Spain's exports went to Western Europe, as opposed to only 11 percent to Latin America and Canada. Forty-eight percent of its imports came from

Europe as opposed to only 8 percent from Latin America. During the period 1959–1973, the flow of European foreign investment to Spain increased to 43 percent of the total, and the percentage has been steadily rising in more recent years. European as well as North American consortia and multinationals have built numerous plants in Iberia, invested heavily there, and absorbed or worked out collaborative arrangements with many smaller Portuguese and Spanish industries; the previously closed banking system of the Iberian nations have been significantly opened to foreign banks and cooperative endeavors. It is clear that given the prominence and direction of these several economic flows and patterns, it was crucial for Spain and Portugal to acquire full membership in the EEC. Indeed, despite the occasional quixotic flirtation with third worldism, Hispanicism, or Luso-tropicalism, the fuller integration of Spain and Portugal into Europe has been the only realistic foreign policy choice since the 1960s.[20]

Not only have Spain and Portugal become more integrated economically with Europe but their societies have come more and more to resemble the European ones as well. They have become more urbanized, modernized, and—at least by economic criteria—middle class. Literacy rates have risen rapidly, industrialization has changed the face of society especially in the urban settings, health care and nutrition are much better, and the full gamut of social programs has been introduced. The same styles and music, and almost the same pornography, are available in Lisbon and Madrid as in Copenhagen or Amsterdam.

While such changes, the concomitants of industrialization and modernization, are familiar and almost comfortable, it should be emphasized, as a loudly discordant note, that these changes have not made Spain and Portugal merely into slightly less-developed versions of the Western or European model, whose path they must necessarily follow and emulate. The fact is, contrary to many social science notions concerning the development process and the expectations of virtually all Europeans and many Spaniards and Portuguese themselves, that Spain and Portugal are *different* and *they will remain so*. The times have changed markedly since the nineteenth century when the northern and more industrialized nations of Europe went through their industrialization-modernization processes and on the basis of which Rostow and other analysts of development fashioned their model of the "stages of growth." The international context has similarly been altered since that earlier time when countries like Britain, Japan, or the United States could develop more or less autonomously in greater or lesser isolation. Finally, it is clear that in Spain and

Portugal many traditional institutions persist and remain strong and that they continue to serve as filters of the Iberian modernization process, often accepting that which is useful and can readily be absorbed, while screening out those elements of modernization that are unacceptable.

The arguments cannot all be developed and fully elaborated here.[21] But what can be said is that because of the circumstances discussed above, Spanish and Portuguese development cannot be expected to mirror or palely and belatedly imitate that of the northern European countries. The social and political concomitants that, based upon the northern European experience, are supposed to follow inevitably from industrialization do not, in the Spanish and Portuguese cases, seem to be following inevitably. For instance, while Spain and Portugal (using family income figures) seem to be becoming more middle class, the presumed middle-class society and middle-class political values—moderation, pragmatic politics, and the like—do not seem to be emerging quickly or even necessarily. Nor are the democratic political institutions, political parties, parliament, and the like as strong or well institutionalized as one might expect, using the earlier European model as chief reference point. Nor has the political behavior of the military or that of other elites come to correspond closely to the presumed Western pattern. These discordant factors force us to introduce some strong reservations about the strength and viability of democratic institutions in both Spain and Portugal and the degree to which these nations will *ever* come to look like the rest of Europe, or their ultimate commitment to it.[22]

The Political Transition in Spain and Portugal. Not only have Spain and Portugal long been isolated from Europe geographically and psychologically but for much of the twentieth century they have been treated as outcasts, virtual pariah states subject to strong disapproval. The authoritarian regimes of Franco and Salazar were viewed as akin to fascism; and particularly in the post-World War II period after fascism's defeat, both were snubbed, sneered at, and condemned as anachronisms. In the Spanish case these sentiments were particularly strong, since Franco, after all, had led the anti-Republican forces in the Civil War in which a number of European social democratic leaders had fought on the Republican side. And even if they had not actually been present in Spain, an entire generation of Europeans in the postwar era, products of the anti-Fascist struggles, had, understandably, carried over these sentiments in their attitudes toward Spain and Portugal. For a long time, therefore, Spain was kept out of the United Nations, NATO, and the European "family" of nations and treated as a poor and disgraceful cousin. Portugal, which suffered similar affronts, did not evoke such strong sentiments as Spain and for strategic reasons was the beneficiary of both British and American insistence that it be more fully integrated into European councils and defense arrangements. In both countries these snubs and isolation grated uncomfortably, not just on the part of the regimes ostensibly being punished but at the level of popular sentiment as well.

In the transition from authoritarianism to liberalism and democracy, in Portugal after the revolution of 1974 and in Spain after Franco's death in 1975,[23] two points merit brief mention, since they bear directly on the relations of these two countries with the EEC and the preeminently *political reasons* both for keeping them out and, eventually, for allowing them in. First, Spain under Franco and Portugal under Salazar and Caetano were never, particularly from 1958 on, quite so authoritarian or "fascistic," and considerably more liberal, as their foreign press coverage and general European sentiment would lead one to believe. Second, in the post-1975 period both Spain and Portugal exhibited more continuities with the past and were hence less "liberal" and "democratic" than that same foreign press and European sentiment would again lead one to believe.[24] One could argue that Spain and Portugal were both ostracized from the European community to some extent under false pretenses, or at least greatly exaggerated ones, and were finally admitted to it under some pretenses that were obviously quite different from the earlier ones but were also, to a degree, false and misleading.

The evidence for these assertions is abundant.[25] For example, under the "old regimes" of Franco and Salazar and Caetano there was very little terror or torture, certainly not enough to call either regime "fascistic"; no racial persecution as in Nazi Germany; no totalitarian "behemoth"—a strong and authoritarian state, yes, but totalitarian, no;[26] a considerable degree of social pluralism, albeit limited; considerable (and sometimes varying) degrees of free speech and press, although clearly not the entirely untrammeled liberty of the democratic countries; considerable trade union activity, although that was not entirely free either;[27] strenuous political activity between the factions of the official party or on the part of some opposition elements, hardly a monolithic single-party system;[28] and vigorous debate on economic policy decisions and on the future political directions of these two regimes.[29] While these and other features obviously do not make for an entirely free and democratic system, they do not really conform to the image we have of a full-fledged totalitarian or fascistic regime either.

In reverse, the post-Franco and post–Salazar and Caetano regimes do not quite conform either to a picture of happy liberalism and triumphant democracy. For example, Spanish and Portuguese "liberalism" continues to exhibit many of the same authoritarian, top-down features as in the past; the presumed agencies of democracy—political parties and parliament—are weakly institutionalized and may not be the main loci of power; there remain many social, cultural, and political continuities with the past—the breaks in 1974 and 1975 were not so sharp as at first imagined; labor relations still largely take place under state auspices and direction; powerful vested interests like the church or the army retain their power and have not been democratized—these, not the parties or parliament, may still be the final arbiters of national politics; public opinion is still often ignored or ridden roughshod over in the making of decisions; the strength of economic elites is still exceedingly powerful in Spain and resurgent in Portugal; and authoritarian tendencies remain strong while the democratic ones are sometimes inchoate.[30]

These observations should not suggest that the regimes of Franco and Salazar and Caetano were, contrary to much evidence, models of sweetness and light, of disguised democracy and hidden liberalism, only that they were far less totalitarian and fascistic than they were usually pictured. Similarly these observations should not imply that since Franco's death and Caetano's ouster there has not been a democratic breakthrough. There has been such a breakthrough, and it is significant. Still, one must be careful not to emphasize the changes at the expense of ignoring the continuities or for that matter to exaggerate the transformation that has occurred. Neither Portugal in 1974 nor Spain after 1975 executed complete about-faces: yet it was *precisely* on such political criteria and the presumption of a complete turnabout in Iberia that the decisions, belatedly, to welcome Spain and Portugal back into the community of "Western," "civilized," "anti-Fascist," and "democratic" nations were made.

The Changing Reigns in Spain and Portugal and the European Involvement. Spain and Portugal no longer exist in isolation. This statement is made not just in the obvious and trivial sense that all nations are interconnected by air and ground transport in ways they were not before. Rather it is meant to say that Spain and Portugal are no longer the absolute sovereigns of their own destinies, having become dependent on and interdependent with a set of worldwide economic forces and international political events over which they have no complete control.

A number of careful studies have shown that the Spanish and Portuguese economies are particularly sensitive to the world economy.[31] Neither has any oil to speak of, which helps explain Portugal's reluctance to allow its Azores air base to be used during the 1973 war as a refueling stop for the resupply of Israel, and Spain's policy which is widely viewed as pro-Arab. Both require the import of many raw materials, and both require most-favored-nation status to market their exports. Both must be able to export surplus labor, and, in the opposite direction, both must pursue policies encouraging a steady stream of foreign tourists. Both also require huge foreign investment flows, both direct and portfolio. Both are absolutely dependent on their imports from and exports to the United States and Western Europe, on loans and foreign aid from these same sources, and on maintaining credit-worthiness from the private banks and international lending institutions dominated by these same nations. All these "dependency variables" point toward stronger links of Iberia with Western Europe and the United States and weaker connections with Africa, Latin America, and the third world (except, for special reasons, its Arabic parts).

These dependency relations also help give the European nations and the United States a number of levers by which to shape, influence, and manipulate Spain and Portugal, which they lacked before. These, plus the sheer affluence of northern Europe that enables these countries to use aid and foreign policy in ways they could not previously, the overweening desire on the part of Spain and Portugal to put their past and their psychological baggage behind and to be accepted within the European family, the special obligation the northern Europeans felt to help the Iberians overcome their "fascistic" past, and finally both U.S. and northern European fears of the Mediterranean becoming a "red sea" and the associated perceived need to shore up NATO's weak and vulnerable southern flank, all combined in the late-1970s to make Spain and Portugal the subjects of much attention and concern.[32] These concerns, plus the economic dependency already examined, dictated that Iberia had to be brought into Europe or the West whether it wished to or not. Both the manifest and hidden agendas of Iberian-European relations require our attention.

Spain and Portugal between Two Worlds

The relations of one-time colonial nations with their former metropoles, Fredrick Pike reminds us, are invariably governed by a love-hate dynamic.[33] Immediately after independence the former metropole is despised for its imperialism and exploitation, and the former colony searches elsewhere for a model to emulate. With the passage of time, however, the model imported from elsewhere often proves unworkable, and the former colony then begins to look inward, to its own past and historical tradition, for a functional framework for development. In the process the former mother country and the institutions it transferred to the colony are examined anew and often resurrected albeit in altered form, and a new pattern of relations is often established between them. Uneasiness and a certain wariness and suspicion, however, continue to color these happier relations.

So it was with Spain and Portugal and their former colonies in the Americas. Immediately after independence early in the nineteenth century, Latin America rejected Spain and Portugal and all they had stood for.[34] The mother countries were strongly derided for holding back progress, keeping Latin America isolated from the main currents of the Western world, shackling Latin America with Catholic and scholastic institutions, impeding industrialization and enlightenment, monopolizing trade, and retarding Latin America's potential for growth and development. Rejecting their Spanish and Portuguese pasts, the countries of Latin America turned to what seemed the best and most progressive, perhaps then the only, alternative: U.S.-style liberalism and republicanism.[35]

Liberalism and republicanism, however, did not work very well in nineteenth century Latin America. They seemed to produce instability, chaos, recurrent breakdowns, and a lack of progress.[36] By the turn of the century, therefore, Latin America began to examine other models, to look with renewed sympathy on its former metropoles, and to search for ways of reconciling its Luso-Hispanic past with its continued aspiration for democratic government. Several ingredients came together to make such a reconciliation possible: the salving effect of time, which softened attitudes toward the former colonial powers; the apparent dysfunctionality of the liberal model;[37] the rise of positivism and corporatism in both Iberia and Latin America, which gave them a new and common ideology of development;[38] a common suspicion of the United States;[39] and the rising sense of *hispanismo* or of a unified Hispanic culture—again in contrast to the United States.[40] Although these themes are analyzed in more detail in chapter 10, the emphasis here is on the main factors that brought Iberia and Latin America back into a closer relationship.

The course of this rapprochement between Iberia and Latin America was never smooth, unilinear, or free from tensions. For one thing, the Latin American countries never embraced *hispanismo* with the same fervor as did Spain; nor were they, as independent nations, some bigger and now more powerful than the mother country, willing to submit to Spanish guidance and direction. Nor were they always willing to give up their New World heritage and sense of distinctiveness, and many were not willing to forsake their liberal-democratic tradition in favor of the vague promises of corporatism. By the same token, many condemned the Fascist-authoritarian regimes of Franco and Salazar, especially as these regimes were ostracized and treated as pariahs in the postwar period. Argentina had leadership aspirations in Latin America often as strong as the Spanish, and Brazil occasionally flirted with the idea of *replacing* Portugal in Africa, not subordinating itself to Portugal. Finally, as many Latin American nations sought to loosen their dependence on the United States, to assert their own indigenous developmental models, and to strengthen their ties to Europe, they developed closer relations with all of Europe, not just Spain and Portugal. The goals were hence consistently pragmatic rather than emotional or ideological. On numerous counts—politics, economics, diplomacy, and trade—the movement for a common Luso-American or Hispano-American grand alliance and community floundered.

Nor were the Iberian nations entirely free of similar difficulties with the very programs they had designed. Spain and Portugal intended to be *leaders* of their respective communities in Africa, Asia, and the Americas, not merely equals. It was they who expected to provide the guidance and ideology, not the Latin Americans. I recall presenting a paper in Spain at one time (ironically, at the very agency the Instituto de Cultura Hispánica—organized initially to help promote *hispanismo*) during which I suggested the utility of employing a common framework for the study of sociopolitical change in Iberia and Latin America. Within days that notion was subjected to a torrent of abuse in the Spanish press and from one of Spain's leading sociologists, who objected that it was an insult to the dignity of Spain to be treated as "just another" Latin American nation.[41]

In the meantime, the trends described earlier were working their inexorable effects. Latin America increasingly went its own way, while Spain and Portugal were drawn closer into Europe. The policy of isolating Franco and Salazar internationally began to wear thin; "Fascist" no longer seemed a wholly accurate adjective to describe these regimes; tourism, fashion, music, and a common youth culture increasingly broke down all national boundaries; the international situation shifted; Iberian trade and finance were increasingly bound up with that of their European neighbors; Spanish and Portuguese workers flooded into Europe; and, overall, Spain and Portugal came to view themselves, and were increasingly seen by Europe, as *European*, not third world, Trans-Pyreneean, Latin American, or Hispano- or Luso-American.

Despite this de facto integration of Iberia into Europe, Spaniards,

Portuguese, and Latin Americans will likely continue to see themselves as somehow different from other Europeans and Americans and to value their common heritage. Although the nature of the relationship between Iberia and Latin America may change, the two regions continue to share a special relationship and Hispanic heritage. The large Latin American community in the Iberian capitals; the common cultural currents of language, law, religion, and politics; the visits of the Spanish monarch and prime minister to Latin America; the trade and commercial patterns that exist and the new agreements and alliances recently forged all testify to the continuing viability of their relationships. Fredrick Pike has put the matter especially well:

> Members of the Iberian community will likely view the differences dividing them as less consequential than those that separate them from the non-Iberian world. While this assessment may be of little moment in shaping diplomatic and economic relations and while it may be challenged occasionally by passing fancies (such as the one that sees Ibero-America's and especially Brazil's affinity as really lying with Africa), it will nonetheless remain important. Belief in the reality of an Iberian community, however elusive of empirical demonstration that community remains, will continue to impart a distinctive hue to one facet of the cultural pluralism and perspective that constitute a glory of human existence, however much they are lamented by the international integrationists.[42]

Iberia, the EEC, and Latin America

By the late 1960s, it is fair to say that Spain and Portugal were already de facto members of Europe—although that fact could not be admitted publicly. The old image of Europe, or civilization, stopping at the Pyrenees no longer carried any meaning or importance. Spain and Portugal were in and of Europe, whether they or Europe were enamored of that reality or not. For political reasons, however, chiefly having to do with European hostility toward what were still viewed as "Fascist regimes," the de jure entry of Spain and Portugal into European councils had to await the overthrow of the Salazar-Caetano regime and the death of Franco.

Spain had actually begun its effort to reenter Europe some three decades earlier. The pace of change was glacial. In 1953 Spain had signed the Bases Agreement with the United States, in 1955 it was admitted to the United Nations, in 1958 it became an associate member of the OEEC, in 1959 it was elevated to full membership in the succeeding OECD and also became a member of the World Bank, and in 1962 it approached the EEC, but only in 1964 did the EEC deign to open "exploratory talks" and then only at the commercial level. A commercial trade pact was finally signed in 1970 after eight years of negotiations and even then over the strenuous objections of some among the membership who opposed Spain's nondemocratic government. Spain thus edged toward the EEC, but the process was dishearteningly slow. It had not by the 1970s achieved full EEC membership, and the negotiations were limited to commercial agreements exclusively. Spain was never invited to join the Council of Europe, and indeed that agency had issued several reports highly critical of the Franco regime. Spain had labored long and hard to be accepted into the EEC, but as long as Franco was alive Spain was not considered "clubbable."[43]

Portugal's path to enter Europe was roughly parallel. Sentiment against Portugal on the part of the European Community was never so strong as it was for Spain, however, chiefly because of the Spanish Civil War, which held an enduring memory for many Europeans. Portugal was admitted to the United Nations earlier and, unlike Spain, became a member of NATO and was never treated as such an outcast. Portugal's economic entry into Europe began about the same time as Spain's, in the mid-1950s in correspondence with Portugal's first five-year economic plan; because of the closed and preferential markets provided by its colonies, though, Portugal's need to join Europe was not so great as Spain's. Portugal's integration into the European markets and economy increased quite dramatically in the 1960s and early 1970s; but, as with Spain and Franco, it required the overthrow of the old regime before Portugal was admitted as a full participant into European councils.[44]

Spain and Portugal had thus been kept from full membership in the European Community on largely political grounds; and their admission to the community was also achieved for preeminently political reasons. The politics governing these relations need to be set forth, since the public discussion and efforts of the various governments concerned to justify Spain's and Portugal's entry into the EEC focused on the economic reasons—trade, tourism, a common currency, expanded markets, complementarity of their economies, and the like. The tacit agenda of political motives includes the following:

• The belief of the German Social Democrats, the French left, British Labor, and Benelux and Scandinavian Socialists that the continuing "Fascist" regimes of Spain and Portugal were unacceptable in the European community of democratic and social democratic nations. Once the "Fascists" had been removed or had left the scene, then both political elites and domestic public opinion in these nations deemed Spain and Portugal acceptable and worthy of admission.[45]

• Much evidence shows that political leaders in France and Germany especially feared the potential for domestic upheaval in their own nations, which the Portuguese revolution seemed to inspire. A variety of European leftists was touting Portugal as a model of revolutionary change in a modern industrial society, as distinct from a third world one, and thus as an example to emulate. Fearing a repeat of the revolutionary events of 1968, or worse, the European leaders sought to moderate Portugal's revolution (and prevent one in Spain) by pushing for their entry into the EEC. Although the fear that France or Germany might explode as Portugal did seems ludicrous in retrospect, at the height of the Portuguese revolution in 1974–1975 the threat of upheaval elsewhere seemed real. At the least, it was feared the leftist opposition or the left wings of the ruling Social-Democratic parties could cause disruptions that these nations' leaders and party heads hoped to avoid.[46]

• Especially worrisome was the fear that in the wake of Franco and Salazar and Caetano, Spain and Portugal (and who knows about Italy, Greece, and Turkey—perhaps the entire southern flank of Europe) might "go Communist." Entry into the EEC and full entry into NATO were seen as heading off the possibility of the Mediterranean flowing red and the immense complications to which such would give rise. As Helmut Schmidt told his EEC colleagues, the admission of Spain and Portugal would both "bolster their democratic regimes and anchor them more firmly to the West." Again in hindsight and with greater knowledge of the Spanish and Portuguese systems, the fears prompting such comments seem preposterous; but in 1975 there was much talk of a "red Mediterranean" in the popular press, scholarly conferences, and government circles. Despite related fears of EEC growers that dropping the barriers against Greek and Iberian produce could hurt them badly, the second enlargement was necessary, said Common Market senior official Fernand Spaak, because it "supports democracy in the soft underbelly of Europe."[47]

• Spain's and Portugal's entry into the EEC and NATO, as a means of defusing the possibility for violent revolution and further turns to the left, were of course a major concern of U.S. foreign policy during this period, as well as that of the Europeans. There is evidence the United States both channeled funds into and exerted pressure on Spain and Portugal, through a number of European Socialist and Social Democratic parties and agencies. In a context (right after Chile and Vietnam) when the United States felt constrained from acting directly or more forcefully and where in any case it had limited levers to manipulate, the use of such European proxies proved advantageous.[48]

• The Europeans naturally had their own foreign policy interests to serve. For some 600 years Portugal has been considered something of a British dependency and its chief continental outpost, and the German foreign policy presence in recent years has also been stronger than before in both Spain and Portugal. The perceived crises in Iberia enabled the European countries, with the blessing and concurrence of the United States, to expand their influence in the peninsula.

• Major domestic political concerns in both Spain and Portugal were also served by dangling the prospect of EEC membership. In Spain that prospect seemed to strengthen the legitimacy of Juan Carlos and the monarchy, as well as the centrist government of Prime Minister Adolfo Suárez, during a time in the immediate post-Franco era when the transition was uncertain, breakdown or extremism seemed possible, and the existing government appeared to offer the best hope for stability and continuity. In Portugal the assurance of EEC membership was used to bolster the prospects of Mario Soares and the Socialist party, which at the time also seemed to the Europeans and the United States to offer the most solid guarantees against chaos on the one hand or a Communist takeover on the other. The possibility of EEC membership was thus used in both countries to affect domestic politics and to secure political outcomes favored by the United States and the EEC.[49]

All these plans required elaborate consultation among the EEC countries, with the United States, within the EEC bureaucracy, and with agencies such as trade unions and party organizations that served as conduits to move funds and assistance into Spain and Portugal. The groups in Iberia that were beneficiaries of the assistance, principally the government of Suárez and the party and then the government of Soares, also had to be involved in the planning. It took years to put the entire set of scenarios into full operation and for the consensus to reach the various bureaucracies affected. By the time the whole scheme was operational and all the tracks greased, however, the conditions in Iberia and southern Europe had changed dramatically from what they had been only a few years earlier. France's later (1980) "bombshell"—to postpone and review the applications of Spain and Portugal for EEC membership—was a realistic recognition of these changed conditions, although to Spain and Portugal it was shocking.

If the entry of Spain and Portugal into the EEC had been rationalized in the mid-1970s largely on political grounds, it would seem to follow that once those political conditions had changed, the perceived need to admit the Iberian nations into the community would also change. In fact, the situation in the 1980s, or the perception thereof, was quite different from that prevailing in 1974–1976 when the concerted campaign to have Spain and Portugal admitted to the EEC was launched in earnest.

By 1980 democracy and antifascism in Spain and Portugal seemed sufficiently well established that European involvement in the struggle no longer seemed so necessary. Nor was Portugal viewed any longer by European leftists as a model of revolutionary transformation in an advanced industrial society whose lessons could be applied threateningly and effectively in the other EEC nations. The possibility of a "red Mediterranean" no longer loomed large; the political crisis in southern Europe seemed to have stabilized. In the absence of such a perceived imminent disaster or threat of a Communist takeover, U.S. concerns were again concentrated elsewhere, while Iberia received less attention. Aid and foreign loans declined; and as Spain and Portugal dropped from the headlines, the rest of Europe also lost interest. Certainly, the crisis atmosphere prevailing in the mid-1970s no longer existed.

The domestic political situation in Spain and Portugal had also been transformed. In Spain elections had been held, the political system seemed to have stabilized, the Communists were isolated, and in the aftermath of the 1977 parliamentary elections Felipe González's Socialist Workers' party came to be looked upon not necessarily as a threat but as a viable and still moderate potential alternative to the government of Suárez. In Portugal the Communists were also isolated and no longer seemed to constitute a threat, the conservative character of the Portuguese electorate had reasserted itself, and, as center-right interests regained strength, Soares's Socialists were no longer seen as the only viable possibility. In the EEC nations in turn, the changed international circumstances and the changed conditions in Spain and Portugal made them pay closer attention now to their own domestic politics, most notably in France where farmers feared that their incomes would suffer as a result of the freer flow of cheaper Iberian agricultural products into their own markets.[50]

To argue that the turnabout in European attitudes toward Spain's and Portugal's entry into the EEC was quite rational, given the domestic and international *political circumstances* on which the decision for admission had originally been reached and the changes in these same conditions by 1980, should not, however, minimize the enormous

195

impact this switch had in Iberia. The French pronouncement (actually supported by Germany and some other EEC members, although the French were held chiefly responsible) came as a tremendous shock to Spain and Portugal. Here they had rid themselves of fascism, held democratic elections, established democratic institutions, and, they thought, satisfied all the other criteria for admission to "Europe"— only to be rejected again. What more could they do? All the old hostilities, prejudices, complexes, inferiorities, and bitterness welled to the surface once more.[51]

In part, of course, this was posturing on the part of Spain and Portugal, a way of seeking to reverse or modify the EEC decision and to mobilize pressure to put their entry into the community back on track. Spain had, in any case, been trying to follow a two-handed policy aimed at both securing entry to Europe *and* maintaining its Latin American ties, so some of its impassioned protestations should be taken with several grains of salt. These qualifications, however, should not blind us to the realities involved and the intense sentiments genuinely felt. Despite some residual ties to Africa and Latin America, Spain and Portugal had made a definitive decision to join Europe. There could be no turning back. In the preceding five years virtually all their economic decisions, trade, even domestic politics had been shaped by that commitment. It was now too late, from their perspectives, to reverse the process or pursue other alternatives. National development planning, foreign policy, and a vast web of international labor, party, business, and other connections had all been fashioned around the assumption of entry into the EEC. Now these hopes seemed dashed.

A vast outpouring of impassioned statements in the press and other media ensued, and in the councils of government anguish and a crisis atmosphere arose. The Spanish and Portuguese felt they had been betrayed, not just by France and the EEC (who received most of the public blame) but also by the United States, which, it was assumed, was the grand architect and ultimate guarantor of the plan. The debate was joined once again over whether Spain and Portugal were a part of Europe or apart from it, whether they were doomed forever to be considered different and unworthy of full participation in Europe, and whether their true destinies lay with Africa, Latin America, and the third world. The discussion was so emotional because it touched on all these historic raw nerves and because it affected the fundamental directions and destinies of the two nations.

To understand this debate and the impassioned cries to which it gave rise, we must recall the context in which they took place and the political symbols and maneuvering involved in the discussion itself. Spain's and Portugal's identities as European nations were still not entirely clear, either to themselves or to foreigners. Strong centripetal and centrifugal forces had long pulled Iberia into Europe and, conversely, pushed it away. Spain and Portugal were certainly different, but their differentness also took on political connotations. Franco, who proclaimed Spain to be "different," used that code word as a prop for his authoritarianism. But during the Franco dictatorship many democratic Spaniards hoped to be less different and more like the European nations. But to speak of Europe in Spain and Portugal had political symbolism as well, for that meant democracy. Joining Europe meant ridding themselves of their old regimes and establishing democratic institutions; Europe and democracy were intimately linked. But, in an intriguing shuffling and juxtaposition of symbols and reality, now that Spain and Portugal actually have democracy, their ardor for Europe, as well as for NATO for that matter, has considerably cooled. This is the emotional debate that French opposition to Iberia's EEC entry brought to a head.[52]

In the meantime, once some of the emotion had died away, more sober and realistic political strategies began to be pursued. Portugal's late Prime Minister Francisco Sá Carneiro traveled to Paris in the summer of 1980 to warn President Valéry Giscard d'Estaing that Portuguese democracy could be endangered by a delay in Common Market membership. It was an obvious effort to revive the political criteria and crisis atmosphere on which Portuguese membership had earlier been encouraged. He was told by the French of the difficulties involved: the fear of farmers that Iberian agricultural products would undermine their own markets and also the sense that the community should solve the problems of its first enlargement (chiefly Britain's demands for a substantial reduction in its EEC budgetary contributions) before it embarked on a second enlargement.

Sá Carneiro emerged from the meeting nevertheless with the reassurance that France favored integration. And domestically, he had turned EEC membership into an electoral promise in the fall 1980 parliamentary campaign, a fact that forced him to put as much pressure on the French as possible. In fact, all the major Portuguese parties were in favor of EEC membership, and both Sá Carneiro and Soares's Socialists had strongly emphasized their commitment to it. Nevertheless, Sá Carneiro did not return from France with any firm guarantee of full membership as scheduled for January 1, 1983, only the reassurance that membership negotiations had already begun and that they would continue in all community domains until the problems had been thoroughly thrashed out. Realistically, Portuguese officials admitted the 1983 deadline was no longer possible or even essential.[53]

After the initial hand wringing, Spain too reiterated its eagerness to join the EEC—and as soon as possible. Spain's interest in EEC membership was thus "total and overwhelming," said its special European Ministry Chef de Cabinet Carlos Westendorp (the creation of this ministry in 1978 was an indication of the importance Spain attaches to its European ties). Spain also reemphasized both its political and its economic ties to the community. "Spain belongs to Western Civilization, Europe, and the democratic system," said Westendorp; "that needs to be supported and consolidated."[54] But membership is also useful economically: Spain could look on Europe as its "natural commercial area." Half its trade was then with the EEC, and Spain looked forward to expanded access to European agricultural and industrial markets. It also sought greater access to European decision making from the inside and no longer from the outside, to freer movement throughout Europe for its surplus labor force, and to access to the EEC regional development fund, a little-used source of finances that Spain hoped to tap in the future. In 1980 Spain exported 65 percent of its agricultural products to the EEC, and 98 percent of the community's apricots come from Spain. For this and a host of other, noneconomic reasons already discussed, Spain had firmly cast its lot with Europe.

In joining the EEC, Spain, as a much bigger nation with far greater agricultural production, faced even greater difficulties than Portugal. In the summer of 1980 there were instances of French farmers burning Spanish trucks transporting cheaper agricultural products into European markets. For both Spain and Portugal the problem of making their heavily subsidized and protected industries competitive in the brisker European markets also bodes severe difficulties. The olive oil and other farm product surpluses to which Spain and Portugal will surely contribute will be a further strain on EEC budgets at a time of tightened finances. In addition, Spain will have to accommodate its foreign policy to a common EEC position, especially regarding Latin America, its special relationship with the Arab world, and its earlier nonrecognition of Israel. Such accommodations might not be so difficult since both Spain and the EEC seem to be gradually evolving toward some common ground.

Spain, like Portugal in its more realistic considerations, however, had accepted the fact that its entry into Europe would be delayed, for a year or longer. It had to deal first with the French and other opposition, the unwillingness of either a Gaullist or a Socialist government to antagonize the farm vote, and the need to restructure both the EEC's finances and its especially burdensome farm subsidies. Spain, however, hoped to settle the terms of its industry's incorporation into Europe fairly rapidly so that it could later proceed with the more difficult negotiations over agriculture once the EEC had straightened out its own internal problems in these areas. Spain hoped that such agreements could be reached quickly so that formal ratification could take place in 1984. Meanwhile, playing its trump, Spain said that its entry into NATO would be contingent upon its admission to the EEC. Finally, in June 1985 Spain and Portugal were formally admitted to the EEC.

Does Europe Still Stop at the Pyrenees?
Retrospect and Prospect

Spain and Portugal have unequivocally, definitively, and probably irreversibly committed themselves to Europe. Overcoming hundreds of years of prejudice and bias—racial, cultural, religious, political, and otherwise—of isolation and separateness, of complexes and inferiorities, the Iberian nations have become a part of Europe. One should not understate the difficulties and wrenching transitions this union involves, not just for the EEC but also for Spain and Portugal, with their strong sense of isolation and historic rejection and with their fierce pride in their own culture and institutions. It is not just commodity agreements that are involved in this transition or worries over apricots and olives but deeper psychological, moral, and cultural contrasts as well. Still, looking at the immense flow of European and American tourists into Iberia, the reverse flow of Spanish and Portuguese workers back into Europe, the impact of European and world culture on Spanish and Portuguese cities and even rural areas, and the long-term and growing incorporation of the Iberian economies into the broader European and world systems, it is difficult to think any longer that Europe stops at the Pyrenees or that the third world begins there.

In crises such as that occasioned by the French suggestion of a postponement of their EEC membership, the Iberian nations tend to fall back on the familiar defenses and to evoke the memory of earlier ties. For example, after Sá Carneiro's trip to France and on the eve of President Carter's 1980 stopover in Lisbon, Portugal emphasized its Atlantic ties with Brazil and the United States. Portugal's President Ramalho Eanes also emphasized the need to build bridges to the Marxist regimes and one-time colonies in Africa. Portuguese government officials noted that "Portugal's membership in the EC is for us not the only possibility of development" and that "the enlargement of the EC appears to be of more interest to Community members than those countries seeking membership." And during the Portuguese Revolution in 1974–1975, we have seen, there was much talk of third world solidarity. But such comments are rather more talk than substance and reflect more the politics of romance and nostalgia than the politics of reality. They are in keeping with that long tradition of defensiveness against repeated European rejections and of saving face by pretending publicly to have other options when in fact there are none.

Privately, the Portuguese know their fate lies with Europe. Their colonies are gone, Brazil has surpassed the former mother country, and the economic handwriting is on the wall. In any case the Portuguese prefer to see themselves as European. With roughly 10 percent of its labor force employed in France, Portugal must rely on other European countries to ameliorate its economic disadvantages. There are also strong emotional and cultural ties. France is thought to be the font of much culture, French is still the second language of most intellectuals and government leaders, *Le Monde* is considered essential reading (or at least for display on coffee tables) in Lisbon, many Portuguese political leaders (including Socialist head Mario Soares) spent long years of exile in France, and, as the famous *fado* (song) says, "Lisbon is a small Paris." The English and American ties are perhaps equally strong. Although Portugal may express such sentiments at times, the country cannot and has no wish really to secede from the West, and the economic bonds cemented in recent years make it impossible to do so even if the wish were strong.

As with Portugal, so with Spain. While negotiating with the EEC Spain also tried strenuously to resurrect its special relationship with Latin America. King Juan Carlos and Prime Minister Suárez made state visits to Latin America, and Spanish trade missions were also aggressive in pursuing contracts and increasing commerce in the area. These ties are to be built not on the older bases of *Hispanismo* implying Spanish paternalism and superiority toward its former colonies but on the basis of a "partnership" whose precise dimensions have never been fully articulated. In this way Spain has sought to have the best of both worlds by pursuing its European and its Latin American connections at the same time.

Recently, however, Spain has annoyed the EEC over precisely these ties. The EEC has said that Spain has failed to specify how its special relationship with Latin America will affect its relations with the European Community. The EEC insists that Spain, as a condition of its membership, define the nature of its relations with Latin America and also agree to accept the commitments made by the EEC with the southern Mediterranean nations and with the African, Caribbean, and Pacific countries that are signatories to the Lomé treaty. The Europeans are concerned that with all its special Latin American relationships Spain may try to bring in its EEC wake a string of "mini-Lomés." Spain, nevertheless, was determined to make relations with Latin America an important ingredient in its overall foreign policy even after it joined the EEC.[55] And in Spain's case there are perhaps stronger arguments, recognized by the EEC, for allowing it to maintain some special relations with Latin America than for Portugal which, with the loss of its colonies, no longer has such special ties.

While there are more advantages than disadvantages for Spain and Portugal in joining the EEC, the implications of their membership for Latin America may not be so happy. With Iberia in the EEC, many other third world nations protected by the Lomé convention, and Latin America's future relations with the EEC, through Spain or directly, still vague and uncertain, Latin America will be left as one of the few "unprotected" areas in the world. There is still some possibility that the world's most powerful economic bloc (the EEC) and the world's most dynamic developing region (Latin America) will work out new arrangements or, alternatively, that Spain's historic and recently expanding ties with Latin America will enable Spain to act as a bridge between the EEC and Latin America. But at this point it seems likely that the enlargement of the EEC will prove detrimental to Latin America, leading to the loss of the European market for many Latin American agricultural products, which will in considerable part be replaced by goods from Iberia. As yet, however, these facts have not quite hit home in Latin America nor their broader implications been fully explored (for example, Latin America's ability to diversify its trade and reduce its dependency may be diminished; Latin America may be further marginalized).[56]

For Spain and Portugal, however, it is clear that their futures lie, not with Africa or the third world and not even so much in Latin America, but in Europe and with Europe, however uncomfortable that may be at times and despite some sacrifice of the Iberian nations' sense of distinctiveness. Psychologically, culturally, politically, and sociologically Europe is where their strongest ties now are; and if these factors are not sufficient, then those all-important economic relations of interdependence must surely make the European bonds definitive.

The terms of the debate have changed, however. European integration is no longer the passionate love affair that it once was but more like a prearranged marriage of convenience. EEC membership, on balance, offers Spain and Portugal more pluses than minuses, and they have no other options for the future. The discussion is hence now more pragmatic than emotional. Iberia will be integrated further into Europe but out of sheer momentum rather than great enthusiasm. Current sentiments are summed up in the slogan, "Europe yes, but not at any price."

Spain and Portugal realistically recognized that the negotiations would be difficult and the transition long. French farmers raised opposition, there was the problem of overdue British payments, and domestic businessmen are still fearful of the effects of lowered tariff barriers on their long-privileged markets. Amid a worldwide economic and energy crisis, which revealed the frailty and fundamental lack of solidarity among the Common Market nations, the time seemed not very propitious for such serious, delicate, and long-term negotiations. The temptations are strong, in these economically troubled times, for the European nations to protect themselves by raising tariffs and building higher trade walls. But the Iberians have long recognized, as any tour of the countryside reveals, that in dangerous circumstances and when under attack, it is far better to face the storm from inside the walls than out. As Spaniards and Portuguese say only half in jest, "May it catch you duly confessed and pardoned."[57]

Notes

1. Stanley Hoffman, "Fragments Floating in the Here and Now: Is There a Europe, Was There a Past, and Will There Be a Future," *Daedalus* (Winter 1979).

2. These themes are discussed more fully in chapter 7 in this book.

3. Bruce M. Russett, *World Handbook of Political and Social Indicators* (New Haven, Conn.: Yale University Press, 1964).

4. Charles W. Anderson, *The Political Economy of Modern Spain* (Madison: University of Wisconsin Press, 1970); Eric N. Baklanoff, "The Political Economy of Portugal's Old Regime: Growth and Change Preceding the 1974 Revolution," *World Development*, vol. 7, no. 8-9 (1979), pp. 799–811; Baklanoff, *The Economic Transformation of Spain and Portugal* (New York: Praeger, 1978); William T. Salisbury and James D. Theberge, eds., *Spain in the 1970s: Economics, Social Structure, Foreign Policy* (New York: Praeger, 1976).

5. These arguments are especially well presented in Juan Linz, "Europe's Southern Frontier: Evolving Trends Toward What?" *Daedalus*, vol. 108 (Winter 1979), pp. 175–209.

6. James W. Cortada, ed., *Spain in the Twentieth Century World* (Westport, Conn.: Greenwood Press, 1980).

7. A fascinating comparative overview is Eric N. Baklanoff, ed., *Mediterranean Europe and the Common Market* (University, Ala.: University of Alabama Press, 1976).

8. On the important role of these geographical determinants, see Fernand Braudel, *The Mediterranean and the Mediterranean World in the Age of Philip II* (New York: Harper and Row, 1972); also, Sax Bradford, *Spain in the World* (Princeton, N.J.: Van Nostrand, 1962).

9. Andre Siegfried, *The Mediterranean* (New York: Duell, Sloan and Pearce, 1948), esp. chap. 6, "The Mediterranean Race"; see also Edward Banfield, *The Moral Bases of a Backward Society* (New York: Free Press, 1958); J. G. Peristiany, ed., *Honor and Shame: The Values of Mediterranean Society* (Chicago: University of Chicago Press, 1966); Julian Pitt-Rivers, *Mediterranean Countrymen: Essays in the Social Anthropology of the Mediterranean* (Paris: Mouton, 1963); and J. Davis, *People of the Mediterranean* (London: Routledge and Kegan Paul, 1976).

10. These themes have all been treated at greater length in other writings by the author: see "Toward a Framework for the Study of Political Change in the Iberic-Latin Tradition: The Corporative Model," *World Politics*, vol. 25 (January 1973), pp. 206–35; "The Ethnocentrism of the Social Sciences: Implications for Research and Policy," *Review of Politics*, vol. 42 (April 1981); "From Corporatism to Neo-Syndicalism: The State, Organized Labor, and the Industrial Relations Systems of Southern Europe," chap. 8 in this volume.

11. J. H. Elliot, *Imperial Spain, 1469–1716* (New York: Mentor Books, 1963); William C. Davis, *The Last Conquistadores* (Athens: University of Georgia Press, 1950); Salvador de Madariaga, *Spain: A Modern History* (New York: Praeger, 1958); Manuel Azaña, "Spain's Place in Europe," *World Review* (June 1934); Gonzalo Fernández de la Mora and Nuno Aguirre de Carcer, "The Foreign Policy of Spain," in Joseph E. Black and Kenneth W. Thompson, eds., *Foreign Policies in a World of Change* (New York: Harper and Row, 1963).

12. The arguments in this and subsequent paragraphs follow closely those of William T. Salisbury, "Western Europe," in Cortada, *Spain in the Twentieth Century World*.

13. Jorge Nadal Oller, *Fracaso de la Revolución Industrial in España, 1814–1913* (Barcelona: Ariel, 1979); based also on materials prepared by Edward Malefakis for a National Endowment for the Humanities seminar, "Comparative History of Southern Europe since 1815," Columbia University, 1977.

14. These themes are treated preliminarily in Wiarda, "Ethnocentrism"; "Toward a Distinct Political Sociology of Latin American Development" (Presentation made at the seminar "Future Directions in Comparative Politics," Center for International Affairs, Harvard University, November 19, 1980); and "Conceptualizing Third World Change: Toward a Non-ethnocentric Theory of Development" (Paper presented at the Annual Meeting of the American Political Science Association, New York, 1981).

15. Howard J. Wiarda, *Corporatism and Development: The Portuguese Experience* (Amherst: University of Massachusetts Press, 1977).

16. A close relationship with Spanish America was also seen as a way of stimulating Spain's regeneration; see Fredrick B. Pike, *Hispanismo, 1898–1936: Spanish Conservatives and Liberals and Their Relations with Spanish America* (Notre Dame, Ind.: University of Notre Dame Press, 1971).

17. Wiarda, "Spain and Portugal"; E. Pitta e Cunha, "Portugal and the European Community" (Paper presented at the Second International Meeting

of the Conference Group on Modern Portugal, University of New Hampshire, Durham, June 21–24, 1979); Ministerio de Comercio y Turismo, "España y la CEE," *Información Comercial Española,* no. 560 (April 1980); Jorge Braga da Macedo, "Portugal and Europe: The Channels of Structural Interdependence," in Lawrence Graham and Douglas Wheeler, eds., *In Search of Modern Portugal* (Madison: University of Wisconsin Press, 1983).

18. Salisbury, "Western Europe"; Linz, "Europe's Southern Frontier"; Baklanoff, *Economic Transformation.*

19. Salisbury, "Western Europe."

20. Banco Comercial Transatlántico, *Spain in Figures* (October 1977); *Información Comercial Española* (January–June 1978); Salisbury, "Western Europe"; World Bank, *Portugal: Current and Prospective Economic Trends* (Washington, D.C.: 1978).

21. See Wiarda, "Toward a Framework"; "Ethnocentrism"; and "From Corporatism to Neo-Syndicalism." A number of these and other writings on parallel themes are brought together in Wiarda, *Corporatism and National Development in Latin America* (Boulder, Colo.: Westview Press, 1981).

22. See the author's skeptical comments in chapter 7 of this volume; also "Toward a Distinct Political Sociology."

23. Lawrence Graham and Harry M. Makler, eds., *Contemporary Portugal: The Revolution and Its Antecedents* (Austin: University of Texas Press, 1979); Howard J. Wiarda, *Transcending Corporatism? The Portuguese Corporative System and the Revolution of 1974* (Columbia: Institute of International Studies, University of South Carolina, 1976). For Spain, there is by now an abundant literature; two accounts by Stanley Meisler in the *Atlantic Monthly* (May 1977), and *Foreign Affairs* (October 1977) offer useful overviews.

24. These points are elaborated in the author's *Corporatism and Development* and *Transcending Corporatism?*

25. For instance, Graham and Makler, eds., *Contemporary Portugal;* Howard J. Wiarda, "The Corporative Origins of the Iberian and Latin American Labor Relations Systems," *Studies in Comparative International Development,* vol. 13 (Spring 1978), pp. 3–37; and, more recently, a great variety of popular media accounts of the malaise and disenchantment with democracy widespread in both Spain and Portugal.

26. On these distinctions see especially Juan Linz, "An Authoritarian Regime: Spain," in E. Allardt and Y. Littunen, eds., *Cleavages, Ideologies, and Party Systems* (Helsinki: Westermarck Society, 1964), pp. 291–342.

27. Wiarda, "Corporative Origins," and *Corporatism and Development.*

28. Juan Linz, "From Falange to Movimiento-Organización: The Spanish Single Party and the Franco Regime," in Samuel P. Huntington and Clement H. Moore, eds., *Authoritarian Politics in Modern Society* (New York: Basic Books, 1970), pp. 128–203.

29. Anderson, *Policy-Making;* Wiarda, *Corporatism and Development.*

30. These themes are discussed in greater detail in Howard J. Wiarda, "The Corporatist Tradition and the Corporative System in Portugal: Structured, Evolving, Transcended, Persistent," in Graham and Makler, eds., *Contemporary Portugal,* chap. 6; "The Transition to Democracy in Portugal: Real or

Wishful?" (Paper presented at the Joint Seminar on Political Development, Harvard and MIT, Cambridge, Mass., December 8, 1976); also the works previously cited: "Spain and Portugal," "From Corporatism to Neo-Syndicalism," and *Transcending Corporatism?*

31. Baklanoff, *Mediterranean Europe;* Salisbury, "Western Europe," p. 115; and the references there cited.

32. For instance, John C. Campbell, "The Mediterranean Crisis," *Foreign Affairs,* vol. 53 (July 1975), pp. 605–24; Douglas Porch, *The Portuguese Armed Forces and the Revolution* (Stanford, Calif.: Hoover Institution, 1977); Michel Salomon, *Méditerranée rouge: un nouvel empire soviétique?* (Paris: Laffant, 1970); Michael Harsgor, *Portugal in Revolution* (Washington, D.C.: Center for Strategic and International Studies, Georgetown University, 1976).

33. "Latin America," in Cortada, ed., *Spain in the Twentieth Century World,* pp. 181–212.

34. Less so for Brazil and its relations with Portugal than for Spanish America and its relations with the former mother country. Independent Brazil remained a monarchy under the Braganzas until 1889, which helps explain its relative stability and progress in the nineteenth century in contrast to the Spanish colonies, and also the fact that it felt less hostility toward the former metropole.

35. But see Glen Dealy, "Prolegomena on the Spanish American Political Tradition," *Hispanic American Historical Review,* vol. 48 (February 1968), pp. 37–58.

36. For some explanations, see Howard J. Wiarda, ed., *Politics and Social Change in Latin America: The Distinct Tradition,* rev. ed. (Amherst: University of Massachusetts Press, 1982); and Claudio Véliz, *The Centralist Tradition in Latin America* (Princeton: Princeton University Press, 1980).

37. The political theory and sociology of the period are treated in Howard J. Wiarda, "Corporatist Theory and Ideology: A Latin American Development Paradigm," *Journal of Church and State,* vol. 20 (Winter 1978), pp. 29–56.

38. Charles W. Anderson, *Politics and Economic Change in Latin America* (Princeton, N.J.: Van Nostrand, 1967).

39. Fredrick B. Pike, "Corporatism and Latin American–United States Relations," in Pike and Thomas Stritch, eds., *The New Corporatism* (Notre Dame, Ind.: University of Notre Dame Press, 1974), pp. 132–70.

40. Pike, *Hispanismo.*

41. Howard J. Wiarda, "Continuities and Parallels in the Study of Iberia and Latin America" (Memorandum presented at the conference "España, América Latina y el Mundo Anglo-Saxón," Instituto de Cultura Hispánica, Madrid, April 4–6, 1974). The Spanish reaction may be followed in the popular press and magazines; see also Amando de Miguel, "España, País Latinoamericano," *Informaciones* (June 12, 1973), which responds to an earlier essay by the author.

42. "Latin America," in Cortada, ed., *Spain in the Twentieth Century World,* p. 208.

43. The history is well summarized in Salisbury, "Western Europe."

44. Baklanoff, "Political Economy of Portugal's Old Regime."

45. To join the nine also meant to have political regimes similar to theirs. So long as Franco and Salazar or Caetano were in power, the door to the EEC was always closed every time they knocked. Political problems were the main obstacles to membership for Spain and Portugal; once those were resolved by Franco's death and Caetano's ouster, Europe also opened the door to membership. See "Opinion on the Portuguese Application for Membership," *Bulletin of the European Communities* (Brussels: European Communities Commission, May 1978); and "Opinion on Spain's Application for Membership," *Bulletin of the European Communities* (November 1978).

46. For some public comments on these issues see Peter Jay, "Europe's Ostrich and America's Eagle," *The Economist* (March 8, 1980), pp. 19–29; and Beate Kohler, "Political Problems of the Southward Expansion," *Intereconomics* (January–February 1979), pp. 3–6.

47. Schmidt's comments are reported in *New York Times* (July 13, 1980); Spaak's in *Wall Street Journal* (October 23, 1980).

48. Tad Szulc, "Behind Portugal's Revolution," *Foreign Policy*, no. 21 (Winter 1975–1976), as well as the items cited in note 32. See also the papers at the conference "Spain and Portugal: The Politics of Economics and Defense," Institute for the Study of Conflict, London, May 29–31, 1975, especially those by Lawrence Martin, "Some Strategic Implications of Events in Iberia"; James Theberge, "Spain's Security in the Western Mediterranean"; Hugh Kay, "The Portuguese Revolution (1974–75)"; and James Holland, "Spain and Portugal in Western Defense." The author's contribution to the discussion was a paper entitled "Can We Learn to Live with a Socialist World? Foreign Policy Implications Stemming from the Portuguese Revolution and Other 'New Forces'." See also the summary of the conference proceedings by Neil Bruce, "Portugal and Spain: Transition Politics," *Conflict Studies* (May 1976).

49. Both Suárez and Soares sought in their election campaigns to use the prospect of EEC membership for maximum political advantage; the issue was heavily reported in the Spanish and Portuguese press during this period. Based also on interviewing with U.S., EEC, and Portuguese and Spanish government officials.

50. Georg Gallus, "Agricultural Problems of the Accession of Greece, Portugal, and Spain to the EC," *Intereconomics* (January–February 1979), pp. 6–10; George Irani, "The Second Enlargement of the European Community: Opportunities and Risks" (Paper presented at the twenty-first Annual Convention of the International Studies Association, Los Angeles, March 19–22, 1980); Irani and Gunnar P. Nielsson, "Greek, Spanish, and Portuguese Memberships of the European Communities: Prospects for States with 'Intermediate Economies'" (Paper presented at the Second Conference of Europeanists, Council of European Studies, Washington, D.C., October 23–25, 1980); Corrado Pirzio-Biroli, "The Community's Development Policy: The View from Inside" (Paper presented at the Second Meeting of the Council of European Studies, Washington, D.C., October 23–25, 1980).

51. See the discussion in the popular Portuguese and Spanish press during the summer and fall of 1980.

52. Perhaps the best, shortest, most informative piece on this whole com-

plex issue is the op-ed statement by *El Pais* editor José Antonio Martínez Soler, "As Spain Joins Europe," *New York Times* (May 21, 1980).

53. *Christian Science Monitor* (July 3, 1980), and (August 4, 1980).

54. Based on an interview in *Christian Science Monitor* (November 24, 1980).

55. *Latin America Weekly Report*, vol. 6 (November 28, 1980); and John Ravenhill, "How Secure a Future? The Lomé Convention and Regionalism in an Era of Complex Interdependence" (Paper presented at the Second Meeting of the Council of European Studies, Washington, D.C., October 23–25, 1980).

56. A much fuller analysis is contained in Georges Landau, "The European Communities and Latin America: The Effects of the Enlargement—A Preliminary Analysis" (Paper presented at the Latin America Program of the Woodrow Wilson International Center for Scholars, Smithsonian Institution, Washington, D.C., October 26, 1981), as well as the larger edited book, *The Impact of an Enlarged European Community on Latin America*, of which Landau's paper and the present chapter form a part. For another slant, see Howard J. Wiarda, "Iberia and Latin America: Reforging the Historical Linkages?" *International Affairs*, vol. 37 (Winter 1981–82).

57. The imagery derives from Martínez Soler, "As Spain Joins Europe."

7
Political Parties in Spain and Portugal

Spain and Portugal are geographically connected to Europe, but in more ways than one they are a long distance from Europe's centers. Lisbon is still four days of solid driving from Paris (if Paris can be considered the continental heart of Europe), and Madrid is three. Distance, however, is not measured just in driving time; in Spain and Portugal it has long been measured in social, cultural, economic, and political ways as well. Henry Kissinger was not the first person to admit that he did not really understand very well those "ungovernable" nations that lay over the Pyrenees (or Italy either).[1]

At least from the time of Charlemagne and Roland,[2] there has existed a certain European prejudice toward Iberia and a certain vague hostility and disdain. As we have seen in previous chapters, this historical prejudice has complex roots. At the same time, the distance and rejection that the people of Iberia feel has simultaneously bred in them a sense of separateness and inferiority as well as a contempt for a Europe to which they nonetheless aspire, because it refused to accept them as equals or to adequately appreciate their Iberian "distinctiveness."

During the long Franco and Salazar eras this sense of isolation, distance, and rejection continued—of course at least as much for the nature of these regimes as for any long-standing prejudices. Spain and Portugal were viewed as outcasts, even outlaws, a view that strengthened their own resolve to maintain their separate ways and that, ironically, enabled Franco and Salazar to rally nationalistic public support around them and thus perpetuate their anachronistic regimes.

But the authoritarian regimes of these two nations have by now been relegated to the past, either by revolution (in the case of Portugal since 1974) or a very rapid evolution (in the case of Spain since 1975). In their place have come the new institutional structures of "democracy," including democracy's various accoutrements: a gamut of political parties, a full-fledged party system, elections, and "party" government. This transition has been accompanied by a new opening toward Europe on the part of the Iberian nations, a sense that they are no longer outcasts but part of the Western democratic community, as well as a new acceptability and legitimacy for Spain and Portugal in European liberal and social democratic circles.[3]

In this chapter we assess the role and functions of political parties and the party systems of Spain and Portugal, focusing specifically on the transition from the authoritarian politics of the Franco and Salazar eras to the more open and democratic period of the present. The questions we will be focusing on are these: What was the nature of "party" politics under the Franco and Salazar regimes? To what degree was this "distinctive"? How well have the newer parties of the post-Franco and post-Salazar eras been institutionalized? What are the role and functions of elections in these systems? To what degree have party government, democracy, and representative rule now been established? Ultimately the questions to which we shall return again are, How accurate is the assessment that Spain and Portugal are now part of the Western democratic community, and to what degree do parties, party government, and systemic politics in Iberia still diverge from, or correspond to, the broader European model?

Parties and the Party System: Their Multifaceted Dimensions

The Spanish and Portuguese party systems, like the party systems of other nations, can be approached from a variety of perspectives. One can, for example, focus on the ideological spectrum and policy goals presented by the parties. One can concentrate on their organizational structure and the classic distinctions between cadre and mass parties. Their electoral bases may be studied to formulate certain theses about voting behavior. Or one may deal with the parliamentary party, as well as its extraparliamentary organization, in the making and unmaking of governments, the passing of legislation, parliamentary debates, and the like.[4]

All these approaches may be constructively used in the examination of the Spanish and Portuguese parties and party systems. But the suspicion remains that these may not necessarily be the only, or the most useful, approaches to studying Iberian parties and politics. The question is still open, in fact, as to whether parties and elections in Iberia stand for or mean the same thing as elsewhere in Europe, whether the "party phenomena" really describe adequately where political power lies and how it is manipulated, whether there are not other more important political arenas and centers of power and decision making to which the parties remain peripheral.[5]

In Spain and Portugal the fact that the parties that have recently burst forth still operate frequently at the periphery rather than at the center of national politics, and do not enjoy much respect or popularity, may in part be explained by the very short history of the parties, their submergence under protracted authoritarian rule, the long-time restrictions on their activities, the downright repression they often felt, and the absence of trained cadres, leaders, and the like. These factors help explain the lack of institutionalization and the relative weakness and fragility of the parties—and of democracy itself—in both Spain and Portugal.

Other explanations as well, however, provide us with a number of provocative approaches, in addition to those already mentioned, for understanding parties and the party systems of Iberia. These have to do with the relations of the parties to a state structure that has historically been far stronger and more important than the parties themselves; the nature of broad, nationwide systems of patron-client relations, which frequently render the parties of secondary importance; the tentative nature of elections in both Spain and Portugal and the fact that other legitimized routes to power (such as the skillfully executed coup d'état, the heroic guerrilla struggle, direct action in streets and factories) also remain open; the existence of other "parties," such as the church, the army, or the financial oligarchy, which may have more importance in domestic politics than do the parties themselves; and the pervasive presence of corporatist and functionalist influences and modes of representation based on a structure of group, regional, or sectoral privileges and rights, hierarchical and inegalitarian assumptions, and hence the denial of some of the fundamental assumptions of democratic rule, such as the principle of one man, one vote.[6] These areas merit our serious attention as much as do the more conventional approaches to parties and party systems.

Intraparty Politics and Factions and the Emergence of a Party System

The origins of the Spanish and Portuguese parties and party systems go back to the nineteenth century. Some would trace their origins even earlier, to the eighteenth century, and the emergence of the "two Spains" or the "two Portugals" phenomena. The one was Catholic, traditionalist, and inward looking; the other more secular, rationalist, "enlightened," and European looking. Although, as we shall see, this fundamental schism in the Spanish (and Portuguese) soul still importantly shapes Iberian politics, parties per se did not emerge until later. When they did, furthermore, they tended to be based on only semi-digested conceptions of British parliamentarism. Right from the beginning the Spanish and Portuguese parties were fundamentally different from their northern European counterparts.[7]

The nineteenth-century Spanish and Portuguese parties were almost exclusively cadre or elitist parties, and they remained so. The suffrage was extended to newer social groups exceedingly slowly and reluctantly. A bow was made to liberalism and republicanism, then in fashion, in the organization of "parties," but the functions performed were quite different. The parties remained the personal mechanisms of rival elite groups, families, and local notables and were almost totally devoid of ideological or programmatic pretensions. They served as the means by which the elites mobilized client support to gain power and to distribute patronage and spoils to the deserving once power was achieved. The "parties" also served as the mechanism for rival *caciques,* or political "bosses," to secure a clientele and to achieve power.[8] The crown served as the "moderating power," balancing, checking, sometimes leading the contending factions.

With social and economic change in Spain and Portugal, principally the gradual development of sizable middle-class and trade union groups toward the end of the nineteenth and the beginning of the twentieth centuries, new political associations began to emerge. These included, in Portugal, not just the liberal, democratic, and republican factions that helped usher in the ill-fated Republic of 1910–1926, but a variety of Catholic, Monarchist, Integralist, Corporatist, Nationalist, Fascist, and Socialist groups as well. In Spain many of the same or similar parties were present, along with the Falange, the Communists, the Anarcho-syndicalists, and various regional groups.

Although we cannot review here the entire history of parties and party politics in Spain and Portugal during this period, carrying us through the establishment of a republic in Spain as well as in Portugal, several features merit particular attention. First, the new parties were among the principal means to power for the emerging Spanish and Portuguese middle sectors and reflected the gradual transition, itself reflective of broad-scale socioeconomic changes, from aristocratic to middle-class dominance of the two nations' major institutions: army, government, universities, bureaucracy, and so forth. Even the Socialist, Communist, and Anarcho-syndicalist groups, while obviously reflecting rising working-class consciousness, tended to be dominated in their executive committees by aspiring middle-class politicians and intellectuals.[9]

Second, while reflecting a growing middle-class society, that middle class in both Spain and Portugal was severely divided internally. It had no consciousness as a class and tended to imitate upper-class ways, while also using an informal alliance with the rising worker elements to wrest control from the old oligarchic groups. Third, reflecting these deep divisions within the middle class, no one party could command a majority, and the ideological distances were so great between these contending factions that lasting coalitions were all but impossible as well. The party spectrum ranged from Communists, Anarcho-syndicalists, and Socialists on the left to Fascists, Monarchists, Falangists, and Integralists on the right—and all of them dominated by emerging, aspiring, ambitious, rival middle-class groups. With a weak or nonexistent center, equally divided, the situation was one of fragmentation and gradual polarization, leading to a condition in both countries of incipient civil war, complicated by rising class consciousness and aspirations (especially in Spain) for regional autonomy.[10]

The result, fourth, was a republican form in which parties and parliament seemed incapable of governing. For its frequent coups, cabinet shuffles, corruption, bombs, and sheer instability and seeming incompetence from 1910 to 1926, Portugal's Republic became the butt of the cruelest national character-based European jokes.[11] The Spanish Republic, 1931–1936, seemed almost equally incapable of concerted, effective government policy making and implementation. And, as the pendulum there swung ever more violently from left to right and back to a left popular front in 1936, with each party faction recruiting large private militias, the civil war seemed to loom inevitably.

It is certainly true that one of the primary characteristics of both the Salazar and the Franco regimes involved their efforts to harness and control this emerging pluralism and particularly to control and suppress if necessary the perceived looming threat (to the middle classes now uncertainly established in power) of organized labor. This posture, however, must be placed in perspective. For based on their experiences under both the elite-dominated systems of the nineteenth century and the chaotic republicanism of the twentieth, Franco and Salazar were not just hostile to the working-class parties but to *all* parties. Like George Washington and De Gaulle, they saw "party" as diminishing the unity, integrity, and grandeur of the nation. Franco and Salazar dissolved, absorbed, or stripped of power both the Socialist and Communist factions *and* the Integralist, Fascist, and Monarchist ones. In keeping with an older Spanish and Portuguese conception going back at least as far as the "golden era" of the sixteenth century, they sought to rule in an authoritative and technocratic fashion, *devoid of all party politics*. The model was that of an organic and corporate state system in which divisive political parties were to have no or little role. Rather than the one-party regimes, with which we are familiar from the literature and which leads sometimes to mistaken labels being applied, the Spanish and Portuguese systems were essentially no-party states dominated by a technocratic-bureaucratic structure, supported by a number of corporate elites (church, army, and landed and industrial wealth) and held together at the top by overpowering and immensely politically skilled *caudillos* (Franco and Salazar), who functioned in ways comparable to the monarchy in the nineteenth century, as the "moderating" or "directing" power.[12] In more than a few quarters, such a model remains a strong ideal in both Spain and Portugal today.

Of course both these regimes did have official appendages, which they called "parties," thus contributing further to our difficulties in categorizing them. But these "parties" did not carry out the functions usually thought of as appropriate for political parties. Only incidentally, almost as an afterthought, did they present candidates for elections, devise party programs, or exercise parliamentary functions. The chief purposes of these "parties" were otherwise. For one thing they served, in the historic fashion, as giant patronage agencies, helping to put both friends and enemies of the regime, as well as virtually the entire emerging middle class, on the public payroll. They served as agencies of charity and benefices, doling out bicycles and toys to children, rocking chairs and sometimes sewing machines to old women, and jobs to aspiring politicians and university graduates as well as compliant labor officials. The party machinery served as a convenient place to test out and bring along rising and politically ambitious persons, as well as to pension off older or out-of-favor ones.

The party was also a fund-raising mechanism and an agency for securing loyalty and service, as all government bureaucrats had to join and pay to it a portion of their salaries. The party hence served as an accommodator of various views as well as an agency to suppress some others. It was the eyes and ears of the regime in the countryside, designed both to tap public opinion (though not necessarily by means of elections) and to help publicize and administer government policies. The party served both to lock out some groups and to absorb others through its monopolization of political acitivity. It was thus more a giant bureaucratic apparatus of the regime than a party per se. It liked to be called a movement, a union, or a civic action association rather than a party. Hence, whereas in one way the Franco and Salazar regimes were one-party states, in another they were not. Even the official parties themselves were in fact antiparty.[13]

Because they absorbed a number of groups and parties that had existed under earlier regimes, the official parties of Franco and Salazar were never quite the monolithic organizations they are often pictured. Rather, the various factions, largely party based, existent within the party always had to be kept in balance. Moreover, as socioeconomic development continued inexorably in the postwar period and as Spain and Portugal became more complex nations and socially differentiated, the number of factions that had to be juggled and balanced in this way also grew. There emerged the leftist Falangists, whose ideology was hardly distinct from that of the Socialists or Anarcho-syndicalists, as well as rightist ones; Christian Democrats, Monarchists, and Social Democrats also found something of a home within the official apparatus.

By the 1950s and 1960s, these factions became critically important in determining the direction of the regime. By studying the makeup of new cabinets, government appointments, and rotations within the top leadership of the party itself, astute observers could determine which faction was rising or falling in power and hence what could be expected in public policies.[14] The Franco and Salazar regimes, in turn, used the party mechanism to raise, check, and balance off these contending factions. The official parties became the agencies to express and reflect, within limits, the growing societal and political pluralism of these two regimes. Moreover, within the official party differences had to be worked out between the rival factions in ways that were not entirely undemocratic. The situation was increasingly analogous to the old one-party American South, where distinct political factions fought it out in the primaries and within the single Democratic party apparatus and where the subsequent general elections served chiefly to ratify the choices already made.[15]

The emerging pluralism of the Franco and Salazar regimes, however, remained a limited pluralism.[16] Not all groups could be accommodated in the traditional cooptive way, particularly the more militant Socialists and Communists. In some instances these groups continued to be persecuted. But in others they too were allowed to function, in a certain grudging recognition of new realities. In Portugal the Socialist opposition was allowed to participate in a series of elections, although its campaign and organizational activities remained severely hamstrung. Socialist leader Mario Soares was allowed into the country on and off, most notably for the 1969 parliamentary elections, which were among the freest Portugal had ever had. During the period of Salazar's successor, Marcello Caetano, successive national "congresses of the democratic opposition" were also held, and even though opposition parties remained largely proscribed, opposition study groups that were in fact the nuclei of the later parties met regularly.[17]

The Communists also remained illegal, but in both countries they had built up a considerable underground apparatus, most notably in the workers' commissions organized parallel to the official syndicates. As the workers' commissions grew in strength, furthermore, the two governments, especially Spain in Franco's last years and Portugal under Caetano, became increasingly inclined to deal with them realistically. Though they remained illegal and, hence, though the government could not admit its dealings with them publicly, it became increasingly inclined to negotiate with the workers' commissions instead of its own official syndicates as the true representatives of labor. Although of course labor relations, like the opposition parties, went through various vicissitudes, this situation is still a considerable distance from a monolithic Fascist structure.[18]

By the 1960s, therefore, the bases for a future, more competitive network of parties and a broader party spectrum had already been laid. These included: the official party with its several major and many minor internal factions; the bureaucratic state apparatus with its divisions and contending elements; the Socialist, Communist, and social democratic opposition, now operating both below and in some areas above ground; and the various exile groups, centered in Paris, London, or, in the case of Portuguese Communist party leader Alvaro Cunhal, Prague. The exile groups tended to be small, personalistic, and highly factionalized, but they also later served as the nuclei for an even broader party spectrum once Franco and the Salazar and Caetano regimes had gone.

Toward the end of the period of authoritarian rule, the dynamics of politics in both Spain and Portugal, and a wrenching internal decision particularly for the opposition groups, revolved increasingly around whether to work within or outside the system. Both the Franco and the Caetano regimes were now sufficiently open for the opposition, on some levels, to function. Agreeing to this, however, involved considerable costs, for by its willingness to participate the opposition not only received certain advantages but also gave added legitimacy to the regime in power that the opposition had long fought. But continuing to work outside the system was also problematic. It enabled the opposition to maintain the purity of its doctrines, but the costs here meant being cut off from the new opportunities, in the new climate, for organization and proselytizing. Most opposition

215

groups opted for varying degrees of both. That is, they chose to try at one level to work within the system and gain certain advantages from it, while at another they sought to maintain their separate existences as "out" and "persecuted" groups. Generally, it can be said that prior to 1974 in Portugal and to a somewhat lesser degree in Spain before 1975, the more moderate democratic opposition tended to be increasingly incorporated and hence co-opted by the existing regimes, while the more radical opposition, principally the Communists, maintained their image of martyrdom. The Socialists, especially in Portugal, were a mixed case, popular at some levels for their heroic opposition but co-opted and compromised at others.[19]

Party Organization

The political parties and the party systems that have recently emerged in Spain and Portugal are fragile and only weakly institutionalized.[20] While many commentators have taken in the past few years to referring to the emerging Spanish and Portuguese "democracies," to a considerable degree, especially as it is based on the presence of parties and a party system, that evaluation represents more wishful thinking than an accurate description of reality. Indeed some other commentators would go so far as to say a party system as such, as the dominant or only means by which political power is mobilized and transferred, does not yet exist in either country.

The weakness, fragility, and lack of institutionalization of the parties and party systems have to do primarily with their short histories and the conditions under which, until recently, they have been obliged to operate. During the thirty-odd years of the Salazar and Franco dictatorships, the parties were illegal, exiled, forced underground, or so hamstrung in their activities that a free and independent existence was impossible. Alternatively, they and their leaders were coopted by the regimes in power, which provided about the only opportunities for employment or survival. The parties were never able to build an effective national organization or to develop grass-roots cadres. These organizational weaknesses continue to plague the parties today and make their continued existence precarious. We shall be considering these organizational problems under four major categories: the relations of the parties to the state, the parties and their parliamentary groups, the parties and their relations with extraparliamentary groups and clienteles, and internal party organization.

Historically, in Iberia it has been difficult for any party to survive, let alone prosper, without state support and assistance. Indeed it is precisely because of the critical importance of official access and favors given the party that dominates the state machinery that the competition for those positions has been so intense. Membership dues are usually insufficient to keep an "out" party alive, jobs and patronage flow usually only from control of the state machinery, and elections are at best tentative and irregular, and thus there is as yet no automatic or institutionalized rotation of the parties into office. Without access to the great public watering trough, the parties tend to atrophy and disappear.[21]

In Portugal the official apparatus of the Salazar-Caetano regime has been disbanded and most of its leading members ousted from official positions or exiled. The period of military rule that came with the revolution of 1974 meant for a time that no party, except the military, had access to the usual spoils and patronage. The formation of a Socialist government in 1976 provided that party with some limited special privileges and jobs, but there was no wholesale reshuffling of the bureaucracy under the Socialists, and they did not use their position in the government to reorganize as a new official party. The precarious nature of the Socialists' mandate was one cause of this; that the Socialists shared power with the armed forces was another. The relation of the parties to the state is hence still weak and uncertain with none of them able to enjoy the wholesale advantages that control of or special access to the state machinery over a long period usually implies.[22]

The situation in Spain is different. That is so both because the transition from the Franco regime was not so abrupt and revolutionary as in Portugal and because the military has not so far stepped overtly into power. Prime Minister Adolfo Suárez inherited most of the governmental machinery, including the largely moribund party machinery, from the old dictatorship. Though himself more a technocrat in the apolitical tradition, in the 1977 election Suárez moved to co-opt the center of the Spanish political spectrum by affiliating his name with, and in a sense taking over, the so-called Union of the Democratic Center (UDC), a hastily formed alliance of fifteen other centrist, moderately Catholic, and bureaucratic groups. In keeping with an older tradition, the Union is not really a party but a movement, alliance, or rally, and it remained of secondary importance in the power structure of the evolving new regime.[23]

The parties' relations with their parliamentary blocs are also weak and uncertain. That is so, especially in Spain, because the Parliament has yet to emerge as a major center of legitimized political authority within the broader system. Spain's is simply not a parliamentary government, and, even though it is uncertain where exactly power does lie in Spain—king, prime minister, armed forces, economic elites—it is certainly not in the Cortes. In Portugal, too, the Parliament had to share power with the armed forces under a pact that allowed elections to be held but reserved for the military a special position as the ultimate arbiters of national affairs. The internal politics of the military and the several armed forces factions are thus at least as important as the rivalries of the parliamentary blocs; in addition, the president, traditionally a military man, had the power to dismiss the prime minister. Within the parliamentary groups, moreover, especially the Socialists and the Popular Democrats, party discipline and organization have been weak, loyalties have frequently been fleeting, and there have been numerous instances of party splits, lack of discipline, and disaffection.

The relations of the parties with their extraparliamentary and clientelist groups are complex. Probably the strongest links have been forged, in both countries, between the Communist parties and the trade unions. This is a long-standing alliance going back a considerable period, even during the era of the dictatorships. In both countries the Socialists have moved recently and with some success to wrest control of the union structure, or at least some unions and some workers, from the Communists. It is likely, though we lack many monographic studies, that the same kinds of links have been fashioned, or at least various attempts made, by other parties with distinct clientelist groups. Each party, however, has sought also to establish a tie with like-thinking groups within the military. Suárez's UDC began to develop a network within the governmental bureaucracy; indeed that is where much of its electoral support in 1977 came from. And in Portugal, the rightist Social Democratic Center (CDS) began to build its support among the conservative, Catholic peasantry in the northern provinces of the country. But the overall impression is that all these links are still weak and tenuous, that the parties have been in existence too briefly for any strong or permanent ties to have been forged, and that the parties' relations with extraparliamentary and clientelist groups are still uncertain, shifting, uninstitutionalized, further retarding the strength and growth of the parties themselves.[24]

The internal structure of the parties presents a similar picture. It is generally conceded that in both countries, because of long, arduous, underground struggles against the dictatorships, the two Communist parties are tough, strong, disciplined, and well-organized. In Portugal some of that strength has been sapped because of the Communists' failures in 1975 and 1976, but in both countries the nuclear organization remains powerful. The rightist parties have been weak and fragmented, both because they represent the now discredited old regime and because in the past their other, more informal connections were such they had little need for a strong party organization or a mass following. They can be expected to begin formulating plans for a political comeback; in both Spain and Portugal, indeed, there are numerous signs that the right is reorganizing.

The two main parties in Portugal are the Socialists (PS) and the Social Democrats (PSD—formerly known as the Popular Democrats, or PPD). Neither is particularly well organized. Both are led by upper-middle-class elements, often more at home in the ideological debates and the social democratic salons of Western Europe than in the harder, "dirtier," nuts-and-bolts activities of party organization.[25] Both are deeply divided internally at the top, and neither has as yet developed the cadres and grass-roots organizations to weld a strong national organization—although, when the Socialists were in power in Portugal, there were some efforts to use the advantage of control of the state machinery to fashion a stronger organization and to lure the workers and peasants away from the Communists.

In Spain Felipe González's Socialist Workers party (PSOE) became a formidable opposition to the Suárez government; in 1982 it came to power. The party has been successful in wresting trade union support away from the Communists (as far as one can tell, the Socialist General Labor Union [UGT] has outdistanced the Workers Commissions [CCOO]; Socialist labor in Spain, unlike Portugal, is number one) and, with 35–45 percent of the vote, it has a sizable mass following. But its organization remains weak; it has lost some support by trying to be all things to all men; it has to some degree more a regional than a genuinely national base; and there are many who question whether without its attractive leader the party would enjoy the same popularity.

Former Prime Minister Suárez's UDC is not really a party at all but a loose collection of local or regional notables, establishmentarians, regime officials, bureaucrats, and others, from a variety of loosely knit centrist, Catholic, and moderately rightist groups. It is really a coalition movement or, as its name implies, a union of diverse interests and of the Spanish people, largely devoid of ideology, program, or strong organization. Indeed it was only after the apolitical prime minister determined to affiliate his name with the UDC and pull it together that it began to flourish and showed signs of becoming the largest party. That step, as the Madrid newspapers prominently played it, also marked the end of the UDC as an independent entity and led to considerable initial resentment on the part of some early UDC leaders.[26] But their resentments were lessened by the benefits immediately showered upon the party as the chosen agent of the once

219

popular prime minister. Although the UDC organization remains weak and though after the election it was consigned to the oblivion that often befalls official machines once their immediate usefulness has expired, a potential though now rusting organizational framework remains that could form a nucleus of a stronger partisan apparatus.

Parties and Their Programs

The emergence of a broad, modern, European-style party spectrum, with a range of left, center, and right parties, is of relatively recent origins in Spain and Portugal. The very newness of the parties and party spectrum contributes to the frequent ambiguity, lack of clarity, and shifting nature of the party ideologies and programs. So does the historical lack of importance afforded parties in the Iberian tradition, as well as the special relationships the parties must maintain vis-à-vis the armed forces or the state machinery. Nevertheless a party spectrum has emerged, and the party phenomenon has gained increasing importance.

Portugal. The party spectrum in Portugal ranges from the right to far left, with (until 1987) no single party able to command a majority, with opinion deeply divided, and with few discernible trends toward a stable, center, middle-of-the-road politics. These features of the new Portuguese party system were particularly evident in the governmental crisis of late 1977 when the ruling (but minority) Socialists suffered a vote of no confidence and the government fell, and hence the unhappy situation developed of a new Socialist-dominated coalition even weaker and more likely to be immobilized and stalemated than the one before. In the summer of 1978 these divisions and the stalemate became such that the government fell again, and this time Socialist Prime Minister Mario Soares was not asked to try to form a new government.

On the left the most prominent party is the Communist party (PCP) led by Alvaro Cunhal and a hard core of able, long-time leaders whose heroic exploits against the old dictatorship are frequently heralded in party propaganda by the combined years (over 300) that these leaders have spent in jail. The PCP is an old-time Moscow-oriented Communist party, which was the only one in Western Europe to applaud the Soviet Union's brutal stifling of liberalism in Czechoslovakia in 1968. The party has so far remained immune to the influences of more liberal Eurocommunism, although in the wake of its debacle in 1975 when the party failed to elbow its way into power and then in 1976 (and subsequently) when it did badly at the polls (16 percent or lower), there is now some evidence that Cunhal may have begun to moderate his position[27]

The PCP has problems on both its right and its left flanks. The Portuguese Socialists have chipped away at its once solid trade union structure. And on the left there are a variety of Maoist, Trotskyite, Fidelista, and Anarcho-syndicalist groups, strong particularly among young people, who argue that the party is old, tired, closed to new influences, bureaucratized, Stalinist, and so illiberal as to be unacceptable. A more accurate reading of the situation, however, is that, while the PCP has some problems, it has retained much of its strength and vigor particularly among the working classes and, in the current situation of societal division and continuing economic problems in Portugal, may well be strengthening its position. Despite the sniping of his numerous critics, whose analysis of the situation is often based on wishful thinking regarding the development of Eurocommunism in the PCP, it may be that Cunhal's harder-line position will prevail and remain the correct one for his party.[28]

Because of the special problems Portugal faces, the Socialist party has not been able to function as a real Socialist party, nor is there much prospect that it will. The Socialists came to power during a period when economic restraints, wage stabilization, and general belt-tightening had to be imposed, but these policies also had the effect of largely eroding its Socialist stance and program. Moreover, because it governed at the suffrance of the army in Portugal and during a period of widespread popular desire for a return to order, the Socialists were cast in a peculiar position. Their Socialist and reformist legitimacy was undermined by the conservative policies that they were forced to follow. For example, it was a Socialist government that began to roll back the agrarian reform, strip the trade unions of their independent bargaining power, return some nationalized properties to private hands, impose police controls on the universities, knuckle under to International Monetary Fund and U.S. embassy advice, and so on.[29] Moreover, there is much doubt as to just how Socialist Mario Soares and his fellow well-coiffed and manicured Socialists are. In the nineteenth century Portuguese liberals were often known as "cafe liberals" because they much preferred the comforts of intellectual discussion in Lisbon's elegant coffee houses to the difficulties of governing. The suspicion lingers that the Soares party consists of "cafe Socialists."

The PSD is similarly somewhat less than meets the eye. Led initially by parliamentary deputy Francisco Sá Carneiro and *Expresso* editor Francisco Pinto Balsemão (both later served as prime minister), the Social Democrats are not really a Social Democratic party but perhaps more the Portuguese equivalents of the liberal wing of the American Republican party (if such a dubious comparison can be made at all). That is, they are classic but conventional and rather bourgeois liberals who favor some reform but not too much. Similarly well-coiffed and manicured, the PSD wants above all else to get to power. It represents a portion of the bourgeoisie who had been excluded from enjoying the benefits and perquisites of governmental position during the Salazar-Caetano era and who desire to make up for these missed opportunities. With the increasingly conservative Portuguese electorate, their wish has now twice come true.

The more conservative CDS is, in effect, the Christian Democratic party of Portugal. It is Catholic (though nonconfessional) and oriented toward the protection of the family, order, stability—although it represents a fairly moderate and mainstream position on these issues, not the extremes. Like some others, it does not consider itself a party but a league or an alliance. Led by Diogo Freitas do Amaral, the CDS slowly gained in strength and for a brief time shared power in a coalition with the Socialists and again with the PSD. It has attracted many government bureaucrats, officials, and others associated with the former regime. Whereas in the immediate postrevolutionary period many of the old *Salazaristas* and *Caetanistas* called themselves Socialists because that was politically the thing to do, now they have begun abandoning the Socialists and joining the CDS, seeing perhaps a brighter future there.

There is still a Monarchist faction alive but not necessarily well in Portugal, and a certain hard core of real Fascists (as distinct from those associated with the old regime who were not Fascists but have been discredited by the use of that label). In addition, there are a number of prominent individuals who someday might attempt a political comeback basing their support on charisma, their name and stature, and a following rather than a party. These include General Antonio de Spínola, the monocled man on horseback whose book helped destroy the old regime and who still harbors ambitions to be the Portuguese De Gaulle; General Kaulza de Arriaga, once Spínola's rival and still with strong ambitions; Franco Nogueira, Caetano's rival, tough and ambitious; Adriano Moreira, a former Caetano protege with ambitions of his own; and perhaps General Ramalho Eanes, the former president, who may become tired of the incessant party bickering, abolish them all, rule directly, and perhaps launch a "movement" of his own.

Spain. In Spain the Communist party (PCE), in contrast to its Portuguese cousin, is most famous for its moderation, its Eurocommunism,[30] and its curious, sometimes mutually supportive relationship with the earlier center-right government of Adolfo Suárez ("if Santiago Carillo can bow and kiss the hands of the king," say Spanish wags, "perhaps the pope will be next"). The party's program is temperate and progressive, calling for the defense of democracy, Spain's withdrawal from NATO, and some (unspecified) nationalizations. Because it largely owes its above-ground existence and legality to a political decision made by the king and former prime minister, it concentrated its attacks on the far right and not the government. The PCE also has a history of long exile and underground activity directed against the Franco regime as well as a strong position within the trade unions. But, under the wily and genial Carillo, its position was moderate indeed. In part at least this has to do with the tactical strategy of the party, for unlike the situation in revolutionary Portugal the Spanish Communists never had a chance to come to power "by fiat," and thus they sought to put their most reasonable and democratic face forward. Then too, the Spanish Communists made a poor electoral showing in 1977 (9 percent of the vote), in contrast with the strong 29 percent polled by the PSOE. To outflank the Socialists and blur their image as the dominant party on the left, the PCE tried to corral the Socialists into a broad popular opposition front (in which the PCE would presumably have a stronger voice than its electoral strength showed it merited), while also working in alliance with the government on crucial parliamentary votes. To this end, Carillo took a curiously familiar "above politics" stance and called for a "government of concentration." This has all given the PCE an acceptability it lacked before, but many Spaniards are either aghast or bewildered at the party's position and some, who recall its hard-line past, not a little bemused. The party remains deeply divided.

With nearly a third of the popular vote, Felipe González's PSOE emerged as the principal opposition group in Spain, to the surprise of the government and even the Socialists themselves. For the 1977 elections the PSOE fashioned a moderate program that was hardly distinguishable from that of the government: a mixed economy, nationalization of "key" but unnamed industries, free unions, and entry into the Common Market. It accused the government of working with the right and the Francoists to defeat the left, and it has been the beneficiary of a widespread desire in Spain for change and a sense of discontent with the existing regime. Since it was the principal opposition, the U.S. embassy and, to a lesser degree, the Common Market Social Democrats have moved quickly to try to co-opt and capture the Spanish Socialists, as they had the Socialists of Portugal. That may not be so easy since the PSOE's basic program, as enunciated in its

223

December 1976 congress, is potentially quite radical, and the party is probably more militant than the Portuguese Socialists and with a stronger basis in the trade union movement. Nevertheless, support for the PSOE may not be all that firm. Felipe González proved a charismatic vote getter who garners considerable support from his personal attractiveness independent of the issues he stands for; and the PSOE, and to some degree the PCE, benefited from a fairly widespread protest vote against the remnants of Francoism, which may prove to be only temporary. After these reservations have been registered, however, the point remains that the PSOE garnered nearly 30 percent in the 1977 balloting and emerged as a major,[31] perhaps *the* major, force to reckon with in any future political consideration.*

So far as can be determined, the UDC, the former prime minister's adopted apparatus, has no clear-cut program of its own. It has sought to capture the broad center and moderate right of the Spanish political spectrum, and with 166 seats in the Cortes (to the PSOE's 118 in 1977) has largely succeeded in doing so. Its ideology, however, is largely the prime minister's ideology, and that means almost no ideology at all. It is pragmatic, vaguely Catholic, technocratic, centrist. As an alliance of some fifteen vaguely liberal, middle-of-the-road, and moderately conservative groups, it is an amalgam of largely middle-class bureaucrats and Social and Christian Democrats. It favors the drafting of a new and somewhat more democratic constitution, economic reform (undefined), a streamlined bureaucracy, free unions, expanded social security, limited regional autonomy, and closer relations with Europe. Seeking to avoid the historical polarizations, it advocates a "safe road to democracy." It favors Spain's gradual entry into NATO and the Common Market but would not be entirely averse to Spain's going it alone. It favors a gradual dismantling of the outdated control mechanisms of the old regime, but without that implying a breakdown of law and order. It recognizes the need to deal with Spain's pressing economic problems but would do so through a mixture of private and state capitalist structures, not socialism. In short, what there is of a "party" here supports the government and its program and is inseparable from them.

The right in Spain is, for now, discredited and without a popular

---

*In 1982 the PSOE won the national elections convincingly; in 1986 the Socialists repeated their earlier victory with an even higher percentage of the vote. Felipe González became prime minister and served effectively, as the other out-of-office parties went through the familiar process of splintering and division. But by 1987 González was himself in trouble with the electorate, his popularity plummeted, his party was torn by factionalism, and the portents of change were in the air.

base. The Popular Alliance (again an alliance rather than a party) of Manuel Fraga Iribarne (considered a liberal when he was in the Franco cabinet) polled only 8 percent of the popular vote (sixteen seats in the Cortes); other rightist groups hardly even bothered to campaign. The alliance advocated retaining "the best of Franco"; called for limited reforms, law and order, and the outlawing of the Communist party; and drew support from Spain's traditional corporate elements—big business, Opus Dei, old-time Francoists, Roman Catholic lay groups, and some sectors of the armed forces. But its poor showing in the 1977 elections should not be taken as the final measure of the right's influence. First, it recognizes that numbers of ballots are not the only measure of political influence in Spain, nor are elections the only route to power. Second, the right feels the early post-Franco euphoria will pass and that as the country settles down again the need for order and discipline will once more become apparent. Third, the right is betting that Suárez's UDC will eventually split up and that it will receive the support of many conservatives, moderates, and Catholics who now support him. Fourth, as indicated, the right remains strong within the army, the church, the economic oligarchy, and some key areas of the state machinery—all of whose strength is considerably greater than the individual votes of its members. The right feels that if the need arises or a crisis situation develops, it can call on the support of any of these key elite groups that can act above and beyond the electoral arena. Although one might wish otherwise, the right in Spain, particularly an updated, refashioned non-Francoist right that by now accepts democratic processes is by no means dead yet.[32]

In addition to these national organizations, Spain also has a number of regional parties with some representation (1977) in the parliament. The chief of these are the Catalan Democratic Pact (eleven seats) and the Basque Nationalist party (eight seats). The regional autonomy issue is of course a volatile one in Spain; contrary to what Karl Deutsch and others have said, national integration, in Spain and elsewhere, is not a necessary and inevitable consequence of modernization.[33] Sentiment in favor of regional autonomy remains very much alive, and especially in Catalonia and the Basque country it is intertwined with complex class and economic issues.[34]

Party Membership and Leadership

There have been few, if any, studies as yet of either Portuguese or Spanish party membership, and probably it is premature for such studies to be done. Although there was remarkable continuity in

225

voting patterns between the 1975 and 1976 elections in Portugal, party membership in both countries nevertheless remains highly unstable and shifting. The tendency to shift party allegiance is still strong, and most Portuguese and Spaniards are not yet inclined to join any party definitively. This helps explain why party membership for all the parties in both countries remains small, although the voting turnout was remarkably heavy. Prudently, most Portuguese and Spanish voters are still waiting to see which way the political winds blow before committing themselves. One is inclined to accept Philip Converse's hypothesis that perhaps several generations of competitive elections and party development are required before fixed party allegiances emerge—whatever the social bases of the cleavages that do eventually develop.[35]

But if the membership remains shifting and the claims of the parties themselves suspect, so much so in both cases that the figures are all but totally worthless, it is nevertheless possible to distinguish between "hard" and "soft" voting patterns. The few opinion surveys and election analyses that have been done in the two countries show the vote for the Communist party to be the "hardest," firmest, and probably most permanent of all the major parties. In Portugal the vote for the PS and in Spain for the PSOE was considerably "softer," although in both cases there was an identifiable "hard core" of party loyalists. These studies and surveys seem to indicate the vote for the Socialist position may be less firm than that for the Communist and hence more fluid, shifting, and susceptible to major changes. The vote for the conservative and Catholic parties seems to occupy an intermediary position between these other two, while the vote for the center parties (Suárez's UDC and Portugal's PSD) seems to be the "softest" of all.[36] What this implies about the possibilities for instability in the middle and the potential for major shifts on the part of the electorate cannot at this time be finally ascertained. This plus other evidence to be presented later, however, provides little optimism for the growth of a stable, happy, bourgeois, middle-of-the-road polity in either Spain or Portugal.

The information on party leadership is much more complete than is that on party membership. Although some few bows have been made by the left parties to the principle of direct worker representation in their executive committees, in fact *all* the party leaderships are dominated by middle-class or middle-sector representatives. Not only are few workers represented but the old oligarchic elites have been largely bypassed as well, even in the conservative parties. This marks a significant class shift in both Spain and Portugal from the aristocratic era preceding the 1930s and is a major indicator of the social changes that occurred inexorably under Franco and Salazar and Caetano regardless of the generally conservative and authoritarian nature of these two regimes. From this point on politics in Spain and Portugal, at least as defined by the social makeup of the various parties' executive committees (and probably also as defined in other important institutions such as the military officer corps and the public service) is essentially middle-class politics. The dynamics of political struggle no longer involve elite versus bourgeoisie but rival factions within the middle classes themselves, obviously taking quite disparate ideological positions and each looking toward the lower classes for electoral mass support.[37]

Voting Strength and Bases of Cleavage

If the data on party membership are often incomplete and misleading, a useful means for determining the class bases of the polity and the sources of other societal cleavages is provided by the voting itself. The data are incomplete, but they nonetheless indicate certain important electoral phenomena characteristic of both countries (see table 7-1). Among the most important of these are the high turnouts and participation, the strong class and regional basis of the balloting, the weakness and isolation of the extreme left and the extreme right, and the relative strength of the center in these early electoral contests, apparently reflecting a desire on the part of the Spanish and Portuguese electorates to avoid the polarization that had previously torn their countries apart.

In both countries the electoral turnout was over 80 percent (90 percent in Portugal in 1975). Although some of the high turnout undoubtedly had to do with the practice of compulsory voting begun under the old dictatorships, the chief factor was simply the desire of the people, after so many years of silence, to express themselves and their opinions at the polls. Election day was a major national holiday, and the campaign itself a long festival of joy, high hopes, and celebration culminating in the vote. For Portugal it was the "first free election in fifty years" (actually the first free election ever),[38] whereas for Spain it was the first free election in forty years. Both countries experienced a sudden and rapid escalation in participation, what Samuel P. Huntington calls a "burst of explosive energy" when civil freedoms are restored after a long period of repression. The longer-range implications of such a sudden burst of popular participation and high expectations provide some interesting hypotheses for comparative study. Huntington speculates that such sudden expansion typically leads to a conservative reaction and renewed efforts by rightist groups to again

TABLE 7–1

SPAIN AND PORTUGAL: VOTING PERCENTAGES, BY PARTY; 1975, 1976, AND 1977

Spain: 1977	
Union of the Democratic Center	34
Socialist Workers party	28
Communist party	9
Popular Alliance	8
Others (Christian Democrats, regional parties, independent socialists, etc.)	20
Portugal: 1975 Constituent Assembly elections	
Socialists	38
Social Democratic party	26
Communist party	12
Center Social Democrats	8
Others (chiefly extreme left or null and blank ballots)	16
Portugal: 1976 elections for the National Assembly[a]	
Socialists	35
Social Democratic party	24
Center Social Democrats	16
Communist party	16
Others	9

a. The most striking changes from 1975 to 1976 are that the Socialists and Social Democrats lost somewhat, the Communists gained (in large part because other extreme left parties chose not to participate), the number of blank ballots and votes for "others" declined significantly, and the CDS doubled in strength (reflecting both a growing conservatism in Portugal and the influx of many embittered "returnees" from Angola and Mozambique).
SOURCE: Author.

reduce political participation and restore a more narrowly based political order.[39] It also generally leads to widespread disillusionment when the hopes generated produce few measurable benefits.

The strongly class and regional basis of the voting is apparent in both countries (see table 7-2). Both demonstrated a comparatively high articulation of class interest, and in both countries the class and regional bases of the parties overlapped. In Portugal the PCP won strongly among rural wage earners in the large estate-dominated provinces of the Alentejo (the southern so-called "red belt") and in the industrial concentrations of the center region, Lisbon, Setúbal, and so on. The more conservative parties—the PSD and CDS—were more attractive to rural smallholders of the northern regions, to Catholics, and to the urban bourgeoisie, both north and south. The PS attracted urban and working class voters in the north who were conservative and comparatively well off, medium-sized farmers in the south, and intellectuals and progressive middle-class elements from the urban areas of Lisbon. The PS attracted probably the widest spectrum of voters; it showed that it could attract moderate, centrist, and middle-class votes as well as working class votes from all areas of the country.[40] A more detailed analysis and breakdown of these voting patterns, crucial for understanding Portuguese politics, is contained in chapter 10.

In Spain in 1977 the patterns were not altogether unlike those in Portugal. First there was a definite regional split, although not so clear-cut as in Portugal, between the more conservative, rural, and agricultural provinces of the south and west and the more urban and industrial concentrations of the north and northeast. The UDC, Prime Minister Suárez's electoral alliance, did well in the more rural, conservative, and Catholic regions and among the urban bourgeoisie and government workers (often synonymous). The left did well in the urban, industrial, and more cosmopolitan centers, sweeping such cities as Barcelona, Valencia, Madrid, Sevilla, and the Basque provinces. A significant correlate of the last was the relative decline of the Basque nationalist party and a sharp move toward the left in these provinces. One conclusion that might be drawn from the vote here is that, while the Basque region seems to be becoming more radicalized by the growing industrialization of its work force, it may be becoming somewhat less inclined toward Basque separatism.[41]

The votes show, in addition, the weaknesses of the extreme left and right in both countries, and the corresponding—and new—strength of the center. Of course, it depends on how one counts. In both countries the combined vote for the left (including Socialist,

TABLE 7–2

DISTRIBUTION OF VOTES BY REGION AND SIZE OF PLACE: PORTUGAL,1975
(percent)

	Socialists	Social Democrats	Communists	Center Democrats
Rural North	29.9	38.6	3.8	1.2
Urban North	41.7	27.4	7.1	9.5
Rural South	41.8	8.5	28.2	2.3
Urban South	45.1	12.4	22.7	4.3

SOURCE: John L. Hammond, "Das Uruas urnas: Electoral Behavior and Non-institutional Militancy Portugal. 1975" (Paper presented at the conference "Crisis in Portugal," Toronto, April 15–17, 1976).

Communist, and some small independent and fringe groups) was over fifty percent. But looked at another way, and given the relative conservativeness and "acceptability" of the Socialists in both countries, as well as the sharp differences between them and the Communists, another and perhaps more valid interpretation is possible. The Communists in Spain polled only 9 percent of the vote and won twenty seats in the Cortes; in Portugal they won only 12–16 percent, and recent indications are that their support has since slipped even further. Indeed, in Portugal the Communists actively campaigned to force a cancellation of the election, not wishing to have their weak electoral strength clearly demonstrated by the votes.

The Portuguese right was discredited and prohibited from participating in the election, whereas in Spain Fraga's Popular Alliance polled only 8 percent of the vote and garnered only seventeen seats in the Cortes. Thus in Spain, if we are correct in assuming that the PSOE is not outside the mainstream and is in fact rather moderate, then the combined moderate or center vote (PSOE and UDC, plus some small parties) runs upward of 80 percent of the electorate. And in Portugal, if the Socialists, liberal-democratic PSD, and Catholic-moderate CDS may similarly be considered all middle-of-the-road and moderate, then the center vote there also surpasses 80 percent. Although the case must not be overstated and one should not underplay the divisions between these parties, as well as the obvious class differences that continue to exist, it could easily be that the lack of support for either extreme and the seeming strength of the center has to do with the increasing *embourgeoisement* of both Spain and Portugal, their increased prosperity, literacy, and overall modernization and the growth in both of a strong middle class since the 1920s and 1930s, when extremes of wealth and the absence of a strong middle class tore both countries apart.[42]

The Electoral System and the Other "Parties"

Although Spain and Portugal have both witnessed the emergence of new political parties and had democratic elections that can and should be celebrated, we should not forget that there are other "parties" in the system and that elections are not viewed as the only means to power. Indeed the case could be made that the parties and elections are sometimes peripheral to the main centers of power and influence in these two systems. The elections thus served as useful opinion polls to gauge the relative strength of the various factions, but real power continued to lie elsewhere, little changed as a result of the elections, and the main arenas of politics had little to do with the votes and
230

parties per se. Let us see what these other arenas, power centers, and "parties" are.

The Electoral System and the Efforts to Circumvent, Regulate, and Control the Election Results. The Spanish electoral system was fashioned in, and was an integral part of, the struggles involving the post-Franco decompression.[43] The principal actors included the king, Juan Carlos; the army; the new generation "liberals" who supported the king; and the old Franco state apparatus, headed by the generalissimo's hand-picked prime minister, Carlos Arías Navarro.

Arías Navarro was willing to hold parliamentary elections, but he insisted that the entire process be tightly controlled and regulated to preserve the continuity of the Franco regime. He proposed a bicameral legislature with the lower house popularly elected by universal suffrage, but the PCE (Spanish Communist party) would be excluded from participating and regime loyalists would be the chief candidates. The upper house was to be appointed from among the traditional corporate interests: the army, the church, central and provisional government authorities, government labor unions, and business associations. In addition, the upper house could veto any action by the lower house, and all legislation would require approval by the prime minister's cabinet.

Moderates and the left claimed the election and a Cortes would be meaningless, however, if they were not democratically based and open to all political groups including the PCE. The king and his supporters concurred, and, in a series of intricate and politically deft steps that followed in 1976, he moved to legalize the PCE, get rid of Arías, diminish the strength of the Francoists (the so-called "bunker"), increase his own standing and popularity, retain the control and support of the army, appoint his own prime minister (Suárez), and promulgate a new electoral law. The Juan Carlos-Suárez Political Reform Act called for a two-house Cortes consisting of a Chamber of Deputies of 350 members elected by universal suffrage, with its membership proportionate to the population of Spain's various provinces and with each province guaranteed a minimum number of seats. The Senate would have 244 members, 204 popularly elected and 40 appointed by the king, and each province would have equal representation. The Senate could still veto legislation of the lower house, and the king was to select the prime minister. Juan Carlos and Suárez then moved to gain the approval of the old Cortes for their plan, which would give it democratic legitimacy but require Cortes members to vote for a proposal that put their own positions at severe risk. Passage was ensured both by subtle threats and by the promise of at least 150 sinecures to those who voted for the measure and then subsequently might themselves be ousted in the balloting. The PCE was also legalized.

Election day brought some surprises, chiefly the low support for the government coalition, the UDC, especially considering *all* (from its own point of view) it had done for "democracy" in Spain. Even though the Political Reform Act ensured a moderate outcome by favoring rural and conservative provinces at the expense of populous and heavily industrial ones (the fifteen smallest provinces with 3.4 million population had fifty-three seats in the Cortes, while the largest province, Catalonia, with 4.5 million population, had only thirty-three seats), the UDC still did not gain its expected parliamentary majority. It won only 34 percent of the popular vote but, because of the electoral system, garnered 47 percent of the parliamentary seats: 166 of 370 in the Chamber and 107 of 204 in the Senate. The results were apparently so disappointing to Juan Carlos and Suárez that they were thereafter despondent and immobilized, slowing considerably the process of Spanish liberalization and reform policy implementation. As another indicator of how the election results have been read, the American embassy began putting some distance between itself and the government while establishing new links with, and thus giving added legitimacy to, Felipe González and the PSOE.

In Portugal of course the situation was different. There was no king or prime minister to provide continuity. Rather, the Salazar-Caetano regime had been destroyed by military *coup d'état*, the so-called "revolution of flowers." The revolution had been led by the Armed Forces Movement (MFA), and, although elections had been promised by the revolution's leaders, the MFA grew increasingly reluctant to hold them on schedule. As discussed in chapter 4, by this time the MFA had created its own set of military *cum* political agencies to bypass the civilian political parties: it felt that it had a better grasp of the public's wishes (that it intuitively knew and even personified the "general will"—again that Rousseauian notion of democracy, which has often been so dangerous and threatening to the real thing) and therefore that its rule should be perpetuated. It continued to throw roadblocks in the way of genuinely democratic elections, invoked the traditional military rights to protect its privileged position, and forced the parties to agree to an accord that limited the importance of the democratic vote and gave the military power to change or annul the results of the electoral process.[44]

Even after the elections were held (with the PS getting 38 percent, the PSD 26 percent, the CDS 8 percent, and the PCP 12.5 percent), the MFA, particularly leftist Prime Minister Vasco Gonçalves and the PCP, continued to disparage their importance. The Constituent Assembly met under a cloud and continuously faced the threat it would be disbanded. The streets remained at least as important a political arena as the ballot box. Only after the turnaround of November 1975, when Gonçalves was forced out and the PCP deprived of some of its special access, did the civilian parties and electioneering (new elections for the parliament were scheduled for 1976) begin to emerge as preeminent. But even with the establishment of a civilian, parliamentary system and the eventual formation of a Socialist government, the president remained a military man and the armed forces continued as the ultimate arbiters of national affairs.

Other "Parties" within the System. In both countries, thus, the party arena, on this and other issues, was not the primary focus, and there were clearly other and often more important "parties" operating in the system.[45] In Spain this meant such nonelected and nondemocratic elements as the king, the armed forces, the bureaucracy, the church, the Francoist element, and the economic elites. In Portugal the principal nonparty "party" was the MFA, but there are other groups and individuals, as we have seen, that must be taken into account.

In Spain also the principal political arenas were not necessarily party related. These included the king and his efforts to build his own popularity, the king's relations with the armed forces, the internal politics of the military institution, the trade union struggle, the changeover in the prime minister's offices, the relations of the government to the Cortes, and so on. In Portugal the principal arenas were also the internal politics of the armed forces and the MFA, the relations of the premier to the Communist party, the struggle for control in streets, factories, and government agencies. All these either took precedence over, or were just as important as, the parties.

Elections are similarly problematic. They are significant to be sure, but one should not read too many implications into them. They tend to be tentative rather than definitive.[46] The elections in Portugal were, in effect, a referendum on the revolution and the MFA; in Spain on the king, the prime minister, and their performance. They were an indication of the current balance of political forces. In Portugal, at least initially, they did not offer a full range of choices (the right groups were excluded, as were prominent personalities like Spínola), and their importance had previously been downgraded by the military. The elections in Spain provided a set of signals, like an opinion poll, which did not convey definitive legitimacy to any groups or party. At best they provided a tentative mandate for Suárez. Hence the elections in both countries may be seen as part of an ongoing political process that afforded new opportunities for some groups and a new

233

defensiveness for others. Other routes to power remained open and were being actively explored by a variety of forces, which again implies that arenas other than the party one must also command our attention. Only gradually have elections begun to enjoy the definitive legitimacy that is the hallmark of a democratic polity.

The Role of Parties within the Spanish and Portuguese Systems

Political parties, a party system, and party government are comparatively new phenomena for Spain and Portugal. Indeed with the exception of the chaotic and short-lived republics of two generations ago, neither country has ever had a functioning party system. In fact, some would go so far as to say that the parties and party systems in Spain and Portugal have been—and remain—mere concessions to foreign fads, or else that they are the contrived and rather synthetic creations for satisfying the a priori conditions for U.S. aid and entry into NATO and the Common Market. They serve—expediently, some argue—to show that the Iberian nations are as "modern" and as "democratic" as the rest of Europe, when in fact a little scratching of the surface reveals the parties to be ephemeral and not central to the functioning of the political system. As the novelist and reporter José Yglesias has written, "In Spain there has been a tendency to think of politics much more as aesthetics than as an attempt at the practical manipulation of reality in a positive determined sense. There has been no effort to fit political formulations to the exigencies of reality in its rambling process of change, but to adapt that reality to an a priori scheme of ideas totally conceived outside its conditions."[47]

The findings in this paper lend support to these contentions, *in part*. With few exceptions, the parties and party systems in both countries are exceedingly weak. To some extent they do seem to represent rather artificial creations, derived from a priori, often foreign criteria. They are not well organized, their leadership is thin, funds are scarce, membership is small, party identification is "soft," loyalties are fleeting, the parties are splintered and fragmented, and party government has not as yet been strongly or irrevocably established. At the same time, the real focuses of power in both countries often lie outside the party arena, with the army, the bureaucracy, the state machinery, the king (in Spain), the president (in Portugal) who is also an army general, powerful economic groups, and other corporate and institutional interests. Elections, similarly, provide one route to power, but other means are also available.

And yet parties and a party system have emerged, and a system of "party government" is evolving. One cannot discount the impressive turnouts at the polls, the "explosion of participation" (to use Huntington's phrase), the new climate of liberty and freedom, and the obvious, often spontaneous joy and outpouring in favor of democratic rule. The parties have been established, and party government and the results of the ballot box have gained new-found legitimacy. That legitimacy is now sufficiently strong and democracy sufficiently well established that no military or civil-military faction, employing some other route to power, could afford to ignore entirely or ride roughshod over these newer expressions of democratic legitimacy.

The result, in both Spain and Portugal, is a dual system of political power and authority. On the one hand, there are the parties and the institutional paraphernalia that go with them: Cortes, elections, campaigns, public opinion, parliamentary maneuvering, and so on. On the other, now submerged under the paraphernalia of "democracy," there is the army, the state structure, and a variety of powerful vested and corporate interests. The political system rests on a complex set of relationships and often an uneasy balance between these two sets of institutional pillars. Hence the old question of the "two Spains" or the "two Portugals," remains: the one largely urban, rationalist, parliamentary democratic, and European looking; the other rural, Catholic, traditionalist, and more inward looking. This fissure in the Spanish and Portuguese soul and society dates back at least to the eighteenth century and is still very much alive. It is changing (in favor of democracy) but still present. What is interesting is to study not only the internal dynamics of each of these clusters of interests but also the involved interactions and potential for conflict between them.[48] Still open to much further analysis is the issue of whether Spain's and Portugal's new affluence, their younger generations, and their rising *embourgeoisement* may have transcended these historic differences. Or, alternatively, will the economic crunch and political crises that both countries are experiencing (Portugal far more so than Spain) bring on a new fragmentation and polarization producing stalemate, conflict, breakdown, and the renewed and familiar turning toward an authoritarian solution?

The signals are mixed, but there are abundant reasons to worry about democracy's future. The social gaps and problems in both countries remain large and seemingly intractable. The Spanish economy is in trouble and the Portuguese in even worse shape. Politically, Portugal has gone through an inconclusive revolution, which has bred increasing governmental paralysis, immobility, fragmentation, and, eventually, a return to more authoritarian methods and a form of military-civilian, "non-partisan," technocratic rule. The "revolution of flowers" has wilted, living standards are declining, the national mood is foul, and there is much weariness of politics. In Spain there is also considerable disillusion that "democracy" has not brought brighter prospects, violence is increasing, and the nation seems adrift. In both countries it has proved far easier to dismantle the structures of the old regimes than to build viable democratic ones to replace them. In both countries there is much malaise and sense of misplaced hopes, if not despair. The political parties in both countries report a sharp drop in enthusiasm, and in both the parties themselves have been increasingly shunted aside in favor of more traditional, "statist" methods of rule. The party-electoral arena may no longer be as important as other arenas, but whether that is the result of a certain lack of interest in parties and platforms in the interregnum between elections or of a deeper and longer-term process of party atrophy it is impossible at this time to say.

The question therefore remains as to just how democratic Portugal and Spain really are—or if the Portuguese and the Spaniards mean the same thing by this term as persons in the United States do. The polls and elections point toward democracy as Iberia's preference, but they also indicate a desire for strong government and authoritative (if not authoritarian) decision making. Many institutions are quite conservative, traditionalist, and non- or ademocratic; and there is considerable doubt as to just how much or how definitively political parties, elections, and democracy have become *the* routes to power. Patronage, familial and clientelistic politics, the statist (technocratic and nonpolitical, in the sense of being nonparty and even antiparty) elements, the military, and the economic elites all represent alternatives to democracy and are by no means subordinate to it or fully under its control.

Democratic institutions, however, are alive and well and have been considerably strengthened since the mid-1970s. They have survived so far, they are being consolidated, and they may hence survive into the future. As former Prime Minister Suárez once noted, "Spain will surprise you." Or alternatively, Spain and Portugal may yet find a formula to balance and reconcile their democratic aspirations and institutions with their nondemocratic ones. Which way the balance will tip is still an open question; and the complex currents, blends, and overlaps between democratic and less-than-democratic forces provide both reasons to be optimistic about the future and reasons to be quite cautious and restrained.

Notes

1. As reported on a not-for-direct-attribution basis during the course of one of the secretary's shuttles about Europe.

2. In the legend of Roland, it is only the Moorish armies of Iberia that are able to defeat the forces of Christendom led by Charlemagne, and Roland himself was killed in Spain, apparently in the Basque country by the "Saracens."

3. Portugal, however, continues to flirt with Third World ideologies, and Spain is not entirely certain it really wants to join NATO.

4. The approach here, as well as the major chapter headings, derive from Raphael Zariski, *The Politics of Uneven Development* (Hinsdale, Ill.: Dryden Press, 1977), chap. 4; and Joseph La Palombara and Myron Weiner, eds., *Political Parties and Political Development* (Princeton, N.J.: Princeton University Press, 1966).

5. On the role of political parties in the Iberic-Latin culture area, see Douglas A. Chalmers, "Parties and Society in Latin America," *Studies in Comparative International Development*, vol. 7 (Summer 1972), pp. 102–28; Robert H. Dix, "Latin America: Opposition and Development," in Robert A. Dahl, ed., *Regimes and Opposition* (New Haven, Conn.: Yale University Press, 1973); and Margaret McLaughlin, "Political Parties in Latin America" (Amherst: University of Massachusetts, Department of Political Science, 1977).

6. See Glen C. Dealy, *The Public Man: An Interpretation of Latin American and Other Catholic Countries* (Amherst: University of Massachusetts Press, 1977); Howard J. Wiarda, "Toward a Framework for the Study of Political Change in the Iberic-Latin Tradition: The Corporative Model," *World Politics*, vol. 25 (January 1973), pp. 206–235; Wiarda, ed., *Politics and Social Change in Latin America* (Amherst: University of Massachusetts Press, 1982); and James M. Malloy, ed., *Authoritarianism and Corporatism in Latin America* (Pittsburgh: University of Pittsburgh Press, 1977).

7. The best historical survey is Stanley G. Payne, *A History of Spain and Portugal,* 2 vols. (Madison: University of Wisconsin Press, 1973).

8. Especially Raymond Carr, *Spain 1808–1939* (Oxford: Clarendon Press, 1966); Miguel M. Cuadrado, *Elecciones y partidos políticos de España, 1868–1931* (Madrid: 1931); Juan Linz, "The Party System of Spain: Past and Future," in S. Lipset and S. Rokkan, eds., *Party Systems and Voter Alignments* (New York: Free Press, 1967), pp. 197–282; Robert Kern, ed., *The Caciques: Oligarchic Politics and the System of Caciquismo in the Luso-Hispanic World* (Albuquerque: University of New Mexico Press, 1973); Marcello Caetano, *Constituções portuguesas* (Coimbra: Coimbra Editora, 1958); A. H. de Oliveira Martins, *History of Portugal*, vol. II (New York: Columbia University Press, 1972); and Douglas L. Wheeler, *Republican Portugal: A Political History, 1910–1926* (Madison: University of Wisconsin Press, 1978).

9. Gerald Brennan's *The Spanish Labyrinth: An Account of the Social and Political Background of the Spanish Civil War* (Cambridge: Cambridge University Press, 1971), is the best book on this period and one of the best ever written about Spain. On the parties, see especially Linz, "The Party System" and Wheeler, *Republican Portugal.* It should be said that some of the Spanish working-class parties, the PSOE-UGT and FAI-CNT, were remarkably free of middle-class intellectual domination.

10. See José Ortega y Gasset, *Invertebrate Spain* (New York: Norton, 1937).

11. Wheeler, *Republican Portugal*.

12. Kenneth N. Medhurst, *Government in Spain* (Oxford: Pergamon Press, 1973); and Lawrence S. Graham, *Portugal: The Decline and Collapse of an Authoritarian Order* (Beverly Hills, Calif.: Sage, 1975).

13. The Spanish Falange became the "Movimiento"; see Juan Linz "From Falange to Movimiento-Organización: The Spanish Single Party and the Franco Regime, 1936–1968," in Samuel P. Huntington and Clement H. Moore, eds., *Authoritarian Politics in Modern Society* (New York: Basic Books, 1970), pp. 128–203. In Portugal it was the União Nacional under Salazar, remodeled and rebaptized as the Aliança Nacional Popular by Caetano; see Howard J. Wiarda, *Corporatism and Development: The Portuguese Experience* (Amherst: University of Massachusetts Press, 1978), chaps. 4, 9, and 10.

14. See especially Graham, *Portugal*.

15. V. O. Key, *Southern Politics in State and Nation* (New York: Knopf, 1949). Specifically, see Charles W. Anderson, *The Political Economy of Modern Spain: Policy-Making in an Authoritarian System* (Madison: University of Wisconsin Press, 1970); and Wiarda, *Corporatism and Development*. An important qualifier should be introduced for Spain. While the description given above holds for the earlier period, it is not a correct description of the Francoist state party mechanism after the late 1950s. By then the Movimiento had become so restricted and limited that the functions described were carried out generally through direct bureaucratic manipulation without normally bothering with the state party as such.

16. Juan Linz, "An Authoritarian Regime: Spain," in E. Allardt and Y. Littunen, eds., *Cleavages, Ideologies and Party Systems* (Helsinki: Westermarck Society, 1964), pp. 291–342 for a discussion of systems of "limited pluralism."

17. For the nature and "givens" of these elections, see Steven Ussach, "The Portuguese Presidential Election of 1958" (Amherst: University of Massachusetts, Department of Political Science, 1974). During a period of extensive research in Portugal in 1972–1973, the author attended several meetings of the Socialist and social-democratic opposition; a major congress of all the "democratic opposition" was more or less freely held at Aveiro.

18. Jon Amsden, *Collective Bargaining and Class Conflict in Spain* (London: Weidenfeld and Nicolson, 1972); and Wiarda, *Corporatism and Development*, chap. 9.

19. For some general comments on the cooptation versus repression strategies, see Howard J. Wiarda and Harvey F. Kline, *Latin American Politics and Development* (Boston: Houghton Mifflin, 1979), part one.

20. The materials in this section are based on field work in Portugal and Spain in 1972–1973, 1974, 1975, 1977.

21. An interesting case study, with broader implications, though not specifically focused on Iberia, is Michael J. Kryzanek, *Political Party Opposition in Latin America: The PRD, Joaquin Balaguer, and Politics in the Dominican Republic, 1966–1973* (Ph.D. diss., University of Massachusetts, 1975).

22. On the importance and role of the state, see Wiarda and Kline, *Latin American Politics*, chap. 5.

23. The author was in Spain in the spring of 1977 when there was much public discussion of the future of the UDC.

24. For Portugal these events may be best followed in *Expresso* and *Jornal Novo;* for Spain, see *Cuadernos para el Diálogo* and *Cambio.*

25. In office Mario Soares proved an abler and tougher politician than most observers anticipated; nevertheless the criticism holds.

26. See the coverage in the daily press for April–May 1977.

27. The most devastating portrayal of Cunhal was his celebrated interview with Oriana Fallaci, *New York Times Magazine,* July 13, 1975; in more recent statements Cunhal has begun to shed some of his "Stalinist" image.

28. Author's assessment, based on field research in Portugal in 1977.

29. These events may be followed in *Expresso* and *Jornal Novo.* During the period preceding the cabinet crisis of December 1977, there was much talk in the Portuguese press about the vacuum of political leadership, the ineffectiveness of the government, and the widespread desire for a "government that really governs." On these and related themes, see Howard J. Wiarda, "The Transition to Democracy in Portugal: Real or Wishful?" (Paper presented to the Joint Seminar on Political Development, Center for International Affairs, Harvard University, Cambridge, Mass., and Center for International Studies, Massachusetts Institute of Technology, Cambridge, Mass., December 8, 1976; excerpts and discussion published in the minutes of that JOSPOD meeting).

30. See Santiago Carillo's recently published book with this title.

31. Based on interviews with U.S. embassy and PSOE officials.

32. Based on the field work in 1977 and interviews with elite group representatives.

33. Deutsch, *Nationalism and Social Communication* (Cambridge: MIT, 1966); but see Milton DaSilva, *The Basque Nationalist Movement: A Case Study in Modernization and Ethnic Conflict* (Ph.D. diss., University of Massachusetts, 1972); and Juan Linz and Amando de Miguel, "Within Nation Differences and Comparisons: The Eight Spains," in R. L. Merritt and S. Rokkan, eds., *Comparing Nations* (New Haven, Conn.: Yale University Press, 1966), pp. 267–319.

34. The upheavals and general strike in the Basque country in May 1977 struck many observers as based on class conflict rather than regional aspirations.

35. Philip Converse, "Of Time and Partisan Stability," *Comparative Political Studies,* vol. 2 (July 1969), pp. 141–42.

36. For Spain, see the Fundación FOESSA surveys and the data and studies done for them by DATA S.A. under the direction of Amando de Miguel, as well as the Gallup surveys; for Portugal, see especially John L. Hammond, "Das Urnas as Ruas: Electoral Behavior and Noninstitutional Political Militancy: Portugal, 1975" (Paper presented at the conference "Crisis in Portugal," Toronto, April 15–17, 1976).

37. On these changes, see Herminio Martins, "Portugal," and Salvador Giner, "Spain," in Margaret Archer and Giner, eds., *Contemporary Europe: Class, Status, and Power* (London: Weidenfeld and Nicolson, 1971); also João B. N. Pereira Neto, "Social Evolution in Portugal since 1945," in R. S. Sayers, ed., *Portugal and Brazil in Transition* (Minneapolis: University of Minnesota Press, 1968); and Amando de Miguel, "Changes in the Spanish Social Structure

239

under Francoism" (New Haven, Conn.: Yale University, Department of Sociology, 1977).

38. Douglas Wheeler, "Portuguese Elections and History" (Durham: University of New Hampshire, Department of History, 1975).

39. Samuel P. Huntington, *Political Order in Changing Societies* (New Haven, Conn.: Yale University Press, 1968), p. 407.

40. Ibid., p. 8. See also *Eleição para a Assembleia Constituinte 1975* (Lisbon: Instituto Nacional de Estatística, 1975).

41. Based on the field research in the spring of 1977, the electoral results as provided by the Spanish embassy in Washington, and an anonymous paper entitled "Some Thoughts on the Meaning of Basque Voting Patterns in the 1977 Spanish Elections."

42. William T. Salisbury and Jonathan Story, "The Economic Positions of Spain and Portugal in 1980: The Official View" (Paper presented at the conference "Spain and Portugal: The Politics of Economics and Defense," Institute for the Study of Conflict, London, May 29–31, 1975); and Juan Linz, "Spain and Portugal: Critical Choices" (Paper presented at the "Mini-Conference on Contemporary Portugal," Yale University, New Haven, Conn., March 28–29, 1975).

43. Two accounts by Stanley Meisler, in the *Atlantic Monthly,* May 1977, and *Foreign Affairs,* October 1977, offer useful overviews of this chronology.

44. See the analysis in Howard J. Wiarda, *Transcending Corporatism? The Portuguese Corporative System and the Revolution of 1974* (Columbia: Institute of International Studies, University of South Carolina, 1976).

45. For a general discussion of this phenomenon, see Wiarda and Kline, *Latin American Politics,* chap. 5.

46. On the role of elections in the political process of Iberia and Latin America, see Charles W. Anderson, "Toward a Theory of Latin American Politics," Occasional Paper no. 2, Graduate Center for Latin American Studies, Vanderbilt University, Nashville, Tenn., February 1964.

47. José Yglesias, *The Franco Years* (Indianapolis, Ind.: Bobbs-Merrill, 1977).

48. On these more general and theoretical issues, see James M. Malloy, ed., *Authoritarianism and Corporatism;* Frederick Pike and Thomas Stritch, eds., *The New Corporatism: Social and Political Structures in the Iberian World* (Notre Dame, Ind.: University of Notre Dame Press, 1974); and Wiarda, ed., *Politics and Social Change.*

8

From Corporatism to Neo-Syndicalism

The State, Organized Labor, and the Changing Industrial Relations Systems of Southern Europe

There are three kinds of democracy in Europe: Anglo-Saxon, Scandinavian, and Mediterranean. Of the three the Mediterranean is the least disciplined and the most difficult to manage.
CONSTANTINE CARAMANLIS

This chapter explores the historic and continuing impact of corporatism in shaping the labor relations systems of southern Europe, now expressed in more "liberal" and even "neo-syndicalist" forms. We shall be concerned not only with the theme of corporatist continuity, however, but also with the distinct forms corporatism may take and with the possibility that the corporatist model may be shunted aside and superseded by other forms of sociopolitical organization.

There are several reasons for undertaking this study in its particular form. First, the study of the role of the state, of state-labor relations, and more broadly of state-society relations in southern Europe is understudied (less so for Italy than the other three countries) and is worthy of serious attention, particularly in this era of change, transition, even crisis that these nations are experiencing.[1] Second, as a scholar whose earlier research concentrated on Iberia and Latin America, I am interested in testing and exploring a number of key concepts—neo-corporatism, organic-statism, delayed-dependent development—in the broader European context.[2] Third, having explored the special character of Iberic-Latin development,[3] I am fascinated by the issue of whether there is in some measure a southern European sociopolitical process distinct from a "northern" one; whether "Europe" should be further disaggregated in terms of a North-South or horizontal dividing line as well as an East-West one;

241

and, if there is such a distinct southern European method or system of dealing with change, what its distinguishing features are and how these are now being altered. Finally, if organic-statism, patrimonialism, and corporatism have been a continuing part of the southern European system and process, how does change occur within that context, what are the long-term consequences of earlier corporatist practice in a period of officially proclaimed "post-corporatism," can one fashion a series of "stages" within a corporatist context (state corporatism, liberal corporatism, and neo-syndicalism) that represents an alternative developmental paradigm to the liberal-pluralist model and others with which we are more familiar, and what are the implications of such a cultural area-specific model of change for our presumption of a universal social science of development?[4] Alternatively, is there a point (as in Italy now, and to a somewhat lesser degree in the other countries) where such political and cultural based explanations begin to lose their validity and where other explanatory paradigms must be used, as complements or perhaps even as substitutes?

This chapter examines two themes simultaneously: the different types and dynamics of corporative systems at different stages of development and an argument about when and how political and cultural elements are important and when and if they may be superseded by other kinds of explanations.

A Distinct Southern European Social and Political Process?

Europe stops at the Pyrenees.

TALLEYRAND

Greece lies beyond the pale.

METTERNICH

I do not understand that nation that lies over the Alps.

HENRY KISSINGER

The question whether there is a unique southern European culture and, by extension, a distinct southern European social and political process is old and controversial.[5] While virtually every visitor is immediately struck by the contrasts between northern and southern Europe, what follows from that is less clear. The problems include specifying these differences precisely and disinterestedly, determining where boundaries should be drawn, assessing the importance and relative weight to be assigned the several perceived cultural differences, going beyond the Weberian and other popular social science notions about the limits of *"weltanschauung"* arguments, and determining if it is in fact the cultural elements or, perhaps more important, the economic and structural ones that ought to be emphasized. Responses to these issues have ranged from vague, often simplistic, and sometimes manifestly racist "national character" studies ("Latins" are violent, tempestuous, and ungovernable[6]) to the "trendy and intemperate" (Robert Packenham's term) dismissal as irrelevant of all political-cultural variables in some recent literature. Between these two extremes there is room both for a good deal more sophisticated political-cultural analysis[7] and for an approach that recognizes the complex multicausality of most historical events.[8]

Defining southern Europe is not easy, nor can its boundaries be determined precisely or with finality. Southern Europe cannot be defined with facile or simplistic criteria that smack of the fallacies and reductionism of the national character studies. Nor can absolute or final borders be drawn for southern Europe, since they are constantly changing. Moreover, any definition of southern Europe must of necessity be ambiguous, since it is based on ideal-type constructs that need not mirror reality exactly to be useful as a research model or a heuristic device.[9] Finally, it should be evident that whatever its bounds southern Europe does not exist in some splendid isolation, entirely apart from the rest of Europe or the world. Rather, it relates to, overlaps with, and is itself a part of other cultural, regional, and transnational systems. Nor can it be thought of as unique or wholly distinctive with development patterns completely unrelated to those occurring in other nations. Indeed, part of the purpose of this chapter is to begin to sort out precisely where, how, and why southern Europe is particular and where its developmental processes are in accord with more universal criteria.

Southern Europe may perhaps best be thought of as a series of concentric circles or rings that begin on the shores of the Mediterranean and radiate outward. Some of these frontiers are political, some economic, some cultural, and some religious; setting the boundaries varies depending on definitions and on which of the criteria are emphasized. Hence the definition of what constitutes southern Europe will always be inexact; nor is a more precise definition needed for our purposes. The fact of variable boundaries corresponds to the real world of fluctuating southern European and Mediterranean civilization historically; moreover, the absence of a precise setting of geographic boundaries need not stand in the way of our elucidating a model of a distinct southern European social and political process. Such a model is meant to approximate political reality, not to mirror it;

it serves as a heuristic device and provides guidelines to our exploration of southern Europe, but it does not have to indicate an exact topographical road map.

By the choice of national systems[10] to be included in this study (Greece, Italy, Portugal, and Spain) some obvious decisions have been made about the definition of southern Europe. Pragmatic as well as scholarly reasons suggest a focus on these four: they are manageable in a research sense; an extant body of literature links them at various levels; they have sufficiently parallel histories to hypothesize some commonalities; all had long experiences with authoritarianism and corporatism and have since evolved more liberal polities; on various social and economic indexes they exhibit some interesting clustering; impressionistically they seem to exhibit numerous common cultural and sociological features; and they are themselves sufficiently cognizant of their common features as well as obvious differences that they perpetually borrow from or imitate each other or in other ways make comparisons among themselves.

The emphasis on the state, corporatism, postcorporatism, and the labor relations systems of these nations also helps focus the research and to concentrate on those more direct factors shaping the role of the state and its efforts, in turn, to control and direct the organized labor movement. Indeed, one of the primary purposes of this chapter is to point to the leading role of the state in all four countries, particularly the crucial issue of who controls the state system and is thereby often able to determine the pattern of labor and industrial relations. In addition, this chapter emphasizes the dynamics of state-labor relations as one of the critical state-society arenas in which the shape and direction of national politics and political economy are forged.

In addition, the theme of "distinctiveness" of the southern European social and political process and its implications for a set of social concepts often presumed to have global validity are of interest here. Of particular significance is the institutionalized corporatism that for a long time seemed endemic to the southern European systems, especially in organized relations governing labor, employers, and the state.

For some, that focus, especially as it applies to labor and industrial relations, will be troubling. At least since Durkheim, political sociologists have assumed that once industrialization begins, its processes and sociopolitical concomitants are more or less universal. Indeed, not only are the processes of change, class behavior, and institutional transformations supposed everywhere to be the same (leading to competitive multiparty systems, pluralist interest groups, and the like), but industrialization and economic growth are thought to eliminate those previously culturally derived differences between nations and regions that once did exist. Such a deterministic and reductionist perspective needs to be closely examined and perhaps challenged in the light of the southern European experience.[11]

Recent research on Iberia and Latin America, for example, has led to an increasing emphasis on the unique or particular in the change and development processes of nations or distinct cultural areas and on the remarkable resiliency and adaptability of traditional institutions under the impact of industrialization and social change. The major institutions of civilizations like those of Iberia and Latin America or a cultural area like that of southern Europe are of course shaped by outside influences, the shared impact of common events, and ties of dependence and interdependence. But such areas may also be distinguished by the persistence of tradition-based institutions, a refusal to adopt "Western" (that is, northwest European) institutions, a selective discrimination among outside influences, only a selective acceptance of the concomitants of modernization, or simply an incompatibility of outside pressures and local wants. Historical and culture-based institutions often serve as filters for the change process, allowing some outside influences in, modifying them in the process, and keeping others out. Moreover, the direction is not always one way, from the modern "West" to the less-developed periphery. Indeed, concepts and models developed or resuscitated in the Iberian and Latin American context, such as corporatism and organic-statism, are now finding their way back into the larger contexts of European and general comparative studies.[12]

This chapter tests a number of hypotheses on corporatism, organic-statism, and patrimonialism to illuminate how change occurs in southern Europe, what models allow us to comprehend these changes, what is unique in the southern European change processes, and where these correspond to more general, global models. Although modern societies, of course, do not differ much in their formal institutional paraphernalia—parties, labor unions, parliaments, bureaucracies, and the like—they do differ significantly in how these institutions actually work, in their relative importance, in the expectations of the citizens, and in the unstated rules and tacit understandings governing the areas of state behavior and state-society relations that often reflect distinct political and cultural influences.

In order to talk about a distinct southern European social and political process, and to draw a more or less horizontal line across Europe, with its imprecisions, vagaries, and mixed areas, distinguishing the southern European civilization from the northern one, we must be careful about the criteria used and be specific about the differences.[13] For organizational purposes these may be considered under four categories: (1) sociogeographic factors marking off the area; (2) socioeconomic features; (3) the political parallels in southern Europe, both before and after the modern era begins in 1815; and (4) the common cultural ingredients that seem to be present throughout the area.

Sociogeographic Factors. Greece, Italy, Portugal, and Spain, both taken individually and viewed as a region, have a number of geographic features, with important sociopolitical implications, that mark them off from other nations or areas.[14] All are or are part of peninsulas, with long coastlines, hence with a considerable history of maritime trade and exploration and with greater occupational differentiation than their comparatively lesser economic development would indicate. Further, all are mountainous, with major barriers to national integration. This characteristic contributes to the perpetuation of regionalism and separatist tendencies and intensifies the difficulties of building internal transportation and communications grids and of knitting together their divisive, fragmented *patrias chicas* ("little societies") into a coherent, integrated, national whole. In addition, the absence of many navigable rivers slowed the development of early trade and travel. Sociologically, a considerable gap existed between highland and plains peoples or between them and coastal (often commercial or maritime) peoples.

The generally mountainous, infertile, chopped-up terrain makes farming difficult, contributes to periodic and frequent food shortages, and prevents much large-scale, intensive, and mechanized agriculture. Unlike the situation in France, Germany, or the Low Countries, the terrain has retarded the growth of agricultural surpluses on which a later commercialization and industrialization might be based. The land and man-land patterns have shaped the particular structure of social, economic, and political relations in southern Europe, fostering distinct forms of "feudalism,"[15] helping preserve patrimonialism, and giving added importance to the central state in fomenting and directing national development.[16]

All four countries, in addition, have Mediterranean climates. They are subject to periodic droughts, which lead again to food shortages. The climate promotes particular crops (wheat, grapes, olives) and crop similarities but also creates a lower ratio of stock breeding to plant growing than in the rest of Europe, the necessity for irrigation, an absence of self-sufficiency in basic foodstuffs, the consequent need to import, and specialization on a narrow range of commercial crops. The southern European nations also lack the mineral resources necessary for the industrial age dawning in the nineteenth century or, as in the Spanish case, the juxtaposition of such key industrial resources as iron and coal. None of them have oil in any quantities and are much more dependent on foreign supplies than the United States. Unlike Eastern Europe, however, that other great European underdeveloped area, southern Europe did have sufficient secondary raw materials to give mining and exports considerable economic importance. Mineral and agricultural exports, coupled with the need to import petroleum as well as industrial metals and products, helped to cast the southern European nations in a relationship of dependency or even "neocolonialism" to their more richly endowed central and northern European neighbors.[17]

One need not be a geographic determinist to recognize the historic and continuing importance of these factors. The nature of the geographic landscape and of the crops grown, respectively, implies certain forms of land tenancy, farm size, need for foreign capital, dependency, and lord-peasant relations. Distinct crops and man-land relations have a sociology—and doubtlessly a politics—of their own. For example, the traditionalism, hierarchy, and rigidity still, apparently, more strongly present in southern than in northern Europe may in part be a product of the south's historical land-holding system, the need to "hold the ranks under discipline" (Braudel), which is what corporatism is all about. The land-holding system itself, based generally on larger estates in the south than in the north, stems in part from the need to drain and clear large swampy areas or to control vast floodplains, which can only be accomplished with large infusions of capital and large-scale (often statist) organization. The plains of the south, therefore, became the property of noblemen and emerging elites and required a large and docile labor force or peasantry. This stands in marked contrast to the north, where the forests could often be cleared and land opened to individuals and families. These features help explain the historically two-class, oligarchic, and non-egalitarian nature of south European society, the absence of a sizable middle class, the difficult path of democratization, and the persistence of a two-class society composed of landlords and peasants. The poor soil of the south ruled out the development of a system of medium-sized family farms, helped prolong feudalism, and made modern capitalism, when it tardily emerged in the late nineteenth century, dependent more on state than on individual initiative.[18]

Socioeconomic Factors. Southern Europe, of course, is something more than a geographic region with certain common features. It is also, to some degree, a distinct social, economic, cultural, and political area as well. Some of its social and economic features are of such historical durability that they may be considered basic characteristics of the area's life.

To begin with, the contrast of the southern European nations with those of both eastern and northern Europe is revealing. The greater occupational variation in southern populations than in eastern populations has already been noted. Both areas were primarily agricultural, but by the 1930s the average proportion of population in agriculture was 66 percent in eastern Europe but only 47 percent in southern Europe (compared with 20 percent in northern Europe).[19] There were significant numbers of commercial and industrial workers, service employees, and fishermen as well as peasants. In addition, at that time southern Europe had a considerably greater mixture in its agricultural sector: both fewer small-to-medium-size individual land holdings than the northern countries but also fewer large-scale estates with servile populations than eastern Europe. Southern Europe may be considered intermediary between these two types, less developed than the north but more developed than the east. It contained a variety of rural occupational groups—large estate owners, free tenants, independent small farm proprietors, servile tenants, sharecroppers, day and permanent laborers—and a variety of rural social orders demanding a say in national politics.

Commercial classes in southern Europe, furthermore, tended to be more important than in eastern Europe, although again less so than in the north. The commercial elites of the south, moreover, despite the region's dependency relations in other economic areas, tended to be national, cohesive, and often interrelated. The elites, in turn, were often tied in closely with their respective states and often dependent on them for protection, tariffs, monopoly privileges, and special access. Hence as southern European capitalism eventually developed, it took on an etatist or neomercantilist rather than a laissez-faire form. Etatism and neomercantilism in the economic sphere were probably related to the persistence of similarly bureaucratic-corporatist forms in the political realm.[20]

Much has been written of the southern European phenomenon of walled enclave cities that predate the Industrial Revolution.[21] Indeed in much of southern Europe it was not industrialization, initially, that produced urbanization. Industrialization and its accompanying social and economic effects were instead superimposed on a set of societies already urban and hence "modern" in this sense. To some degree, at least in southern Europe the sociocultural arrangements already in place have often shaped the particular form that industrialization took.[22]

The form of adaptation of the southern European nations to industrialization was also distinct from that of both northern and eastern Europe. Industrialization in the south, while lagging behind that of the north and taking somewhat different forms, was facilitated by the prevalence of earlier handicraft manufacturing, by the long history of urban life (in contrast with the village or hamlet pattern of eastern Europe), by comparatively less ethnic and linguistic conflict than in the east, and by a long history of etatist leadership and intervention in trade, hydraulic projects, shipping, and commerce. Malefakis maintains that the absence of such a strong and all-encompassing feudal tradition and of a servile class (as in eastern Europe) made southern Europe both more responsive to and rebellious against industrialization and its effects.

All of these factors helped construct in southern Europe a situation of "dualities" of the sort later ascribed to developing nations. The southern European societies did not experience such complete transformations after 1800 as did northern Europe but considerably more than eastern Europe. The economies and societies of southern Europe were neither traditional nor modern but complex and overlapping combinations. Political and social institutions as well as individual personalities exhibited these split characteristics. Instead of modernity superseding tradition, they continued to exist side by side. Rather than disintegrating as modernization went forward, indeed, traditional institutions tended to bend to it and absorb it, meanwhile strengthening themselves in the process.

Just as there are many similarities of social and economic structures in southern Europe, so are there commonalities in the patterns of national development. The mere coincidence of these parallel chronologies, especially during the fast-changing industrial era when so many factors are involved, is itself significant in fashioning a model of southern European development.

During the first several decades of the nineteenth century, political instability generally ruled out sustained and systematic efforts at economic development. The southern European nations lagged ever farther behind the north. In the 1850s and 1860s, the first stages of modernization began, and by the 1870s, development began to accelerate. These changes combined indigenous factors (the establishment, finally, of political stability and national infrastructure development) with alterations in the international economy with which southern Europe had now become more closely intertwined.

The period from 1870 to World War I was a time of economic "take-off" for all southern European countries. Italy's growth was the most impressive, but Greece, Portugal, and Spain also registered strong, steady gains during the period. The bases for the development of more modern economies were laid.

The interwar period proved to be a time of economic uncertainty, considerable disruption, and uneven growth. This was due in part to the political instability of the time, the economic upheavals, and the uncertainties occasioned by the experiments with manifestly corporative economic planning and national restructuring. Nevertheless, despite general hostility toward the interwar experiments with corporatism, this period also saw a definitive break with the oligarchic, rural, and agricultural order that had been dominant to that point and the consolidation of a more centralized, bureaucratic, middle-class, urban, and commercial-industrial order. These changes in turn helped pave the way for the economic "miracles" of the postwar period, first in Italy, then in Greece and Spain, and eventually though to a lesser extent in Portugal, which finally brought the more or less "sustained economic growth" that had been interrupted earlier.[23]

By the dawn of the 1980s all four countries, again following Malefakis's commentary, displayed some glittering industries, a considerably modernized agriculture, and booming tourism. But many of the old problems also remained: "duality," immense social and economic gaps, many inefficient family-based firms requiring protectionism, vast backward areas, large numbers of émigré workers, major lags in social capital investment, and uncertain and insecure middle class, a restive and sometimes volatile trade union movement, inadequate social programs, persistent paternalism and patrimonialism on the part of the elites, an overblown and inefficient bureaucracy not designed to serve the public weal, debilitating dependency on outside capital and markets, and a state system still torn by its desire to maintain the web of controls over the economy and societal groups on the one hand and the pressures to liberalize still further on the other.

The formulations of Alexander Gerschenkron with regard to these late developing nations of southern Europe provide a useful beginning point for explaining these tendencies. Ranking the major European countries (unfortunately Italy was the only southern European country to receive attention) according to their level of economic development as of the mid-nineteenth century (in order: Britain, France, Germany, Austria, Italy, and Russia), Gerschenkron stated that "the more delayed the industrial development of a country, the more explosive was the great spurt of its industrialization if and when it came."[24] Particularly relevant are Gerschenkron's propositions that the "late developers" had a stronger tendency to foster economic growth by monopolistic compacts regulated and supervised by the state (the essence of corporatism), proceeded with industrialization under state direction, employed investment banks acting under the aegis of the state or a web of bureaucratic controls both to promote and to coordinate development, and in general had a stronger need for controlling potentially disruptive societal sectors in order to achieve the development desired. Gerschenkron talked principally of the state's role in promoting economic growth, but I would extend his language of "controls," "regulation," "monopoly," and "discipline" to the realm of sociopolitical groups as well. Economic development in southern Europe was too precarious and too easily upset, and the regimes presiding over it too unstable, for a laissez-faire marketplace to be allowed—either in the economic arena or in the sociopolitical. Indeed, in the southern European context especially, these two seemed inseparable: systems of neo-mercantilism, statism, and corporatism in the economic sphere necessarily had as corollaries social and political corporatism and bureaucratic-authoritarianism. We conclude with Gerschenkron that the industrial history of Europe "appears not as a series of mere repetitions of the 'first' industrialization but as an orderly system of graduated deviations from that industrialization."

In the late industrializers, in contrast to the earlier ones, the network of industrial cartels, investment banks, government bureaucracies, and, at least during the corporative regimes and probably for a longer time, organized labor and other groups were closely integrated with the state system and helped provide for "integral," "organic," "coordinated" national development. Accordingly, the importance of parliament, political parties, and other accoutrements usually associated with Western notions of democracy and republicanism was notably less in southern Europe, at least during these early stages.[25] Further, the need of both industrial and agricultural elites for high tariffs led to a wedding of older and newer wealth rather than its greater differentiation and concomitant social pluralism, helping to strengthen and perpetuate both elitist rule and a more closed and authoritarian political regime.

In contrast to the more laissez-faire systems emerging elsewhere, the industrialists of southern Europe produced mainly consumer goods in a market protected by the state. High agricultural tariffs also led to the greater commercialization of agriculture, which in turn produced even greater land concentrations and the proliferation of landless workers strongly attracted to anarchist and syndicalist ide-

251

ologies. When these workers migrated to the industrial centers, they took their ideologies with them, increasing the strength of the anarchist and syndicalist labor movements against the industrial elites and eventually calling forth even stronger corporatist control mechanisms to handle the "social question." These conflicting pressures exacerbated the social and political tensions leading to the fragmentation and breakdown of the interwar period.

The Gerschenkron model of late, delayed, often dependent industrialization provides a useful but incomplete framework for explaining the particular path of southern European development. Our special concern has been the social and political corollates of late development, particularly the role of the state in fostering, coordinating, and shaping the process, and the explanatory power of this formulation in helping account for the later emergence of manifestly corporate-authoritarian regimes (as distinguished from the earlier "natural corporatism") during the 1920s and 1930s.

Political Parallels since 1815. It would be simpler if political forces could consistently and unambiguously be explained by economic factors or if political behavior were the exact mirror of its presumed class determinants. Unfortunately reality, no less in southern Europe than elsewhere, is often more complex.[26] The Gerschenkron model, for instance, useful for analyzing European development in the 1850–1930 period, is perhaps less helpful for understanding subsequent decades. And while the economic and class determinants of state behavior may hold to a large degree in the earlier context, the Gerschenkron analysis seems less useful for more recent decades as the modern bureaucratic state has become increasingly independent from *all* classes[27] and when, as in the case of neosyndicalist Italy, labor elements have succeeded in capturing some parts of a "bourgeois" state system (chiefly the Labor Ministry and Social Security Institute) for themselves. Hence this study hypothesizes a degree of autonomy in the political and economic functions of state systems and examines changing as opposed to fixed patterns of state-society relations.[28]

Nevertheless, even in a brief survey of the political parallels and divergences in the development of the southern European nations since 1815, it is possible to discern four broad phases (in Italy perhaps a fifth phase has been entered) in the development process during this time frame in which the political histories of these four nations ran remarkably parallel. Indeed, given the rather obvious differences between these countries, the developmental parallels are both singular and probably not coincidental: similar results are likely due to similar causes.

The first phase, ushered in with the conquests, new ideas, and new institutions of the Napoleonic era, encompasses the period from the 1810s to the 1870s.[29] It was a period, in Spain and Portugal, of *pronunciamientos* (barracks revolts) and civil wars; in Greece and Italy, of liberation, conflict, and efforts at unification. With variations from country to country this half-century was a period of considerable fragmentation and chaos, of civil strife and frequent foreign intervention, of the lack of either much consensus on political institutionalization or economic growth, and of falling farther behind the more developed nations of the north. The traditional corporate-authoritarian forms often persisted, but a nascent liberal order also began to emerge.

The second phase, 1870s–1910s, was characterized in all four countries by a settling or fading away of many of the earlier conflicts; the consolidation of more liberal regimes; the building of much national infrastructure (roads, highways, ports, railroads, telegraph, and telephone), economic growth and incipient industrialization, and considerable development of political institutions (armies, bureaucracies, and the like) and of the national associational life. The organizational void (*falta de organización*, to employ the familiar Spanish lament) now began to be filled. These changes, however, came generally under elite and often authoritarian auspices, guided, led, and directed by the state. But by this time there were two sociopolitical forms of organization becoming roughly equivalent in strength: the older corporate and elitist one and the newer republican-liberal form.

The third phase, 1920s–1940s, represented both a break with the past and an extension of it. The older, elite-dominated system, increasingly under challenge, broke down and eventually gave way to a new middle-class order. Although the middle sectors were deeply divided on both the ends and the means of political action, eventually in all four countries, middle-sector dominance was consolidated in the form of corporatist-authoritarian-bureaucratic regimes: Carmona, Salazar, and Caetano in Portugal; Mussolini in Italy; Metaxas and the monarchy in Greece; and Primo de Rivera and then Franco in Spain.[30] Continuing the rationalization and organization of national life begun in the earlier period and extending that to new sectors of organized labor, commerce, and industry, these regimes sought both to promote development and to regulate or harness the national economic life and the emerging associational groups that seemed to threaten systemic stability, with even stronger state controls than before. Although the new corporative mechanism was aimed at regulating all groups, the controls were directed and applied more strongly toward organized labor than toward business, since labor was where the greatest perceived threat to continued middle-sector dominance lay. Corporatism and authoritarianism were restored and resurrected, albeit now under middle-class auspices, while liberalism and nascent Socialist movements were suppressed, often with a vengeance.[31]

Corporatism in this context has two different meanings. The older traditional form of natural corporatism had been supplanted by a more defined and self-conscious form. The new corporatism owed something to the historic and political-cultural form, often seeking to identify itself with the nation's earlier traditions; but it also represented a response to the economic and organizational pressures of the time. These included trends toward greater centralization of decision making, the rising threat of mass demands, the economic crisis of the 1930s, the growth of state planning, greater economic interdependence among nations, a host of new social programs that called for consultation with various socioeconomic interests, efforts to control the lower classes, and the like. In some countries the older (political-cultural) and the newer (self-conscious) forms of corporatism merged, while in others such a disjunction developed that corporatism as an ideology and form of national sociopolitical organization was, perhaps permanently, discredited.[32]

Marking the beginning and end of the next phase, that of official liberalism, is more difficult. Italian fascism collapsed in 1944–1945 along with Italy's defeat in the war. Corporatism hung on, though considerably transformed, in Portugal until the revolution of 1974, in Spain until Franco's death in 1975, but only intermittently in Greece until the overthrow of the colonels in 1974. While the formal structures of corporatism were in their turn abolished in all four countries, paving the way to a new, more liberal era, the changes, dramatic though they are, should not completely overshadow the perhaps equally important continuities. Another interesting point is the relative weight of indigenous forces as opposed to external ones (the United States, NATO, the Common Market countries, and international public opinion) in precipitating the change from corporatist to more liberal regimes or the degree to which democracy and liberalization are part of southern European reality or merely the façade it shows to the rest of the world. Clearly while considerable liberalization has occurred, far more in Italy than elsewhere, it is also clear that the corporative control mechanisms by which the state tries to license and regulate journalists, judges, farm workers, and labor remain extensive. The effectiveness of such residual controls, however, varies considerably from country to country.[33]

One key element of continuity (again Italy may constitute a major exception) from the era of state-corporatism to that of officially sanctioned liberalism is the role played by the state. In Spain it was strong power at the center (the king and his prime minister) that presided over the transition from Francoist authoritarianism to liberalism; in Greece and Portugal, capture of the state apparatus was crucial in the struggle of antiregime forces to shift national directions. In all three countries the central state has continued to play a leading, guiding, and directing role, seeking to regulate the change process and to harness, if not control, the group life that swirls about it. In state-society relations, therefore, there were both change and continuity, with the state and the shifting coalitions of groups supporting it seeking to maintain a tutelary role, while the various societal actors, including organized labor, sought to use their new freedom either to assert their autonomy from the state or to capture, if possible, part of a fragmented, paralyzed, often ineffective state (the Italian case) for themselves. Hence, in Italy, domination of state and corporative controls has been more an aspiration than a reality, since the postwar era "society" has emerged as triumphant over a generally weak state. Although in the other countries in the new liberal era societal groups have also obviously gained some greater strength vis-à-vis the state, the arenas of state-society political struggle are still largely the same, and the equation is subject to virtually constant redefinition.

A principal hypothesis here, therefore, is that while the older etatist and bureaucratic-authoritarian form of corporatism has been overthrown or superseded, corporatism in other forms continues to exist. I have designated these newer forms "liberal corporatism" and "neo-syndicalism." The tendencies toward corporatism and organic-statism in all these forms appear to reflect both a powerful political-cultural tradition and a response to real, objective problems and conditions in the present. Corporatism and etatism, I suggest, are essential ingredients in the southern European development process. The particular form these may take no matter whether overt or disguised can vary considerably, reflecting differences in the balance of power between state and society and in various combinations between the authoritarian-etatist and the liberal and newer Socialist features. I see a progression in the form taken by corporatism from state corporatism to liberal corporatism to neosyndicalism. These changes appear to reflect broader-scale social and economic transformations and may correspond to shifts in the governing coalitions. Hence when change in southern European society and polity comes, it is likely to take place within this corporative-organic-statist context rather than necessarily as a contest between corporatism and something else.

Some have argued that corporatism, etatism, and a modernized, updated patrimonialism constitute the natural political system in southern Europe and that these nations have an "elective affinity" for these particular forms. Certainly the longevity of corporatism in these countries provides some empirical evidence for the point.[34]

Patrimonial authority, organic statism, and corporatism, are not just epiphenomena of traditional society and thus of merely historic or passing interest, but may be continuing, perhaps permanent features of diversely modernizing societies.[35] Rather than being swept away under the impact of change, they may instead be reinforced by the establishment of new government agencies, by the judicious doling out of state contracts or even whole programs or offices, by the creation of officially sanctioned interest groups tied in with these agencies, and by the restructuring of earlier forms of localized patron-client relations on a national, larger, and better-organized basis.

Many of the political phenomena in southern Europe may be viewed as the likely concomitants of economic and social development occuring within the context of a patrimonialist, organic-statist, corporatist system. Economic development produces large numbers of persons with no connection to established patron-client networks but who demand either their share of the spoils or the system's replacement. They may be co-opted through the creation of new branch organizations and officially sanctioned interest associations, a process with its own regularities.[36] Or they will rebel against it, in praetorian fashion, with each group employing the technique giving it a comparative political advantage: In Huntington's pungent, epigrammatic, punning comment on this phenomenon, the wealthy will bribe (and turn to state corporatism), the students will riot, the workers will strike, the mobs will demonstrate, and the military will stage a coup.[37]

What passes for frequent "revolutions" in Greece, Portugal, or Spain, or ideological squabblings among the rival Christian Democratic factions in Italy, may more accurately be seen as the efforts of contending elites to gain access to the benefits and patronage opportunities that control of the state system affords. In modern times the state has become the great national patron, replacing the local landlords, notables, clerics, or royal agents of the past. But the practices and patterns of systemwide patrimonialism remain almost a constant. "Politics" therefore consists chiefly of the efforts of competing middle-sector groups—often allied with rival labor groups and sometimes encompassing one or another military clique, party or faction thereof, university student federation, farmers' association, and moneyed interest—to capture the pinnacles of the system for themselves or to hive off a section of it for particular advantage. The groups and coalitions may change, new actors may emerge, upheavals may occur; but both the patrimonialist-organicist-corporatist state system *and* the struggle to dominate all or parts or it for private and clientelistic advantage seem continuous.[38]

James Kurth argues that such corporatist-authoritarian regimes are the "ideal type" and "normal form" of patrimonial politics in the industrializing nations of southern Europe. He states that the description of a traditional patrimonial ruler is remarkably parallel to the recent descriptions of modern neo-corporatism. If France is the heartland of feudalism and the Middle East that of sultanism, to use Max Weber's familiar categories, southern Europe is the area where patrimonialism and corporatism have been especially strong. For a country with a patrimonialist tradition, Kurth says, the *normal* path of development and modernization is a corporatist regime.

Corporatism may exist in a variety of forms, however, both temporally and spatially. The temporal dimension is encompassed in the model of the three forms of state corporatism, liberal corporatism, and neo-syndicalism; spatially, quite distinct forms may be found in the Iberian systems of updated "Hapsburgian monarchy" (Franco and Salazar) as opposed to the "parliamentary republics" of Italy and Greece dominated for a long time by a single conservative party.[39] As the permanent (to date) postwar government party, the Christian Democrats of Italy are the beneficiaries as well as current repositories of the historic preference for organic unity, monism, social harmony, and an elaborate, now national patron-client system; and as a Catholic party, they also retain the legacy of the corporatist encyclicals *Rerum Novarum* and *Quadragesimo Anno,* even though most Christian Democrats no longer accept that older corporative formula. Constantine Caramanlis's New Democratic party is a newer and perhaps less stable, but similarly conservative-centrist party that has cleverly built upon, reinforced, and perpetuated Greece's enduring patrimonialist and patronage-dominated institutions. Kurth concluded that given the propensity in southern Europe for patrimonialism and organic unity, systems of corporatist-authoritarian Bonapartist rule or of one-party dominance—or perhaps some combination of or alternation between the two—were likely to be the area's most persistent and stable form of political order in the modern era.

Kurth's arguments lend support to my earlier analysis of the Iberic-Latin political process and seem to square, more than other formulations, with the observable realities of southern Europe. Several reservations, however, should be introduced. First, Kurth's term "natural form" to describe the corporatism of southern Europe may be overly deterministic; I would prefer to use "propensity" or "tendencies" instead, thus making allowance for other possible forms. Second, while there may be a propensity for patrimonialism, corporatism, and organic-statism in southern Europe, it is worth exploring whether this is always the case or if it exists only during times of change and crisis[40] and whether all groups share these propensities *or* only those elites and middle sectors that stand to gain the most advantage from it.[41] Third, while corporatism and etatism may still be due in part to the political-cultural factors Kurth mentions, newer economic and objective causes may also figure. Fourth, while there is something of a "natural" propensity for corporatism and etatism, the class, partisan, and systemic biases that this implies should command attention as well.[42] Finally, the Portuguese revolution and the possibility in Italy of a "historic compromise" between the Christian Democrats and the Communists to include the Communists in power force us to allow for the contingency that radical new structures could render the argument for historical continuity meaningless or nearly so. While Kurth's analysis therefore carries considerable explanatory power, it should not be seen as a complete explanation. Kurth in fact would be among the first to argue for a more complex, multicausal explanation rather than one that reduces all variables to a single cause.[43]

Corporatism. Anthropologist Eric Wolf[44] has traced the origins of southern European corporatism not just to the interwar period or even to the early writings on corporatism in the nineteenth century[45] but to the very origins of Mediterranean civil society in the family, kinship group, clan, and village community. During the thousand year interval between the collapse of the Roman empire and the rise of the new absolute states along the south European littoral, a host of corporately organized bodies—monastic orders, merchant and artisan guilds, communities and leagues, military-religious orders—provided the initial interstitial framework for group associability and consolidation and served as intermediaries between the individual and the rising state system.[46]

Society came to be essentially a confederation of such corporate units, which were at once both public and private, political agencies as well as religious ones. A "corporation" may be defined as an entity or body recognized in law as constituted by one or more persons and having various rights and duties as a juridical person whose relations with the state are governed by both informal understandings and, often, formal contracts. "Corporatism" refers to a system of interest intermediation and national sociopolitical organization based upon these entities and governing the relations between the state, with its licensing and regulating powers, and various societal groups.[47] Corporatism may of course take societal forms as well as statist ones,[48] and is compatible with a considerable variety of regimes. In early modern times corporatism had a singular advantage, again particularly in southern Europe where this tradition was strongest, since the division of men according to estates and.occupational groups was, in the immensely influential work of Thomas Aquinas, thought to represent the immutable will of divine providence.[49]

The earliest corporate bodies of southern Europe grew in importance by feeding on the duality between church and state, which was one of the cultural and structural hallmarks of Latin Christianity. Eventually the state emerged triumphant both in its struggle with the church and in its assertion of supremacy over corporate interests, but even then the Mediterranean Christian states (Wolf's term) tended to oscillate between the assertions of absolute despotism on the part of the ruler (monarch, *caudillo*, or *duce*) and the often de facto delegation of the maintenance of law, order, and internal discipline to the separate corporate bodies that made up political society. These arenas of state-society or state-corporate group relations, it is hypothesized, still constitute some of the principal pivots of southern European politics, which assume importance in its change and development process. While acknowledging the disruptions in the structure and roles of various historic and formal corporate groups in the early nineteenth century and the new impact of economic and structural as well as political-cultural factors in shaping corporatism, Wolf sees continuity between the venerated corporately organized state-society systems of earlier times and the manifestly corporatist regimes fashioned in the interwar period.

Patrimonialism. Patrimonialism, one of Weber's forms of traditional authority,[50] refers to the creation and maintenance of a paternalistic political system, dominated by elites and middle-sector elements, characterized by elaborate networks of patron-client relations operating at the national as well as the local levels, and dedicated to the preservation of the existing system and flexibly preserving as much national unity as possible, even under the impact of the twentieth century's mass challenges. Patrimonialism implies a structure of top-down rule, a political system organized rather on an extended family basis with accepted rights and responsibilities, a tutelary regime that brings new social elements into the system but does so under elite and state regulation and guidance. The patrimonial regime tends to be bureaucratic and administrative, a "cartelist" or "sinecure" state in which public employment and programs serve as means of co-optation and political control. A patrimonial state is centralized and authoritarian, with the main elites generally acting jointly to maintain social peace through heavy reliance on conciliation and paternalism. A patrimonialist system tries to limit and channel social mobilization, but it is by no means incompatible with modernization and the incorporation of new social groups into the political system.

Patrimonialist systems tend, thus, to be continuous over time regardless of the changing composition of the elites who occupy decision-making roles. A patrimonial regime may be either conservative or modernizing; it may, similarly, exist in monarchist or republican forms, in *caudillo*-dominated systems (Portugal, Spain) as well as parliamentary forms (Italy), and in various combinations of or oscillations between them (Greece).

A further important point to emphasize is the close connection between patrimonialism and corporatism, especially as corporatism is defined in its political-cultural sense by Philippe Schmitter. "Corporatism," Schmitter says, "is a belief in and acceptance of a natural hierarchy of social groups, each with its ordained place and its own set of perquisites and responsibilities." "These orders," he goes on to say, "have and accept voluntary restrictions on their autonomy and horizontal interaction. They are seen as linked by vertical lines of subordination directly to higher social institutions, which are conceded the right and duty to intervene in intergroup conflicts for the sake of social peace." Schmitter says that while such a corporatist-patrimonialist system stresses permanence and immutability, it does accept new interest associations provided they accept limits on their independence and agree to accept the rules of the existing political "game." Schmitter also concludes that while corporatism seeks to limit and control change, it is not opposed to change per se and may indeed be quite adaptable.[51]

Organic statism. When the state in southern Europe, after a long and tortuous struggle for ascendancy,[52] eventually emerged as the dominant national institution, its forms tended to be centralist (or centralizing), corporative, organic, patrimonialist, and bureaucratic. It was based on patron-client ties of reciprocity and eventually extended from highly personal and individualistic links binding monarch and vassals to a much larger-scale and more impersonal network where the bureaucratic state became the great national patron and its clients consisted of the major corporative agencies within the system: church, army, elites, bourgeoisie, and eventually farm groups and the labor movement. It sought to mobilize the economic and social resources of its subjects without at the same time granting them political roles that could be used to challenge the system or even influence policy. The state bureaucracy thus administers and legislates, often impervious to parliamentary debate or political party struggle; the state shapes or dominates, rather than merely umpiring, as in interest-group liberalism, the structure and activities of the various factions. The guiding, directing, tutelary role of the state and the concept of group rights as vested in the major corporative bodies both derive from Roman law.[53]

Long ago Hegel saw that the emphasis on corporate or group law rather than law as applied to individuals would have the practical effect of producing divisiveness, fragmentation, and "an utter lack of law."[54] In fashioning a system of what Hegel termed "imageless jural relations" between the state and its component corporate groups, the new states of the Mediterranean built upon an earlier Roman tradition during their early periods of territorial and eventual national consolidation. Roman law not only provided a guide to help determine the contractual relations between the state and "society" (defined as the major, legitimized, or duly recognized corporate groups) but also required a host of intermediaries, mediators, negotiators, conciliators, and "champions at law."[55] It helped make necessary the growth of what Wolf calls "interstitial patron-client sets" to bridge the gap between decision makers and those who suffer the consequences. The latter, like the peasants of southern Italy and elsewhere in southern Europe, or like the trade unions in the early decades of their existence, experience "the state only present as 'the law,' not as a symbol or object of social obligation." The state of law becomes instead the state of "the Machiavellians"—those elites who control or manipulate the state system.[56]

Organic statism in this context refers to a tradition of political thought and a system of sociopolitical organization in which the component parts of the national society and polity are combined in a unified, harmonious, integral relationship. The organic unity of civil society is brought about by the architectonic action of public authorities—hence "organic statism." The state in such a system is interventionist and, at least in design and aspiration, strong. Organic unity at the same time requires a monistic system in which there is little separation of powers; nor can interest groups be allowed to exist

261

in a laissez-faire context wholly independent from the state. Rather such groups must be chartered and guided by the state, in theory if not always in reality, to achieve the common good of integral, harmonious national development.[57]

In these ways organic statism is usually closely associated with a patrimonialist and corporatist political order. Nevertheless, organic-statist systems are, again like corporatism, quite compatible with a variety of political regimes including *caudillo*-led dictatorships, one-party dominant or national-unity regimes, and monarchism as well as socialism.

The three main sociocultural and sociopolitical currents discussed above—corporatism, patrimonialism, and organic statism—carry important implications for understanding the patterns of southern European development.[58] During the first phase, roughly from the revival of Roman law beginning in the late eleventh century until the consolidation of larger city and territorial states in the fifteenth century, civilization and public order were advanced through the growth of corporate communities and a network of associations evolving into an institutionalized sociopolitical infrastructure integrating church, state, and society. Various kinds of corporate bodies, in the face of a still weak state (itself viewed then as one among several "corporations") meshed to provide a social, political, and religious systemic base. "Society" (its component corporate units) dominated.

In the second phase of development, beginning about the fifteenth century, the state and the public sphere began to emerge as dominant. Using Roman law and its related pattern of patron-clientele, benefiting (at least through the sixteenth century) from the growing economic prosperity in the Mediterranean world, and employing the absolutist doctrines then current, the bureaucratic state began to emerge as a consolidating, integrating force. Thereafter state-society relations would be dominated by the efforts of the state to expand its authority over societal or corporate groups and the struggle of the corporate groups to maintain some autonomy, define their place in the system through corporate contracts, secure special access for themselves or their members, or else capture the state system or some parts of it. From the age of emerging absolutism to that of republicanism this state-society tension has been at the heart of politics in the southern European world.

These findings of the cultural and social anthropologists enable us to go beyond the simplistic, obsolete, and now deservedly discredited "national character" studies. They also enable us to distinguish more carefully between what is universal in the development process thus conforming more or less to our Western-derived social science notions *and* what is particular, unique, or distinctive in individual nations or cultural areas.

Complex societies in the modern world seem not to differ a great deal in the formal organization of their economic, legal, or political systems. All tend to become rationalized and bureaucratized, greater differentiation occurs, political parties and interest groups are organized, capitalism and market economies tend to displace feudalism, and so on. Yet while these similarities appear in formal organization, it is equally clear that behavior patterns, norms, attitudes, and characteristic ways of doing things may remain quite distinct.

Thus, while the formal institutional structures may evolve in accord with some universal patterns of development, the behavior patterns of individuals, kin and corporate groups, larger corporate communities, coalitions, family and friendship patterns, cliques, patron-client ties, co-optation mechanisms, and the like may exhibit more continuity, persistence, and distinctiveness. The problem has often come when the features of these behavior patterns have been stereotyped as national political behavior or "national character."[59] Furthermore, it is these behavior patterns that make possible the functioning of the "great institutions" (parties, bureaucracies, and the state) and condition their often distinct behavior in distinct societies and cultural areas. Of course, as the great institutions change character historically, so in part do the behavior patterns of groups and individuals.

A large body of research has accumulated in recent years, however, demonstrating that these behavior patterns (for example, Indian caste associations, Islamic fundamentalism, African tribalism, Latin American or south European corporatism, patrimonialism, or organic statism) change far less rapidly than the political and institutional superstructure. That same evidence indicates that such traditional behavoir patterns have proved to be far more flexible, adaptable, accommodative, and persistent than was previously thought possible or that our major social science models presume.

One important aspect that helps explain such continuity is the transfer of the values, norms, and behavior patterns of the dominant groups to the newer emerging groups in the society. As Wolf observes, just as the early integration of society was promoted by certain dominant elites who drew after them the rising elements, so some groups set the tone and pace in forging a social and political etiquette that is then emulated by others. Thus, a group's behavioral etiquette and the direction of its influence reflect its degree of dominance over other groups in society. Examples of the downward circulation of such etiquettes include the transfer of elite values to the rising business-

263

industrial and, later, middle-sector elements, the communication of urban forms to rural groups via the kinship network in Greece, the spread of courtly manners in France or Spain, or the acceptance of assumptions of hierarchy and "natural" inequalities among some lower-class elements in Portugal and Spain. This theory helps explain how and why the values and behavior patterns of the historically dominant group—the elite—may be transferred both to other, newer groups and to the society as a whole.

Equally fascinating—and crucial for understanding southern Europe—is the process by which the politics (broadly defined) of the dominant groups shapes national politics or the politics of the great institutions. Political parties may develop, but their behavior and functions are often devoid of ideology or program and are frequently patterned after the extended family, where loyalty, service, and the mutual ties of patronage and clientage may be more important than issues and theories. Interest groups such as trade unions may form; but they are often chartered and sponsored by the state, receiving certain benefits from it and—in classic patronage fashion—owing it loyalty and service in return. The great institutions may reflect quite distinct cultural traditions.

Especially important is the way the patron-client system has been transferred and retained in national politics. The central state has now become the great national patron, replacing the *caciques* or local notables of the past. Entire agencies, programs, ministries, or parts thereof may be doled out to different groups in return for the traditional reciprocity involving loyalty and service (perhaps votes at election time, agreement to maintain social peace within the group's own membership, perhaps acquiescence in the latest social pact). Client groups may seek to gain special access to the patronal state or to take over state agencies or programs, or portions of them, for themselves. The transition from elite or business dominance of the state system, including the Labor Ministry, to a situation (as in Italy) where the labor federations have themselves captured or hived off parts of the Labor Ministry and Social Security Institute exemplifies this process. The same values and norms governing an earlier, simpler patron-client pattern at local levels have by now been transferred to and persist at the national level. The beneficiaries of the state's largesse and opportunities for sinecures have been altered but not so much the system per se. (Actually in Italy the situation is complicated by the fact that all three of the major labor federations—Socialist, Communist, and Christian Democrat—have each carved out separate patronage niches within the Labor Ministry–Social Security Institute network.)

Description and analysis of the behavior patterns and values discussed here thus reveal much about what might be termed the "hidden mechanisms" (what goes on behind the curtain rather than in front of it) of some modern complex societies in southern Europe. An understanding of the models of etiquette structuring behavior in the dominant groups and then transferred to the newer, rising classes or to the system as a whole also explains much about the social and political dynamic, the changing distribution of forces in the body politic, and, at the same time, the persistence of traditional norms. Similarly, the inculcation of the norms or patterns of one dominant group (for example, elite-dominated patron-client patterns) into the national political system enables us to understand why, although the formal institutional paraphernalia or great institutions seem to conform to universal developmental criteria, the actual behavior and functioning of these institutions may be quite particular or specific to a cultural area. As the cultural and social anthropologists have concluded, this approach need not necessarily lead to definitions of national character as the term has simplistically been employed in the past, but they do indicate the way in which the behavior patterns of one society or cultural area may shape state or bureaucratic behavior and even the structure of social and political forces in ways that are quite different from those of another.

The State and Development in Mediterranean Polities

The extensive regulatory apparatus of public authority seems to have been a salient and continuing characteristic of the Mediterranean economies from at least the days of Diocletian.

WILLIAM GLADE

The notion that southern Europe might be something more than merely a set of boundary lines on a map encompassing a geographic region, that it may be to some degree a cultural whole is undoubtedly a fascinating one.[60] If there is something to the notion of a distinct southern European cultural area and social and political process, some underlying similarities in the operations of that area's core institutions, such as the trade unions and the state-bureaucratic system are also likely.

The leading role of the state in Mediterranean Europe, from Roman times to the present, is suggested in these words cited from William Glade. In Iberia during its centuries of reconquest, integration, and centralization, a type of "Caesaropapist" infrastructure extended the boundaries of the public sector well beyond the range of civil bureaucracy. The state was neither merely a benign filter mechanism through which competing interest groups expressed their views nor merely the reflection of underlying class structure. Rather, the

265

state emerged as a leading, guiding, directing force, imposing order and often its own preferences above those of the rival groups and shaping class relations as well as being shaped by them. Moreover, in the sixteenth century the state became the principal entrepreneur throughout the Mediterranean world. Among the components of this emerging state capitalism or mercantilism were mints, arsenals, vast public works, state banks, state industries and import-export concerns, trade monopolies, regulatory agencies, and various mixed public-private enterprises. Braudel comments:

> The state in the sixteenth century was increasingly emerging as the great collector and redistributor of revenue; it derived income from taxation, the sale of offices, government bonds, and confiscation of an enormous share of the various "national products". . . . It was on the state that warfare depended . . . as did the biggest economic enterprises.[61]

It was not just in the economic sphere that the state emerged as dominant, however, but in the sociopolitical as well. Administrative paternalism, the elaborate regulation of the relations among social and political groups and between them and the state, pervasive intervention in various spheres of activity, and a general conferring on the state of primary responsibility for structuring the social order—these were some of the main features of the southern European state systems. As would be expected, the economic facts of a strong etatist tradition and system went hand in hand with similarly strong sociopolitical ones. Mercantilism in the economic sphere was closely related to the requirements of authoritarianism, centralism, a form of corporatism, and bureaucratic-patrimonialism in the sociopolitical sphere.[62]

Pluralism, therefore, in the free-wheeling and unstructured sense of the U.S. polity or in the only slightly more constrained form of northern Europe failed to develop in southern Europe. The nations of southern Europe (postwar Italy is the major exception) were characterized by systems of "limited pluralism."[63] The distinct groups and classes were, in part, created, nurtured, and sustained in their special privileges and rights by the state. It was the state that organized both public opinion and the dynamic equilibrium of interests. The interest groups generally remained of secondary importance to the state. They might influence the state, gain special access to the privileges it dispersed, or gain control for private advantage of some of its branches; but it was the state that remained the key, with broad areas of discretion and autonomy, not the parties, cliques, or interest groups. A decade ago, in making a link between this historic model and contemporary politics in Iberia and Latin America, I wrote the following:

> It is the state . . . that serves as the instrument of national integration, incorporating diverse groups, guilds, and interests, and functioning as the regulator and filter through which the legitimacy of new social and political forces is recognized and through which they are admitted into the system. Power tends to be concentrated in the executive and in the bureaucratic-patrimonialist state machinery. The bureaucracy serves to dispense the available goods, favors, and spoils to the deserving.[64]

Both a historical and a comparative study of political society in southern Europe indicate the traditional prominence of the state in economic organization and as the major arbiter of distributional relationships among a variety of power contenders. Economically, the state in southern Europe was activist and interventionist, dispensing assorted types of financial assistance to private entrepreneurial groups, mobilizing investment capital, fomenting trade and commerce, passing out contracts and monopolies, and shielding domestic industry, banks, and the like from outside competition. Combining stimulation and protection, the state in southern Europe was vastly more entangled in the economy than it was in England, Germany, or the United States.

The same armamentarium of interventionist devices and expedients used in the economic sphere also gave the state vast political powers. Through patron-client relationships it distributed rewards and resources to its followers and withdrew them from the opposition or from threatening social groups. These devices helped make the southern European systems resistant both to laissez-faire and to the possibilities for domestic revolution. The state was organized on a unitary, centralized, monist, corporatist, and bureaucratic-patrimonialist basis, and to a large extent it remains so today. Although to reify this interpretation of cultural continuity cannot be justified (for in all these countries there are sharp breaks with the past and contrasting, often conflicting, cultural currents), the past dies slowly in southern Europe; the hand of history still weighs especially heavily there. In this light the expanded postwar economic role of the state and its continued leadership (or effort to assert such) in labor and industrial relations do not represent drastic changes in governmental activity.[65]

In the four countries studied in detail—Greece, Italy, Portugal, and Spain—research has revealed that those in control of the state systems still feel a strong compulsion to control and regulate the trade union movements. For example, although the older corporative structures have considerably eroded in Portugal since the 1974 revolution, in Spain since Franco's death, and in Greece since the colonels, the control mechanisms available to the state bureaucracy are still powerful. While there has been some bending both to domestic pressures and to the pressures of the International Labor Organization to liberalize and provide freedom for the trade unions, in fact the instruments available to the respective labor ministries or to an adept prime minister seeking to enforce some form of austerity program remain extensive. Even liberal regimes, while not employing them so often or so heavy handedly as in the past, like to maintain a battery of corporative control mechanisms in reserve. These encompass both legal controls and requirements left over from the corporative era as well as the more informal means by which government may exercise leverage over the trade unions.

In Spain the legal controls on labor activity are still powerful (although at present subject to further negotiation); in Portugal the radical revolution has failed, and the bourgeois one triumphed, with various efforts now under way to restore "discipline" to the work place and break the dominance of the Communist-dominated Intersindical; in Greece the unions have been kept weak and divided by state intervention and favoritism. Italy is of course another story: while the government still retains the capacity to manipulate labor to some degree and has various levers available for reaching accommodations with it, organized labor has virtually complete subsystem autonomy; it exists in what is here termed a "neo-syndicalist" relationship (as contrasted with the "liberal corporatism" of the other countries) to the state; and, despite the fumings and voluminous writings of scores of Christian Democratic constitutional lawyers still seeking to place labor under some legal restraints, it remains powerful, independent, virtually a separate sovereignty within the broader national system.[66]

To point to the continuities in the southern European systems is not, therefore, to deny change. But change, even drastic and fundamental or structural change, has often been handled within some quite familiar boundaries. What was once merely a cartelist state where virtually everyone, including almost the entire middle class, was put on the public payroll has now become a "neo-Bismarckian" system through the grafting on of new functions. In the past these changes have generally been gradual, a response to the evolving situation: the growth of a more complex system of state capitalism, the fostering of national consolidation and development, the growth of vast new social services, the requirements of arbitrating among and imposing solutions on social and political groups to preserve stability and the conditions for economic growth, and the increased economic interdependency and consequent need for greater coordination among diverse interests.

Such changes, however, have implied more an expansion and elaboration of state functions than any fundamental alteration in the leading, guiding, or directing role of the state. Obviously one must distinguish between the *caudillo*-led systems so long persistent in Portugal and Spain and the single-party-dominant system of postwar Italy and between the liberal corporatism of Greece, Portugal, and Spain and the neo-syndicalism of Italy. Still, the parallels between them may be as interesting as the differences, particularly as they relate to the key role played by the state in interaction with organized labor and the changing balances in state-society relations.

There remains the question of the causes for the longevity and sheer survival of such etatist, *dirigiste,* or neo-mercantilist systems. While no complete answer is yet possible, two lines of inquiry seem especially promising. One has to do with political culture, style, historical tradition, and certain characteristic sociopolitical forms. This approach looks at the legal, political-sociological, religious, and historical-cultural bases of southern European society, particularly its historical corporatist, patrimonialist, and organic-statist features. Shorn of the simplistic national character stereotypes and representing systematic research rather than a haphazard approach to history, this method is a useful though still partial one, carrying considerable explanatory power.

The second avenue worthy of further exploration has to do with the patterns and sociopolitical implications of the delayed and, to some extent, dependent development of the southern European area. The persistence of a neo-mercantilist state system also seems to reflect historical lags in development and the comparative weakness and fragmentation of the private sector in the domestic polity and economy, causing the state to fill the void. This pattern derives from the kind of nonhegemonic class and interest arrangement that Marx saw as the structural basis of Bonapartism in France and that led to the development of a strong state apparatus largely autonomous from all classes. The need to maintain order and social peace during times of transition helps explain the corporatist features of these systems, which are to some degree the products of crisis. Although such explanations are useful, they should be viewed as the beginning and not the end of research. They are more useful during some periods than others: they tell us little about why southern Europe lagged in the first place, why statism and corporatism were characteristic long

269

before the nineteenth century onset of industrialization, why in all "crises" corporatist solutions seem preferred, or why corporatism, organic statism, and patrimonialism persist even after their historical epoch has passed. For purposes of this analysis, therefore, we prefer to keep open the question of ultimate causation, since we are not sure that is even a very interesting or significant issue and we prefer to let the data speak for themselves rather than seeking to impose some artificial restraints on them a priori.

Southern European Labor and Labor Relations

Southern European unions are not based on the same principles Americans take for granted.

AMERICAN LABOR ATTACHÉ

The southern European sociopolitical systems may be pictured, at least historically, as pyramidal, hierarchically stratified, and authoritarian. In these systems power tended to be concentrated rather than dispersed and unitary rather than pluralistic, with the central state apparatus dominating the pinnacles of the system. Divided horizontally in rigid class layers, these systems have also been organized vertically into a variety of corporate sectors. While southern European society is thus organized on both a class and a corporative basis, it is the corporative that is our main concern here. By now, organized labor, along with the church, the army, the bureaucracy, the entrepreneurial groups and others, has come to constitute one of the major societal or corporate pillars in this vertical, pyramidal arrangement in all four countries.[67]

A former American labor attaché, in what seems a naive and elementary insight but was clearly an eye-opening experience for him, has written that the southern European unions are not based on the same principles that Americans take for granted. They are so "different," he says, that knowledge of the U.S. system of labor relations may be more a hindrance than a help in understanding them. Among the features he singled out as making the southern European labor movements distinctive were their strong political, ideological, and even religious base; the persistent and pervasive sense of class differences, hierarchy, and conflict that the society helped engender; the corporatively based nature of the southern European labor systems; the highly centralized structure of labor bargaining; the preeminent role of the state in overseeing labor relations; the seemingly greater importance of prolabor legislation than of collective contracts; the political dependence of the unions on the state, rather than on employers, for greater benefits, increased wages, and better working conditions; the comparatively greater strength of the unions at the national level and their close relations with political parties compared with their weakness at the plant level; and their greater emphasis on political action than on collective bargaining. These features not only made the southern European unions different, he said, but also were related to the stratified, hierarchical, pyramidal, and etatist nature of their national societies.[68]

A study published by the International Institute for Labor Studies in Geneva focused on parallel themes.[69] Among the common features of the industrial relations systems of France, Italy, Portugal, and Spain (Greece was not included), which, in the author's words, "set them apart from most of the advanced industrial countries, or at any rate from those of the Nordic or Anglo-Saxon types," were the following: (1) recurrent political instability, recourse to violence and political action on the part of the unions, and a tendency toward one-party or state authoritarianism; (2) church- and society-upheld values of authority and hierarchy, which, this author believed, helped produce both the anarchy of the lower classes and the efforts of the upper classes to hold them in check through corporative controls; (3) an emphasis on the paternalism of the state and of a national system of patron-client relations; (4) therefore, the unions' use of political rather than collective bargaining strategies, stemming both from the need to win, by political means, long-denied labor "rights" *and* from resentments concerning class barriers that often outweigh issues of modestly higher wage benefits; and (5) a context combining a weak national consensus with the unions' lack of confidence in the ability of the industrial ruling class to provide balanced economic growth and little faith in the fairness of the state that has historically upheld employer interests at the expense of labor.

A wealth of such anecdotal, semi-impressionistic, semi-systematic data all point to the same conclusion: the largely distinct systems of labor relations of southern Europe. Recently, more rigorously systematic and empirical studies have pointed toward a number of the same or similar themes. A major example is David Snyder's comparative studies of strikes and the strike process in France, Italy, and the United States.[70] Snyder argues that in the past conceptual models stressing economic factors have dominated studies of industrial conflict. Among the factors that he says have influenced the formation of such economic models are protests resulting from rapid social change, failed negotiations, and forms of collective action. But recent investigations of French and Italian strikes, he states, point toward the greater importance of political and institutional factors in explaining labor action. A comparison of the United States with these two countries indicates that the key differences lie in the institutional context of labor relations, specifically in the role of the state. The state in France and Italy has long been an important actor in the system of industrial relations—some would say the most important actor. Workers' action in France and Italy was designed to bring pressure on the government rather than on employers because the government could exert maximum leverage on otherwise reluctant employers or grant concessions to labor unilaterally; stikes therefore were the means by which unions contended for political power. While the contrasting collective bargaining model holds for the United States, for France and Italy (and southern Europe more generally) the entire framework of the assumptions undergirding such models fails to apply.

The differences have to do with (1) the extent and stability of union membership (low and weak, at least in the past, in France and Italy); (2) the national political position of labor (historically not legitimized as a full or equal participant in national life); and (3) the low degree of institutionalization of collective bargaining. Where union membership is extensive and stable, where labor's position has been long legitimate, and where collective bargainiing is well institutionalized, as in the United States, Great Britain, West Germany, Scandinavia, and Holland, the collective bargaining model usually taken as the norm for other nations generally holds. But where these institutional features are comparatively weak or conversely where the state's role in the national life including labor relations has historically been strong, as in southern Europe generally, a political model must be used. Thus Snyder concludes that one cannot use a simple economic model to explain labor behavior without regard to the legal, political-cultural, and institutional settings in which they occur and that in southern Europe a political-institutional model carries more explanatory power than a simple economic one.

Much of the literature points toward the same general conclusion as Snyder's: the need to adapt the explanatory models we use to the political and institutional settings of the country or group of countries we investigate.[71] In my earlier work on the origins of the Iberian and Latin American labor relations systems, I found that the modern structure of labor relations in these countries was still importantly shaped by their distinctively corporatist, patrimonialist, and organic-statist origins and traditions.[72] That is, the labor relations systems of these nations have from the beginning largely been cast in an etatist, corporatist, and patrimonialist mold as distinct from a liberal and laissez-faire one and that these have continued to influence the nature of class relations, the role of the state and state-society relations, the

political structure and system and the way these have characteristically dealt with change, and the nature of public policy. Corporatism of course has both multiple causes and multiple effects. If we
would understand these systems, we must examine their hypothesized corporative origins closely, their evolution, and their movement away from manifestly corporative systems toward something
else.

In exploring and verifying the hypothesis of corporative origins,
this research investigated the contents of the first labor codes, the
social legislation and constitutional clauses relating to work life and
labor, and the earliest state agencies established to deal with the rising
labor movements. The questions posed in this research are, Were the
early official labor relations systems in fact corporative in origin? What
was the impact of this form of structuring on the labor relations
systems? What were the dynamics of change within these systems?
What were the varieties of forms within the corporative context and
those seeking to transcend it, in both theory and practice? And what
are the consequent implications for southern European society, politics, development, and the state system?

Based on these data, a political bargaining model of labor relations is set forth, as distinct from the familiar economic or collective
bargaining model. In southern Europe the social gaps and class differences remain sufficiently large that the idea that workers and
employers can sit down as equals on opposite sides of the bargaining
table and resolve their differences amicably is still only weakly established. In such a context of hierarchy and inequality, workers must
generally look to the state for relief, largesse, and protection. These
conditions arising from economic and class differences and the past
weakness of labor are reinforced by those historical predilections for
corporatism, patrimonialism, and organic statism. The state remains—even in Italy, which has to a considerable extent transcended
its corporatist past and evolved toward the collective or economic
bargaining model[73]—the third party in virtually all labor disputes.
Hence for southern Europe, a labor relations model derived from the
Latin American or perhaps Iberic-Latin context and based on a political bargaining system with a number of distinct and persistent corporatist features is a feasible construct. This model is probably as useful
as one derived from the northern European experience, which (except
perhaps for Italy) southern Europe has not yet known.[74]

Although the origins of the Iberian, Latin American, and southern European systems are corporatist in the broadest sense, patrimonialist, and organic statist (albeit with interesting variations and
quite a mixture of other influences), the more interesting issue is the

degree to which they remain so today. Hence a series of indexes may be applied to measure change within, or away from, such corporately shaped, etatist, and patrimonialist systems of labor relations. The variables used included:

- time factors: when the codes or labor charters were adopted and their subsequent institutional evolution
- whether corporatism took a state or more societal form
- the degree of such corporative structuring and control and the changes in this over time in different nations
- the political context: that is, competitive or closed, authoritarian or democratic, multi- or single-party
- degree of economic development and industrialization and the growth and comparative organizational strength and structural base of the respective labor movements
- the dynamics of change within these labor relations systems: that is, change induced from within or without, changing governmental and societal orientations to labor and labor issues, use of labor violence and political action, and evolution within a corporative system or its shunting aside

These measures imply a far greater variety and range of corporatism than previously assumed.[75] They also offer a way of comparing more or less systematically the southern European labor relations systems here under review. They provide, further, a means to assess some interpretations of the phenomenon of corporatism—political-cultural, liberal, and structuralist—that are often perceived as being at variance but may in fact be compatible. Finally, they offer us a method of exploring one of the key topics of the study, namely if to some degree southern European labor relations are still cast in one or another form of corporatism or if they have by now changed to something else.

From Political Culture to Political Economy in Southern Europe?

I would suggest that Italy's labor relations today have more in common with the traditions of Northern Europe than the traditions of the South. If corporatist practices develop, it will be through a process more similar to that in Sweden or Holland than that in Spain.

PETER LANGE

Economic, objective, and organizational factors may now be as important in determining southern Europe's persistent corporatist features as its earlier historical and cultural tradition. A nascent liberal order had grown up alongside the traditional corporatist structures, gradually gaining in strength until by the early twentieth century it was roughly equivalent to the corporatist one. Such regimes as Franco's, Salazar's, Mussolini's, and Metaxas's, therefore, while in one sense in accord with their countries' historical traditions, were outside the liberal framework of those traditions forcing the regimes to use a high degree of repression ("fascism") to suppress the liberal elements. Not only have the earlier trends toward greater structural transformation continued and accelerated in recent years (Italy in the postwar period, Spain after Franco, Portugal since the 1974 revolution, Greece since the colonels), but also a third or "Socialist" option and framework has now grown up along with the other two. As the older corporatist organization of society and its accompanying explanatory model have been gradually supplanted by these newer models, therefore, it seems appropriate to shift the focus from political-cultural explanations to political-economic ones, or at least to some combination of these. This shift would seem to be a pragmatic and empirical matter, not a political or ideological one.[76]

These changes, coupled with other forces of international interdependence, imply that at some levels southern Europe is now less a distinct cultural area and more an area experiencing the same forces propelling change in northern Europe. In Portugal, the revolution basically set aside the older corporative model in favor of one, for a time, that was revolutionary and Socialist. Given the division of opinion in Greece, that country can obviously no longer be looked at wholly in terms of its earlier corporatist and paternalistic structures. The transition to democracy in Spain, while limited and incomplete in some areas, is nevertheless real. Since the late-1960s, Italy may well have a labor relations system more closely comparable to the most advanced systems of northern Europe than to an earlier corporatist model.[77]

The case of Italy merits special and perhaps separate attention. In Italy, and in varying degrees in the other countries as well, it may no longer be the Mediterranean or southern European aspects that are crucial but broader economic forces. At Italy's stage of development, and perhaps only slightly less in the other countries, there may well be a transfer from culture-based explanations to political-economic ones. In all these countries different traditions may now be called upon, not just the corporatist one. There is by now a real liberal tradition as well as one oriented toward socialism. Thus, the interrelations between state and society, particularly labor groups, may be considerably more complex than previously indicated. As societal groups grow in influence and autonomy, the historic commanding and tutelary role of the state diminishes. The equation may have shifted by now away from corporatism and the state and toward society.

Provisionally, I suggest that the corporatist model put forward here as an explanatory paradigm works best for the period of early unionism and of liberal or middle-class incorporation into, or conquest of, the system, from the 1890s to the 1930s. At this stage the unions were still generally led and governed by middle-class elites, the state system itself was dominated by its emerging middle sectors, and the unions were relatively weak. Some of these changes are summarized in table 8–1. At a later stage, when the unions had become stronger and more militant, when real issues of class and interest politics took precedence over the older paternalism, and when Socialist pressures became strong, the earlier corporative model lost some of its explanatory strength or was combined with something else (liberal corporatism or neo-syndicalism). At this stage, although the corporative framework still has some utility, the other models are clearly called for.

At this stage also, one must distinguish between the type of corporatism espoused by the elites and the program supported by the unions. In Italy, for example, the so-called Pandolfi Plan put forward by a Christian Democratic–dominated government provided for the familiar triangular collaboration and harmony between labor, employers, and the state; called for a kind of institutionalized consultation on policy measures that contained strong corporative ingredients; and advocated the incorporation of both labor and capital into the state system. It was a full-fledged, although updated, corporative scheme.[78] But worker groups opposed the plan and offered in response a system of what might be called "pan-syndicalism." In short, different classes in the system may have quite distinct notions of the kind of corporatism to be put in place or about whether the state is to be corporatist at all.

The implications are several, both theoretical and practical. First, these comments may force us to look at Italy and to some extent at the other countries in terms of the neo-corporatism of the advanced industrial societies of northern Europe and not in terms of their historical Mediterranean ethos.[79] Second, we must be aware of how in the present more pluralist circumstances of these societies, corporatist solutions may be manipulated for class and partisan reasons that may have little to do with historical political culture. Third, we must understand the complex overlaps of corporatist, liberal, Socialist, and perhaps other institutional forms—the varied combinations that exist.

276

TABLE 8–1

THE TRANSITION FROM STATE CORPORATISM TO LIBERAL CORPORATISM TO NEO-SYNDICALISM: SOME GUIDEPOSTS

Point of Comparison	State Corporatism	Liberal Corporatism	Neo-syndicalism
Role of state	Authoritarian	Limited	Fragmented, immobilized
Nature of economic system	State capitalist/ plutocratic	Mixed/ modernizing	High public ownership
Class base	Elite and bourgeois dominance	Middle class, pluralist	Mass mobilization
Status of the unions	State dominated	Juridically independent	Union penetration of state
Legal-constitutional controls over unions	Extensive web of controls	Limited controls	Virtually no controls
Role of Labor Ministry	Manipulates labor	Administrative roles	Servant of labor
Degree of union independence	Dependent on state	Autonomous from state	"State" within a state
Labor's response to austerity	Labor shoulders austerity's burdens	Labor a strong pressure group, bargaining situation	Labor resistance
Political strength of unions	Weak	One group among several, pluralism	Can sometimes topple a government or minister or impose its will
Percent organized	10–30	20–50	Over 40
Degree of labor unity	Labor kept divided	Pluralism of labor groups; Socialists predominate	Common front; labor united and strong

SOURCE: Author.

In addition, the theory must be realistic, capable of providing an organizational and theoretical principle for our case studies, but sufficiently flexible to indicate divergence and new departures as well. Finally, having made the case for at least the partial homogenization of southern Europe's "distinct" political culture under the impact of modern forces of change, the contrary argument must also be recognized. For not only is political culture at this transitional stage still an important, though probably reduced, explanatory factor, but also the hypothesis has been advanced recently that once nations become advanced industrial societies, political culture may again become important in explaining the persistent differences among them.

Conclusions, Hypotheses, and Propositions

Can it be said that the Mediterranean is an internally coherent zone? On the whole the answer is yes.

FERNAND BRAUDEL

From geography, history, religion, climate, commerce, law, language, culture, economics, and agriculture, the southern European region has a certain unity, constitutes a certain *civilization*. One can observe it on the map, see it, feel it, smell it. Yet it is also a part of a larger Europe as well. Is it, then, sufficiently distinct from the rest of Europe to constitute a subject of specifically regional politics, economics, or, in the case of this study, labor and industrial relations?[80]

In its formal structures and the great institutions—parties, parliaments, bureaucracies, unions, and the like—southern Europe often bears striking similarities to northern Europe. But while the formal institutions are often similar, the differences in the informal rules and patterns that govern behavior, the group values, and the ways in which the formal institutions actually function are often still important. The main themes are summarized in the following propositions.

• Southern Europe may, to some degree and at least historically, be considered a distinct cultural area. This obviously is not to negate its overlaps with other areas; its position within the broader European, Mediterranean, or other transnational contexts; the quite different patterns prevailing between and even within the separate political systems of the area; or the difficulties and ambiguities of delineating precise boundaries. The degree to which we can specify a distinct southern European cultural area depends, it seems apparent, on what we seek to explain and the level of generality we wish to achieve. Our focus here is the national political and labor and industrial relations systems of southern Europe: hence our definition of the area, arbitrary in some ways but reasonable in others, as encompassing Greece, Italy, Portugal, and Spain. This definition does not solve all our problems, but it does have considerable intellectual justification: it provides a plausible beginning point for the research, and it helps resolve pragmatically some research problems of time and comprehensiveness.

• Among the distinctive historical, political-cultural, and sociological features of the nations of this cultural area are a continuing and comparatively high degree of corporatism, patrimonialism, and organic statism. This is not to imply that these features are not present in other nations or that they are unique to southern Europe. Rather what this proposition suggests is the comparatively high *degree* to which these features are present and their combination in what is likely a *syndrome of traits*, specific to this cultural area.

• Within the southern European context, the role and function of the central state and state system are pivotal. The state performs, historically and often continuing at present, a set of guiding, leading, directing, controlling, and tutelary roles. The state is still, to some degree, organized and functions within corporatist, patrimonialist, and organicist forms and characteristics noted above. This stands in fairly stark contrast to the laissez-faire principles (political as well as economic) on which the North American polity is organized; it also necessitates some revisions in Marxian interpretation to account for the "relative autonomy" of the state.[81]

• "Society" in southern Europe has been largely defined by its major organized or "corporate" units, including organized labor. Such groups have generally been subordinate to and dependent on the power of the central state, although they may assert and struggle for varying degrees of autonomy from it. The political options of these groups in this context have been to seek to gain legal recognition from the state for their existence and activities, to secure greater benefits in return for the classic patron-client contractual obligation of loyalty and service, then to seek to gain greater "liberties" and special access to the state system, and perhaps eventually to "hive off" or capture a part or all of the state system for themselves.

• Change generally has taken place within these systems, historically and continuing in important ways at present, under state auspices and control.

• The state generally seeks to structure, license, and regulate the participation of new groups and social classes within the system to maintain existing structures and prevent radical departures.

• The institutional framework for such structuring and control has traditionally been bureaucratic-patrimonialist; for organized labor the specific institutional structure used by the state to control its participation was state corporatism. Examples include Portugal under Salazar and, to a lesser degree, Caetano; Spain under Primo de Rivera and Franco; Greece under Metaxas and the colonels; and Italy under Mussolini.

• While state corporatism may be employed to control labor during its early stages, sooner or later, reflecting changed circumstances and the growing strength of labor, a more "liberal" form replaces the earlier authoritarian form. But while the system is "more liberal," it may also retain various of its corporatist features. Change generally continues to take place within an organicist, patrimonialist, corporatist, and bureaucratic-etatist framework and does not necessarily imply a transition to a fully laissez-faire society and polity. Labor is freer than before but not entirely free; it is still often subject to state control, regulation, manipulation, or discipline. The polity at this stage is more liberal than under state corporatism but the pluralism that exists is still often a form of limited pluralism and bears little resemblance to the free-wheeling interest group struggle and unfettered associability of the United States. Examples include Greece under Caramanlis, Spain under Suárez, Portugal under Soares, and, with reservations, Italy from 1948 to 1968.

• The next stage in this progression is a system of neo-syndicalism.[82] Neo-syndicalism is defined here as trade union action to control directly all or part of the state machinery. The labor ministry and social security institutes are ordinarily the main targets for labor to seek to capture in this way. Organized labor is at this stage no longer so much subject to state discipline and regulation (although the state may still be not entirely without other means to manipulate and seek to control labor) but is itself a part of the state and its bureaucratic-patrimonialist machinery. It has hived off one sector of the state system for itself and for its own advantage. Examples include Portugal, 1974–1975, when the Communist party was given control of the Labor Ministry and used it to benefit its own labor sector and political position, while keeping the authoritarian-pyramidal and hierarchical-bureaucratic structure of the old regime and its top-down labor structure largely intact;[83] and Italy from 1968 to the present, when organized labor moved "from marginality to centrality" and took direct control of some parts of the Labor Ministry–Social Security apparatus. These changes—from state-corporatism, to liberal-corporatism, to neo-syndicalism—are summarized in the accompanying table 8–1.

• In this way change—even quite radical change involving structural transformations—has come to southern Europe; but change has come in ways that have often served to retain, even enhance, the central role of the bureaucratic-patrimonialist state, within an organicist, unitary, and corporatist (broadly defined) framework more than an unfettered laissez-faire one. Of course it must be recognized that other explanatory frameworks must be used as complements or supplements to the one suggested here, that change may take place at times outside the corporatist-etatist framework as well as within it, and that corporatism in the present circumstances of southern Europe is as much due to economic and objective circumstances as to historical and political-cultural traditions. Still there remains a special affinity in southern Europe for corporatist-etatist forms of socioeconomic organization, sometimes more an aspiration than actual operating procedures, more behavior and habit than formalized institution. In this way much of the distinctiveness of the southern European social and political process has been preserved, not so much its formal institutional structures, which resemble those elsewhere, but its informal ways of operating.

• At present the precise implications of this form of change for the countries affected are unclear. Four major possibilities, which may however not be mutually exclusive, present themselves.

—a full-fledged transition from the present system of growing corporate pluralism or neo-syndicalism to revolutionary socialism, implying the likely resurrection or perpetuation of an etatist system but with new groups or parties in control at the top of the pyramid who have captured not just the labor and social security agencies for themselves and their clients but the entire state system

—a perpetuation of the status quo: that is, of a more or less stable but pluralist and probably increasingly disorganized and immobilized system in which each major corporate or societal group captures or hives off a part of the state machinery, and the patronage and other benefits flowing from it, for itself

—a further fragmentation and disintegration of the social and political fabric until a stage is reached of almost complete subsystem autonomy, little attachment to a central core or consensual nucleus, virtually constant conflict, accelerating violence, morbific politics, competing group militias, and the potential for much greater civil strife (Italy may be reaching that condition; Argentina may have reached it some time ago.)

—the demand and possibilities for an authoritarian solution becoming stronger (But such authoritarianism, in a condition of advanced social mobilization and neo-syndicalism, would likely require for its success extremely repressive measures. Again, Argentina or perhaps Chile or Uruguay serve as illustrations.)

These propositions summarize the changing industrial and labor relations systems of southern Europe. The study has both major empirical implications for a comparative understanding of how these systems work and theoretical implications for such key issues as the presumed universality of the social sciences, whether southern Europe constitutes a distinct cultural area, the role of the state and state-society relations in comparative perspective, and corporatism and its various forms, stages, and permutations.

Notes

1. The role of the state, not as a more or less neutral referee of the interest group struggle as in American pluralist theory but as a guiding, directing, controlling force in society, has recently been the subject of renewed attention by social scientists. A useful collection on this theme is the special issue of *Daedalus*, vol. 108 (Fall 1979), devoted to "the state"; see also the author's "State-Society Relations and Public Policy in Latin America" (Paper presented at the Center for Latin American and Iberian Studies, Harvard University, April, 1980), forthcoming.

2. Howard J. Wiarda, *Corporatism and Development: The Portuguese Experience* (Amherst: University of Massachusetts Press, 1977); also Wiarda, "Spain and Portugal," in Peter Merkl, ed., *Western European Party Systems* (New York: Free Press, 1980), pp. 298–328.

3. Howard J. Wiarda, *Politics and Social Change in Latin America: The Distinct Tradition* (Amherst: University of Massachusetts Press, 1982); Wiarda, "Toward a Framework for the Study of Political Change in the Iberic-Latin Tradition: The Corporative Model," *World Politics*, vol. 25 (January 1973), pp. 206–35; Wiarda, *Corporatism and National Development in Latin America* (Boulder, Colo.: Westview Press, 1981).

4. Some preliminary explorations of these themes include Howard J. Wiarda's *Transcending Corporatism? The Portuguese Corporative System and the Revolution of 1974* (Columbia: Institute of International Studies, University of South Carolina, 1976); and "The Ethnocentrism of the Social Sciences: Implications for Research and Policy," *The Review of Politics*, vol. 43 (April 1981).

5. Only a few of the modern and more general studies on this theme are listed here: Andre Siegfried, *The Mediterranean* (New York: Duell, Sloan and Pearce, 1948); Edward C. Banfield, *The Moral Basis of a Backward Society* (New York: The Free Press, 1958); Michael Banton, ed., *The Social Anthropology of Complex Societies* (London: Tavistock, 1966); J. G. Peristiany, ed., *Honor and Shame: The Values of Mediterranean Society* (Chicago: University of Chicago Press, 1966); Julian Pitt-Rivers, *Mediterranean Countrymen: Essays in the Social Anthropology of the Mediterranean* (Paris: Mouton, 1963); Sidney Tarrow, *Peasant Communism in Southern Italy* (New Haven, Conn.: Yale University Press, 1967); the special edition of the *Anthropological Quarterly*, vol. 36 (July 1963), on the theme of "The Old World Peoples," especially the article by Donald Pitkin on "Mediterranean Europe"; J. Davis, *People of the Mediterranean: An Essay in Comparative Social History* (London: Routledge and Kegan Paul, 1976); Ernest

Gellner and John Waterbury, eds., *Patrons and Clients in Mediterranean Societies* (London: Duckworth, 1977); and, to my mind, the best study on the subject, Fernand Braudel, *The Mediterranean and the Mediterranean World in the Age of Philip II* (New York: Harper and Row, 1972).

6. See, for instance, Siegfried's chap. 4 "The Mediterranean Race."

7. Gabriel A. Almond and Sidney Verba, eds., *The Civic Culture Revisited* (Boston: Little, Brown, 1980).

8. Robert T. Holt and John E. Truner, eds., *The Methodology of Comparative Research* (New York: Free Press, 1970).

9. Still useful on "ideal types" is the classic formulation by Max Weber, *The Theory of Social and Economic Organization* (New York: Free Press, 1964).

10. But keeping in mind, of course, the immense differences between the north and the south of Italy.

11. Emile Durkheim, *The Division of Labor in Society* (New York: Free Press, 1947). The emphasis on the universal homogenizing effects of capitalism and industrialization on culture, society, and politics dominates both much Marxian and non-Marxian economics and sociology. While clearly valid at some times, such homogenization seems less so at others, as illustrated in the discussion that follows.

12. These themes are treated in greater detail in Wiarda, *Corporatism and National Development* and "Ethnocentrism."

13. The East/West division of Europe is both more familiar and easier to draw than the North/South one. There are, in addition, political and strategic reasons—NATO, the "common defense," the indivisibility of "Western democracy"—as well as intellectual ones for wishing to mute or deny the latter while emphasizing the former.

14. The discussion in this section borrows heavily from materials prepared by Edward Malefakis for an NEH seminar "Comparative History of Southern Europe since 1815" (Columbia University, 1977), which in turn derives in part from Braudel's extensive treatment.

15. See especially Braudel's discussion of how Mediterranean feudalism differed from the paradigmatic case of France and the implications of this for contrasting social structures.

16. Richard M. Morse, "The Heritage of Latin America," in Louis Hartz, ed., *The Founding of New Societies* (New York: Harcourt, Brace, 1964).

17. Dudley Seers et al., eds., *Underdeveloped Europe: Studies in Core-Periphery Relations* (Sussex: Harvester, 1979).

18. Again, Braudel's comments on these themes seem both carefully researched and judiciously balanced.

19. The figures and analysis derive from and follow closely the materials prepared by Malefakis; see also Syles Labini, *Saggio sulle clasi sociali* (Rome: Laterza, 1975).

20. Stanley Hoffmann, "Impressions, Depressions, Repressions, Expressions: France 1980" (Speech given at the Center for European Studies, Harvard University, January, 1980), in which he referred similarly to France as a "bureaucratic monarchy" politically, with a "neo-mercantilist" economy. For further elaboration of these connections between political and economic

structures see Howard J. Wiarda, "The Political Economy of Latin American Development: The Mercantilist Model" (Paper presented at the Harvard-MIT Joint Seminar on Political Development, Cambridge, Massachussetts, February 27, 1980), parts of which were published in *Corporatism and National Development*. For a discussion of a nation that sought to separate the two, where Keynesianism was accepted in the economic sphere but not—until recently perhaps—in the political one, see Wiarda, "The Latin Americanization of the United States," *The New Scholar*, vol. 7 (1979), pp. 51–85.

21. Gideon Sjoberg, *The Preindustrial City* (New York: Free Press, 1960).

22. An especially good analysis of these processes, equally relevant to southern Europe, is Claudio Véliz, *The Centralist Tradition in Latin America* (Princeton: Princeton University Press, 1980).

23. Charles W. Anderson, *The Political Economy of Modern Spain* (Madison: University of Wisconsin Press, 1970); Roland Sarti, *Fascism and the Industrial Leadership in Italy* (Berkeley: University of California Press, 1971); Keith R. Legg, *Politics in Modern Greece* (Stanford: Stanford University Press, 1969); Wiarda, *Corporatism and National Development*.

24. Alexander Gerschenkron, *Economic Backwardness in Historical Perspective* (Cambridge, Mass.: Harvard University Press, 1962).

25. James Kurth, "Political Parallelisms in Southern Europe Since 1815" (paper prepared for delivery at the Conference on southern Europe, Columbia University, New York, March 21–23, 1977).

26. I have discussed elsewhere the particularism, the parochialism, and the less-than-universal character of some major social science models; see Wiarda, "Ethnocentrism."

27. The classic statement is by Marx, *The Eighteenth Brumaire of Louis Bonaparte* (Moscow: Progress Publishers, 1972).

28. For a general and conceptual overview of the state-society approach see Wiarda, "State-Society Relations."

29. The analysis here closely follows that of Kurth, "Political Parallelisms." Actually, my own preference would be to push the analysis of parallels in southern Europe back much farther, to the revival of Roman law, the formulation of the first "corporations" (church orders, military brotherhoods, universities, towns, and other associations), and the emergence of new, struggling state systems and their interrelations with these equally new societal groups. The study of the origins of these "state" and "societal" systems is part of another research project currently being undertaken.

30. The term "middle sectors" is used to indicate the divisions and lack of agreed upon principles characterizing this sector. For some parallels as well as differences with other countries see Charles Maier, *Recasting Bourgeois Europe* (Princeton: Princeton University Press, 1975).

31. Sarti, *Fascism;* Wiarda, *Corporatism and Development*.

32. Howard J. Wiarda, "Corporatism and Development in the Iberic-Latin World: Persistent Strains and New Possibilities," *Review of Politics*, vol. 36 (January 1974), pp. 3–33.

33. Further differentiation between the four countries is of course neces-

sary. In the spring and summer of 1980 what impressed me was the attention given these continuing control mechanisms, especially in Spain.

34. Kurth, "Political Parallelisms"; Hartz, *The Founding of New Societies;* Wiarda, "Toward a Framework."

35. S. N. Eisenstadt, "Post-Traditional Society and the Continuity and Reconstruction of Tradition," *Daedalus,* vol. 102 (Winter 1973), pp. 1–27; Lloyd I. Rudolph and Susanne Hoeber Rudolph, *The Modernity of Tradition* (Chicago: University of Chicago Press, 1967).

36. Charles W. Anderson, "Toward a Theory of Latin American Politics," in Wiarda, ed., *Politics and Social Change.*

37. Samuel P. Huntington, *Political Order in Changing Societies* (New Haven: Yale University Press, 1968), p. 196.

38. The description of how such systems work is elaborated in Howard J. Wiarda and Harvey F. Kline, *Latin American Politics and Development* (Boston: Houghton-Mifflin, 1979).

39. The imagery and analysis derive from Kurth, "Political Parallelisms."

40. Corporatism does seem to be something of an elite response to crisis, but that begs the question of why corporatism is consistently the favored response and why other groups may favor it besides the elites; see the discussion in the text below.

41. On the one hand, one can easily picture a society that is corporatist-authoritarian in its beliefs at the top and Lockean-participatory at the bottom. On the other hand, one should not underestimate the capacity of some groups to set the pace in forging a social "etiquette," which is then emulated by others and becomes a shared societal value system. The matter is discussed in the text, but further research is needed.

42. Franco, for instance, was very clever at projecting his particular values as the national values and *only* cultural tradition of Spain; but then one suspects all political groups in their own way seek to promote the concept put forward by former cabinet secretary (and GM president) Charles Wilson, "What's good for General Motors is good for the U.S.A."

43. These and other reservations have been treated at greater length in Wiarda, *Corporatism and National Development.*

44. Eric Wolf, "Cultural Dissonance in the Italian Alps," *Comparative Studies in Society and History,* vol. 5 (1962), pp. 1–14; Wolf, "Kinship, Friendship, and Patron-Client Relations in Complex Societies," in Banton, ed., *Social Anthropology,* pp. 1–22; Wolf, "Society and Symbols in Latin Europe and in the Islamic Near East: Some Comparisons," *Anthropological Quarterly,* vol. 42 (July 1969), pp. 287–301.

45. Howard J. Wiarda, "Corporatist Theory and Ideology," *Journal of Church and State,* vol. 20 (Winter 1978), pp. 29–56.

46. Angus MacKay, *Spain in the Middle Ages: From Frontier to Empire, 1000–1500* (London: Macmillan, 1977).

47. These and other definitions are offered in Wiarda, *Corporatism and National Development.* For a consensus definition of corporatism, with which the present author more or less concurs, that offers a way out of the termi-

nological morass into which some writers have fallen, see David Collier and Ruth Berins Collier, "Who Does What, to Whom, and How: Toward a Comparative Analysis of Latin American Corporatism," in James M. Malloy, ed., *Authoritarianism and Corporatism in Latin America* (Pittsburgh, Penn.: University of Pittsburgh Press, 1977), pp. 489–512; another consensus definition, focusing on corporatism's main traits and expressing the desire to quit quarreling over terms and get on with the research, is Daniel Levy, "Corporatist and Pluralist Principles in Government-University Relations: Chile, Mexico and the U.S." (Paper presented at the Fourth International Conference on Higher Education, University of Lancaster, August 29–September 1, 1978).

48. The distinction is Manoïlesco's, *Le siècle du corporatisme* (Paris: Félix Alcan, 1934).

49. Thomas Gilby, *The Political Thought of Thomas Aquinas* (Chicago: University of Chicago Press, 1958).

50. Weber, *The Theory of Social and Economic Organization*, p. 346ff.

51. Philippe Schmitter, *Interest Conflict and Political Change in Brazil* (Stanford: Stanford University Press, 1971), pp. 98–99. Close readers will note that this definition corresponds closely to my own formulation in "Toward a Framework."

52. The best study is, again, Braudel, *The Mediterranean.*

53. Wolf, "Society and Symbols."

54. Quoted in Wolf.

55. The literature is vast; especially useful on the themes presented here are Gaines Post, *Studies in Medieval Legal Thought: Public Law and the State, 1100–1322* (Princeton: Princeton University Press, 1964); and MacKay, *Spain in the Middle Ages.*

56. James Burnham, *The Machiavellians* (Chicago: Regnery, 1943).

57. The definition and corollaries of organic-statism derive from Alfred Stepan, *The State and Society: Peru in Comparative Perspective* (Princeton: Princeton University Press, 1978). But see also Wiarda, "Toward a Framework" and "Corporatist Theory and Ideology" for earlier statements of many of these same ideas, and Robert Packenham's critical review of the Stepan book in *American Political Science Review,* vol. 74 (September 1980), pp. 864–66.

58. Wolf, "Society and Symbols" and "Kinship, Friendship, and Patron-Client Relations."

59. Classic examples include Ruth Benedict, *The Chrysanthemum and the Sword* (Boston: Houghton-Mifflin, 1946); or Geoffrey Gorer, *The American People* (New York: Norton, 1948).

60. A. L. Kroeber, *The Nature of Culture* (Chicago: University of Chicago Press, 1952). The analysis in this and succeeding paragraphs follows closely that of William P. Glade, "The State and Economic Development in Mediterranean Politics" (Paper presented at the 1973 Annual Meeting of the American Political Science Association, New Orleans, September 4–8).

61. Braudel, *The Mediterranean,* p. 449.

62. An elaboration of this "neo-mercantilist" model and its main traits is in Wiarda, "The Political Economy."

63. Juan Linz, "An Authoritarian Regime: Spain," in E. Allardt and Y.

Littunen, eds., *Cleavages, Ideologies and Party Systems* (Helsinki: Westermarck Society, 1964), pp. 291–342.

64. Wiarda, "Toward a Framework," pp. 221–22.

65. For some comparisons see Andrew Shonfield, *Modern Capitalism: The Changing Balance of Public and Private Power* (London: Oxford University Press, 1965).

66. Peter Lange, "Neo-Corporatism in Italy? A Case in European Perspective" (Paper presented at the Workshop on Neo-Corporatism and Public Policy, Center for International Studies, Cornell University, April 3–5, 1980); and Lange and Maurizio Vannicelli, "Strategy under Stress: The Italian Union Movement and the Italian Crisis in Developmental Perspective," in Peter Lange, George Ross, and Maurizio Vannicelli, *Labor Unions and Change in France and Italy* (London: Allen and Unwin, 1982).

67. Based on materials, interviews, and reports supplied the author during a period of research, July–September 1979, at the International Labor Organization headquarters in Geneva.

68. Also, Carroll Hawkins, "Reflections on Labor's Relations to Government and Politics in Latin America," *Western Political Quarterly*, vol. 20 (December 1967), pp. 930–40.

69. F. Sellier, *Future Industrial Relations: France, Italy, Portugal and Spain* (Geneva, IILS, 1972).

70. David Snyder, "Institutional Setting and Industrial Conflict: Comparative Analyses of France, Italy, and the United States," *American Sociological Review*, vol. 40 (June 1975), pp. 259–78; also Douglas A. Hibbs, Jr., "On the Political Economy of Long-Run Trends in Strike Activity," *British Journal of Political Science*, vol. 8 (1978), p. 169.

71. Among others, see Hawkins, "Reflections on Labor's Relations to Government and Politics"; Martin A. Schain, "The Dynamics of Labor Policy in France: Industrial Relations and the French Trade Union Movement," as well as Jean-Daniel Reynaud, "Commentaire: Déviation ou autre modèle," *Tocqueville Review*, vol. 2 (Winter 1980), pp. 77–115.

72. Wiarda, "The Corporative Origins of the Iberian and Latin American Labor Relations Systems," *Studies in Comparative International Development*, vol. 13 (Spring 1978), pp. 3–37.

73. Lange and Vannicelli, "Strategy."

74. James L. Payne, *Labor and Politics in Peru: The System of Political Bargaining* (New Haven: Yale University Press, 1965).

75. David Collier et al., "Varieties of Latin American 'Corporatism' " (Paper presented at the Annual Meeting of the American Political Science Association, San Francisco, September 2–5, 1975); and Ruth Berins Collier and David Collier, "Inducements versus Constraints: Disaggregating 'Corporatism,' " *American Political Science Review*, vol. 73 (December 1979), pp. 967–986.

76. Abraham Kaplan, "Systems Theory and Political Science," *Social Research*, vol. 35 (July 1968), pp. 30–47.

77. Wiarda, *Transcending Corporatism?*; Lange and Vannicelli, "Strategy."

78. K. Robert Nilsson, "The EUR Accords and the Historic Compromise: Italian Labor and Eurocommunism," *Polity*, vol. 14 (Fall 1981).

79. Lange, "Neo-Corporatism in Italy?"

80. For some comments on this theme, which however allow a political and national security bias favoring "Westernism" and "Europeanism" to detract from a more realistic analysis, see John C. Campbell, "The Mediterranean Crisis," *Foreign Affairs*, vol. 53 (July 1975), pp. 605–24.

81. Ralph Miliband, *The State in Capitalist Society* (New York: Basic Books, 1969); Nicos Poulantzas, *Political Power and Social Classes* (London: Sheed and Ward, 1973); Antonio Gramsci, *The Modern Prince and Other Writings* (New York: International Publishers, 1970); Santiago Carrillo, *Eurocommunism and the State* (London: Lawrence and Wishart, 1977). It is probably not coincidental that the major efforts by Marxists to deal with the issue of the state and its "relative autonomy" have been by southern Europeans.

82. The process has been traced especially well by Peter Lange, "Unions, Parties, the State and Liberal Corporatism: Some Reflections Growing out of the Italian Experience" (Paper presented at the First National Meeting of the Council of European Studies, Washington, D.C., March 30, 1979); and Lange and Maurizio Vannicelli, "From Marginality to Centrality: Italian Unionism in the 1970s" (Paper presented at the Annual Meeting of the American Political Science Association, Washington, D.C., September 1979). Lange shows how the concept of "liberal corporatism" is now of limited utility in comprehending Italian state-labor relations; his use of the term "pan-syndicalism," though not fully defined, seems comparable to my "neo-syndicalism."

83. Wiarda, *Transcending Corporatism?*; and Wiarda, "Portugal: The Two Revolutions" (Paper presented at the seventeenth Annual Convention of the International Studies Association, Toronto, February 1976).

9

Interpreting Iberian-Latin American Interrelations

Paradigm Consensus and Conflict

The title of this chapter may seem abstract, arcane, overtheoretical, and removed from the realities of foreign policy analysis. In fact, it is none of these things. It has to do with the kinds of intellectual models and conceptual frameworks that Iberia and Latin America employ to interpret themselves, each other, and their international relations. It thus has very practical as well as theoretical consequences. Indeed, one could make the case that since it is on the basis of these conceptual models and paradigms, whether explicitly recognized or implicitly held, that the realities of relations between Iberia and Latin America, as well as with the outside world, are based, an understanding of these conceptual considerations may precede and even overshadow the more concrete and presumably more practical issues. That, in any case, is the basis on which this discussion proceeds.

As defined by Thomas Kuhn, a paradigm is the way a scientific or professional community views a field of study or a policy area, identifies appropriate problems for study and analysis, and specifies legitimate concepts, methods, and approaches.[1] Paradigm conflict refers to disagreement and dissension within that community over the dominant sociopolitical models or conceptual frameworks used to interpret the field or policy area. Paradigm consensus obviously refers to a basic agreement on these same themes and approaches. The paradigms discussed here encompass not just the intellectual and social science models applicable to the *internal* development and dynamics in Iberia and Latin America but also the models relevant to their domestic sociopolitical order and pattern of development *and* the perceptions that govern their views of relations with each other and with other nations. It is my purpose to trace the evolution of these dominant paradigms, to offer some observations on how these have changed over time and circumstances, and to demonstrate how this approach enables us to understand better Iberian and Latin American internal development and their complex international ties.

Iberia and Latin America: Unity Forged and Unity Lost

Unity Forged. By the beginning of the sixteenth century—that era that we and our History of Western Civilization courses take as the beginning of the modern era—Spain and Portugal had forged the world's first genuinely global empires, encompassing vast holdings in Africa, Asia, and Latin America and even in Europe (Austria, the Netherlands, and Naples, as well as Iberia itself) through the Hapsburg dynasty and the Holy Roman Empire.[2] By the indexes we commonly use to gauge modernization, they were also the most advanced nations of that time. Long before England or France, to say nothing of Germany, Italy, the Scandinavian, or the Benelux countries, Spain and Portugal had achieved territorial unity, become centralized nation-states, acquired a common law, language, and religion, and developed highly rationalized armies, bureaucracies, and political institutions.[3]

Institutionalization in Iberia—often organized on a predominantly authoritarian, hierarchical, elitist, corporatist, and organic-statist basis—took a form different from the form it later took in England and northwest Europe, those countries we now think of as the most "developed." Nor have the heirs of this latter developmental tradition, either in northwest Europe or in North America, always appreciated the nature of the political, social, religious, and military institutions established and solidified in Iberia. The Iberian tradition constituted an alternative route to development—Catholic, corporatist, elitist, hierarchical, authoritarian, organicist—and not one with which we have always been comfortable. But of the fact that they were "modern" and "modernizing"—indeed the most modern in Europe of that time—there can be no doubt.[4]

The panoply of institutions solidly established in the Spanish and Portuguese states around 1500 was then transferred to their American colonies (as well as their African and Asian domains). We await an updated comparative study of the impact of Spanish and Portuguese institutions on such nations as the Philippines, Angola, and Mozambique and those of Latin America. In the Americas, together with the two Iberian mother countries, these institutions not only survived but thrived and were even revitalized. The efforts of Spain and Portugal in subduing, conquering, colonizing, and transferring their institutions to the New World in a mere seventy years (by 1570 the conquest had been essentially completed) was one of the great epic adventures of all times. It began the process of the Europeanization and Westernization of the globe, though in the Spanish and Portuguese cases we are clearly dealing with a particular "fragment" (to use Louis Hartz's term)[5] of the West. The scope and speed of the Spanish and Portuguese conquests make the centuries-long struggle of the Birtish and French to colonize North America seem incompetent and interminable by comparison.

Spain and Portugal sought, with remarkable success, to create in the Americas a system of society and polity modeled on their own. The main instructions brought to the New World were an authoritarian, centralized, absolutist political system; a two-class, hierarchical, elitist social structure; an exploitive, mercantilist, and "neofeudal" economic system; a corporatist system of societal institutions and state-society relations (especially centered in such corporate bodies as the church, the army, the bureaucracy, the university, or the local community); a rigid and absolutist religious system that paralleled and buttressed the state concept; and a system of learning grounded in rote memorization, scholasticism, and deductive reasoning. The structure of the indigenous Indian civilizations, similarly absolutist and theocratic, often served to bolster the Spanish system of domination, and in the New World these institutions had, of course, to be adapted to local conditions and to the requirements of vast distances and empty spaces. But that meant that to be effective in the far reaches of the empire, Spain's institutions sometimes had to be even more authoritarian in the New World than they were in the old.

The main point, however, is the remarkable accomplishment of the Iberian nations in transferring and establishing so strongly their own institutions in the Americas in such a short period of time. That feat may be unmatched in the long history of colonialism.[6]

The Iberian influence was not only strong but remarkably long lasting. Despite depressions, attempted foreign interventions, incompetent kings, changing dynasties, and various efforts at reform, the Spanish and Portuguese imperial systems remained stable for over three centuries. They lasted, without serious revolt or upheaval, from 1500 until the emergence of strong independence movements in the years between 1800 and 1825. In somewhat modified form, they also survived the transition to independence, the divisive nineteenth century, and even the deeper structural changes of the twentieth. Many scholars would suggest they survive even today, though the subject has now become much more controversial—a matter that lies at the heart of this analysis.

Unity Lost—and Revived. All countries, it seems, that were once colonies of another country have a contentious, up-and-down relationship with their former colonial masters. Normally it goes through three stages.[7] The first stage is a period of bitterness toward the colonial power and rejection of it. Then as the postindependence years often prove rocky, unstable, and disappointing, a certain nostalgia and romance for the colonial past may set in. This transition may last a generation or more. Finally, a new, more realistic basis for stable relations is established, implying not only renewed, albeit still limited, contact but also a new set of institutional arrangements and cultural ties. Ideally, they would combine what is worthwhile from the colonial past with what is viable from the postindependence present.

In Latin America the very strength and longevity of the Spanish (and to a lesser extent the Portuguese) colonial system help explain the intense rejection of it after independence. Not only was Spanish colonial officialdom thrown out, but the Spanish *system,* in all its facets, was also repudiated. True, there were creole conservatives throughout the colonies who wished to retain their ties to Spain, and some felt they could have the best of both worlds by importing a Bourbon or Hapsburg prince and establishing an independent monarchy. But those were minority views. After independence the Spanish-Portuguese monopoly systems of trade and commerce were quickly abolished. The Roman Catholic church was disestablished in most countries and lost the bulk of its landholdings. The Spanish-Portuguese system of colonial administration crumbled. New constitutions were promulgated that proclaimed liberalism and republicanism. Legislation providing for equality was enacted to replace the colonial system of hierarchy, authority, and ascribed status. The Latin Americans felt a strong need to *de*-Hispanicize their cultures and societies.[8]

There was also, in the terms used here, a paradigm shift. The older paradigm had been based on notions of hierarchy, rank, organic statism, Catholicism, orthodoxy, authority, and revealed truth. The newer *official* paradigm was based on liberalism and republicanism and was heir to the eighteenth-century ideas of inevitable progress, democracy, liberty, empiricism, fraternity, and equality. Whereas the older paradigm had it roots in the ancient and revered Hispanic tradition in all its aspects, the newer one obviously derived from the French and U.S. experiences of democratic revolution. This paradigm came to constitute a new orthodoxy. Virtually all discourse now had to be within the framework of liberalism and republicanism. The shift was thoroughgoing and complete, encompassing all aspects; the consensus that had existed on the earlier paradigm now gave way—at least on the surface—to consensus on a quite different one.[9]

It is, by now, part of the conventional wisdom that much of the new liberal legislation, the new constitutions with their elaborate bills of rights and separations of power, had little effect on the way Latin America continued to be governed. The church remained powerful, the landholding system remained oligarchic, and a small white elite continued to rule. Most recently the interpretation has been offered that Latin America's founding fathers never intended to go in a liberal direction but only to pay lip service to the republican precepts. Even in the new "liberal" constitutions numerous clauses provided for executive caesarism, the armed forces were given a special place as almost a fourth branch of government, Catholicism remained the official religion, most elections were indirect, and the suffrage was severely restricted. In these ways there was more continuity in the shift to independence than a sharp break or a repudiation of the past.[10] Nonetheless, at the formal and institutional level a major restructuring had occurred, and certainly among the intellectual classes the Spanish and Portuguese systems and all they stood for had to be rejected while liberalism and republicanism were championed.

These attitudes persisted at least through the first generation of Latin America's postindependence leaders. But by the 1850s these early leaders had largely passed from the scene. New conservative parties and leaders emerged around mid-century seeking to restore the position of the church and the older social system of hierarchy and caste. The stimulus given to the economy about the same time by investment and commerce also gave rise to renewed calls for strong government that could preserve order, for centralized banks, for more powerful armies and bureaucracies, for stronger protectionist measures, and for trade monopolies and charters from a strong and authoritative, if not authoritarian, state. The conservative paradigm, in short, had made a comeback. Of course the restoration of the Spanish and Portuguese system, in all its aspects, was still taboo, but sentiment favoring a renewal of the historic institutions—without specifically identifying them with the former colonial powers—was certainly gaining strength. From this point on, there were two dominant and competing paradigms in Latin America (as well as Iberia): a conservative one that was largely rural, Catholic, agrarian, creole-Hispanic, and inward looking *and* a liberal one that was largely urban, secular, commercial, middle class, republican, and oriented outward toward Europe and the United States.[11]

By the 1890s attitudes toward the mother countries, Spain and

Portugal, had been almost entirely reversed from what they were earlier in the century. These attitudes became even more inexorably intertwined with the domestic politics of Latin America and with the prevailing intellectual paradigms. Many Latin American intellectuals now looked on Spain with respect and sympathy rather than with the disdain of the past. Increasingly, under the influence of positivism and social Darwinism, they came to emphasize their Hispanic, European, and hence Western roots instead of their indigenous, *criollo*, or often *mestizo* ones. Feelings were often mixed, and the legacy of bitterness toward Spain and the colonial era remained. Still there was definitely a new—often romantic or romanticized—attitude toward the mother countries.[12]

Among the reasons for this change of view was, first, simply the passage of time. After seventy or eighty years Spain was no longer so deeply resented as it had been in the early postindependence period. Then it had been seen as an exploitive power, an instrument of ruin, or an "enemy of change."[13] Now Latin America was less inclined to blame its Spanish legacy for all its troubles. Indeed, by this point there were renewed pride in the Spanish system and various efforts to resurrect Hispanic institutions and restore the "glory" of the Spanish language, religion, and culture.

A second, related factor was that many Latin Americans had become thoroughly disillusioned with the liberal-republican model imported from the United States. Although liberalism still dominated the political discourse and constitutions of the area, more and more intellectuals and political leaders came to view the liberal laws and precepts they had earlier adopted as imported institutions, not entirely appropriate in their place and circumstance. Liberalism was suited to the "Anglo-Saxon" democracies, they argued, but was often inappropriate in Latin America. Strong criticisms of liberal democracy were falling on receptive ears in Europe at this time from the pens of Pareto, Mosca, Sorel, Michels, and Gumplowicz, a fashion that many Latin American intellectuals were quick to follow. The new "science of positivism" was in its heyday; throughout Latin America the influence of positivism was reflected in efforts to restructure government on a more organized, rationalized, and scientific base, which implied the restoration of the Spanish principles of order, authority, and hierarchy. The new positivist order was to be led by a "scientific and technocratic elite," a concept that has seldom been criticized by the scientists, intellectuals, and technocrats who themselves are likely to do the leading.[14]

The disillusionment with liberalism was, third, accompanied by profound fear, suspicion, and dislike of the apparent embodiment itself of liberalism, the United States. By the turn of the century the United States had emerged as the hemisphere's dominant power: it had seized Cuba and Puerto Rico from Spain in the war of 1898, it was about to acquire the rights to build the Panama Canal, and it had intervened or threatened to intervene in a number of countries in Central America and the Caribbean. Secretary of State Richard Olney had proclaimed the United States "practically sovereign" in the Western Hemisphere. Hence both liberalism and liberalism's imperial agent had to be opposed.

In the writings of the Cuban independence leader José Martí, the great Nicaraguan poet Ruben Darío, and the Uruguayan essayist José Enrique Rodó (to name only some of the most prominent), the United States was condemned for its crass materialism, its rampant and inorganic individualism, its lack of humanism, its imperialistic intervention in Central America and the Caribbean, and now for its humiliating defeat of "mother Spain" (even the metaphors change) in the war of 1898. Rodó's *Ariel* was the foremost expression of this view; it went through twelve editions and may have been Latin America's best-selling book for all time. Liberalism, materialism, and all that was evil and philistine were now pictured as emanating from the United States.[15]

Fourth, Spain's "generation of '98" also helped stimulate greater ties between Latin America and the mother country. This generation of especially prominent intellectuals (Unamuno, Ortega, and many others) had reacted strongly against Spain's defeat by the United States, and their writings elicited great sympathy in Latin America. These intellectuals, in the wake of defeat and humiliation and the agonizing self-examination these events prompted, began to wrestle with the same questions that had long preoccupied their Latin American counterparts: Who are we as a nation and a people? What is our destiny? Are we different from other peoples, and how? In their search for answers, as we shall see, some common solutions were put forward on both sides of the Atlantic.

A fifth cementing factor was the new preoccupation with the elements that bound Iberia and Latin America together rather than, as in the past, the things that separated them. The elements of unity included law, language, a rich literature, religion, and culture in its broadest sense. There were new cultural exchanges of dancers, musicians, artists, and intellectuals. These ties were further expressed in more abstract concepts: the elaboration of philosophical and even psychological orientations that were presumably "unique" to the Iberian–Latin American peoples, a new respect for and preoccupation with *lo hispano* (everything that was Hispanic), and the widespread celebration of October 12, Columbus Day, the day of Spain's discovery of America, as a major pan-Hispanic holiday, known in the Iberian-Latin world as *día de la raza* (*raza* was used here more in a cultural than in a racial sense).

Finally, what bound Iberia and Latin America together again during this period was the search for a new political formula. Liberalism was now more widely viewed as appropriate for the northern democracies, but in Iberia and Latin America it was generally perceived—and celebrated—that their histories and traditions were "different." Liberalism was increasingly rejected, as was Marxism, for they were seen to be equally antithetical to the main currents of Catholic-Hispanic civilization. Iberia and Latin America wanted a formula that would help overcome their legacies of instability and lack of progress, fill their historical organizational and institutional void, and enable them to modernize and adjust to twentieth-century realities, while providing for continuity with revered institutions from the past. The formula settled on and widely adopted, albeit in different forms, in the countries of Iberia and Latin America was corporatism and an updated organic statism.[16] This topic will be discussed further in the next section.

Although these signs all pointed toward greater unity and harmony between Iberia and Latin America as the twentieth century unfolded, in fact little in the way of more concrete bonds resulted, at least initially. There were no diplomatic, military, or political alliances, no economic common market or even much increase in trade or tourism, no common military efforts, not many more ties of any sort—except at the level of romance, or what Fredrick Pike calls "lyrical *Hispanismo*"[17]—than before. There was a new *spirit* of unity, however imprecisely that may be gauged, and, as indicated, there was a considerable flurry of new cultural activities. But the grand dreams of a Lusitanian, Hispanic, or Iberian empire or commonwealth never materialized. Why? The answers to this question are not only fascinating but also helpful in understanding the complexities of Iberian–Latin American relations today and the confusion over how to interpret these relations appropriately, which is the heart of the analysis here.

To begin with, we must recognize that there is far more diversity in this area than the terms "Iberian-Latin culture" or "Hispanic world" imply. Bolivia is very different from Argentina, Costa Rica from Nicaragua, Chile from Peru, Venezuela from Colombia, Portugal from Spain, and Brazil and Mexico from all the rest. Whether one looks at levels of development, racial and social composition, history and resources, or political institutions, the many differences between and among the Iberian and Latin American nations make it difficult to find one single model or interpretive framework that fits them all. Only with difficulty, and what Giovanni Sartori called considerable "concept stretching," can these nations all be made to fit into any one dominant paradigm.[18] Often this leads to simplistic and hence inappropriate labels or to the use of an ideological straitjacket that fits, imperfectly at best, and implies the imposition of forced unity on a cultural area that is in fact quite diverse. The sheer diversity of the area makes the unity of Iberia and Latin America, as well as any attempt at common interpretation, more and more problematic.

Second, the relationship, again, between colony and mother country is an important factor. It is a story perhaps familiar to North Americans: former colonies grew larger and stronger than their mother countries, and the mother countries were unable or unwilling to accept that fact. Brazil and Portugal provide the most obvious example. Brazil, with over 130 million people, is the seventh most populous and the fifth largest nation in the world. Economically it is a major manufacturing as well as agricultural country, with vast resources and potential. Portugal, with fewer than 10 million people, occupies a small space on the western fringes of Europe, is poor in resources, and has an economy producing only about 10 percent of Brazil's gross national product. It is simply not realistic to expect big, powerful Brazil to subordinate its policies to small, weak Portugal or even to coordinate them with Portugal. And, although both are Portuguese speaking and share a certain common heritage, they cannot easily or consistently be interpreted in the same intellectual terms either. The contrasts in size and resources are not so glaring in the case of Spain and some of its larger former colonies, but it seems quite unrealistic for nations like Argentina, Mexico, or Venezuela, or even Colombia, Chile, or Peru to return to a position of less than equality with the former metropole. Nor would the efforts to interpret them using the same categories be any less problematic than for Portugal and Brazil.

Early in the twentieth century and through the Franco period and beyond, when Spain launched a more aggressive strategy of *hispanismo* (defined here as an effort to resurrect and spread Hispanic culture, pride, and also hegemony throughout its former colonies), it was clear that Spain perceived the Latin American nations as a community that Spain would guide and direct, not as part of a community of nations equal to itself. That is a third reason why a commonwealth or federation with Latin America failed to develop. *Hispanismo* was an extension and revival of Spain's historic, self-perceived "civilizing" mission. Although Spain sometimes proclaimed that its former colonies were now to be dealt with fraternally rather than paternally, it did not really believe that, nor would its citizens accept the premise. People from the "Indies" were still viewed in Spain as undeveloped, racially impure, and often uncivilized. To most Spaniards it was unthinkable that those native to the Americas ("creoles") should be treated as equals. The Portuguese, despite the self-perpetuated myth of greater racial tolerance and ability to bridge the gap with native peoples, maintained the same air of superiority toward Brazilians. Hence if there was to be a new Hispanic or Lusitanian confederation, it was, from the Iberian viewpoint, to be one under Spanish and Portuguese hegemony, not a fraternity of equals. If Spain and Portugal wanted to associate with anyone as equals, it would have to be with Europe and not with Latin America. The Latin Americans, of course, felt these prejudices and resented them. Indeed, it was in large part because the so-called Fascist regimes of Franco and Salazar had been rejected by Europe that Spain and Portugal reemphasized their Atlantic, Latin American, and, especially in the Portuguese case, African ties in the first place.[19]

Practical economic realities also stood in the way of the development of a stronger Hispanic, Lusitanian, or perhaps combined Iberian–Latin American confederation. Through midcentury Spain and Portugal were among the poorest countries in Europe. It was only in the late 1950s and in the 1960s that they began to develop rapidly. Before that they lacked the resources to do much more than pay lip service to the Hispanic or Lusitanian commonwealth ideal. They lacked the military, diplomatic, and economic might to follow an expansive, hegemonic policy seriously. Hence, while there was much talk of a Hispanic and Lusitanian community and quite a bit of cultural exchange and sympathy, few more concrete ties were developed. That came later when Spain, especially, emerged as a middle-level industrial power with a commensurately more ambitious foreign policy. At this point, however, economic underdevelopment and lack of resources made greater interchange between Iberia and Latin America unrealistic.

In addition, there were practical political reasons why the *hispanismo* and *lusitanismo* ideas failed to gain much ground. In the postwar era, with Franco and Salazar still entrenched in power despite various efforts to unseat them, Spain and Portugal held on to their uniquely corporatist forms, often mislabeled "Fascist," and sought to update and refurbish them. In fact, corporatism was one of the key ingredients in the concept of *hispanismo* and one of the features that helped make Spain and Portugal "different." The Franco and Salazar regimes took considerable pride in their corporately inspired systems, however incompletely these had been implemented

298

and despite the increased emphasis as time went by on institutions other than the corporatist ones.[20]

Latin America, in contrast, which had also experimented extensively with corporatist forms and institutions in the 1930s (Vargas in Brazil, Ibañez in Chile, Cárdenas in Mexico, and others) now largely abandoned corporatism, at least formally, and reverted to its liberal republican tradition or else covered over corporatist practice with liberal labels. This had to do in part with the New World setting where corporatism had never been so in vogue as it was in Europe between the wars, in part because of U.S. influence, which was instrumental in forcing Latin America to repudiate corporatism and statism, and in part because the corporatist historical tradition and institutions were considerably weaker in Latin America than in Iberia. The point is, however, that many Latin American nations, particularly Brazil vis-à-vis Portugal and Mexico and others vis-à-vis Spain, came to look down on, feel superior to, and in some cases even publicly denounce their motherlands for their persistent fascism. That was hardly the basis for a close and lasting "family" of nations.

Last, but hardly unimportant, were the economic relationships. Latin America's trade ties, its patterns of exports, imports, and dependency relations were overwhelmingly with the United States and not with Iberia. These trends became stronger in the post-World War II period. The situation varied somewhat from country to country, but by virtually any index—aid, capital investment, tourism, or the like— Latin America was enveloped within the U.S. orbit; its economic and commercial ties with Spain and Portugal were quite insignificant. A comparable situation existed in Iberia. Despite the romantic talk of *hispanismo*, a Lusitanian federation, Atlanticism, or even third worldism, Spain's and Portugal's economies from at least the 1950s and 1960s on were intimately connected with those of Western Europe. Patterns of trade, commerce, and banking were increasingly oriented toward Europe. The flood of tourists that began to inundate Spain in the 1960s, stimulating its economy further, came from Europe, not Latin America; the movies and culture were European; and the waves of Spanish and Portuguese migrants who left the peninsula seeking greater opportunities also went primarily to Europe instead of, as historically, to Latin America. While Spain and Portugal thus talked of the unity of the Latin peoples and cultures in Iberia and the Americas, the actual numbers pointed increasingly in other directions.[21] To a considerable extent that remains true today.

Corporatism and the Corporative Model

This period of change, sometimes rivalry and conflict, provided the context for the formulation of a new conceptual framework or paradigm, called the corporative model. This model was set forth in the middle to late 1960s and early 1970s as an explanation of the common developmental features of Iberia and Latin America.[22]

As presented here, the corporative model is to be distinguished from the often unhappy actual practice and experience of corporatism under Salazar and Franco. The corporative model sought to present a conceptual framework within which to understand Iberia and Latin America, to describe an ideal type, not to argue that the model corresponds exactly to any existing regime or movement. Nor should the corporative model be confused with Spain's earlier efforts to propagate corporatism as part of its broader campaign of *hispanismo*. The corporative model is an intellectual construct, a heuristic device, not a part of any nation's foreign policy initiatives or institutional apparatus. In actual practice, as we shall see, however, the corporative model *did* become confused with these other things, thus producing both intellectual confusion and political controversy. Here I shall first describe the corporative framework and then analyze the politicization that occurred.

Rationale for the Corporative Model. The corporative model or framework was fashioned largely in response to dissatisfaction with the older dominant paradigms, the liberal developmentalist and the Marxian approaches. The liberal developmentalist approach, which grew out of the Kennedy era, the general development literature of the early 1960s, and the Peace Corps mood of the time, sought to bring U.S.-style development to the third world, particularly to Latin America. It posited a path of inevitable, unilinear progress toward a social and political system just like our own—or just like what we imagined ourselves to be: liberal, democratic, pluralistic, socially just, and politically moderate. But the model derived exclusively from the Western European and U.S. experiences of development and had only limited utility in enabling us to understand Latin America. It failed to explain why such key Latin American actors as the military, the oligarchy, and the middle class failed to conform to the expectations assumed by the model. And it neglected many important aspects of Latin American social, political, and institutional life.

The Marxian paradigm seemed equally problematic. The Marxian class categories were useful in providing a broad outline of Latin America's transition from feudalism to a kind of capitalism. But their utility diminished in examining the specifics of individual country differences in the contemporary context and in seeking to explain the behavior of such diverse groups (and their internal factions) as the army, the church, and the trade unions. Among many Latin Americanists the sense was strong that neither the liberal developmentalist nor the Marxian approach was a sufficient explanation by itself or adequately attuned to the distinctive features of Latin America.

Hence the corporative model was proffered not as a substitute for these other two but as a useful complement to them. Using those features of the liberal developmentalist and Marxian models that did apply in Latin America, the corporative framework filled in some dimensions that these others treated inadequately, if at all. The corporative model seemed especially useful in explaining aspects of Iberian and Latin American group relations, the patrimonialist role of the state,[23] trade union structure, several aspects of political culture, state-society relations, and public policy in such areas as social security and labor legislation.

Here, corporatism means the tendency to view the political community as the sum total of the functional interests in the society, with each of those interests deemed to have a defined position and, under the proper circumstances, a legitimate right to participate in the political society.[24] Under a corporatist system, however, participation is determined largely by sector rather than by the egalitarian liberal calculation of one-man-one-vote. The typical "corporations" or "corporate interests" in such a system are the landowners, the armed forces, the church, businessmen and industrialists, university students, professionals, and, most recently, organized labor, peasants, and women. In practice, the Iberian and most Latin American states have combined a corporatist system of funtional representation with one form or another of electoral or geographic representation.

Corporatist systems tend to be dominated by notions of hierarchy and elites and to leave much of the rest of the population—chiefly unorganized peasant, worker, and indigenous elements—unrepresented. Corporatism also limits participation within the system to those whom the state recognizes as having a legitimate right to bargain in the political process. In practice, the hierarchical, organicist, and personalist principles on which the separate corporations and the entire national system generally are organized ensure that the real decision makers are usually few. The system is frankly undemocratic and nonegalitarian, features that make corporatism anathema to liberals. But it should be noted further that Latin American corporatism could take left-wing and syndicalist directions as well as right-wing ones. Thus, seen in terms of its corporatist, vertical, and authoritarian institutions, the Mexico of left-of-center President Cárdenas was not much different structurally and institutionally from its more conservative successors.

The purpose of those who advanced the corporative model, however, was not to champion hierarchy and authoritarianism, or any particular political or ideological orientation, but simply to try to comprehend Latin America in its own terms. Whatever our personal sentiments regarding these features of the Iberian and Latin American systems, it was felt that the models used to interpret these societies had to reflect their own realities rather than our private or political preferences for them.

Iberia and Latin America are, of course, a part of the Western tradition, but a fragment that broke off from the main currents of the West around 1500 and pursued a separate path.[25] The Iberian and Latin American nations were thus isolated and cut off from what is commonly seen as the main currents of the modern Western world: the Protestant Reformation and industrialism, religious pluralism, representative government, the Enlightenment, and the movement toward greater social differentiation and pluralism. In the period of the Counter-Reformation and beyond, Iberia, to say nothing of its isolated colonies in the New World, remained apart from these modernizing currents and locked into a feudal and medieval pre-1500 model.

Components of the Corporative Model. The designers of the corporative model sought to trace the roots and origins of the Iberian-Latin systems in the late feudal period and to analyze their subsequent developmental paths. They began with the theoretical underpinnings.[26] These included the biblical concepts of an organic society with all its arms and branches related; the Greek and Roman notions of a hierarchy of classes and rank orders; the stoic concepts of Seneca; the Christian corporate injunctions of Augustine and Thomas; the justifications for Christian, state-building, royal authority in Suárez and the sixteenth-century Thomists; and the subsequent revival of Catholic corporate ideology and forms of sociopolitical organization in the nineteenth and twentieth centuries. Corporatism hence connotes the political world view of what we might call the Aristotelian-Thomistic synthesis, now updated to deal with the newer contingencies reflecting an industrialized, socially differentiated world. Corporatism in this sense is a general pattern of political cognition like liberalism and Marxism but quite distinct from the other two. One could say that while Locke's doctrine lies at the heart of the liberal tradition and Marx's, obviously, at the heart of the Socialist one, Suárez's lies at the heart of the Iberian-Latin corporatist one. Indeed, it would make an interesting study to contrast these three giants in their respective intellectual traditions and to trace the subsequent permutations of these philosophies as well as the current challenges to each of them. Because of its particular history and traditions, the Iberian-Latin cultural area has been especially heavily affected by the corporative political cognition. Hence a proper interpretation of Iberia and Latin America, the corporative approach argued, must start with an examination of these constructs and their accompanying societal forms rather than with the political assumptions of the Lockean and Anglo-American experience.

From the political theory of Iberia and Latin America, interpreters of the corporative model moved to a discussion of the dominant sociopolitical features. Again, these were pictured as quite different from those prevailing in the Lockean and Anglo-American tradition. Iberia and Latin America were seen as rooted in notions of hierarchy, rank, position, status, authority, and a vertical corporate organization of society and power. These systems were steeply pyramidal, divided hierarchically by classes, castes, and rank orders and vertically by corporate segments: army, church, oligarchy, and so on.

Firmly institutionalized during three centuries of colonial rule, these systems underwent not revolutionary but actually quite modest adjustments as Latin America achieved independence. The pinnacle of this hierarchical system was removed, but the essential organization of society and polity was not greatly altered in its realities. Change began first with the birth of a commercial elite, then a middle class developed, and eventually trade unions emerged. But the basic structure of society remained two classed and quasi-feudal. "Modernization" thus occurred, but the ancient and revered system of power and hierarchy was modified only in its particulars. New groups were added, but the *system* of a corporately structured society and polity persisted.

In the original formulation of the corporative model, little attention was devoted to economic factors. These clearly deserve greater attention. For the fact is that the notions of hierarchy, rank, authority, and corporate organization so strongly present in Iberia and Latin America in the social and political spheres are also dominant in the economic sphere. These factors are reflected in the statist, neo-mercantilist, autarchic, state capitalist nature of these nations' economies. The autarchy and corporatism found in the prevailing sociopolitical institutions of this cultural area are also reflected in the economic, serving to reinforce each other. Just as liberalism implies a large measure of freedom in both the political and the economic spheres, so under corporatism and organic statism are these two mutually joined—albeit implying quite different kinds of systems. In subsequent writings this earlier oversight was corrected by adding an explicitly economic component to the model.[27]

Having addressed the religio-cultural, sociopolitical, and economic dimensions of Iberian–Latin American society, the model then moved to a discussion of the change process. It emphasized the importance of such institutions as patronage, bureaucracy, *compadrazgo* (political kinship), and personalism within the system. It showed how gradual and incremental change could go forward without altering the basic structures of society in their fundamentals. The enduring features of presidential authority, elite dominance, top-down rule, and the corporate hierarchical organization of society were stressed. These features have demonstrated remarkable continuity and staying power. Although incorporating new social elements, the basic structure of society was not changed. The corporative framework helped maintain the traditional structure while providing for limited change through the co-optation of new social and political units into the administrative apparatus of the central state system. This system was pictured as quite rational and logical in its own terms, though obviously quite different from the liberal democratic model.

Challenges to the Corporative Model. Because it served to explain and in part to rationalize the seemingly inherent corporate-organic structure of society and polity in Iberia and Latin America, the model offered was sometimes interpreted as justifying these features. In fact, the pitfalls in such a societal model were elaborately discussed, and the forces undermining the system were pointed out in a separate section of the presentation entitled "The Crisis of the Traditional System."[28] First, the historical consensus on the value and worth of these more traditional institutions was declining. Second, the institutional structure on which the system had been based—the landowning pattern, the institution of the *hacienda* (landed estate), and the extended family—was breaking down or undergoing major changes. Third, a variety of new forces—political parties, trade unions, and the like—had emerged to challenge the traditional system. Fourth, politics in Iberia and Latin America had become increasingly more oriented to class, issues, and interests. These and other trends had combined to provoke a challenge of unprecedented proportions throughout the area.

Although the model had been formulated and presented before Allende's ascent in Chile, several years before the Portuguese Revolution of 1974, before the death of Franco, before the Nicaraguan revolution, and before the revolutionary upheaval in El Salvador, the traditional system of society and power seemed to demonstrate remarkable resilience and perseverance in all but a few nations of the area. In the late 1960s it showed considerable strength and perhaps even the capacity to survive the contemporary crisis as it had survived others in the past. At the least, the corporative model of society and polity in Iberia and Latin America merited attention as a continuing major, if not still *the* major, principle and system of national sociopolitical organization.

Nevertheless, the presentation ended pessimistically.[29] It suggested that the outcome of the change process in Iberia and Latin America would be neither the persistence of viable traditional or historical corporative institutions nor the definitive triumph of more "modern" ones organized on the basis of some other model, whether liberal or Marxian. Rather, what seemed more likely was an increasingly conflictive, fragmented, even in some cases disintegrating society as modernization went forward. At that time Argentina provided the paradigm case of a nation so deeply divided among rival societal and political conceptions that no government—left or right, civilian or military—seemed able to govern effectively and well. Similarly, Uruguay and Chile, which are among the most modern of the Latin American societies, appeared to be especially vulnerable to the polarization and breakdown resulting from modernization and seemed to follow Argentina. Hence the future for Iberia and Latin America was seen to lie not in traditionalism and a pre-twentieth-century corporatism nor in democracy or socialism but in a continued polarizing, disintegrative pattern of conflict and breakdown among, between, and within *all* of these. That was a sad prognosis but, unfortunately, probably realistic.

Politics and Paradigms:
The Politicization of the Model

The model presented above and in a number of other variations was diffused widely throughout the U.S. academic community in the early to mid-1970s and in Iberia and Latin America. This model seemed to be an alternative to the liberal developmentalism favored by the United States and to the Marxian categories favored by some intellectuals and other groups. It also explicitly linked Iberia and Latin America as a distinct cultural area whose dominant development model had been both common to the nations of this area and distinctive from those of other nations. It thus attracted major attention.

My concern here is not the receptivity the model was accorded in the United States; that has been dealt with elsewhere and is not the major focus of this analysis.[30] Rather, I will focus on its reception in Iberia and Latin America and on what this may tell us about the relations between these two areas. For the fact is, the corporative model was at different times received differently by various groups in these societies and was used and sometimes exploited for quite partisan political purposes. Such partisan use of significant scholarly and intellectual paradigms is not at all unusual in the social sciences—or in politics, for that matter. This case offers some interesting variations and nuances on these themes, however, and sheds light on the internal politics and political relations of these two regions in the last quarter century.

Domestic Reception of the Model in Latin America. In Latin America conservative groups sometimes used the model to justify their legitimacy and right to remain in power. They liked the emphasis on hierarchy and rank and the notion of everyone in his or her place. They had long favored a kind of Catholic conservative corporatism that seemed to be implied in the model. But conservatives were not altogether happy with the model's emphasis on elite venality, the dissection of the elites' methods of control, or the prediction of breakdown if the system continued unaltered.[31]

Such diverse regimes and systems as those of Mexico, Brazil, Colombia, Peru under its left-wing military, and Chile and Argentina under their right-wing militaries also found elements in the model that helped rationalize their rule and activities. All these regimes had similarly corporative or quasi-corporative features. But they also had liberal, democratic, and republican institutions or aspirations alongside their corporative ones. In these countries the reaction to the corporative model was sometimes mixed: its utility in interpreting and comprehending certain areas of the national life was recognized, but some understandably resisted the idea of elevating corporatism to the status of a single, complete, and all-encompassing explanation. That had not, in any case, been the intention of those who first advanced the corporative model.

Liberals and democrats, with the major exception of Christian Democrats, who tended to be supportive, were often more critical because the model suggested that democracy and liberalism were not inevitable in Latin America and might not even be desired or feasible. They preferred to erase corporatism from their history, to ignore it, or to forget about it. They often wished to have their countries identified with a liberal and social democratic present and not with what they viewed as a corporatism of the past. In doing so, however, they glossed over or ignored many elements integral to their own national realities.

Latin American intellectuals also had mixed feelings. Most applauded the effort to fashion a distinctively Latin American, or Iberian-Latin, model of development. It appealed to their pride, their nationalism, and their desire for an important place in the sun. But they were often opposed to the particular form that it took, since the authoritarianism, elitism, and corporatism at the heart of the model were not the most popular forms of sociopolitical organization in the social democratic salons of Europe and the United States where these intellectuals looked for acceptability. In addition, Latin American intellectuals were not attracted to a model that seemed to place most of the responsibility for the area's authoritarianism and lack of development on domestic, internal structures and traditions. From their point of view, it was much preferable and more comfortable, as in Marxism-Leninism and dependency theory, to place all the blame on external forces—that is, on U.S. "imperialism."[32]

Domestic Reception of the Model in Spain and Portugal. In Spain and Portugal the reactions were parallel but reflected the particular circumstances of these two nations. First, the model was presented, disseminated, and discussed in Iberia when the Franco and Salazar-Caetano regimes were still in power.[33] These regimes had, after all, been founded on an authoritarian corporatist basis in the 1930s. Regime supporters and the regimes themselves seized upon the model almost desperately as a last-ditch way to justify and perpetuate an ideology and system increasingly viewed as moribund by their own populations. Second, the Spanish and Portuguese elites reveled in the notion that their countries could be a model of anything. After the many humiliations these nations had been forced to bear, their centuries-long decline from influence in the world, and the rejection by Europe, the notion that they had something of interest to offer, even to export, was enormously welcome.[34]

Third, these elites of Spain and Portugal were particularly enthusiastic that their systems were still the models for Latin America. In recent decades, in both Latin America and the peninsula, that notion had been strongly challenged. The colonial powers had been driven out and their institutions repudiated; Latin America had gone its separate ways. Now came a theory that suggested that the Iberian influence was still powerful—even more, that it constituted a *model*. For vanquished but still proud elites and governments in Iberia, that was welcome news indeed.

But the opposition to the corporative model was at least equally strong, and for some powerful political—and sometimes unexpected—reasons. First, many Portuguese and Spaniards resented being grouped together with the Latin American nations.[35] To understand this reaction, one must know something of Iberian history, pride, and attitudes toward race. The Spanish and Portuguese prefer to think of themselves as Europeans, advanced, Western, white, and cultured. Many of them see Latin America as part of the third world, uncivilized, only partially Western, and racially mixed. For them to be classified with the Latin Americans was therefore an insult to the national pride, to their belief in their advanced status, and to their *limpieza de sangre* (purity of blood). Across the political spectrum, from right to left, nationalistic, even xenophobic, sentiment was nearly unanimous on this point.

Second, the model was entangled in Iberian domestic politics. Corporatism was not a neutral term in Spain and Portugal. Both the Franco and the Salazar-Caetano regimes had been founded on corporative principles; corporatism remained a main ingredient in their ideology. At the time the model was formulated in the late 1960s, both these regimes seemed to offer ongoing examples of functioning, more or less efficient, and stable corporative-authoritarian regimes.[36] At the time no one foresaw that Portugal would be engulfed in a revolution in 1974 that would sweep away its corporative institutions or that Franco's death in 1975 would also be accompanied by thoroughgoing change. But even then, corporatism had to be—and was—strongly repudiated on political grounds by the oppositions to these two regimes. The model presented seemed in part to rationalize and justify the existing system and had been seized upon by apologists for the regime for just that purpose. But that was precisely why those in opposition—of whatever stripe—had to oppose it. They took no pride in corporatism regardless of its nationalistic roots, could not countenance its continuance, and above all could not accept it as a model. From their viewpoint, if there were to be an ideology of *hispanismo*, they wanted a *hispanismo democrático* rather than that of Franco or Salazar or of an older historical tradition they preferred to forget. From their reaction it becomes easy to see why in this case a social science paradigm formulated and presented as an abstract, an ideal type, or a heuristic theory should become embroiled with domestic, partisan politics.[37]

Third, there was an economic dimension to the debate. At this time both Spain and Portugal were embarked on vigorous development programs and were trying to escape their earlier status as underdeveloped nations, the most backward in Europe. Spain especially had made major economic strides forward (but Portugal was also advancing), and part of Spain's economic development strategy had been to drop the outdated autarchic mercantilist system that was a key ingredient in the corporative model.[38] Spain and Portugal wanted to be a part of Europe and the first world, not Latin America and the third world. Classifying them together in a single Iberian-Latin model obscured these differences and the immense economic changes under way in both Iberian nations since the late 1950s. The use of a common framework for both Iberia and Latin America seemed to force the former backward into the third world and therefore had to be repudiated by all forward-looking Spaniards and Portuguese. Again, the repudiation ranged broadly across the political spectrum.

Finally, the elaboration of the corporative model became entwined with Iberia's efforts to join Europe—not just economically through the European Economic Community (EEC) but politically and psychologically as well. The corporative model implied that Spain and Portugal were "different," a theme that both the advertisements for tourism and the Franco and Salazar-Caetano regimes had exploited for political purposes. The terms were loaded, and they became code words for other things. Many Spaniards and Portuguese, whatever their wishes in the past, no longer wished to be different. They wanted to be Europeans. By "European," however, they meant their politics, society, and culture, not just integration into the EEC. That of course implied democracy; and being a Europeanist in Spain and Portugal carried political connotations at this time. Being "different" was a code word for supporting the Franco and Salazar-Caetano regimes; being "European" was a code word for opposition to them and for favoring European-style democracy. In this context a social science model that seemed to emphasize the different was bound to meet resistance.[39]

Overall, intellectuals in Spain, and to a lesser extent in Portugal, seemed to feel that they had already left corporatism and corporatist models behind them at precisely the time some American social scientists were promulgating them anew. Many intellectuals and political leaders felt that they had superseded their corporatist past and embarked on a new, more democratic and "European" route. They did not want to be reminded of what to them seemed ancient history; they preferred to shunt corporatism aside and not think about it. Such sentiment was widespread while Franco and Salazar were still alive despite the existence in both their countries of quite strong corporative institutions. Those ideas gathered even greater strength once the Salazar-Caetano regime was removed through revolution and Franco had died. Corporatism was probably stronger in these two regimes even in their later years than their critics were willing to admit, and it remains present today in many social and political institutions. But in the charged political context of those days, it is easy to see why the corporative model was such a sensitive—and highly politicized—matter.

Relations between Iberia and Latin America. Not all the issues to which the corporative model gave rise or in which it became entwined were exclusively in the domain of domestic Latin American or domestic Iberian politics and society. Other issues stemmed from the relations *between* Iberia and Latin America.[40] These also had to do with the appropriate models these nations should follow. Some background, however, is needed for an understanding of these complex matters.

In an earlier section of this chapter I traced the broad outlines of Iberian–Latin American relations, from 1492 until approximately the mid-twentieth century. I stressed that while *hispanismo* and a grand Hispanic or Lusitanian federation had often been expressed as an ideal, numerous more mundane realities—mutual jealousies, lack of economic resources, political incapacity, and the like—had often stood in the way. But in the past three decades the relations between the Iberian mother countries and their former colonies in the Americas have undergone some radical transformations, reflecting the political upheavals that have taken place both internally in these nations and in their changing relations with each other. Throughout the period, regardless of the precise nature of the particular regimes in power, the long-term trend has been toward a discernible, perhaps irreversible increase in the ties binding the Iberian and Latin American nations together.

While several of the Latin American nations, most prominently Mexico, persisted in their estrangement from "fascistic" Spain, others, particularly the military regimes that surged to power from about the mid-1960s, now looked upon the mother country in quite a different light. Their perspective was one of admiration quite independent of any strengthened commmercial relations. Particularly for the "bureaucratic-authoritarians"[41] in power in Brazil, Argentina, and then Chile and Uruguay, Franco's Spain was viewed not as the pariah as it continued to be treated in the democracies of Western Europe and North America, but as a nation that had *successfully* managed the transition to industrialization and modernization. It had done so apparently without sacrificing its authoritarian, conservative, and traditionalist features. Spain (and Portugal, as always, to a lesser extent) was thus seen as a model of a functioning, viable, stable authoritarian corporatist regime. To the not dissimilar authoritarian corporatist regimes in Argentina, Brazil, Chile, and other countries, the Spanish model of stimulating economic growth, increasing educational opportunities, and providing expanded social servicies—seemingly without a resulting demand for greater pluralism, liberalism, and democratization—was very attractive. Modernization and national development could thus be achieved, which the Latin American bureaucratic authoritarians also desired, but without the social and political concomitants—mass mobilization, social upheaval, even revolutions—to which in other nations these had given rise. A variety of Latin American authoritarian regimes hence studied and sought to emulate the Spanish example. Those who lived and worked in Spain and Portugal during the early 1970s were witness to a virtually continuous parade of Latin American heads of state, military officers, and civilian technocrats all eager to learn the Spanish system.[42]

Although Spain's attractiveness as a model did not diminish greatly with Franco's death in 1975 and the subsequent evolution toward more democratic politics, the terms of reference were now obviously somewhat altered. For by the mid-1970s the bloom was also off the bureaucratic authoritarian model in Latin America, and several of the most powerful military regimes were scrambling to get out of power before the discredit for political and economic mismanagement in their countries was placed entirely on the military's shoulders.

For many in the United States, as well as for some Latin Americans, Spain now provided a model of how to bridge the transition from authoritarianism to democracy successfully. After all, a new political party system had emerged in Spain, the press was free, elections had been held, and a more or less democratic system was evolving.[43] Of course, what made the Spanish model so attractive to the United States was that this transition had been accomplished peacefully and gradually, without revolutionary turmoil. The Spanish transition stood in marked contrast to the situation in Portugal, where only a year earlier a revolution that threatened to come under Communist control had engulfed the country. That is why the Spanish model was strongly pushed by the U.S. government, especially during the period in the late 1970s of the so-called *retorno*, when it was often hoped and assumed by the Americans that such countries as Peru, Ecuador, Bolivia, Brazil, Argentina, Uruguay, and maybe even Chile would "return" to democratic rule. That hope was sometimes wishful, but it sparked a lot of attention in official circles to the "Spanish model."[44]

Although many Latin American military leaders also looked with some admiration at the newest, post-Franco Spanish model, they saw it in terms quite different from those in which the United States saw it. The Latin American military authoritarians were not necessarily enamored of democracy, but they could appreciate Spain's efforts at postauthoritarian "decompression" without wholesale abandonment of authoritarian controls.[45] That is, they believed that Spain had successfully evolved beyond the most offensive features of the old regime, which had invited international ostracism and censure, a position in which a number of the Latin American authoritarian regimes also found themselves. But the Spanish transition did not completely remove controls over labor and other groups, was not disorderly, did not result in breakdown or left-wing threats, and did not involve a purge of the armed forces themselves. All these features were attractive to the Latin American militaries, which wanted to go in the same direction or were being forced by circumstances to do so: that is, to loosen the controls and liberalize somewhat (as often to qualify for U.S. and other aid as to satisfy their domestic populations), but without letting go of all the controls or paving the way for precipitous change. Authoritarianism might thus be continued in some areas of the national life, but it would be given a new and more acceptable face; the military could retire to the barracks without discredit or reason to feel threatened. Indeed the armed forces could reap glory by restoring democracy and thus diverting attention from their numerous incapacities and misdeeds. The success of this strategy is still in doubt: Brazil's *abertura* was managed efficiently from the military's point of view, but in Argentina some key leaders of former military regimes may not fare so well in the hands of the civilian government inaugurated in 1983.[46]

This perception of Spain's transition, however, was not universal in Latin America. Spain's transition could be either a good or a bad example, depending on one's point of view. Each group was inclined to support those tendencies in Spain that reinforced its own political orientation. Some thought the Spanish transition too fast, helping give rise to Basque terrorism and other undesirable features; others (principally the opposition to Latin America's military regimes) saw Spain's evolution as too slow. The Spanish metaphor was used by diverse groups for different purposes.[47]

The Brazilian case is complicated by Brazil's special relationship with Portugal. Actually, Brazil's trade, commercial, and political ties with Spain are by now greater than its ties with its former mother country. Nevertheless, strong cultural affinities between Brazil and Portugal encourage close attention to each other's affairs. Brazil provides a classic case of the former colony that surpasses the former colonizer on virtually all indexes and the difficult, discordant relations to which such a reversal of position and power often gives rise. To a considerable extent, the corporative institutions established by Brazil's President Getulio Vargas between 1930 and 1945, which continued long after his removal from the scene, were patterned after those of corporative Portugal, although they were never so completely or so vigorously applied. In the post-World War II period, however, Brazil restored some republican institutions and took considerable pride in denigrating Portugal for its continued "fascistic" forms. After 1964, as Brazil itself moved back in a corporative and authoritarian direction, its affinities with the Portuguese regime of Salazar-Caetano were again manifest.[48] During this same period, while Portugal was involved in a series of guerrilla wars in Africa and sought to pressure Brazil into supporting its cause of maintaining a grand Lusitanian empire under Portuguese control, Brazil as the more powerful of the two was instead following an independent course, seeking to establish its own leadership in the Portuguese-speaking world rather than subordinating its interests to those of its former metropole.

The Portuguese revolution of 1974 also elicited mixed feelings in Brazil. To the extent that the revolution succeeded in establishing liberty and democracy, Brazilian liberals and others opposed to Brazil's own military regime were cheered. But to the extent that the revolution produced anarchy, economic disruptions, and the possibility of a Communist takeover, proregime forces in Brazil were strengthened. On balance, the Portuguese revolution was perceived in Brazil as producing more undesirable features, and the Portuguese revolutionary model therefore proved not very attractive in Brazil.[49]

Spain, meanwhile, was increasing its ties with Latin America. The older, rather romantic concept of *hispanismo,* which implied Spanish leadership and dominance of the Latin American nations, was replaced by a concept of brotherhood and equality among the partners—although privately many Spaniards still could not accept their Latin American "children" as equals. The transformation was reflected in a change of names of the Spanish government agency responsible for dealing with Latin America: from the Instituto de Cultura Hispánica to the Instituto de Cooperación Iberoamericana. The new strategy, furthermore, was much more pragmatic, concrete, and realistic than the older one had been. *Hispanismo,* the shared unity of the Hispanic nations, had sounded attractive, even noble, as a concept; but other than in fiery declamations, a romantic yearning, or an occasional conference, it had never been adequately developed. The newer thrust had a more solid base, and it produced more significant results.[50]

The Spanish initiatives were in the realms of politics, diplomacy, economics, culture, and social science. King Juan Carlos and Prime Ministers Adolfo Suárez and Felipe González made state and political visits to Latin America accompanied by much pomp and rhetoric

313

concerning the Hispanic soul and the unity of Hispanic soil—as well as the more important trade and commercial relations. These were followed by visits of foreign ministers and a steady procession of other Spanish officials. Diplomatically, Spain sought, with some success, support for its policies in Europe and the Middle East and also tried to weld a United Nations bloc of Spanish-speaking countries. Economically, Spain increased its trade with Latin America, provided technical assistance and aid, sent its businessmen to seek contracts throughout the hemisphere, and signed state contracts with numerous Latin American governments for the building of roads, dams, port facilities, factories, and other large projects. Culturally, Spain sent its orchestras, artists, and dancers on Latin American tours. It loudly trumpeted its accomplishments, as, for example, its passing from a "less developed" to an "industrial market" economy, as well as its successful transition from authoritarianism to democracy. And in the social sciences, the Spaniards continued to push for and sought to propagate the notions of common sociological and even political unity among the Hispanic nations—however they might still disagree about which traits in their tradition they preferred to emphasize. Included in this conception was an underlying and longstanding hostility to U.S.-style liberalism as well as continued attachment to the idea of a distinct Iberian-Latin development model—again, variously defined.[51]

Spain's renewed and more aggressive policies in these areas, which bore considerable fruit, were fueled by the dramatic surge of the Spanish economy between 1960 and 1980. The Spanish "miracle," almost as impressive as the better-known postwar West German and Japanese miracles, propelled Spain from backwardness and underdevelopment to a position as a major industrial power with the tenth largest gross national product in the world. Its per capita income rose rapidly, a new middle class emerged, and with these changes Spain, in contrast with its ambitious but largely futile efforts during earlier epochs, acquired the desire to play a larger role in international affairs and the means to do so. In part also, Spain's subsequent successes in expanding its influence could be attributed to the corresponding declining attention given Latin America by the United States in the 1970s and to the increasing desire of Latin American nations to diversify their own international connections and thus reduce their dependence on the United States.[52]

Spain's foreign policy thrusts into Latin America in the 1970s may also be viewed in the light of its other great foreign policy objective: to secure entry into Europe and the EEC. During this period Spain followed a two-pronged strategy of wooing both Europe and Latin

America and attempting to use each of these as a lever to help accomplish its other goals. That is, Spain used its expanding ties with Latin America to help bolster its case for entry into the EEC. Likewise, it used its growing European ties to strengthen its position in Latin America. By the same token, when Spain seemed poised on the verge of acceptance into Europe (and thus into the community of advanced and democratic nations thus implied) and then later when it actually joined the EEC, it neglected its Latin American connections. But when Spain was rebuffed by Europe (as when it executed several Basque terrorists, thus provoking a European outcry and the familiar hints that Spain was still "uncivilized") or when its entry into the EEC was postponed or blocked temporarily by European (primarily French) intransigence, it tended to compensate by reemphasizing its Atlantic and Latin American ties. These shifts in emphasis were closely related to the lingering debate in Spain about whether it was of the first world or the third world, a European developed nation or a still underdeveloped one, a part of "the West" or apart from it. This debate, in turn, was reflected in the argument over paradigms and models that Spanish intellectuals used to define their nation and its international role.[53]

The Socialist Government in Spain. Another major paradigm shift occurred with the advent of a Socialist government in Spain in 1982 under Felipe González. Although that process remains incomplete, its implications are potentially large, and it deserves attention. The shift was important both domestically and internationally.

Domestically, it meant that Spain had definitively shunted aside (at least for now) the older corporative political model.[54] That model, despite criticism, had continued to survive in the early post-Franco period and through the term of Prime Minister Adolfo Suárez because it did in fact correspond to many Spanish realities. After 1975 Spain had embarked on a transition to democracy, but it had not completely bridged that gap. During the transition many Spanish institutions— labor relations, public policy, the position of the army or the church— continued to represent a mixture of older corporatist and newer democratizing features. Although progressive Spaniards preferred to emphasize the democratic elements over the corporatist ones, corporatism remained a major institutional form even after Franco had passed from the scene. Hence the case could be made that a proper interpretation of Spanish realities required attention both to corporative principles and modes of interpretation and to the newer liberal and social democratic ones.

With the triumph of socialism in Spain, however, the corporative model and interpretation could be eliminated—or so at least the prevailing intellectual currents preferred to think. Spain seemed, at last, to have caught up with Europe. The model for Spaniards remained, as always, France. With Socialist François Mitterrand in power in Paris and a Socialist government installed in Madrid, a new era of harmony between the two countries—progressivism in their interpretations of self and others, and, probably, anti-Americanism—seemed in the works. The dominant motifs in Spanish interpretation, in cultural aspects and in the social sciences, became Socialist, social democratic, Marxist, and quasi-Marxist dependency theory. France's flamboyant (and anti-American) cultural minister Jack Lang and Mitterrand's adviser on Latin America Regis Débray seemed to point the way. But the romance went out of this relationship fairly quickly when it proved to be fellow Socialist Mitterrand who held up Spain's entry into the EEC and when González traveled to Latin America and found the situation there not always in accord with Débray's interpretations. The estrangement was reinforced by Spain's sober realization that it needed its U.S. connections and could not afford to pursue anti-American policies too vigorously.[55] One wonders too about the efficacy and wisdom of many Spanish intellectuals in emphasizing only one body of interpretation (Socialist, social democratic, and Marxist) to the exclusion of all others. Historically, we have said, when one part of Spain, however temporarily dominant, has tried to rule entirely without the other—even to the point of excluding it from any legitimacy—it has created a sure formula for resentment, polarization, and even civil war.

International Repercussions of Socialist Rule. Internationally, particularly with regard to Latin America, some major shifts occurred with the advent of Socialist rule. It would be tempting to place the responsibility for these shifts on the shoulders of then Foreign Minister Fernando Morán, who struck many observers as having a naive and romantic view of the world. But in fact the problem goes deeper, reflecting a major paradigm shift in Spanish thinking, or at least that of its intellectuals. The new Spanish policy in Latin America was based on a strongly held and rather rigid Marxian class analysis, a belief in dependency theory, the traditional Spanish disdain for all things American, and a new combination of *hispanismo* and third worldism, the latter derived in part from González's close friend and mentor Willy Brandt. Spain now presented itself as a bridge to the third world, or maybe a leader of it. While thinking of itself as "advanced" and fully European, with heavy emphasis on the theme of "social democracy," and as a leader of the Socialist International,

Spain also sought to project in Latin America a form of *hispanismo* that identified it with the New World Economic Order and as an ally of "the South" in the great North-South dispute. Moreover, it offered itself as a model of the successful transition from authoritarianism to democracy, socialism, and social justice for others to emulate. Human rights were also prominent on the agenda.[56]

This combination of ingredients constituted a rather potent brew—and was not entirely in accord with U.S. thinking and policy. Indeed, in some quarters the Spanish view, again like the French, was downright hostile to the American presence and role in Latin America. Latin Americans were not necessarily very happy with the new Spanish role either: many found it patronizing, and they resented Spain's offer to serve as a bridge to Europe and to the industrialized world. Nations such as Venezuela, Argentina, Mexico, and Brazil felt that they could handle those relations well enough by themselves without any Spanish intermediation. Spain sought somewhat arrogantly to offer "lessons" to Argentina, Chile, and other nations; the last thing it wanted to admit was that it might still have common features with them. That stance also caused resentment in some places.

In practice, however, Spanish policy was quite sophisticated, nonideological, realistic, pragmatic, and discriminating. In Venezuela, Colombia, and Peru, where Spain had major investments, various development assistance programs, and other economic stakes (not the least being a desire for oil), its Marxism, third worldism, and criticisms of the domestic politics and social realities of these countries remained muted—to the point of silence.[57] With Cuba, Spain had long had important relations, even under Franco; now these were largely continued as before without what some had feared would be an official embrace of Castro.[58] Spain expanded its trade and relations with Brazil, largely ignoring the fact that it was still a military regime.

Some of Spain's most complex relations were in the Southern Cone.[59] It was there especially that Spain wished to serve as a model for the observance of human rights and to offer lessons in the transition to democracy. But those ideas confronted the reality, especially in Argentina, of its major commercial stakes. The commercial interests quickly emerged as paramount over the political and ideological ones. But in this case Spain was able to have its cake and eat it too; when populist radical Raúl Alfonsín was elected president and Argentina restored to democracy, Spain could claim that *it* was the model followed.

This left Central America, where Spain had neither economic nor strategic interests, as a test for its new, independent, and anti-American foreign policy. Even here Spanish policy proved remarkably restrained, though. In large part that restraint was due to the views of Felipe González, which were quite pragmatic in comparison with the more romantic and sometimes wishful notions held by some of his advisers. González recognized immediately that Nicaragua's rulers were not just a happy band of fellow social democrats but also included strong Marxist-Leninist elements intent on setting up a monolithic state; moreover, he led both his own party and the Socialist International to distance themselves from the Nicaraguan regime and to apply pressure on the regime to hold elections and restore pluralims. He was not entirely sympathetic to U.S. policy in El Salvador, but he was cognizant of the complexities of the issues. Moreover, González recognized realistically that ideological posturing on Central America, while somewhat useful in pleasing one sector of Spanish domestic opinion, would needlessly antagonize the United States and that the costs of doing so were simply not worth it. The Spanish government was sensitive to the resentment that would be engendered it if pursued too prominent and disagreeable a role in Latin America, one that might bring Spain into conflict with the United States.[60] Hence, although with the inauguration of socialism there was revealed a paradigm shift in the prevailing circles of Spanish intellectuals, at the policy level the shift has been far less dramatic. In that sphere prudence, pragmatism, and moderation still prevail.

Conclusion and Implications

Paradigms, models, and ways of interpreting and thus simplifying the world seem to be with us always, in all areas of human relations.[61] Such paradigms may be recognized or unrecognized in our thinking, explicit or implicit; but they are forever present. They guide our thoughts, they serve as heuristic devices, they map a research or cognitive terrain. They help order diverse information, and they also shape policy decisions. In the case under consideration here, we have been considering the dominant paradigms and models by which Iberia and Latin America interpret themselves and also how they look at each other and the outside world.

Over time, the historical ties between Iberia and Latin America have waxed and waned, as seems to be true of the relations between all metropoles and their former colonies. In the body of this chapter I traced this evolution from colonial times to the present. Particularly in the past two decades, some notable shifts have occurred in these relations as Spain sought to expand its influence in Latin America and as the Latin American nations themselves sought to diversify their international connections and reduce their dependency on the United States. These shifts were related to major domestic economic, social, and political transformations in Latin America and in Iberia, especially Spain. Since 1974 Portugal has been so preoccupied with its internal political situation and with the downward turn of its economy that it has not been such a significant force in these new equations.

The renewed and greater ties between Spain and Latin America in the past twenty-odd years could be considered natural, almost inevitable. Despite the frequent oscillations in these relations, the Spaniards, Portuguese, and Latin Americans have always viewed themselves as sharing many basic features and as being different from their northern neighbors, whether in Europe or in the Americas. They have regularly proceeded *as if* there were a shared community between them and have resented assertions to the contrary. That Iberia and Latin America have shared and will continue to share a special relationship no one could doubt. The common cultural currents of law, language, religion, sociology, and politics; the attention that they pay to each other's affairs; their now extensive commercial and diplomatic interdependence; and the sizable Latin American expatriate communities always present in Madrid and Lisbon all testify to the historic and continuing importance of these ties. Hence as Fredrick Pike says, Spain, Portugal, and the nations of Latin America are almost certain to continue—despite their ideological and paradigm shifts—to see value in their common histories and traditions and to emphasize these particularly as they contrast with U.S. policy and institutions. Loyalty to the concept of a distinct Iberian–Latin American community, Pike emphasizes, is thus certain to be a continuing principle of their complex interrelations, although, as we have seen, the precise nature of those relations may vary over time.[62]

In this chapter I have highlighted the changing conceptual and paradigmatic relations of Iberia and Latin America. Originally that was a relationship of metropoles to colonies, but since independence the relations between Iberia and Latin America have been both confusing and complex. Although there has long been a search for a common framework or a common grounding, most easily summarized in the concept of *hispanismo*, different nations and groups within those nations at various times have seen the relationship in dissimilar ways and have used it for disparate, usually private purposes. That was clearly the case with corporatism and the corporatist model highlighted here. Viewed by various groups for diverse political purposes, that concept was not at all seen as a neutral, more or less benign social science construct. Rather it involved deeply felt political and sociological sensitivities, it became enmeshed in the domestic politics of these nations, and it affected how they viewed each other and hence their international politics as well. The concept became highly controversial, the debate over it was highly politicized, and it was used for intensely partisan purposes. Although that had not been the intention of those who first offered the model, in retrospect it is possible to see why that was the result.

Currently the corporatist paradigm, so long dominant in Iberia and Latin America, is both out of favor and out of power in Madrid, Lisbon, and some of the Latin American capitals. That has as much to do with the shifting and often fickle political winds as it does with any more objective assessment of its utility as a conceptual model. We do know, however, that beneath the surface in Portugal, Spain, and these other countries are currents that are very ancient and not particularly social-democratic and that may again be restored to prominence if not to power.[63] We do not yet know when or to what degree these countercurrents will make themselves felt again in coming years in Iberia and Latin America, as some parallel stirrings are already making themselves felt in Mitterrand's France, or whether they will again become the prevailing view. One suspects that in the future in Iberia and Latin America we are more likely to see a pluralism and probable fragmentation of both political views and of the paradigms used to interpret these events than the overwhelming dominance of any one of them. In that case there may be reason to regret that the issue became so intensely politicized and that the prevailing paradigms were so closely tied to political movements and particular regimes in power. The very diversity and complexity of these nations and their domestic and international systems demand that the models we use to interpret them reflect pragmatically that diversity and complexity, rather than be tied too closely to any currently prevailing regime or intellectual orthodoxy.[64]

Notes

1. Thomas Kuhn, *The Structure of Scientific Revolutions* (Chicago: University of Chicago Press, 1971).

2. The materials in this section were treated first in Howard J. Wiarda, "Iberia and Latin America: Reforging the Historic Link," *International Journal*, vol. 37 (Winter 1981–1982), pp. 132–48.

3. J. H. Elliot, *Imperial Spain 1469–1716* (New York: St. Martin's Press, 1963); and Fernand Braudel, *The Mediterranean and the Mediterranean World in the Age of Philip II* (New York: Harper and Row, 1972).

4. Charles Tilly, ed., *The Formation of the Nation State in Western Europe* (Princeton, N.J.: Princeton University Press, 1975); see also Charles Gibson, ed., *The Black Legend: Anti-Spanish Attitudes in the Old World and the New* (New

York: Knopf, 1971); and Richard Morse, "The Heritage of Latin America," in Louis Hartz, ed., *The Founding of New Societies* (New York: Harcourt, Brace and World, 1964).

5. Hartz, "Introduction," *The Founding of New Societies.*

6. Charles Gibson, *Spain in America* (New York: Harper, 1966); and C. H. Haring, *The Spanish Empire in America* (New York: Harcourt, Brace and World, 1947).

7. Fredrick B. Pike, "Latin America," in Jaime Cortada, ed., *Spain in the Twentieth Century World* (Greenwood, Conn.: Greenwood Press, 1980), pp. 181–212.

8. T. Halperin Donghi, *The Aftermath of Revolution in Latin America* (New York: Harper and Row, 1973). It should be said that the initial independence movements in Latin America were conservative and pro-Spanish, designed to hold the colonies for the Spanish crown against the French usurper imposed by Napoleon. Only later did they become republican and anti-Spanish.

9. James Busey, "Observations on Latin American Constitutionalism," *The Americas,* vol. 24 (July 1967), pp. 46–66.

10. Glen Dealy, "Prolegomena on the Spanish American Political Tradition," *Hispanic American Historical Review,* vol. 48 (1968), pp. 37–58.

11. Charles Hale, *Mexican Liberalism in the Age of Mora, 1821–1853* (New Haven, Conn.: Yale University Press, 1968). Also chap. 11, "Does the Future Still Lie in Bolivia? Politics and the Stages of Corporative Development in Latin America," in Howard J. Wiarda, *Corporatism and National Development in Latin America* (Boulder, Colo.: Westview Press, 1981), pp. 211–34.

12. Fredrick Pike, *Hispanismo, 1898–1936: Spanish Conservatives and Liberals and Their Relations with Spanish America* (Notre Dame, Ind.: Notre Dame University Press, 1971).

13. Donald C. Worcester, "The Spanish American Past: Enemy of Change," *Journal of Inter-American Studies,* vol. 11 (January 1969), pp. 66–75.

14. W. Rex Crawford, *A Century of Latin American Thought* (New York: Praeger Publishers, 1966), chaps. 4 and 5.

15. José Enrique Rodó, *Ariel,* first published in Montevideo in 1900; English translation by F. J. Stimson (Boston: Houghton-Mifflin, 1922).

16. Fredrick Pike and Thomas Stritch, eds., *The New Corporatism: Social and Political Structures in the Iberian World* (Notre Dame, Ind.: Notre Dame University Press, 1974).

17. Fredrick B. Pike, "Spanish-Latin American Relations: Two Centuries of Divergence—and a New Beginning?" in Wiarda, ed., *The Iberian-Latin American Connection* (Boulder, Colo.: Westview Press, 1977).

18. Giovanni Sartori, "Concept Misinformation in Comparative Politics," *American Political Science Review,* vol. 64 (December 1970), pp. 1033–53.

19. Howard J. Wiarda, "Does Europe Still Stop at the Pyrenees or Does Latin America Begin There? Iberia, Latin America, and the Second Enlargement of the European Community," chap. 6 in this volume.

20. Howard J. Wiarda, *Corporatism and Development: The Portuguese Experience* (Amherst: University of Massachusetts Press, 1977).

21. Eric Baklanoff, *The Economic Transformation of Spain and Portugal* (New

York: Praeger Publishers, 1978).

22. The model was formulated in the late 1960s, presented at professional meetings in 1970 and 1971, and published in early 1973; see Howard J. Wiarda, "Toward a Framework for the Study of Political Change in the Iberic-Latin Tradition: The Corporative Model," *World Politics,* vol. 25 (January, 1973), pp. 206–35. An elaboration, with qualifications, several case studies, additional theoretical materials, and a response to critics, is Wiarda, *Corporatism and National Development.* See also Philippe Schmitter, "Paths to Political Development in Latin America," in Douglas A. Chalmers, ed., *Changing Latin America* (New York: Columbia University, Academy of Political Science, 1972); and James Malloy, ed., *Authoritarianism and Corporatism in Latin America* (Pittsburgh, Penn.: University of Pittsburgh Press, 1977).

23. Riordan Roett, *Brazil: Politics in a Patrimonial Society,* 3d ed. (New York: Praeger Publishers, 1983).

24. Mark Falcoff, "The Politics of Latin America," in R. Daniel McMichael and John D. Paulus, eds., *Western Hemisphere Stability: The Latin American Connection* (Pittsburgh, Penn.: World Affairs Council of Pittsburgh, nineteenth World Affairs Forum, 1983); also Howard J. Wiarda, "The Political Systems of Latin America: Developmental Models and a Taxonomy of Regimes," in Jack W. Hopkins, ed., *Latin America: Perspectives on a Region* (New York: Homes and Meier, 1986).

25. Hartz, *The Founding of New Societies.*

26. Howard J. Wiarda, "Corporatist Theory and Ideology: A Latin American Developmental Paradigm," *A Journal of Church and State,* vol. 13 (Winter 1978), pp. 29–56; also published as chapter 7 in *Corporatism and National Development.*

27. Howard J. Wiarda, "The Political Economy of Latin American Development: The Mercantilist Model," in *Corporatism and National Development,* pp. 245–48.

28. Included in Wiarda, "Toward a Frameowrk for the Study of Political Change in the Iberic-Latin Tradition."

29. Ibid., pp. 234–35.

30. See the final chapter of Wiarda, *Corporatism and National Development.*

31. For example, Gerhard W. Goldberg, "La Función Política de las Fuerzas Armadas en América Latina," *Realidad* [Chile], vol. 3 (December 1981), pp. 13–23; Dieter Blumenwitz et al., *Política y Educación en la Democracía del Futuro* (Santiago: Ediciones Universidad Católica de Chile, 1982); Fernando Escalante, book review in *Foro Internacional* [Mexico] (October–December 1982), pp. 206–8.

32. See, especially, the author's introduction to the Portuguese edition of *Corporatism and National Development,* published as *O Modelo Corporativo na America Latina e a Latinoamericanizgcão dos Estados Unidos* (Rio de Janeiro: Ed. Vozes, 1983). Something of the flavor of the degbate may be found in the exchange between the author and Brazilian sociologist Simon Schwartzman in *Dados: Revista de Ciencias Sociais* [Rio de Janeiro], vol. 25 (1982), pp. 229–56.

33. The model was presented at a series of conferences in Portugal in 1972–1973. See also Howard J. Wiarda, "Corporative Theory and Organization: The

Portuguese Model" (Paper prepared for delivery at the sixth Annual Meeting of the Iberian Social Studies Association, Balliol College, Oxford, England, April 9–12, 1973); "The Portuguese Corporative System: Basic Structures and Current Functions" (Paper prepared for a meeting of the Conference Group on Modern Portugal, University of New Hampshire, Durham, October 14, 1973); and especially "Continuities and Parallels in the Study of Iberia and Latin America" (Memorandum presented at a conference on "España, América Latina, y el Mundo Anglo-Sajón," Instituto de Cultura Hispánica, Madrid, April 4–6, 1974).

34. See, for example, Manuel de Lucena, *A evolução do sistema corporativo portugues*, 2 vols. (Lisbon: Perspectivas e Realidades, 1976). Based also on interviews in Spain and Portugal in 1972–1973, 1974, 1977, 1979.

35. Amando de Miguel, "España, País Latinoamericano," *Informaciones*, June 12, 1973.

36. The argument was forcefully put forth in Philippe C. Schmitter, "Still the Century of Corporatism?" *Review of Politics*, vol. 43 (April 1981), pp. 85–131.

37. Richard M. Nuccio, "The Family as Political Metaphor in Authoritarian-Conservative Regimes: The Case of Spain" (Amherst: University of Massachusetts, Program in Latin American Studies, Occasional Papers Series no. 9, 1978). See also Nuccio "The Socialization of Political Values: The Context of Official Education in Spain" (Ph.D. diss., University of Massachusetts, 1977).

38. Charles W. Anderson, *The Political Economy of Modern Spain: Policy-making in an Authoritarian System* (Madison: University of Wisconsin Press, 1970).

39. Nuccio, "The Family as Political Metaphor"; Wiarda, "Does Europe Still Stop at the Pyrenees?"

40. The materials in this section are derived from Wiarda, "Iberia and Latin America."

41. Guillermo O'Donnell, *Modernization and Bureaucratic Authoritarianism* (Berkeley: University of California, Institute of International Studies, 1973); David Collier, *The New Authoritarianism in Latin America* (Princeton, N.J.: Princeton University Press, 1979).

42. Pike, "Spanish-Latin American Relations"; based also on field research and participant observation in Brazil, Argentina, Venezuela, Chile, Portugal, and Spain during this period.

43. David S. Bell, ed., *Democratic Politics in Spain* (New York: St. Martin's Press, 1983); John Coverdale, *The Political Transformation of Spain after Franco* (New York: Praeger Publishers, 1979); Victor Alba, *Transition in Spain: Franco to Democracy* (New Brunswick, N.J.: Transaction Books, 1978); José Maravall, *The Transition to Democracy in Spain* (London: Croom Helm, 1982). A more skeptical and less celebratory view is Howard J. Wiarda, "Spain and Portugal," in Peter Merkl, ed., *Western European Party Systems* (New York: Free Press, 1980), pp. 298–328.

44. See the report of one such study group by Richard Sholk, "Comparative Aspects of the Transition from Authoritarian Rule: A Rapporteur's Report" (Washington, D.C.: Woodrow Wilson International Center for Schol-

ars, Latin America Program, Occasional Paper no. 114, 1982). Again, dissenting views may be found in Howard J. Wiarda, "Electoral Competition and Participation in Portugal: Has Democracy Been Institutionalized?" in Myron Weiner and Ergun Ozbudun, eds., *Elections in Developing Countries* (Durham, N.C.: Duke University Press, 1987), chap. 11; and Wiarda, "Can Democracy Be Exported? The Quest for Democracy in United States Latin America Policy," in Kevin Middlebrook and Carlos Rico, eds., *The United States and Latin America in the 1980s* (Pittsburgh, Penn.: University of Pittsburgh Press, 1986).

45. A superb theoretical statement long preceding the "transition to democracy" literature and more realistic is Arpad von Lazar, "Latin America and the Politics of Post-Authoritariansim: A Model for Decompression," *Comparative Political Studies*, vol. 1 (October 1968), pp. 419–29.

46. Peter Snow, "Argentina: Politics in a Conflict Society," in Howard J. Wiarda and Harvey F. Kline, eds., *Latin American Politics and Development*, 2d rev. ed. (Boulder, Colo.: Westview Press, 1985).

47. Mark Falcoff, "Spain and the Southern Cone," in Wiarda, ed., *The Iberian-Latin American Connection*.

48. Philippe Schmitter, "The 'Portugalization' of Brazil," in Alfred Stepan, ed., *Authoritarian Brazil* (New Haven, Conn.: Yale University Press, 1973).

49. Based on a review of Brazilian newspapers during 1974–1976.

50. For example, *Las relaciones económicas entre España e Iberoamérica* (Madrid: Ediciones Cultura Hispánica de Instituto de Cooperación Iberoamericana, 1982); based also on materials generated by the Task Force on Scholarly Relations with Spain of the Latin American Studies Association, on which the author served as a member.

51. Enrique Baloyra and Rafael López Pintor, *Iberoamérica en los años 80: Perspectivas de cambio social y político* (Madrid: Centro de Investigaciones Sociologicas con la colaboración del Instituto de Cooperación Iberoamericana, 1983).

52. Eric Baklanoff, "Spain's Emergence as a Middle Industrial Power: The Basis and Structure of Spanish-Latin American Economic Relations," in Wiarda, ed., *The Iberian-Latin American Connection*.

53. Wiarda, "Does Europe Stop at the Pyrenees?" and "Electoral Competition and Participation in Portugal."

54. Based on interviews in Spain in 1979 and 1984; see also Howard J. Wiarda, *From Corporatism to Neo-Syndicalism: The State, Organized Labor, and the Changing Industrial Relations Systems of Southern Europe*, chap. 8 in this volume.

55. See William T. Salisbury and Richard V. Salisbury, "Spain, the United States, and Latin America," in Wiarda, ed., *The Iberian-Latin American Connection*. Based also on a regular reading of the international edition of Spain's *El País*, 1983–1984.

56. Based on interviews in Spain during 1984; also Eusebio Mujal-León, "Rei(g)ning in Spain," *Foreign Policy*, no. 51 (Summer 1983), pp. 101–17.

57. David Blank, "Spain and the Andean Republics," in Wiarda, ed., *The Iberian-Latin American Connection*.

58. Alistair Hennessey, "Spanish-Cuban Relations," in Ibid.

59. Falcoff, "Spain and the Southern Cone."

60. Eusebio Mujal-León, "Continuity and Change in the Foreign Policy of a Socialist Spain," in Wiarda, ed., *The Iberian-Latin American Connection,* as well as his "European Socialism and the Crisis in Central America," in Howard J. Wiarda, ed., *Rift and Revolution: The Central American Imbroglio* (Washington, D.C.: American Enterprise Institute, 1984).

61. William Connolly, *The Terms of Political Discourse* (Princeton, N.J.: Princeton University Press, 1984); also Connolly and Glen Gordon, *Social Structure and Political Theory* (Lexington, Mass.: D. C. Heath, 1974).

62. Pike, "Latin America," p. 208.

63. Wiarda, "Electoral Competition and Participation in Portugal" and "Can Democracy Be Exported?"

64. Wiarda, *Corporatism and National Development;* also Abraham Kaplan, "Systems Theory and Political Science," *Social Research,* vol. 35 (July 1968), pp. 30–47.

10
How Well Institutionalized Are Portuguese Elections and Democracy?

No good wind or happy marriage ever comes from Spain.
OLD PORTUGUESE SAYING

If you gather all the data—the inflation, the unemployment, the number of returnees from Africa—the situation is explosive. . . . But in Portugal nothing happens.
FORMER PRIME MINISTER FRANCISCO BALSEMÃO

In 1974 in the so-called Revolution of Carnations, Portugal overthrew the longest-lived authoritarian-corporate regime in Western Europe and subsequently moved to establish democracy. Democracy had never before been strongly institutionalized in Portugal; and a mere ten years later, Portugal's fledgling democratic system and institutions were strongly under attack again. The Portuguese economy was a shambles, inflation and unemployment were unacceptably high, the society and polity were deeply fissured and fragmented, and the bloom was off both the revolution and Portugal's struggling democratic regime.

There was much disillusion with politics and parties; a political malaise and paralysis had set in; stagnation, drift, and political weariness had produced a foul public mood; and the graffiti and posters of revolution and democracy had faded or were in tatters, prompting numerous unkind visitors to call Lisbon "the dirtiest capital in Europe." The insult grates on the Portuguese, whose whitewashed villages and scrubbed sidewalks were in the past a source of great national pride. When widespread alienation, intensifying class conflict, political polarization, nostalgia for earlier, less frenetic times, and a threadbare economy—to say nothing of those "no good winds" blowing from Spain in the form of sporadic but serious assaults on that nation's democratic institutions—are added to this simmering cauldron of woes, one would expect the pot soon to boil over. That may of course still occur, but for now at least the former prime minister's words still hold: "The situation is explosive. . . . But in Portugal nothing happens."[1]

This chapter explores these trends in Portugal's politics, its liberal and its authoritarian currents, the present, more complex sources of social and political cleavages, the recent establishment of democracy, and the prospects for its continuation and institutionalization. Portugal is a special case in this regard: although it is a European and a Western country, it has not throughout its history definitively been considered by its neighbors or considered itself fully a part of Europe; and although by many socioeconomic indexes it could—at least historically—be grouped with the third world, it is geographically, psychologically, and now economically, sociologically, and perhaps politically as well, a part of Europe. Ultimately, the questions to be posed are these: Why is it that "nothing happens" in Portugal? Will Portugal's present democratic system survive and prove lasting? If not, what options, if any, does Portugal have besides democracy? Finally, what are the possibilities for an indigenous, home-grown brand of democracy as contrasted with the largely imported and hence only weakly institutionalized variety now sprouting but lacking either deep roots or budding flowers?[2]

The Portuguese Background

Although Portugal is a "Western" and a "European" country, the precise meaning of those terms has never been entirely clear to the Portuguese. Furthermore, although Portugal has all the formal trappings of democracy, its deep regional, religious, class, rural-urban, and ideological cleavages often seem more like those of various third world nations and unlike those of Western Europe, where such intensely divisive politics as Portugal still experiences have generally diminshed in recent decades. Even the questions whether democracy is viable, institutionalized, and lasting and whether alternatives exist—issues still heatedly debated in Portugal—make that country more akin to the third world than to most of Western Europe. Hence the first set of questions to be answered here is whether Portugal is a part of Europe or apart from it and whether it is developed or developing, Western or non-Western, or perhaps—and most likely—occupying some intermediary position between these alternative models and polar points.

European or Something Else? Portugal is not only attached physically to Europe but it also faces west across the Atlantic and south toward Africa. It has long been torn between its European attachments and its overseas settlements; but now, with the independence of Brazil and its former African colonies and the end of the dream of a grand Lusitanian empire (stylized maps that once adorned Lisbon's telephone poles showed the country, along with its African colonies, superimposed on a map of Europe and proclaimed, "You're as big as any of these"), it may well be that Portugal no longer has that choice. With modern communications and transportation, the effects of a flood of European tourists and of the reverse torrent of Portuguese workers into other European countries and the equally impressive impact of Western culture (democracy as well as Coke and rock music), the psychological and geographic distance of Portugal from Europe has also diminished significantly.[3]

Portugal's entry into the European Economic Community (EEC) has also brought the country closer to Europe—not so much for the ostensible economic reasons usually cited but even more important for drawing a floundering, potentially unstable, and revolutionary Portugal closer to the West militarily, strategically, and politically. Indeed, one of the most important developments since the 1974 Revolution was the role of the Western European nations in steering Portugal in a multiparty, parliamentary, and social democratic direction, a strategy that merits applause on the one hand but gives rise to the disquieting question on the other of to what degree democracy in Portugal, or its present and particular form, reflects genuine, indigenous Portuguese desires or whether it represents the preferred and to some extent imposed solution of the outside powers. Hence we ask, Has the choice forced on Portugal in recent years between dictatorship and democracy been a falsely dichotomous choice? Would the Portuguese themselves if left alone have posed the issue in such stark either-or terms? Might there not be other alternatives? Could the Portuguese develop a form of democracy that would be in accord with Portuguese tradition and experience and that would therefore have a greater potential for institutionalization than the present somewhat pale imitations of European parliamentarism? Equally disturbing are these additional questions, which emerge from the same set of considerations: Will the Western nations be as concerned as before with helping sustain Portuguese democracy now that the most radical and, to them, threatening phase of the Portuguese Revolution seems to have run its course? Alternatively, will Portugal itself, now that the romance of "joining Europe" has worn off and the hard realities have set in, have a lesser commitment to those democratic institutions that, in part at least, it adopted earlier so as to be more "acceptable" to Europe? All these questions cannot be fully answered here, but they do not augur well for the future of Portuguese democracy.[4]

Developed or Developing? By the criteria either of dependency analysis or of Immanuel Wallerstein's capitalist "world system," Portugal is a dependent, underdeveloped nation. By virtually all economic indexes Portugal has, next to Albania, the lowest standard of living in Europe. Long a continental outpost and dependency of Britain, only in the twentieth century did Portugal begin to use its resources for greater internal development. But as the crisis brought on by simultaneously fighting three colonial wars (in Angola, Guinea-Bissau, and Mozambique) accelerated in the 1960s, as Portugal lost these colonies and was torn by revolution in the 1970s, and as its economy slid downhill in the early 1980s, it exchanged its dependence on Britain for a new and different dependence on the United States and the EEC. Today Portugal is in much the same situation in world economic affairs as it has been for three centuries: weak, dependent, its industries in need of protection, and its economy in perilous straits.[5]

Although Portugal is economically underdeveloped by European standards (which is the measure by which it is compared and compares itself), it is far ahead of most of the developing world. Its per capita income of $1,840 per year (1977) means that it long ago passed the threshold separating the developed from the developing nations. Although it is not closing the gaps with the more advanced nations of Europe (on most indexes it is falling further behind), Portugal is no longer the backward, underdeveloped, ninetheenth-century society it was until twenty-five years ago. It has industrialized, urbanized, and become more middle class. Both economically and sociologically, it now approximates the nations of Western Europe and aspires thereto.[6] Hence by one set of indexes Portugal belongs to the developing world; by another it approaches the developed one.

Third, First, or Second World? Similar confusion exists about which "world of development" Portugal belongs with.[7] Portugal sometimes thinks of itself as a third world nation. These are usually fleeting ideas, however, for with the loss of its colonies and the increasingly close economic, banking, and trade ties since the 1960s between Portugal and the EEC, Portugal is now closely integrated with the first world of European nations whether it wishes to be or not. "Third worldism" continues to be expressed from time to time, but that may no longer be a feasible choice for Portugal and may reflect more the politics of romance and nostalgia than the politics of reality.[8]

At least as interesting is the debate over "first worldism" versus "second worldism." Long a retarded capitalist country whose economic system was more akin to a nineteenth-century (or earlier) form of capitalism and neo-mercantilism, in its revolution of the mid-1970s Portugal lurched precipitiously toward socialism. For a time there was much talk of Yugoslav, Cuban, and Soviet models as well as West German or Scandinavian ones. Portugal nationalized many firms, converted others to cooperatives run by employees who were often mainly interested in keeping their jobs, and established a "mixed" economy dominated as always by the state—but now tipping away from socialism and back toward greater private ownership. At present it would be safest to say that Portugal is not first or second or third world, that its economy is neither capitalist nor Socialist but rather a mixture of these and, perhaps most accurately, a system chiefly in disarray: inflation rates of 30 percent, exhausted foreign exchange reserves, immense foreign debt, and considerable economic chaos.[9]

Western or Non-Western? Portugal is of course a geographical part of the West and tied to it by trade and diplomacy, as well as by its religious, cultural, legal, and political traditions. But Portugal is a late developer whose modernization is taking place in a different time, in a changed international context, and not necessarily in accord with the same sequences of stages as occurred in the rest of Europe; indeed, its own traditional social and political institutions have proved remarkably resilient and flexible, selecting which sociopolitical concomitants of industrialization to incorporate and which to filter out. Portugal, in fact, fails to conform very well to the Western model.[10]

Portugal remains a part of the West but apart from it, a Western country in its major institutions but one whose development experience does not in all ways conform to the northwest European pattern. In examining the Portuguese social and political system, therefore, we must note where it fits the Western model that our social sciences often presumptuously think of as universal and where it is distinct.

By all these criteria—a part of Europe or apart from it; developed or developing; first, second, or third world; Western or non-Western—Portugal occupies an intermediary position. It tips primarily toward the European, developed, first world, and Western pattern, but not exclusively; particularly in times of crisis, it may lean in other, quite different directions. It will be interesting to see if the intermediary position Portugal occupies economically, socially, and psychologically is also reflected in its political system, the degree of institutionalization of its democracy, and the nature of its societal and voting divisions.

The Institutionalization of Parties and Elections in Portugal

The Portuguese experience with elections, democracy, and parliamentary rule has been brief, sporadic, uncertain, and frequently interrupted. The irregular and only weakly institutionalized nature of parties, elections, parliament, and democracy, together with abundant recent survey data showing widespread disillusionment with all parties and the present democratic system, forces us to consider whether democracy is the best and most appropriate form of government for Portugal or whether it is even the system to which most Portuguese aspire.[11] I shall return to this issue later; now let me simply say that despite repeated crises and long periods of authoritarian rule, elections and democracy survive, thrive, and have been joyfully reinstated in Portugal—even if they do not always correspond to the British parliamentary model from which, in Portugal's long dependency, they largely derive.

Origins of the Party System. The origins of the Portuguese party system go back to the eighteenth century or even earlier, to Pombal and the Enlightenment, to that fundamental division in the Portuguese soul and society between a Portugal that was rural, two class, traditional, "feudal," Catholic, inward looking, hierarchical, and authoritarian *and* a Portugal that is urban, bourgeois, modernizing, secular and rationalist, outward and European looking, nascently egalitarian, and democratic.[12] This split, whose origins predate the development of modern political parties, divides Portugal, as it does or did France, into two great "nations" or "families," a "family of order" and a "family of change."[13] The division into two Portugals, poles apart in politics and in virtually all areas of life, pertaining to quite different historical epochs and not just to fleeting party programs, not only continued to divide Portugal throughout the nineteenth century and into the twentieth but still lies at the roots of the regional, religious, ideological, and class cleavages that even now pull the country apart.

After the Napoleonic wars Portugal moved to establish a constitutional monarchy patterned after that of Britain.[14] But socioeconomic conditions in Portugal were quite different from those prevailing in the world's first industrializing nation, and it is not clear that the Portuguese entirely understood the finer points of British parliamentarism. Nor were the changes ushered in with parliamentarism very radical, for many of Portugal's historical elitist and authoritarian assumptions continued to prevail. The suffrage was limited, and voting was indirect. Only males twenty-five years of age or older, heads of families, priests, officers, and graduates with higher degrees could vote for provincial electors. These electors were required to have an annual income of at least 200,000 *reis*, and it was they who chose the deputies.[15] Both wealth and political power remained highly concentrated.

Portuguese politics during the nineteenth century was in many respects like that of Spain: chaotic, divisive, torn by revolt and civil war. The fissures that had emerged in the eighteenth century became open conflicts, but they reached deeper into society, gradually involved more persons, and were eventually covered over with the forms, language, and paraphernalia of party and parliamentary politics. The parties that emerged represented rival elite cliques, but gradually they acquired a genuine programmatic base and a wider appeal. Coups, revolutions, and assassinations were often the means of seeking or seizing power, but some of these movements began to have a political program behind them and to take on more "democratic" features. Clientelism, colonelism (rule by local military elites), and rotativism (gentlemen's agreements among these elites providing for rotation in office) served as the means by which various factions held their followers and circulated in and out of power; but eventually the clientelistic networks also formed a larger and more massive base, and rotation enabled a variety of shifting cliques and their clienteles to take a turn at the great public watering trough. The system was hardly democratic, but the tendency was in that direction.[16]

These developments came to a head with the establishment of the First Portuguese Republic (1910–1926). The republic was highly unstable. But its accomplishments, as Douglas S. Wheeler's book has emphasized, should not be ignored: elections were held regularly, human rights were respected, some reforms were carried out, the suffrage was extended, and more people than ever before were brought into national politics. In addition, a host of new democratic parties came into existence, largely replacing (though in some cases fusing with) the old elitist nineteenth-century cliques and cadres, and a modern political party system and a full ideological spectrum emerged for the first time. The parties, party system, and democracy itself had little chance to institutionalize themselves, however; in 1926 a military coup led to the creation and restitution of full-fledged authoritarianism. Chaos and corruption had by then become so wide-spread that at the time the republic was overthrown few lamented its passing. But republicanism and democracy nonetheless remained ideals, although it was half a century before they were restored.[17]

The era of Salazar (1928–1968) and Caetano (1968–1974) has been treated at length earlier,[18] but three major topics merit some attention here. One is the nature of the Salazar-Caetano regime; the second has to do with elections, one-party politics, and the functions of the party "system" in an authoritarian regime of "elections without choice"; and the third concerns the nascent emergence of a more broadly based party spectrum even while the old regime was still in power.

The Salazar-Caetano Regime. The Salazar-Caetano regime has been widely misrepresented in the literature, and the record needs to be set straight if we are to understand properly the nature of parties, elections, parliament, and democracy during that era and subse-quently. The Salazar-Caetano regime has been denounced as reaction-ary; fascistic; a throwback to an earlier, sleepier era; a regime seeking to turn the clock back; one dedicated to putting and keeping workers and peasants in their place; a hierarchical, elitist, authoritarian, Catholic-corporatist system opposed to the main currents of twen-tieth-century life; a Portuguese form of Poujadism (a French ultracon-servative movement of the 1950s); akin to the Hitler, Mussolini, and Franco regimes; antidemocratic; and a revolt against modern mass society and a nostalgic longing for the past. All these interpretations, with some qualifications, have a considerable basis in fact. (For exam-ple, Portugal was not really like the Nazi behemoth; it had parallels with Fascist Italy but was not like Germany.) The trouble is that they are not the only interpretations that might be offered.

Although the Salazar-Caetano regime *was* in one sense a reaction-ary throwback, its corporative-authoritarian forms should also be looked at as an alternative way of dealing with the great forces of twentieth-century modernization and not just a way of turning its face against them.[19] Similarly, although we may not like corporatism as an ideology and a type of national sociopolitical organization, we must recognize and deal with it realistically, study its dynamics, and under-stand it as the twentieth century's other great and often forgotten "ism," perhaps as significant as its major alternatives, liberalism and socialism, particularly in the Latin and Catholic countries of Europe and Latin America. Further, although Portugal was admittedly anti-democratic, we must recognize that historically it never had de-veloped the doctrines of parliamentary democracy comparable to the British tradition and that in Portuguese, terms of constitutional law

such as popular sovereignty, elections, rights, participation, representation, and the like convey quite different meanings or imply different
institutional arrangements from those in the Anglo-American tradition.

Nor should the Portuguese regime be viewed in simplistic Marxian terms as governed by its landed elites and bourgeois plutocrats
(although to some degree that came to be true also) but as one in
which rival middle-sector elements competed for power and influence. The middle sectors who governed during the Salazar-Caetano
regime were different from those who governed during the republic
and were often rivals of them. Moreover, the class configuration of the
regime also changed over time, becoming somewhat less elitist and
somewhat more responsive to the newer social forces. Finally, it is
important to understand Portuguese corporatism—particularly at the
beginning—as in part a nationalistic rejection of what were considered
inappropriate foreign models, particularly British parliamentarism,
which seemed to have produced so much chaos. The corporatists in
Portugal were seeking to develop an indigenous (Catholic and southern European) model based on their own history and traditions,
rather than one imported from the outside, and resurrecting and
reinstituting homegrown, national institutions and sociopolitical
structures—however unsuccessful that experiment proved in the
end.[20]

Elections and One-Party Politics. The second theme important here is
the role of parties and elections in such a system. Upon taking power
in 1926, the military regime moved, in the familiar way, against the
existing political parties and was especially harsh to those associated
with republicanism and the left. In the early 1930s Salazar created a
single official party, the União Nacional, rebaptized by Caetano as the
Aliança Nacional Popular, which from that time on monopolized
elections, patronage, and the political machinery of the state and
offered voters only the option of ratifying the regime in power.
Through these and other means the left was stripped of the possibility
of coming to power or even voicing much opposition, real political
choice among several alternatives was eliminated, participation was
limited, and the population was demobilized. The system was undemocratic and antidemocratic; indeed, it made no pretense of being
otherwise.[21]

All this is disturbing from a democratic perspective, but in the
Portuguese context of that time it may be understandable. To understand it, one must bear in mind, first, the distinct political-cultural
tradition of Portugal already referred to—the disastrous experience

with British parliamentarism and the chaos of the First Republic, Portuguese nationalism, and the desire to create an indigenous model rather than just a pale imitation of the West, the special meaning of *popular sovereignty* and other terms within the Portuguese political tradition—and, second, Portugal's level of socioeconomic development and the intermediary position it occupies between the developed and the developing worlds. For although, after several decades of significant economic growth, Portugal is now approaching the lower end of the European spectrum economically, sociologically, and politically, in the 1920s and 1930s it showed more characteristics of a developing nation with all its attendant features and problems: backwardness, high illiteracy, social fragmentation, instability, inchoate political institutions, and the like.

Thus the single-party system and the absence of much electoral choice can be understood as a response to the urgent need to unify a developing but badly fragmented nation on the brink of disintegration, to forge coherence out of chaos, to achieve a measure of economic growth and stability before full democracy could be attempted, to pull together disparate and fractious groups into a common effort at national development, and to build a true nation out of contending, centrifugal factions. Although a single-party regime could perhaps be justified in Portugal in the 1920s and 1930s, however, particularly given the country's underdevelopment as compared with its northern European counterparts, the same rationalizations no longer served in the 1960s and 1970s, when the earlier problems of achieving national integration and development had been largely overcome and the nation had become socially more pluralistic and multiclass, yet when the regime itself had become ossified and "sclerotic."[22]

The Nascent Emergence of a Party System. The third theme has to do with the emergence of a new and more modern party system even while the old regime was still in power. Portugal under Salazar and Caetano was never so fascistic or totalitarian that *some* limited pluralism and party activity could not take place.[23] By the late 1960s the Communists, though illegal, had gained a position of dominance in the underground labor organization and in the south among the peasants. The Socialists functioned in a limited, on-again, off-again fashion, chiefly from exile but also within the country through a variety of fronts and "study groups." The Social Democrats and Christian Democrats were operating more or less openly as opposition within the country, although their freedom and activities were also circumscribed; but they did publish a newspaper highly critical of the government and even, for a time, had a small bloc in the parliament.

335

Moreover, the official party, as a large bureaucratic apparatus, encompassed a variety of factions within its loose structure; and it was here that the major centrist, Catholic, rightist, and monarchist groups found a home. All these factions, as well as the exile, underground, and study groups, served as the nuclei of a multiparty system once the Salazar-Caetano regime was overthrown.[24]

By the beginning of the 1970s, then, Portugal was a decidedly mixed or intermediate case, both in its level of socioeconomic development and, correspondingly, in its political culture and institutions. The following observations summarize these currents, as Portugal reached the end of one era and was about to embark upon another:

• Socioeconomically Portugal by the early 1960s was suspended between the advanced industrial societies of Western Europe and the developing societies of the third world. With the new economic growth and interdependence forged during the 1960s and 1970s, Portugal was drawn more into the former orbit than into the latter.[25]

• Portugese political culture, historically conservative, had changed radically in the post–World War II era, especially in the urban-industrial areas. There was no longer just one Portugal or two but now three: a conservative-traditional Portugal, a liberal one, and most recently a more radical and Socialist one, within which there were several subcurrents. These changes reflected the transformation in class structure that had occurred in the country.[26]

• The voting act, historically plebiscitary and designed chiefly to ratify a government already in power, was now seen both in that traditional sense and in a newer one, which implied genuine mass participation and the demand for real choice among several alternatives.[27]

• Historically and under Salazar and Caetano the suffrage had been limited, restricted mainly to male heads of households; now there occurred a sudden explosion of political participation, mobilizing particularly the cities but also, to a considerable degree and in some areas, the countryside as well—and encompassing women as well as men.[28]

• Elections in Portugal had always been viewed as providing tentative and limited mandates; now elections were strongly viewed as *the* route to power, carrying more definitive legitimacy. Politics still took place in the barracks and in the streets as well as at the polls; but the concept of legitimized routes to power besides the electoral one was fading. This was especially true for Portugal, given the long denial of democratic choice.[29]

• In the historical Portuguese model political parties had always operated at the margins, enjoying neither much popularity nor much legitimacy. Now the parties achieved greater importance as articulators of rival programs and ideologies and as the bases for parliamentary representation and governance.[30]

• At the same time the other "parties"—army, church, elites—that had historically played such an important role in the Portuguese system became more functionally specific and, to some degree, were marginalized and shunted aside as the main power contenders. This is not to deny the continuing importance of these groups within the system but only to point out that they now had to contend with other blocs, such as organized labor, that were enjoying widespread legitimacy—to say nothing of the real parties.[31]

• As a mixed system, politically as well as socioeconomically, Portuguese politics had become more open, fluid. New routes to power had evolved. In another study I have sought to show how in the transitional systems of Iberia and Latin America both "critical elections" and "critical coups," or various combinations of them, could serve as the triggering forces in a radical, epochal transformation of society. In Portugal in the early 1970s these currents were very much in the air.[32]

It is clear, therefore, that Portugal was undergoing some profound transformations—sociologically, economically, politically— even before the revolution of 1974. The revolution demonstrated just how profound the changes had already been; it also served as the catalyst and triggering mechanism for a major restructuring of the entire national system.

Democratic Portugal: Electoral Mobilization and the Emergence of a New Party System

The Portuguese revolution that began in 1974 was, as we have seen, one of the major epochal events of the 1970s. It was important not only because of its effects on Portugal but because it attracted international attention. At first the revolution was seen by some groups as the possible herald of a wave of revolutions throughout Western Europe. But Portugal proved not to be the wave of the future for Western Europe: as an intermediate and semideveloped nation it was hardly a model for the already developed ones, let alone the cutting edge for advanced social change. Eventually it was agreed that its revolution conformed to earlier notions of revolution as a phenom-

337

enon of transitional nations, neither wholly backward nor advanced.[33]

The revolt was initiated by some generally younger officers of the Portuguese armed forces, but from the beginning it had widespread civilian participation and support as well. It could be seen as a critical coup in the sense that it ushered in an epochal or sea change, which was later ratified and redirected in a series of elections that could also be described as critical. In this way it was in keeping with a number of the transitional characteristics outlined: the army was the major "party," but other civilian party elements were involved as well; it combined electoral choice with a form of plebiscitary confirmation; and it united action in the barracks with action in the streets with action at the polls.

The revolution had begun as a military coup, but it had quickly taken on many features of a popular social revolution. The instruments of repression of the old dictatorship were quickly toppled; soon all institutions associated with the old order were under attack. The people, principally those of the capital and the industrial centers, poured into the streets in a joyful victory celebration, placing carnations in the guns of their "liberators." In the Alentejo, an area in the south with large estates still organized on a kind of feudal, two-class basis where the Communist party had a considerable following, there were also peasant uprisings; but in general the Portuguese countryside—more traditional and Catholic than the urban centers—remained subdued.[34]

The main coup of April 1974 was soon followed by other, lower-level rebellions. These are what effectively converted the military revolt into a profounder, deeper social revolution. Employees of private firms demanded the overthrow of managers and employers; government workers "sanitized" their agencies of "Fascist" influences; peasants seized private lands and threw out the owners; maids and servants denounced their employers; children rebelled against their parents. It was not just the old regime that was attacked but all symbols of hierarchy, authority, and "fascism." Most of these turnovers were the result of popular action in the streets, firms, or offices; they were later ratified by decree-law and in elections.[35]

Although the changes were major, they should not be emphasized at the expense of ignoring the persistencies. The older authoritarian-corporatist regime had been destroyed, but Portugal did not become a full-fledged participatory democracy overnight. Many structures of hierarchy and authority remained, although often with new heads. The *saneamento* (literally, "cleansing") of the public service was sporadic and incomplete and varied in its thoroughness from ministry to ministry. At the crucial Ministry of Labor, for instance, which was given over to the Portuguese Communist party (PCP) immediately after the revolution, the same "sleepy" bureaucrats often continued to shuffle the same mountains of paper in the same sleepy way. The PCP did not democratize the ministry; on the contrary, it kept in place and used the top-down structures and instruments of the old regime to cement its control over the trade unions and to keep the revolution from going too far.[36] In these and numerous other ways Portugal remained a transitional system, liberated in some ways but merely adhering to new authority patterns in others, and a complex, often chaotic mixture, fusion, and hodgepodge of traditional and modern.

Parties and the New Party System: The Ideological Spectrum. This period also saw the emergence of a host of new parties and of a full-fledged party system in Portugal. The exiles returned, organizations that had been underground emerged into the open, and the former study groups were reorganized as political parties. The fact that the parties and the party system have been in existence for only a short time, however, helps explain why they have so far been quite unstable and why the system has not yet "settled down." The electorate in Portugal remained quite volatile, with major shifts in voting behavior registered over the next decade. The instability and lack of institutionalization may also be explained by the inexperience of the Portuguese with democratic institutions, the fact that competitive parties had not previously played a major role in the nation's political life, and that other institutions (the military, for example) and political arenas (the streets, for example) loomed at least as important—if not more so—as the electoral one. There are now, nonetheless, a full-fledged party spectrum and system (including democratic elections, parliament, and party government) that have gained greater importance and legitimacy.[37]

The Portuguese party system is broad. It encompasses Communists on the far left and monarchists and Fascists (now rebaptized under new labels) on the far right. A large number of smaller and personalistic parties come and go, usually around election time, but they are seldom large nor do they exhibit many signs of permanence. For a long time following the revolution there were few discernible trends toward stable, center, middle-of-the-road politics. But in 1987 a centrist party won an absolute majority for the first time *ever* in Portuguese republican history. (A fuller description of the main parties and their programs appears in chapter 7.)

The Portuguese Communist party is tough, disciplined, well

organized, and strongly Moscow oriented. It shows few signs of becoming a more pragmatic "Eurocommunist" party. Although the party has been steadily losing electoral support since the mid-1970s, it remains a major force.[38]

The Portuguese Socialist party (PS) is similar to the European Socialist and Social Democratic parties. It is bourgeois, moderate, and established, although it enjoys considerable lower-class support. It also has the same deep rifts between its left and its more centrist wings as the other European members of the Socialist International.

The Socialists, led by Mario Soares, are an important party, and for a time had the largest share of the vote. After the earliest, most radical stages of the revolution in 1974–1975, the Socialists came to power in 1976, and Soares became prime minister. They had a difficult time, caught between their desires to implement a Socialist program and the need to institute an austerity program, hold down wages, roll back agrarian reform, and bow to pressure from the International Monetary Fund for stabilization. The Socialists have developed close ties with their European counterparts and have been the beneficiaries of considerable assistance, financial and other, from various West European Socialist parties. They are also besieged—accused by the Communists of being insufficiently revolutionary but prisoners of an electorate that seems to be becoming increasingly conservative. In 1979 the party was defeated at the polls, but in 1983, again under Mario Soares, it returned to power. Later, it lost its parliamentary majority again, but in 1986 the popular Soares was elected president.

The Social Democratic party (PSD, which early on merged with the small Popular Democratic party, or PPD, and is sometimes referred to by the initials of both groups, PPD/PSD) is a center party led by bourgeois and moderate liberals. At one point it formed the democratic opposition to Caetano, operating within the parliament; it is oriented toward the classic liberal freedoms and favors some, though limited, reform. After 1974 it served as a check on the more radical elements within the revolutionary movement, and after 1976 it formed the principal opposition to the Soares government. As the electorate turned to the right by the late 1970s, the PSD campaigned actively; in 1979 it emerged as the dominant party and won the December 1979 elections (in a coalition, which it headed, called the Democratic Alliance), and its leader, Francisco Sá Carneiro, became prime minister. But Sá Carneiro was killed in 1980 in a plane crash; Francisco Pinto Balsemão, editor of the weekly newspaper *Expresso* and an untested leader, became prime minister and party head. The PS and PSD subsequently formed a coalition government in mid-1983 under the leadership of Socialist leader Mario Soares. The precarious coalition lasted until 1985, when new elections were held. The PSD overtook the PS to become the largest single party in the Assembly, and in October 1985 the PSD leader, Cavaco Silva, was appointed prime minister of a minority PSD government. In 1987 Cavaco Silva won an absolute majority.

The Christian Democratic party (CDS) is the main conservative party of Portugal. It is somewhat right of center and still within the country's political mainstreams. Headed by Diogo Freitas do Amaral, the CDS has gained in stength in the years since the revolution. It has the support and financial backing of several individuals and family groups associated with the old regime, a number of whom have begun to launch political comebacks.

There is an active monarchist party, the Popular Monarchists, in Portugal; as a member of the Democratic Alliance that came to power in 1979, the party received a cabinet position, making Portugal the only country in Europe where monarchists were actually in government. There is no Fascist party in Portugal (it has been outlawed since the revolution), but there is some limited Fascist sentiment.

Also on the right are a number of persons formerly associated with the Salazar regime who conceivably might lead a rightist resurgence. These persons tend to be more important as individual, charismatic personalities than for any party affiliation they might have. General Antonio Ramalho Eanes, the former president and considerably more than a figurehead, is the most prominent of the personalistic party leaders.

The Institutionalization of Free Elections. The suffrage has always been limited in Portugal; historically various qualifications were based on wealth and property, and under Salazar's system, in which the family was considered the basic corporate unit of society, only heads of households could vote. The 1975 elections, therefore, in which universal suffrage prevailed for the first time, could be thought of as the first free elections in fifty years or, as historian Douglas Wheeler argues, perhaps the first ever.[39]

But even then the process was not entirely open or the elections wholly free. The right-wing groups, those associated with the old regime and "fascism," were formally excluded from participation in the election, and many high-ranking officials, civilian and military, had either been forced into exile or been stripped of their political rights and forbidden to run in the elections. The other set of problems had to do with the Armed Forces Movement (MFA), which had led the 1974 revolution. Elections had been promised in the wake of the old regime's overthrow, but throughout 1974 and early 1975 evidence

341

mounted that the MFA officers enjoyed their position as leaders of the revolution and wanted to continue it.[40]

The MFA thus began to issue statements denigrating the scheduled elections and to make efforts to control the results. First it postponed the election—to April 25, 1975, the anniversary of the revolution and the last possible day it could live up to its promise to hold elections within a year. It elevated its own role to an extra-constitutional position above and beyond the party competition. It demanded that the soon-to-be-elected Constituent Assembly give the MFA veto power over its actions.[41] Some MFA officers flirted with the idea of forming a party of their own, and Premier Vasco Gonçalves, a brigadier general and leader of the extreme left faction within the MFA, vowed that the military would discount or ignore any electoral vote that "did not express the will of the people"—presumably as defined not by the people themselves at the polls but by the MFA.

The MFA continued to place barriers in the way of an open and democratic process. Even after the voting it tried to ignore the results, to pressure the parties, and to influence the work of the Constituent Assembly. It was plain that the military barracks was still where decisions were being made. The military and the central squares of Lisbon, where the largest demonstrations were held, remained as important in reaching political decisions as was the ballot box. But eventually the revolutionary street demonstrations subsided, and the armed forces more or less went back to their quarters. Nevertheless democracy was far less firmly established than one would have preferred.

In this as in other areas, therefore, Portugal remains a mixed system. Democracy has been established; elections are free and open; there is universal suffrage; there are no religious, regional, ethnic, or other barriers to participation; the parties may campaign freely; and the party spectrum is wide. But at the same time barriers remain: the right still faces restrictions, there are other legitimized routes to power besides elections, it is not clear that the parliament is the only or even the most important locus of political decision making, politics still takes place in the streets and other informal arenas as much as in the voting booth or the parliament, and there are other powerful "parties" besides the formal parties. In these ways the system still puts some, though limited, restrictions on competitiveness; seeks to manage some facets of intraelite competition; and imposes rules, though not necessarily the time-honored ones, for permitting new groups of elites to participate in the political process.[42]

Electoral Mobilization and Election Campaigns. In Portugal, because it is Western, European, and relatively highly developed, at least in

TABLE 10–1

PARTICIPATION IN GENERAL ELECTIONS UNDER SALAZAR AND
CAETANO, 1934–1973

Year of Election	Voters	Voters as Percentage of Total Population
1934	506,575	7.6
1938	743,930	10.6
1945	909,456	12.0
1949	1,140,000	14.6
1953	1,161,932	14.4
1957	1,213,381	14.5
1961	1,236,000	14.5
1965	1,278,387	14.8
1969	1,809,780	18.9
1973	2,096,020	20.0

SOURCE: Richard A. H. Robinson, *Contemporary Portugal: A History* (London: Allen and Unwin, 1979), p. 68.

comparison with most third world countries, the standard socioeconomic status model of the Western democracies is probably the dominant indicator and mechanism of electoral mobilization. That is, higher socioeconomic status generally leads to greater amounts of political information and awareness and consequently to greater political participation.[43]

This hypothesis is borne out by the data on electoral participation in Portugal. In the rural, sleepy Portugal of the nineteenth century the suffrage was limited, and participation rose gradually from about 2 percent at the beginning of the century to approximately 4 percent at the end. Electoral laws passed under the republic after 1910 led to a major increase in political participation, but voters had to be literate, male, and twenty-one or older. These restrictions, especially in a country with as high an illiteracy rate as Portugal (upward of 80 percent at that time), effectively kept the suffrage limited. Salazar sought to demobilize the population by limiting the vote to heads of households (a few women were thus able to vote) and by providing for no electoral choice. Table 10–1 shows a gradual increase in the number of voters during the Salazar-Caetano era, from 7.6 percent of the total national population in 1934 to a high of 20 percent in 1973. Table 10–2 shows the degree to which the official party monopolized (or nearly so) even the limited suffrage allowed during this period.

The revolution of 1974 served as a particular spur to Portugal's explosion of participation. A country that had been sleepy, morose,

TABLE 10–2
RESULTS OF NATIONAL ASSEMBLY ELECTION, 1969

Party	Percentage of Vote	Seats
União Nacional (government)	80.0	120
CDE (democratic opposition)	10.0	0
CEUD	1.9	0
CEM (monarchists)	0.1	0

SOURCE: Author.

and known for its bittersweet, long-suffering *fado* music became suddenly alive, dynamic, clamoring for change and a new style in political affairs. People poured into the streets in joy and celebration. Long-bottled-up emotions were released. Every wall and building in Lisbon was plastered with slogans and posters. The censorship was also ended, and dozens of new newspapers, radio programs, and party information sheets were launched. The level of mobilization and political consciousness increased dramatically. Women were given the vote for the first time. It is no accident that participation in the elections after 1974 was in the range of 85 to 90 percent of the eligible electorate (see table 10–3).[44] This was a nearly threefold increase in political participation since the last election under Caetano.

The general consciousness raising and mobilization were uneven, however. As would be expected, the capital, Lisbon, was the center and hotbed of political action. Lisbon is where the universities and activist young people are concentrated; it is where rallies and

TABLE 10–3
VOTING TURNOUT, 1975–1980

Date	Election	Registered Voters	Number Voting	Percentage Voting
1975	Constituent Assembly	6,231,372	5,711,829	91.7
1976	National Assembly	6,042,035	5,482,723	85.6
1976	President of the Council of Ministers	6,467,480	4,881,125	75.5
1979	National Assembly	6,894,636	6,007,453	87.1
1980	National Assembly	7,179,023	6,026,395	83.9
1980	President of the Council of Ministers	6,920,869	5,840,332	84.4

SOURCE: Author.

demonstrations take place; it is the seat of government and of all political party headquarters and the location of most of the country's newspapers and radio stations.

But if one takes Lisbon as the center of a series of concentric circles, the level of mobilization and aroused political consciousness generally decreases from the center to the rural and provincial areas. The exceptions to this rule, however, are especially noteworthy. The city of Setúbal and the surrounding area, heavily industrial, are also highly politicized and traditionally a Communist party stronghold. The university town of Coimbra is a hotbed of political activity. In the north, Porto, the country's second largest city, is generally calmer, more conservative, more traditional, less intense, and less politicized than the capital. It serves as a kind of conservative counterbalance to the frenetic life of the capital. In the south, in contrast, the rural "red belt" that stretches from Evora through the Alentejo, the political mobilization of the peasants and day laborers has been intensive, led again by the Communist party.[45]

The rest of the countryside, particularly in the north, is more traditional. The people of these areas are aware of the alternative political ideologies of the parties, but they tend also to be small landowners, Catholic, and conservative—and they vote accordingly. They resist and are often hostile to the parties of the left. The political mobilization teams sent out by the government and the parties of the left in the early, heady, most radical days of the revolution met with generally strong silence and sometimes violent or armed resistance. Efforts to convince these "peasants" that their conservative or moderate political preferences reflected "false consciousness" fell on unreceptive ears. The mobilization or *concientização* campaign ended in failure.[46]

But the standard socioeconomic model of the Western democracies and the party system are not the only political mobilization mechanisms that apply in Portugal. Neighborhood associations, local notables, community organizations, and clientelistic networks constitute alternative ways to mobilize the electorate. That is to be expected in view of the generally assumed relationship between such factors as clientelism and intermediate levels of socioeconomic modernization. In the attention that has been devoted to parties, ideologies, and programs, however, these other mechanisms have been almost entirely neglected in the literature.

Impressionistically one gathers that the clientelistic networks operating during the Salazar-Caetano era, not just local ones but the larger national ones as well, have been severely disrupted since 1974.

Many have been destroyed, as the older *patrões* were ousted or forced to flee. At the same time the country has been so disturbed politically since the revolution and the parties operating are so new that they have not yet had the chance to build up a newer and stable web of clientelistic networks—as the Christian Democratic party of Italy has, for example. For Portugal another ill effect of being a transitional nation is that its older patron-client networks have been disrupted and in many cases destroyed, and no stable newer ones have yet been created to replace them. The situation is one of disorder, chaos, transition, and institutional void. This vacuum lies at the heart of Portugal's problems of instability and institutional incompleteness.

Elections since 1974: Who Won, Party Shifts, the Changing Balance of Political Power. The most obvious answer to the question who won the elections in Portugal since 1974 is the moderates and the centrists. The extremes have, thus far, been kept isolated, and the broad middle of the political spectrum has emerged triumphant. Within this framework, however, there have been subtle shifts in the locus of power and several possibilities for new and potentially destabilizing coalitions. The election returns bear out these contentions.

Immediately after the revolt against the rightist Salazar-Caetano regime, left-wing militants seemed to dominate both the MFA and the streets. The elections from 1975 on, however, have served as a check on left-wing activities and an indicator of far left weakness. They have also demonstrated the lack of support for the far right. The real strength electorally has been in the center. Since the Socialist party tends to be quite conservative and to hate the Communists, it should be included with the more or less acceptable and centrist ranks. The extremist groups have not proved to be very popular, and they have been kept isolated.[47]

The Communists in Portugal in the 1970s rather consistently won about 15 percent of the vote; even when allied with some of the other fringe and independent leftist factions, their vote total has not risen more than two or three percentage points above that figure. More recently their voting strength has declined. The right was discredited by the Salazar experience and legally barred from presenting slates of candidates in elections; even had it been allowed to participate, it is doubtful if it would have garnered more than a few percentage points of the vote—at least in the first elections after 1974. Hence, if it is fair (as I think it is) to characterize the Socialists, the liberal PSD, and the Catholic moderate CDS as generally middle of the road and within the mainstream of Portuguese politics, then this broad center encompasses some 80 percent or more of the popular vote.

Although the case should not be overstated and one should certainly not underplay either the often bitter differences between these parties or the distinct class interests they represent, it may be that something of a centrist consensus—heretofore lacking in all the nation's history—has begun to develop in Portugal. Such a centrist consensus, it may be hypothesized, has to do with the increasing *embourgeoisement* of Portuguese society since World War II; its increased literacy, prosperity, and overall modernization; and the growth of a now sizable middle class since the 1920s, when extremes of wealth and poverty and the absence of a strong middle class tore the country apart, contributing both to the chaos of the First Republic and to the far rightist-Salazarista reaction to it.[48]

But the qualifications to this thesis may be as important as the thesis itself. These are related to the gradual shift in Portuguese voting behavior, since the 1974 revolution, away from the left and toward the right. After the revolution, we have seen, the left initially seemed dominant. Then, for the first two postrevolution elections in 1975 and 1976 the Socialists gained the upper hand. Later the PSD emerged as dominant, working at first in alliance with the Socialists and then scoring impressive triumphs on its own. As it gained independent strength and as conservative sentiment flourished, the PSD abandoned the Socialists and allied itself with the CDS. In the Democratic Alliance, which emerged victorious in 1979, the PSD and the CDS were the main parties in the coalition, but it now included the Monarchists and some Salazarista loyalists as well. That represented a major conservative shift since the revolutionary upheaval of 1974–1975. Even when the Socialists returned to power in 1983, they did so because the PSD was in chaos and the Socialists were deemed an "acceptable" alternative, not because the electorate had become less conservative. Later, the PSD came back to power with an impressive majority.

As these electoral shifts have taken place, at least three currents have developed that may well upset the thesis of an emerging middle-of-the-road consensus. One is the growing antipathy between the PSD and the Socialists, who are no longer allies but often bitter antagonists. Second, the Socialists, because of their isolation and apparently decreasing strength, might well be pushed into an alliance of the left with the Communists, who had previously been their sworn enemies. The third concern is the resurgence of the right, now stronger than before, whose call for an authoritarian solution finds increasing acceptance in the current Portuguese context of political and administrative chaos and spiraling economic downturn. These elements of dissent may well prove to be as important as the indicators of centrism and consensus discussed earlier.

Social Cleavages and Voter Alignments

Portugal takes pride in calling itself the oldest nation-state in Western Europe and one of the most integrated. It is not a country of major ethnic, linguistic, or racial cleavages. Portuguese is *the* language (although there are regional accents and dialects), the culture is south western European and fairly uniform throughout the country (again, with some regional variations), and the overwhelmingly dominant racial strain is Caucasian. There are unassimilated Gypsies who are often treated with condescension and hostility, and especially in Lisbon, there are small numnbers of Indians, blacks, mulattoes, Timorese, and others who are a legacy of Portugal's colonial past. But these are insignificant numerically; hence, ethnic and racial cleavages do not loom large in this analysis.

But other kinds of cleavages, which are related to Portugal's geography and socioeconomic and political development, do exist and are important for understanding electoral behavior. The most important of these are regional (the north-south split), class based (for voting and often for other purposes Portugal remains to a large degree a two-class society), religious (Catholic versus secular), and rural-urban. Data from the 1975 Constituent Assembly election and, with a consistency that is little short of amazing, from subsequent elections clearly demonstrate these cleavages and their political importance.[49]

The data show a clear correspondence between voting for the four major political factions (Communists, Socialists, Social Democrats, and Christian Democrats) and regional, class, religious, and rural-urban factors. The vote for these four parties is rather neatly distributed into regions of quite distinct social background and characteristics. Continental Portugal is divided into 274 *concelhos,* or districts, for which it is possible to gather both voting statistics and socioeconomic data.[50] The analysis is further based on the relations between the electoral data and the distribution of the economically active population into primary, secondary, and tertiary sectors and, further, the primary sector is broken down into the self-employed and those employed by others.

Regional Differences. For the purposes of this analysis, continental Portugal may be divided into four regions: north and south, rural and urban. Urban *concelhos* are defined here, following the criteria of the Portuguese National Statistics Institute, as those containing a district capital or a city of 10,000 persons or more; rural provinces have no district capital nor a city of 10,000 or more. The south includes the Algarve, the Alentejo, and the urban *concelhos* of Lisbon and its environs. The north includes virtually all the territory north of the Tejo (or Tagus) River, encompassing the Ribatejo, Beira, Douro, Minho, and Tras-os-Montes provinces, and the rural *concelhos* of Estremadura (see figure 10-1). The importance of the rural-urban distinction may be self-evident; the north-south split calls for some explanation.

Portugal's two major political regions, north and south, are quite distinctive socially, culturally, economically, and politically. Their particular characteristics are determined in large part by their distinct histories and socioeconomic structures and reflected in their ideological preferences and voting choices. The north is more traditional, conservative (culturally as well as politically), and Catholic. Its language and accents are often closer to Spanish—or more accurately, Galician—than to the Portuguese spoken in the south. In the premodern era, some of these northern and northeastern areas were part of Spain, or of León—perhaps, with the religious center at Santiago de Campostela and the famous medieval pilgrimages there, the most Catholic region in Iberia. It is out of the north also that the reconquest of the peninsula from the Moors began and from which the Portuguese nation, the oldest centralized state in Western Europe, began. Hence many Portuguese still think of (and idealize) the virtues of the northerners—determination, self-reliance, capacity for hard work, independence, Catholicism, individualism—as *the* national virtues.[51]

The landholding pattern of the north reflects and reinforces—perhaps even helped create—these prevailing characteristcs. The predominant pattern is of small holdings manned by strong, independent yeoman farmers who by struggle, persistence, hard work, and determination manage to eke out a "poor but noble" existence on the area's rocky hillsides. The chief products are vegetables and grapes, both of which may be efficiently and profitably grown on small parcels of land. Both are labor-intensive rather than capital-intensive, so that whole families are put to work on the land and the traditional family structure and traditional Catholicism have remained strong. The church is a major voice institutionally and in its hold on the population. Even the main urban industrial center of the north, Porto, reflects this prevailing regional pattern: business firms tend to be small, family dominated, and traditional. The northern urban workers' allegiance to the land and their traditional orientation are such

FIGURE 10–1
The Regions and Provinces of Portugal

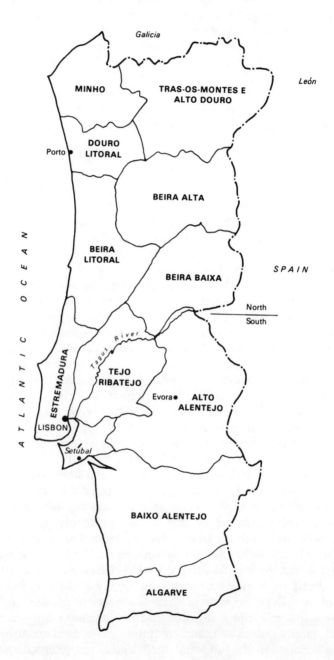

that many also maintain small plots of land, thus helping to preserve the prevailing land patterns and also maintaining the self-reliance, close-knit families, and individualism that elsewhere seem to be among the casualties of modern, urban mass society.

The south, in contrast, is a land of large estates and of larger, more impersonal industry. In the rural areas of the Alentejo, a sharp two-class society persists, consisting of landowners and their estate managers and a large landless class of peasants and day laborers. The southern proletariat, rural and urban, is both more conscious of its inferior class position and more amenable to the appeals of class revolution.[52] The working class is more concentrated than in the north, particularly in the Lisbon-Setúbal area; and, unlike their northern counterparts, southern workers seldom own small plots of land. The southerners—again, rural and urban—also seem to be less traditional, less Catholic, and clearly less conservative politically. Northerners tend to look down on them not just for these reasons but also because the southerners are presumed to have been "tainted," both religiously and racially, by their longer and more intimate contact with the Moors. Finally, it is worth noting the different attitudes maintained in these two areas during the nearly half-century, 1926–1974, of rule of corporatist authoritarianism: the north tended generally to support the regime in power or was neutral toward it (until opposition mounted near the end); the south was a focal point of opposition, often radical and rebellious opposition.

Voting Alignments in the 1975 Elections. Tables 10–4 and 10–5 show the patterns of voting for the five largest parties (PS, PPD/PSD, PCP, CDS, MDP) in the critical 1975 elections, as well as what John Hammond calls the "party of abstainers"—those who cast blank or void ballots. It is important to remember that in 1975, still at the height of the radical phase of the revolution, the PS should be thought of as the center party, with the PCP and the MDP to its left and the PPD/PSD and the CDS to its right. The regional distribution of the voting is most obvious. The CDS and the PPD/PSD, the two parties on the right, did considerably better in the north. The PCP and the MDP, the two parties on the left, did significantly better (almost twice as well) in the south. Within the regions the differences are also striking: the two parties of the right did better in the rural north than in the urban north; in the south the right did better in the urban than in the rural areas. The parties of the left did better in the rural south than in the urban south; up north, as would be expected, the left did better in urban than in rural areas. The number of abstentions was higher in

351

TABLE 10–4

RESULTS OF THE CONSTITUENT ASSEMBLY ELECTION, APRIL 25, 1975

Party	Percentage of Vote	Seats
Socialist party (PS)	37.9	115
Social Democrats (PPD, later PSD)	26.4	80
Portuguese Communist party (PCP)	12.5	30
Christian-Democratic party (CDS)	7.6	16
Portuguese Democratic Movement (MDP) (independent Marxists)	4.1	5
People's Democratic Union (UDP) (left of PCP)	0.8	1
Abstentions, blanks, and void ballots	10.0	

SOURCE: *Diario do Governo*, May 19, 1975.

the north than in the south, and within both regions there were more abstentions in rural than in urban areas.[53]

The PS was the largest vote getter in this election and in the 1976 parliamentary elections. It did somewhat better in the south than in the north; in both areas it did better in urban than in rural areas (and was alone among the parties in this regard). The PS was also thought of differently in north and south: in the more conservative north it was looked upon as the only acceptable leftist alternative; in the more

TABLE 10–5

RESULTS OF CONSTITUENT ASSEMBLY ELECTION, BY REGION AND SIZE OF PLACE, 1975
(percent)

Region	CDS	PPD/PSD	PS	PCP	MDP	Abstentions	Number of concelhos
Rural north	11.0	28.2	30.1	4.2	3.3	17.3	156
Urban north	9.7	27.5	41.6	7.2	3.8	12.7	25
Rural south	2.4	8.6	41.5	28.1	6.8	14.6	72
Urban south	4.3	12.6	45.1	22.3	4.7	12.9	21
Continent	7.7	24.7	38.6	13.1	4.2	14.6	274

NOTE: CDS = Christian-Democratic party; PPD/PSD = Popular Democratic party/Social Democratic party; PS = Socialist party; PCP = Portuguese Communist party; MDP = Portuguese Democratic Movement. Party votes are percentage of valid vote. Percentages do not add to 100 because of rounding.
SOURCE: John Hammond, "Das ruas as urnas," cited in full in n. 29 at end of chapter.

radical south it was thought of as the only acceptable rightist alternative.

This regional difference is crucial in understanding the breakdown of the party vote by sector and socioeconomic characteristics. Indeed, Hammond, who is an authority on Portuguese voting behavior, argues that the regional difference overshadows class distinctions as an explanatory paradigm. My own reading of the data leads me to see these in mutually complementary and reinforcing relationships, and I am less confident of elevating the regional one to a preeminent position—although I am willing to grant it major importance.[54]

The party vote in 1975 may also be broken down sectorally.[55] Table 10–6 shows the voting returns by economic or labor force sectors. The analysis shows that tertiary-sector workers (chiefly government bureaucrats) tended to vote Socialist and, to a considerably smaller extent, Communist. Primary-sector workers (agricultural and manufacturing sectors) must be further sudivided into two groups: those who were self-employed (encompassing both owners and renters) tended to vote for the parties of the right; those who were employed by others voted primarily for the parties of the left. Workers in the secondary or service sector were also divided, and the division reflected much the same regional split as noted earlier in the analysis of the PS vote. Secondary workers in the north, like rural proprietors, tended to vote for the parties of the right; in the south they tended to vote left, more like that region's rural workers. In both areas, however, secondary-sector workers moved increasingly toward a center vote.

The correlations in the voting between region, class, and cultural-religious variables were great. In general, the parties of the right garnered much of their support from rural, traditional areas in the north, regions of lower prosperity and of stronger Catholicism. The parties of the left gained much of their support from urban and rural areas of the south that had high concentrations of employed workers and had become more secularized. These patterns require closer analysis.

The parties of the right and those of the left contrasted sharply, Hammond correctly notes, on virtually every dimension. Here we shall consider the votes for the PPD/PSD and the CDS together, for even though the two had considerable differences, which later became accentuated, and the PPD/PSD outpolled the CDS by a large margin, the vote distribution for the two was remarkably parallel. The vote for the parties of the right is contrasted with that for the left, the PCP and the MDP (which later merged into the PCP), and both of these are then compared with the vote for the PS.

TABLE 10–6
Labor Force Distribution and the Vote, 1975
(percent)

	CDS	PPD/PSD	PS	PCP	MDP	Abstentions
Rural North						
Primary, self-employed	20	63	2	−3	3	24
Primary, by others	13	45	22	2	0	21
Secondary	18	45	25	3	2	9
Tertiary	−16	−20	92	21	10	17
Multiple R	.314	.522	.666	.411	.243	.552
Urban north						
Primary, self-employed	25	51	9	−3	12	13
Primary, by others	−5	9	40	16	−1	37
Secondary	12	24	48	5	3	7
Tertiary	5	30	44	11	4	15
Multiple R	.335	.330	.545	.401	.385	.814
Rural south						
Primary, self-employed	4	20	45	−18	14	38
Primary, by others	2	2	32	55	4	7
Secondary	3	16	46	15	10	13
Tertiary	2	8	60	9	7	15
Multiple R	.179	.503	.329	.558	.210	.692
Urban south						
Primary	6	14	59	1	4	16
Secondary	−4	−3	30	59	6	11
Tertiary	9	20	51	7	5	13
Multiple R	.756	.524	.448	.554	.187	.300

Note: CDS = Christian Democratic party; PPD/PSD = Popular Democratic party/Social Democratic party; PS = Socialist party; PCP = Portuguese Communist party; MDP = Portuguese Democratic Movement.

The figures in this table represent estimates of the percentage of voters in each labor-force category who voted for each party. The estimates are derived from a regression analysis of each dependent variable by three variables representing the percentage of each *concelho*'s labor force in three of the labor force categories. That the method provides an estimate rather than a precise figure is demonstrated by occasional anomalous values less than zero. For further discussion of the methodology and its limits, see Hammond. For most of the categories, however, the figures may be considered reasonably accurate. Because of their small numbers in the urban south, it was not possible to obtain reliable figures differentiating self-employed primary workers.

Source: Hammond, "Das ruas as urnas," cited in full in n. 29 at end of chapter.

The two parties of the right were especially strong among self-employed or proprietary farmers both in the south and in the north. Most of these voted PPD/PSD, although they also constituted the backbone of the CDS. In the south agricultural workers voted strongly for the PCP; but in the north they gave a large vote to the PPD/PSD and to the PS. Secondary workers voted strongly PPD/PSD in the north, but in the south they voted for neither of the two conservative parties. Instead, they supported the Socialists and, especially in the south's urban areas, the Communist party.

Looked at another way, the rightist vote was strongest in the poorest, most traditional, most remote, most Catholic, most backward areas of the country—although the differentiation along these lines was stronger in the north than in the south. Survey data indicate that these poorer elements preferred to conserve what they had, however marginal that might be, rather than risk all by a more violent change.[56] These were also the areas that had experienced the greatest outward migration of workers to Europe.[57] Poverty and the absence of a brighter future for them or their children were among the principal reasons for the massive Portuguese emigration of the 1960s and 1970s; the areas that produced the most emigrants, Hammond notes, also produced the largest concentrations of conservative voters.[58]

Urbanization was also differentially related to the vote in the two regions of the country. In the south the vote for the two more conservative parties was somewhat more urban than rural; in the north it was overwhelmingly the reverse. This accounts for the fact that in the nation as a whole, the conservative parties were backed more strongly in the rural areas—although the pattern was not uniform and in the south failed to apply. The reverse was true for the PCP and its ally, the MDP: they were strongest in the urban areas of the north and in the rural areas of the south.

Catholicism and the Catholic church were also major influences in the voting. The church played an active role in the campaign and had taken the lead in opposing what it feared might be an imminent Communist takeover. The church concentrated its efforts in the north, where its strength was, and the campaign clearly succeeded. Catholic voters overwhelmingly supported the two parties of the right and correspondingly repudiated the PCP. Hammond notes again that in the north the relation between religion and party preference was greater in the rural areas, whereas in the south (where in any case the relation was weaker) it was stronger in urban areas.

The two smaller parties in these major blocs merit some separate attention in these regards. The vote for the CDS, though generally parallel to that for the PPD/PSD, varied enormously from district to

355

district, even among those whose regional or socioeconomic conditions were similar. Gaspar and Vitorino hypothesize that the variations in these districts may be a result of the exercise of the historic Portuguese *caciquismo* (a native chief), particularly the influence of a local notable or priest.[59] The MDP vote, unlike that for the Communist party, also varied more from district to district and again in ways that seem unrelated to socioeconomic variables. Gaspar and Vitorino surmise that for the MDP the considerable variation is less likely to be due to the traditional *caciquismo* than to particular and localized conditions prevailing under the old dictatorship.

Although the vote for the major parties and blocs of the left and the right shows some remarkable consistencies across and within regions, the same cannot be said for the Socialist party (PS), which was, after all, the largest vote getter. In part the lack of homogeneity and consistency in the vote for the PS was due to its representing in this election a center position, so that it could be expected to attract a wide variety of support along a considerable range of the spectrum; but in part the PS vote also reflected the class, regional, and urban-rural differences that have rather consistently emerged from the data. The PS tended to be a conservative choice in the south and a leftist choice in the north. Nationwide, the only constant in the PS vote appears to be its support from persons in the tertiary sector. Among other sectors, support for the PS varied remarkably from north to south. It was supported by rural proprietors in the south and by rural employed workers in the north. It garnered relatively large numbers of votes by secondary-sector workers in the north, but among these same workers in the south it was considerably outpolled by the PCP. In both regions these secondary-sector workers voted like primary-sector workers, that is, for parties of the right in the north and for parties of the left in the south. But if such voters were disinclined to vote for either left or right and inclined to move toward the center, in both areas that meant a vote for the PS.

The PS also won in the more prosperous districts of the north and the less prosperous ones of the south. It was rejected in the more Catholic areas of the north (whose votes went to the PPD/PSD or CDS), though to a lesser extent than was true for the PCP, but in the urban south the vote for the PS in Catholic districts was higher than for the PPD/PSD or the CDS, even though the latter was the Catholic party. The conclusion seems obvious: the PS victory was fashioned not by appealing to any narrow class, regional, or urban-rural constituency but by trying to be all things to all persons in all parts of the country, different things to different persons in different parts of the country, a modern, pragmatic, multiclass, middle-of-the-road, catchall party that commanded the broad center of the political spectrum and took a great many votes from the leftist and rightist blocs on both sides of it.[60]

Finally, mention should be made of the abstentions and blank ballots (together, about 15 percent of registered voters), which rather closely reflected the patterns already noted. That is, there were strong correlations between abstentions and blank ballots and the PPD/PSD vote; the correlation with the PCP vote was also high but negative, and that with the PS vote negative but not so high. Abstentions and blank ballots were high among rural proprietors, low among secondary-sector workers, and even lower among agricultural workers in the south. Abstentions and blank votes were greatest in the poorest regions, the remotest regions, and the most Catholic regions. The pattern of abstentions and blank ballots lends further support to Hammond's finding that the PS vote was a vote for the left in the north and for the right in the south, since the PS vote was related to abstentions negatively in the north and positively in the south.[61]

This analysis of the cleavages within the Portuguese electorate and the distribution of the vote suggests that the parties (the PS being the major exception) presented some quite consistent national images to voters in their programs and ideologies and that the voters reacted fairly consistently to these according to their regional, religious, class, and rural-urban statuses. The PCP won strongly in those areas where it had long been active and among voters who might be thought of as potentially its primary supporters: rural wage earners in the large-estate-dominated areas of the south and industrial wage earners in the more secular, urban areas of the south and center (Lisbon-Setúbal). Indeed, the support for the PCP was so consistently strong in this and subsequent elections that the area commencing with Lisbon and Setúbal and stretching east through the Alentejo to Evora became known as the red belt.

The PPD/PSD and the CDS were more attractive to the rural self-employed in the primary sector, to Catholics, and to more traditional elements. They also did well among the urban bourgeoisie in the south. It is therefore clear that the class bases of these parties, their regional bases, and the cultural-religious as well as socioeconomic characteristics of the distinct regions overlap and are strongly correlated. The support of all the major parties was concentrated in the region where the regional characteristics themselves, the dominant cultural patterns, and the dominant mode of agricultural or other forms of production were closely correlated with the class bases and appeals of the respective parties. Furthermore, the parties won a disproportionate share of support from other classes in the regions where they enjoyed maximum strength.

The PS won votes among several classes but was particularly and consistently strong among tertiary-sector workers. The PS attracted a large proportion of votes from those outside the regionally dominant mode of production: the rural self-employed in the south and industrial workers in the north. Hammond's important conclusion is that a PS vote appears to have been a vote against the party of each region's numerically strongest class, in favor of the alternative nearest on the spectrum in the direction in which that constituency's interests would lead it—that is, to the left for nonproprietors in the north and to the right for voters other than industrial or agricultural workers in the south. This will help explain the subsequent decline of the PS as the dominant party and the confusion and lack of clarity in voters' minds concerning what it stood for. As Hammond acidly concludes, "The PS's campaign and the electorate's response appear to have led it to victory by turning it into a residual category."[62]

The Portuguese electorate in 1975 thus voted in clear and well-defined terms, according to fairly neat class, regional, religious, and rural-urban differences. The voters chose parties or blocs largely in accord with their own preconceived self-interest or appropriate to their own status and distinct from other parties or blocs, whether defined by economic, cultural, regional, or rural-urban criteria or some combination of these. Given the absence of free and competitive elections in the preceding fifty years—or ever—the results of this election and the consistency with which these positions were maintained in subsequent elections were quite remarkable. The outcome, as Hammond says, was therefore orderly in both process and outcome.[63] The process was orderly in that an extremely high turnout was coupled with an active, relatively peaceful campaign, a wide range of choice among competing parties, and the general observance of democratic procedures. The outcome was also orderly in demonstrating a system of well-defined parties appealing with success to distinct class and sectoral elements within the electorate on the basis of their perceived interests. All parties, including the MFA, eventually accepted the results of the election as legitimate and definitive.

Patterns in Subsequent Elections. Subsequent elections in Portugal through the 1970s did not alter these fundamental patterns in major ways and therefore may be summarized briefly. The results shifted somewhat, generally toward the right, but the core patterns continued largely as before. Thus in the 1976 elections for the National

TABLE 10–7

RESULTS OF THE NATIONAL ASSEMBLY ELECTIONS, APRIL 25, 1976

Party	Percentage of Vote	Seats
Socialist party (PS)	35.0	107
Social Democrats (PPD/PSD)	24.0	71
Christian Democratic party (CDS)	15.9	41
Portuguese Communist party (PCP)	15.9	40
People's Democratic Union (UDP)	1.7	1
Abstentions	16.0	—

SOURCE: *Diario da república,* May 25, 1976.

Assembly (see table 10–7), the PS and PPD/PSD vote was almost identical with what it had been in 1975. The Communist party vote increased by 3.4 percentage points, almost entirely because of the absence of the MDP, whose supporters cast their ballots for the PCP. The big gainer was the CDS, whose support increased more than 100 percent, on the one hand because of the vote of the "returnees," Portuguese colonists (about half a million) from Angola and Mozambique, who tended to vote for conservative positions, and on the other because of a gradual resurgence of conservative strength now that the euphoria of the revolution was wearing off. Since party support in Portugal is linked clearly to the class, cultural, religious, and regional ecologies of north and south, it seems unlikely that the vote received by the several parties would change fundamentally unless there were basic alterations in the distinct ecologies.[64]

In the 1976 presidential election (see table 10–8), General Antonio Ramalho Eanes, backed by the center parties (PS, PPD/PSD, CDS), gained 62 percent of the vote, and another centrist, Prime Minister José Pinheiro de Azevedo, who had suffered a heart attack just before the election, won another 14 percent—the combined total being approximately what we have defined as the center vote in Portugal. The candidates of the left, however, won one vote in every four.

In the local elections of December 12, 1976 (see table 10–9), all the parties virtually repeated their vote totals from the 1975 Constituent Assembly and 1976 National Assembly elections, the PS continuing to decline slightly while the PPD/PSD and CDS held their own or gained modestly. This election for local officials was looked on as an endorsement of the Socialist government formed earlier in the year. The analysis of the voting behavior offered earlier is reinforced by these results: the Socialists won in the main cities of Lisbon, Oporto, Santarem, Setúbal, Portalegre, and Faro; the PSD won the town halls in

TABLE 10–8
Results of Presidential Election, June 27, 1976

Candidate	Percentage of Vote
Antonio Ramalho Eanes (backed by Socialists, Social Democrats, and Christian Democrats)	62.0
Otelo Saraiva de Carvalho (populist left, backed by People's Democratic Union)	16.0
José Pinheiro de Azevedo (ailing, independent, acting prime minister)	14.0
Octavio Pato (backed by Communist party)	8.0

Source: *Diario da república,* July 6, 1976.

the rural districts of Aveiro, Leiria, and Vila Real as well as in the Azores and Madeira Islands; the CDS won in the northern towns of Bragança and Guarda; the Communists elected a majority of the mayors in the southern red belt districts of Beja, Evora, and Setúbal (although they failed to capture the city of Setúbal); and the Monarchists won the mayorship of Ribeira da Pena in the northern district of Vila Real.

A minority Socialist government had meantime been formed in 1976, which with different colorations governed until 1979. The Socialists had come to power with a mandate to carry out democratic reforms aimed at achieving social justice, but in government the PS was forced to carry out a necessary but unpopular belt tightening that gradually undermined its support and sacrificed its claims to Socialist legitimacy. Public opinion, meanwhile, in the face of a continued economic downturn and perpetual political discord, continued to

TABLE 10–9
Results of Local Elections, December 12, 1976

Party	Percentage of Vote
Socialist party (PS)	33.0
Social Democratic party (PSD)	24.5
Portuguese Communist party (PCP)	17.6
Christian Democratic party (CDS)	16.6
People's Democratic Union (UDP)	2.4

Source: Author.

shift gradually toward the right as the more conservative characteristics of Portuguese political culture began to reassert themselves.[65] At first the Socialists had relied on an uncomfortable alliance with the PCP, some independent Marxists, and the left wing of the PPD/PSD to carry out their program; by 1977 the Communists were in eclipse, and the PPD/PSD formed a more centrist voting alliance with the PS; in 1978 the PSD, seeing the PS government as a sinking ship and fortified by polls showing its own growing popularity, abandoned the Socialists, who then formed a coalition with the more conservative CDS. Only three years earlier Socialist Prime Minister Soares had been touting his party as the "furthest left of any of the European socialist parties" and the CDS as "reactionary and a refuge for capitalists and former fascists." But since then both parties had moved closer to the center, and in any case the alliance was purely a pragmatic one, which observers predicted could break up at any time—and it did.[66]

The CDS gained legitimacy and respectability from its participation in government with the Socialists; but when its own polls confirmed the rightward trend of public opinion and the fading popularity of the PS, the CDS also abandoned the government, forcing new elections. Sensing the possibility of achieving a working majority, the PSD and the CDS, along with the small Popular Monarchist party, formed a coalition, the Democratic Alliance. In the National Assembly elections of December 2, 1979, which were confirmed in the National Assembly elections of October 5, 1980, the Democratic Alliance won an absolute majority of seats with 45 percent (128 seats) and 47 percent (134 seats) of the vote, respectively. The Socialists, reflecting trends at work at least since 1976, fell back to 26 percent (74 seats) and 28 percent (74 seats), respectively. The Communists remained consistent at about 17 percent of the vote, 47 and 41 seats, respectively.[67]

There had clearly been a conservative swing in Portugal since the revolutionary upheaval of the mid-1970s. Whether this constituted a long-term and more or less permanent tendency or merely a short-term one was impossible to say on the basis of only two elections. In the 1979 and 1980 National Assembly elections, however, nationwide voting patterns indicated that support for the Democratic Alliance cut across the earlier cleavage lines of class and region. The alliance maintained and strengthened its position in the north, largely at Socialist expense, but it also made gains in the previously Communist-dominated red belt in the Alentejo and in the working-class neighborhoods of Lisbon and other industrial towns. It was too early to know whether this reflected a fundamental shift in Portugal's basic regional and "ecological" bases of politics or only a passing phase. Certainly the presidential election of December 7, 1980, offered scant support for the "fundamental shift" thesis. General Eanes, backed by the PS and the PCP, won handily with 55 percent of the vote. But he was a popular figure in his own right regardless of the party support; he benefited from a national sense of the need for stability and continuity when Prime Minister Francisco Sá Carneiro, the PSD president, was killed in a plane crash while campaigning for his candidate; and the Democratic Alliance's candidate, though lackluster, nevertheless managed to win 42 percent of the vote. In 1983 the Socialists returned to power. So far, therefore, any firm conclusion on the sometimes alleged sea change in Portuguese voting behavior would be premature.[68]

Later votes did in fact confirm the conservative trend. The Democratic Alliance (center-right) had been the first coalition in postrevolutonary Portugal to gain an absolute majority in the parliament. In subsequent elections the Communists suffered a 50 percent drop by going from roughly 15–18 percent in the early elections after the Revolution to 8–9 percent in 1987. The PS continued as a major party, but by the 1980s it had lost its hegemonic position. It returned to power in 1983 but only because the Democratic Alliance split, broke up, and lost its leadership. Socialist leader Mario Soares won the presidency in 1986, but he was almost defeated by conservative (CDS) candidate Freitas do Amaral.

The big winner in these transitions was the moderate-conservative PSD. The PSD had been the major and dominant partner in the Democratic Alliance. It had provided the prime ministers (Sá Carneiro and Pinto Balsemão) when the alliance governed. When the alliance split, it enabled the Socialists to return to power, although the PSD remained part of the governing coalition. The PSD continued to gain in strength until it became the largest single party in the parliament, and in 1985 new PSD leader Cavaco Silva (another "apolitical" technocrat, severe and stern) became the prime minister, even though the party still lacked a parliamentary majority. But in July 1987 that was changed when the PSD won its absolute majority and became, replacing the PS, the country's main or hegemonic party.

These trends may be summarized as follows: the PCP has been the big electoral loser since 1975, while the PS has suffered moderate losses. The big winners have been the PSD and, to a somewhat lesser extent, the CDS. Hence it appears that after the leftward thrust of the mid-1970s, Portugal has returned to its historic conservative and moderately conservative roots. Cavaco Silva was frequently pictured as a "democratic Salazar."

One further aspect of this voting shift merits mention. In 1975 and 1976 many officials of the former regime voted for the PS because, as pragmatists, they saw it as the dominant party, a strong alternative to the Communists, and a way of keeping their government jobs. But by 1979–1980, for the same pragmatic reasons, they had abandoned the PS and voted for the Democratic Alliance. Given the heavily bureaucratic and statist nature of the Portuguese system, that shift represented a sizable percentage of the electorate. It also indicated that Portuguese voting behavior reflects factors other than the ideological, class, religious, or regional ones already described. Finally, this resurgence by the more conservative parties served as a means by which some former officials of the old regime, such as Adriano Moreira, could gain reentry into the government.

Voting Cleavages and Development. With regard to Seymour Martin Lipset and Stein Rokkan's more general comments on the nature of voting cleavages and development and the place of Portugal within this scheme, the following comments may be offered.[69] Portugal, in contrast to many less-developed countries, appears to have passed out of stage one of the Lipset-Rokkan model. That is, it is not torn by separatist tribal or factional movements that would separate from the central state; there are no serious territorial or functional efforts (for instance, on the part of the church) to rebel against national government authority; there are no cleavages over the nature of the national political culture, no particularistic or kin-centered separatist movements, and no efforts at undermining the national community. There was a time in the mid-1970s, at the height of the most radical phase of the revolution, when the sentiment for independence gained ground in the conservative Azores; and there was even some talk, when in 1975 the Communists seemed close to seizing power in Lisbon, of forming a separate, more conservative Portuguese nation in the north. The Azorian independence movement had a considerable history behind it, however; and the northern Portugal one faded as soon as the election returns came in and the moderates turned out to be overwhelmingly victorious. Cleavages such as these seem to be characteristic of an earlier phase of national consolidation; and although Portugal still has some residual features of these, they do not at this point appear to offer a serious challenge to the central state or the integrity of the nation.

Portugal is not in Lipset and Rokkan's stage three either, however, where the cleavages have to do chiefly with issues of postindustrial distribution and quality of life. There is new and rising concern for such issues in Portugal, but they are still of secondary importance and do not yet constitute a major basis for electoral cleavage, as they do in the more advanced industrial nations of Western Europe and in the United States.

Portugal, rather, seems to be in a stage two, or an intermediate, phase. It has some of the cleavages of stage one and some of stage three. But its chief cleavages result from the sudden and dramatic explosion of participation in a country inexperienced in democratic procedures and governance; from the recent establishment (or re-establishment) of democracy but where democracy is not yet consolidated or institutionalized; from still strong conflicts over religion, class and regional issues, the nature of pluralism and tolerance, and the precise configuration of the national political system. Ideological passions have not yet declined in Portugal; the party spectrum is still wide and exceedingly diverse; there are few signs of the full consolidation of stable middle-of-the-road politics. There are still forces that would replace Portugal's democratic institutions with some others, still forces (à la Poujadism in France) that would rebel against the main currents of the twentieth century. Worker-employer conflicts remain highly volatile, there is still much conflict between the primary and secondary economies, and the question whether "progress toward socialism" should remain the constitutional leitmotif is a hotly contested one. The military has the potential to intervene; politics may once again center in the streets more than in the parliament; rebellion and revolution remain possibilities. In all these ways Portugal seems still to occupy an intermediary position, in keeping with its level of socioeconomic development and the yet inchoate nature and functioning of its parties and party system.

Conclusion: Elections, Voting, and Democracy in Portugal

Since 1974 democracy has been reestablished in Portugal—or, depending on the criteria used, democracy may be said to have been established really for the first time. But the issues of how established, consolidated, and institutionalized democracy is in Portugal remain open to considerable discussion and debate. Let me try to pose some of the more important questions pertaining to this issue, even if we are not yet in a position to answer them with certainty.

Portugal now has all the paraphernalia of a modern democratic system: freely expressed public opinion, political parties, a party spectrum, parliamentary rule, coalition government, and the like. But the question remains whether the party-parliament arena is the only or even the most important arena of national politics, *the* locus of politics and power. It seems clear from this analysis that other actors (the army or the church, for example) may be as important as the parties as political influences, and other arenas (the civil-military one, for instance) as important as the party arena in determining the direction of Portuguese politics.[70]

A second question has to do with where we classify Portugal: with the developing world or the developed one, with Europe or apart from it. The question is critical because it has to do with Portugal's fundamental identity (this is far less true by now for Spain) and its future direction as a nation. In this analysis Portugal has been pictured as intermediary in a number of socioeconomic indicators of development, but some time ago it had crossed the threshold into the ranks of the developed nations—albeit at the lower end. Similarly, with regard to Europe: Portugal was long ambivalent about whether it was properly European or, alternatively, Atlanticist and third world; but now, for good or ill, it seems to have cast its lot with Europe. Its economy is so intertwined with and dependent on Europe that the historical choice open to Portugal may by now have been definitively decided. Politically as well, the Europeans and the United States have sought since 1975 to envelop Portugal within the Western family of democratic nations, and clever politicians such as Soares and Sá Carneiro adroitly used these connections to strengthen democracy in Portugal as well as their own party and personal positions. Although the issue for now seems decided—Europe and the first world—the existing undercurrents are sufficient that the book should not be closed on this issue, nor should the questions it poses be entirely forgotten.[71]

A third set of questions relates to the sources of conflict and cleavage in Portugal, how deep the divisions remain, and how they have changed. Portugal is clearly deeply divided on a wide range of ideological, class, regional, religious, and public policy issues. These issues do not pertain to the nation-creating and nation-building cleavages of stage one of the developmentalist scheme of Lipset and Rokkan or to the stage three cleavages characteristic of advanced industrial nations. Rather, they correspond more to the kinds of cleavages identified with political systems at an intermediate or transitional stage, and they seem to correlate rather well with Portugal's intermediate and "mixed" levels of socioeconomic development. Although the country has long been divided between the "two Portugals," for example, rural, conservative, Catholic, feudal, traditionalist versus urban, liberal, secular, bourgeois, modern—a third Portugal may now have been added, one that is radical, Marxist, and revolutionary and therefore adds a new and fundamental source of cleavage to the older division. Achieving a reconciliation or even some

365

working arrangements between these three Portugals is exceedingly difficult because all three emerged from and may be identified with different historical epochs that are so far apart on such a wide range of issues that the gaps are virtually unbridgeable.[72]

Again there is the question of the institutionalization of democracy, elections, and parliamentary rule in Portugal. Clearly, elections have been established as one route to power in Portugal, and at present they are widely viewed as the only legitimate one. Similarly parties and parliament have in the post-1974 era gained legitimacy. But the situation is fluid, subject to change; and other routes to power, it must be remembered, such as a skillfully executed coup d'état, protest marches and street violence, or a heroic revolutionary act, also have a long history within the Portuguese tradition and may acquire renewed legitimacy. We also know that other "parties" within the system are capable of acting independently of the formal parties and parliament. Although these alternative routes to and agencies of political power seem for now to have been eclipsed in favor of the triumvirate of parties, elections, and parliament, that may not be a permanent condition. Portugal could still experience a violent clash among contending groups, a military coup, a left-wing or right-wing takeover, or some combination or sequence of these—any one or all of which constitute a major threat to the party system and the democratic electoral process.

Portuguese politics ebb and flow, with different forms of institutions enjoying different degrees of legitimacy at different times. What may well be a temporary and ephemeral set of political arrangements at present should not be afforded a permanence they may not deserve.[73] It is important in this connection to remember those "no good winds" that blow from Spain, especially the earlier coup attempts there or rumors of coup attempts, which find their reflection in discontent among some Portuguese officers over efforts to return them to the barracks after their "heroic" leadership roles in the revolution, and in the constitutional debate over the special position of the armed forces. Troublesome too for Portuguese democracy are the diminishing Western European and U.S. interest in its outcome, the rebuffs the Portuguese have sometimes received from the EEC, and hence the renewal of the age-old debate about whether Portugal really wants to be in and like Europe or will follow its own alternative route.

Finally, there is the question of the indigenous roots of Portuguese democracy—of crisis, the possibilities for survival, and the future directions of the Portuguese political system. Democracy in Portugal has only recently been revived, after some fifty years of authoritarianism, corporatism, and dictatorship. Certainly the joy and happiness with which democracy was revived (at least before the gloom, drift, and disillusion that have since set it) attest to its continued popularity and capacity to survive. The particular form that the renewal of democracy took in Portugal, however, was modeled almost exclusively on the parliamentary systems of the EEC nations. Hence the nagging question remains whether democracy in Portugal is really based on homegrown institutions and traditions or is a form imposed or copied from the outside and therefore lacking strong roots. Is Portuguese democracy, like so many things Portuguese historically, chiefly *para Inglés ver*—for the English (or Americans or the EEC) to see?

One might even ask whether posing the question in terms of a constant, either-or, dichotomous struggle between democracy and dictatorship is the best means of framing the issues, whether that might not be a false or too restrictive choice for Portugal, one that fails to encompass all or the most viable and realistic alternatives. Are there other possibilities, indigenous and truly Portuguese, that might combine and better reconcile Portugal's authoritarian and democratic traditions, that might serve as an alternative to the highly fragmented and polarized system that still exists, that might enable Portugal to begin closing and healing the deep divisions that continue to tear the nation apart? One suspects that there are such indigenous institutions or that they could be developed, perhaps combining Portugal's corporatist with its liberal traditions, its organicist with its individualistic orientations, its desire for strong leadership with its commitment to democratic values; but whether they would prove functional and stable is still unknown.[74] That is, however, the one system and solution that Portugal has not yet tried, although in the ongoing constitutional debate about the role of the military in Portuguese national life, the powers of the presidency, and the role of the parties and parliament, there is evidence that the country has begun to come to grips with these issues.[75]

Notes

1. The recent changes are especially well surveyed in Lawrence S. Graham and Harry M. Makler, eds., *Contemporary Portugal: The Revolution and Its Antecedents* (Austin: University of Texas Press, 1979); and Lawrence S. Graham and Douglas Wheeler, eds., *In Search of Modern Portugal* (Madison: University of Wisconsin Press, 1983).

2. The issues raised here are a continuation of a discussion of Portuguese political culture, the change process, and the appropriateness of democracy begun in Howard J. Wiarda, *Corporatism and Development: The Portuguese Experience* (Amherst: University of Massachusetts Press, 1977). The more

general theoretical issues are elaborated in Howard J. Wiarda, ed., *The Continuing Struggle for Democracy in Latin America* (Boulder, Colo.: Westview Press, 1980); and Howard J. Wiarda, *Corporatism and National Development in Latin America* (Boulder, Colo.: Westview Press, 1981).

3. The issue of whether Portugal is a part of Europe or apart from it is discussed in more detail in Howard J. Wiarda, "Spain and Portugal," in Peter H. Merkl, ed., *Western European Party Systems* (New York: Free Press, 1980), pp. 298–328.

4. These themes are more fully elaborated in Howard J. Wiarda, "Does Europe Still Stop at the Pyrenees? Or Does Latin America Begin There? Iberia, Latin America, and the Second Enlargement of the European Community," in Georges D. Landau and G. Harvey Summ, eds., *The Impact of an Enlarged European Community on Latin America* (forthcoming); published initially as Occasional Paper no. 2, Center for Hemispheric Studies, American Enterprise Institute, Washington, D.C., 1981.

5. These arguments are stated forcefully in a Ph.D. thesis being written at the Massachusetts Institute of Technology by Elizabeth Leeds; see also Immanuel Wallerstein, *The Modern World-System: Capitalist Agriculture and the Origins of the European World-Economy in the Sixteenth Century* (New York: Academic Press, 1976).

6. The more recent changes are summarized in Juan Linz, "Europe's Southern Frontier: Evolving toward What?" *Daedalus*, vol. 108 (Winter 1979), pp. 175–209.

7. Irving Louis Horowitz, *Three Worlds of Development: The Theory and Practice of International Stratification* (New York: Oxford University Press, 1966).

8. Eric N. Baklanoff, "The Political Economy of Portugal's Old Regime: Growth and Change Preceding the 1974 Revolution," *World Development*, vol. 7 (1979), pp. 799–811; and *The Economic Transformation of Spain and Portugal* (New York: Praeger, 1978). For some parallel comments on Spain, see William T. Salisbury, "Western Europe," in James W. Cortada, ed., *Spain in the Twentieth Century World* (Westport, Conn.: Greenview Press, 1980).

9. See the chapters by David Raby on populism and the Portuguese left, Bill Lomax on ideology and illusion in the Portuguese revolution, John Logan on worker mobilization, Walter Opello on the persistence of Portuguese political culture, Lawrence Graham on the state system, Harry Makler on the survival and revival of the industrial bourgeoisie, and Pitta e Cunha on Portugal and the EEC, in Graham and Wheeler, *In Search of Modern Portugal.*

10. Alexander Gerschenkron, *Economic Backwardness in Historical Perspective* (Cambridge, Mass.: Harvard University Press, 1962); for a general discussion see Howard J. Wiarda, "The Ethnocentrism of the Social Sciences: Implications for Theory and Research," *Review of Politics*, vol. 42 (April 1981); and Howard J. Wiarda, *From Corporatism to Neo-Syndicalism: The State, Organized Labor, and the Changing Industrial Relations Systems of Southern Europe* (Cambridge, Mass.: Harvard University, Center for European Studies Monograph Series, 1981).

11. Douglas L. Wheeler, "Portuguese Elections and History" (Paper presented at the Conference on Modern Portugal, Yale University, 1975); Howard

J. Wiarda, "The Transition to Democracy in Portugal, Real or Wishful?" (Paper presented at the Joint Seminar on Political Development, Center for International Affairs, Harvard University, and Center for International Studies, Massachusetts Institute of Technology, December 8, 1976); Thomas Bruneau and Mario Bacalhau, *Os portugueses e a política quartro anos depois do 25 de Abril* (The Portuguese and Politics Four Years after 25 April) (Lisbon: Meseta, 1978); and Mario Bacalhau, *Inqúerito a situação politica: Eanes a solução?* (Inquiry into the Political Situation: Eanes the Solution?) (Lisbon: Heptagono, 1980).

12. For a more detailed discussion, see Wiarda, "Spain and Portugal."

13. Henry Ehrmann, *Politics in France*, 3d ed. (Boston: Little, Brown, 1976).

14. Douglas L. Wheeler, *Republican Portugal* (Madison: University of Wisconsin Press, 1978).

15. Stanley G. Payne, *A History of Spain and Portugal* (Madison: University of Wisconsin Press, 1973), p. 523.

16. A. H. de Oliveira Marques, *History of Portugal* (New York: Columbia University Press, 1972); but see also Wiarda, *Corporatism and Development*, chap. 2.

17. Wheeler, *Republican Portugal*; and Richard A. H. Robinson, *Contemporary Portugal: A History* (London: Allen and Unwin, 1979).

18. Wiarda, *Corporatism and Development*; Neil Bruce, *Portugal: The Last Empire* (New York: Wiley, 1975); Antonio de Figueiredo, *Portugal: Fifty Years of Dictatorship* (New York: Holmes and Meier, 1975); Hugh Kay, *Salazar and Modern Portugal* (London: Eyrie and Spottiswoode, 1970); Peter Fryer and Patricia McGowan-Pinheiro, *Oldest Ally: A Portrait of Salazar's Portugal* (London: Dobson, 1961); and Graham and Makler, *Contemporary Portugal*.

19. Wiarda, *Corporatism and Development*; Wiarda, "The Corporatist Tradition and the Corporative System in Portugal: Structured, Evolving, Transcended, Persistent," in Graham and Makler, *Contemporary Portugal*, pp. 89–122; and especially and most recently, Wiarda, *Corporatism and National Development in Latin America*.

20. For further elaboration see Howard J. Wiarda, "Corporatist Theory and Ideology: A Latin American Development Paradigm," *Journal of Church and State*, vol. 20 (Winter 1978), pp. 29–56; Wiarda, "Democracy and Human Rights in Latin America: Toward a New Conceptualization," *Orbis*, vol. 22 (Spring 1978), pp. 137–60; Wiarda, "Toward a Framework for the Study of Political Change in the Iberic-Latin Tradition: The Corporative Model," *World Politics*, vol. 25 (January 1973), pp. 206–35.

21. For more discussion see Wiarda, "Spain and Portugal"; a more general and theoretical statement by the author was published as a monograph under the title *Critical Elections and Critical Coups: State, Society, and the Military in the Process of Latin American Development* (Athens: Center for International Studies, Ohio University, 1979).

22. José Pires Cardosos, *Dinossauro excelentíssimo* (Most Excellent Dinosaur) (Lisbon: Arcadia, 1972); and Francisco Sarsfield Cabral, *Una perspectiva sobre Portugal* (A Perspective on Portugal) (Lisbon: Moraes, 1973).

23. The concept of "limited pluralism" derives from Juan Linz, "An Authoritarian Regime: Spain," in E. Allardt and Y. Luttunen, eds., *Cleavages,*

Ideologies, and Party Systems (Helsinki: Westermarck Society, 1964), pp. 291–342.

24. Based on field research and participant observation in Portugal during a nine-month period in 1972–1973.

25. Baklanoff, "Political Economy"; Baklanoff, *Economic Transformation*; and Wiarda, "Does Europe Still Stop at the Pyrenees?"

26. Herminio Martins, "Portugal," in Margaret Archer and Salvador Ginner, eds., *Contemporary Europe: Class, Status, and Power* (London: Weidenfeld and Nicolson, 1971); and João B. Nunes Pereira Neto, "Social Evolution in Portugal since 1945," in R. S. Sayers, ed., *Portugal and Brazil in Transition* (Minneapolis: University of Minnesota Press, 1968), pp. 212–41.

27. Marcello Caetano, *Manual de ciencia política e direito constitucional* (Manual of Political Science and Constitutional Law) (Coimbra: Ed. Coimbra, numerous eds.). Caetano was not only prime minister but also the country's leading political scientist.

28. See Samuel P. Huntington, *Political Order in Changing Societies* (New Haven, Conn.: Yale University Press, 1968), p. 407, for a discussion of the implications of such a dramatic increase in political participation.

29. Charles W. Anderson, "Toward a Theory of Latin American Politics," in Howard J. Wiarda, ed., *Politics and Social Change in Latin America: The Distinct Tradition*, rev. ed. (Amherst: University of Massachusetts Press, 1982); and John Hammond, "Das ruas as urnas [From the Streets to the Polling Booth]: Electoral Behavior and Noninstitutional Political Militancy, Portugal, 1975" (Paper presented at the Third Meeting of the Conference Group on Modern Portugal, Toronto, April 16–17, 1976, published under the less descriptive title "Electoral Behavior and Political Militancy," in Graham and Makler, *Contemporary Portugal*, pp. 257–80).

30. Wiarda, "Spain and Portugal."

31. For a discussion of the army and other actors as "parties," see Howard J. Wiarda and Harvey F. Kline, *Latin American Politics and Development* (Boston: Houghton Mifflin, 1979), pt. I.

32. Wiarda, *Critical Elections and Critical Coups*.

33. Douglas Porch, *The Portuguese Armed Forces and the Revolution* (Stanford, Calif.: Hoover Institution, 1977).

34. For a solid, scholarly account, see Robinson, *Contemporary Portugal*, chaps. 5–7.

35. Howard J. Wiarda, *Transcending Corporatism? The Portuguese Corporative System and the Revolution of 1974* (Columbia: Institute of International Studies, University of South Carolina, 1976).

36. Based on field research and interviews in the Ministry of Labor in 1972–1973, 1974, 1975, 1977, and 1979.

37. The discussion here and in the following paragraphs is based on Wiarda, "Spain and Portugal."

38. See, for instance, Cunhal's celebrated interview with Oriana Fallachi, *New York Times Magazine*, July 13, 1975; in more recent statements Cunhal has sought to shed his Stalinist image. See also John L. Hammond, "Portugal's Communists and the Revolution," *Radical History Review*, vol. 23 (Spring

1980), pp. 140–61; and Eusebio M. Mujal-Leon, "The PCP and the Portuguese Revolution," *Problems of Communism*, vol. 26 (Jan.–Feb. 1977), pp. 31–34.

39. Wheeler, "Portuguese Elections," p. 2.

40. After the overthrow of the monarchy in 1910, the Portuguese armed forces generally exercised the "moderative power" formerly exercised by the crown. The MFA sought to resurrect this tradition after 1974, but it was divided between those officers who wanted to "moderate" the political process and others who wished to direct it more strongly.

41. Portugal has both a prime minister and a president. The prime minister is the effective head of government and a civilian; the president, ordinarily a leading military man, exercises chiefly ceremonial duties but may, under particular circumstances and depending on the person occupying the position, play a stronger role.

42. Anderson, "Toward a Theory"; and Wiarda, *Transcending Corporatism?*

43. Richard Rose, ed., *Electoral Behavior: A Comparative Handbook* (New York: Free Press, 1974); and Seymour Martin Lipset and Stein Rokkan, eds., *Party Systems and Voter Alignments: Cross-National Perspectives* (New York: Free Press, 1967).

44. Hammond, "Das ruas as urnas."

45. Electoral data in Portugal are published by the Instituto Nacional de Estatística; see also Thomas C. Bruneau, "Popular Support for Democracy in Post-Revolutionary Portugal: Results from a Survey," in Graham, *Portuguese Revolution*.

46. Ben Pimlott and Jean Seaton, "Political Power and the Portuguese Media," and Bill Lomax, "Ideology and Illusion in the Portuguese Revolution: The Role of the Left," both in Graham and Wheeler, *In Search of Modern Portugal*.

47. The discussion is based on the analysis in Wiarda, "Spain and Portugal."

48. Pereira Neto, "Social Evolution," and Linz, "Europe's Southern Frontier."

49. The analysis here and in subsequent pages follows closely the pioneering work on Portuguese electoral behavior carried out by Hammond, "Das ruas as urnas."

50. The Azores and Madeira are excluded from the analysis.

51. Oliveira Marques, *History of Portugal*; William C. Atkinson, *A History of Spain and Portugal* (Middlesex: Penguin, 1960); and Harold V. Livermore, *A New History of Portugal* (London: Cambridge University Press, 1969).

52. José Cutileiro, *A Portuguese Rural Society* (Oxford: Oxford University Press, 1971).

53. The analysis follows that of Hammond, "Das ruas as urnas"; see also Jorgé Gaspar and Nuno Vitorino, *As eleições de 25 de Abril: Geografiá e imagem dos partidos* (The Elections of 25 April: Geography and Image of the Parties) (Lisbon: Horizonte, 1976); and Jorge Gaspar, *Eleições Portuguesas, 1975–1976* (Portuguese Elections, 1975–1976) (Lisbon: Centro de Estudos Geograficos, 1979).

54. Hammond also qualifies his position by emphasizing the in-

completeness of his class data.

55. The analysis here and subsequently continues to follow that of Hammond.

56. The best survey data and political analyses were published in the journal *Expresso* during this period.

57. Caroline B. Brettel, "Emigration and Its Implications," in Graham and Makler, eds., *Contemporary Portugal.·*

58. The urban south was also an exception to the pattern of inverse relations between prosperity and conservatism: there the conservative vote was not in the poorer *concelhos* but mainly in the wealthier ones; see Hammond, "Das ruas as urnas," p. 265.

59. Gaspar and Vitorino, *As eleições*, pp. 48–49.

60. Hammond notes that the PS ran a U.S.-style campaign; its pragmatism and multiclass appeal may have been due in part to U.S. influence and that of the Western European Socialists and Social Democrats who helped advise and financially bolster the party.

61. Hammond, "Das ruas as urnas," p. 267.

62. Ibid., p. 268.

63. Ibid., p. 269. Hammond's conclusion may be contrasted with that of Philip Converse ("Of Time and Partisan Stability," *Comparative Political Studies*, vol. 2 [July 1969], pp. 137–71), who argues that such stable electoral patterns may require two or three generations.

64. Ben Pimlott, "Parties and Voters in the Portuguese Revolution: The Elections of 1975 and 1976," *Parliamentary Affairs*, vol. 3 (Winter 1977), pp. 35–58; and Juan Carlos González Hernández, "El proceso electoral portugues: Analises cuantitivo del comportamiento político, 1975–1976" (The Portuguese Electoral Process: A Quantitative Analysis of Political Behavior, 1975–1976), *Revista Española de Opinión Pública*, vol. 48 (1977), pp. 205–70.

65. Bruneau and Bacalhau, *Os portugueses e a política.*

66. Good analyses may be found in *Expresso* and *Jornal Novo* for this period.

67. *Diario da República*, December 24, 1979; Comissão Nacional de Eleições, October 31, 1980.

68. Bruneau's survey data tend to support the conservative trend thesis. He found a renewed pride in Portuguese historical and cultural institutions; considerable public sentiment in favor of the old (Salazar-Caetano) regime, primarily on economic grounds; low regard for the results of the 1974 Revolution; and much unhappiness and disillusionment with the Socialist government then in power. In fact Bruneau's survey, carried out in the spring of 1978, foretold the Democratic Alliance victories of 1979 and 1980. See Bruneau, "Popular Support for Democracy."

69. Seymour Martin Lipset and Stein Rokkan, "Cleavage Structures, Party Systems, and Voter Alignments: An Introduction," in Lipset and Rokkan, *Party Systems and Voter Alignments*, pp. 1–64.

70. For fuller discussion see Wiarda, "Spain and Portugal."

71. See Wiarda, "Does Europe Still Stop at the Pyrenees?"

72. See Anderson, "Toward a Theory"; and Wiarda, "Law and Political Development in Latin America: Toward a Framework for Analysis," *American*

Journal of Comparative Law, vol. 19 (Summer 1971), pp. 434–63, for more on these stages.

73. Bruneau's survey data, for instance, show that the Portuguese people are only mildly supportive of democracy and that they both do not yet strongly identify with the structures of the present regime and are unhappy with the results. There seems to be little direct or immediate link between the wishes of the population and the government, which is perceived as not functioning effectively. The parties, according to Bruneau's survey, have not demonstrated their ability to govern, and there is reason to think the failure of the parties has decreased the legitimacy of the constitution and the democratic system. Popular support for a democratic system in Portugal still does not exist if that system is identified with the governments that have come and gone since April 25, 1974. Bruneau concludes that the electorate would support what amounts to a nondemocratic alternative that promised to provide what the population clearly desires: peace, stability, and economic growth. He therefore calls for some more "indirect" forms of democracy but without specifying precisely what that means; see Bruneau, "Popular Support for Democracy."

74. Although liberal or social democracy has not worked very well or garnered overwhelming support in Portugal, revolutionary socialism of the Marxist-Leninist type has also been rejected at the polls; and corporatism, which did have some strong indigenous roots, was thoroughly discredited by its practice under Salazar. Portugal therefore seems likely to limp along as a divided and fractured nation with no single system of rule enjoying widespread popularity. It will continue to tinker with its existing institutions to make them more functional and will probably show considerable genius in improvising solutions in response to one crisis or another; but Portugal remains a country in search of a legitimized governing formula, and it is likely to remain so for some time. See the author's "Conclusion," in *Corporatism and Development*.

75. Thomas C. Bruneau explores these more recent efforts to strike a constitutional and institutional balance in "Politics in Portugal, 1976–81, and Revision of the Constitution" (Paper prepared for presentation to Social Science Research Council Conference on Contemporary Change in Southern Europe, Madrid, November 25–28, 1981).

11
Spanish and Portuguese Foreign Policy in Latin America

Spain and Portugal have long histories in Latin America. In 1992 we will celebrate the 500th anniversary of Columbus's discovery of the Americas for Spain; the 500th anniversary of Portugal's discovery of Brazil will be in the year 2000. The involvement of both Spain and Portugal in Latin America reaches into centuries past, and the ties between Iberia and Latin America remain powerful today.

The influence of Spain and Portugal in Latin America has been deep as well as long. Spain and Portugal were the first modern imperial nations, and their emergence in the sixteenth century as leading world powers was intimately related to their American conquests. Ibero-America provided the gold and silver that enabled Spain and Portugal to play leading roles on the world's stage and, for a time, to achieve eminence (even preeminence in the Spanish case) among the European powers. But as the readily available wealth of the Americas was depleted in the seventeenth and eighteenth centuries, the mother countries went into a long period of decline from which they have only recently begun to recover.

The influence of Spain and Portugal on their American colonies was strong. In the political, legal, religious, economic, sociological, and intellectual spheres the Iberian nations stamped their mark indelibly on the American continent. There have been other cultural influences—France, the United States—since that time, and at various points in history the Latin American nations have sought to reject and turn their backs on their colonial past. But the heavy hand of Spanish and Portuguese institutional arrangements and behavioral patterns— by no means democratic historically—still hangs over the area, either as a legacy still to be overcome or, perhaps more realistically, as a culture and set of givens to which to adapt and accommodate.

Part of Spain's and Portugal's decline as nations involved the loss of the majority of their American colonies early in the nineteenth century. The two processes—Iberia's decline, even decadence, and Latin America's independence—were related. For a long time Latin

374

America bitterly rejected not only Spanish colonialism (Brazil never felt as bitter about its mother country as did the Hispanic countries) but all the cultural and institutional features imposed by the former metropole. It was not until the end of the century that normal diplomatic relations between Spain and Latin America were resumed. The Spanish-American War of 1898 was a major catalyst in reviving cultural ties and the idea of the fundamental unity of the Hispanic nations. The growing rapprochement continued during the first third of the twentieth century, though in neither Spain nor Latin America did this emerging accommodation produce many concrete results.

The Franco regime used the evolving notions of *hispanismo* to try to increase Spain's influence in Latin America and to compensate for Spain's ostracism from Europe after World War II.[1] This effort to strengthen its European hand by playing its Latin American card and to augment its Latin American presence in order to increase its European position is not new in Spanish foreign policy, and it continues to this day. In addition, Franco, and Salazar as well, sought to export the model of a conservative, authoritarian, corporative polity to Latin America and achieved a considerable degree of success for a time in such countries as Argentina, Brazil, Chile, the Dominican Republic, Bolivia, Guatemala, Honduras, Peru, Panama, Cuba, Mexico, Columbia, Ecuador, Costa Rica, Paraguay, Venezuela, El Salvador, and Nicaragua. But after the war the attraction of corporatism faded; in fact corporatism and corporatist forms were never as popular in Latin America as they were in Iberia.[2]

The transition of Portugal and Spain from authoritarianism to democracy also had a major impact on Latin America, especially in those countries where the military in politics and a bureaucratic-authoritarian model of development had seized hold. The more-or-less successful transition, especially in Spain, gave that country considerable coin to use in furthering its foreign policy objectives. Spain, unlike Portugal, had made the transition without social upheaval or the destruction of such traditional institutions as the church, the monarchy, or the army. That achievement was enormously attractive to the governing elites in Latin America. Hence, since the mid-1970s Latin America has become one of the major focuses of Spanish foreign policy. Spain has made strong efforts in the political, diplomatic, economic, and cultural realms to expand its ties and influence in Latin America.

Both the centrist governments of Adolfo Suárez and Calvo Sotelo and the Socialist one of Felipe González have made Latin America a primary concern, indicating that this is not a partisan but a permanent feature of Spanish foreign policy. At the same time (and for reasons that include cultural and historic ties, the attractiveness of the Spanish transition to democracy, augmented commercial ties, greater access to Europe, and a desire to reduce their dependency on the United States) the Latin American states have increased their links with Spain. The result is a new culture-area condominium with strong implications for Iberia, for Latin America, and for the United States.

Current Policies

The Spanish presence has been growing significantly in Latin America, especially over the past twenty years, independent of the nature of the regime in Madrid. Spain has become a significant actor within the region. For Latin America also, Spain has become of growing importance.

Spain's interests in Latin America stem from a variety of factors. First are the historical ties of language, culture, religion, sociology, and politics: in many areas Spain and Latin America can be interpreted—at heast historically—in terms of a common framework and developmental model. Spain and Spanish America (and Portugal and Brazil) share many cultural features, and the common Spanish (or Portuguese) language is an important means of opening political, diplomatic, and other doors.[3]

Second, Spain now has major political and economic investments (discussed in more detail below) in Latin America. Third, 3 million Latin Americans hold Spanish citizenship, and the Latin American community in Madrid has become sizable, a haven not just for political exiles but also for Latin Americans who send their children for university training or for some European refinement. Fourth, there is *realpolitik:* Spain looks on Latin America as a strong bargaining chip that it can continue to use in its negotiations with the EEC; Spain would similarly like to serve as a "bridge" between Latin America and the European community.

These basic interests are relatively constant in Spanish foreign policy, but there have been changes over time and nuances from administration to administration. Franco sought to use the Latin American connection to expand Spanish influence abroad, to gain support and legitimacy for his often beleaguered regime, and to ameliorate the isolation of Spain by the European nations. The centrist government of Adolfo Suárez (1976–1981) viewed Latin America chiefly as a political and diplomatic means to gain further leverage in Spain's preeminent foreign policy goal of securing entry into the European community. Prime Minister Leopoldo Calvo Sotelo continued that strategy, while seeking to use the Latin American connection to secure greater prestige and authority for the Spainsh crown.

Under Socialist Prime Minister Felipe González, some new initiatives were added to what had been a quite traditional approach to Latin America. The more substantive nuances included a much more activist foreign policy in Central America and the Southern Cone, the creation of a multiparty senatorial commission within Spain to study the problem of the "disappeared persons" in Argentina and Chile, and the holding of congressional hearings in the Cortes on the situation in Central America. In addition, González visited the area on several occasions on behalf of the Socialist International and his own substantive foreign policy. These were not just ceremonial trips but also reflected Spanish efforts at mediation in the Central American conflicts. The government viewed Latin America as a testing ground for its efforts to promote transitions to democracy (as in Spain) in the third world; in addition, it would like to play the role of intermediary between Latin America and Europe, between the United States and Latin America, and between "the South" (or at least its Latin American parts) and "the North" (Europe *and* the United States). It will be recalled, for example, that Spain had before offered to serve as a go-between in the El Salvador conflict, an initiative that was at one point picked up by the U.S. Department of State in its so-called two-track strategy (that is, to strengthen the El Salvadoran government and security forces and at the same time talk to the guerrillas, using Spain as intermediary). But the architect of the policy, Assistant Secretary Thomas Enders, was forced to resign when these initiatives became public knowledge; ironically perhaps, Enders was then named ambassador to Spain.

There has been a flurry of Spanish activity in Latin America in the past twenty years, even though Spain has no security or military interests in the region. Spain's military and security interests are largely focused on Western Europe, NATO, Gibraltar and the Straits thereof, North Africa (Ceuta, Morocco), and the Middle East, from which Spain derives the overwhelming share of its energy resources. The Spanish military-strategic dimension in Latin America is therefore limited. Spain sells military equipment to several Latin American countries, and Spanish military sales to the region are increasing dramatically. But so far as can be determined, Spain has no military involvement in the region, either overt or covert. It is not direct strategic interests that motivates Spain's Latin American policy; there are none.

Spain's diplomatic ties are more extensive. Spain has established normal bilateral relations with *all* the Spanish-speaking nations of Latin America. This includes the smaller countries of Central America (except Guatemala with which Spain broke relations in 1980 when police stormed the Spanish embassy in order to end a peasant occupation; those relations have since been resumed), where Spain has but limited commercial and other interests. The Spanish king and a succession of prime ministers have made numerous trips to the area, extolling Spain, the unity and brotherhood of the Hispanic peoples and soils, the glories and potential of Hispanic unity, the inviolability of the Spanish soul and "race." More substantively they have talked of trade, aid, commercial relations, Spain as a "bridge" to Europe, Spain as a model for the achievement of a democracy and human rights, Spain as a mediator, Spain as a growing presence. In the king's words, Spain has a Latin American "vocation."

These diplomatic initiatives have not quite produced the Hispanic commonwealth or confederation that some Spanish foreign policy officials, in their unguarded and doubtlessly romantic moments, have talked of. But they have produced something of a Hispanic voting bloc at the United Nations (although that bloc remains "floating" and is not as monolithic as some other UN blocs). They have achieved some common unity of purpose on issues such as intervention in the internal affairs of other nations or the need to reduce dependency on any one particular power bloc; some sense of shared destiny and purpose; some common strategies in seeking to achieve democracy and human rights; and some sense of the need to elevate in importance those institutions that are uniquely Hispanic or that point toward a Hispanic (as distinct from Anglo-Saxon) model of development. These achievements for Spanish foreign policy are often symbolic, sometimes fuzzy and intangible, sometimes vague and imprecise, but they are no less important for being so. Of such gradual alterations in the tides are more fundamental sea changes often made.

Spain has also become a growing economic presence in Latin America. Spain's commercial and economic interests in the area must be viewed in terms of Spain's recent transformation into a middle-level industrial power, Latin America's own desires to diversify its trade relations, and Spain's efforts to give concrete economic content to its still limited political and diplomatic initiatives. In these ways, as Fredrick Pike put it, "practical" *hispanismo* could be substituted for "lyrical" *hispanismo*.[4]

Spain is a relatively new member of the World Bank's category of "industrialized market economies," and its exports to Latin America consist chiefly (90 percent) of manufactured goods. At the same time,

Latin America supplies about 25 percent of Spain's primary commodity imports. Spanish banks have also made substantial loans to some of Latin America's principal debtor nations, a matter that is of as much concern to Spain as to the major U.S. and West German banks. Nevertheless, despite the dramatic increase in the *volume* of trade between Spain and Latin America since the 1950s, the *relative* percentages have changed very little. That is, Spanish exports to Latin America constitute between 9 and 11 percent of the total; imports from the region have held steady at about 11 percent. Spain still occupies a relatively minor role in Latin America's world trade, providing the destination for about 3 percent of the region's exports and the source of only 2.5 percent of its imports. The United States continues to be Latin America's dominant trade partner and is likely to remain so; the European Economic Community is a distant second and will remain in that position. Spain is thus a growing but still quite modest economic presence in Latin America. It should also be said that Latin America is a more important market for Spain than Spain is for Latin America.

Spain's cultural ties to Latin America have also expanded significantly in recent decades. Spanish artists and intellectuals as well as shows of Spanish art, theater, music, and dance have been sent on tour in Latin America, and Latin American artists and intellectuals have been invited to Spain in unprecedented numbers. The number of books by Spaniards being published or distributed in Latin America and the works by Latin Americans published or distributed in Spain is at an all-time high. Spain is also undertaking a major effort to influence Latin American intellectuals and now offers upwards of 500 scholarships per year to Latin American young people to study in Spain. These ties of culture and scholarship have undoubtedly helped cement a stronger relationship between Spain and Latin America.

Our main concern in this chapter, however, is not culture per se but the *political-cultural* ties forged between Iberia and Latin America. We have earlier traced the long, difficult, convoluted history of these links. Chapter 9 discussed the efforts to fashion a common political-cultural framework for the study of development in both Iberia and Latin America—and the political machinations, the divergent views, and the personal, partisan, and private political uses of the model, or models, that have been put forward. The concepts advanced now seem to change with each administration in Madrid—or in the Latin American countries. At one point it might have been said that the organization of a common sociopolitical and developmental framework for the Iberian-Latin nations was possible, but recent events and experiences leave one far less sanguine about the prospects.

Spain's political interests in Latin America are more extensive and perhaps constitute the most important set of ties among those listed. These relations in turn can be divided into two categories: those that are long term and independent of any particular regime of the moment and those that appear to be the initiatives of a single administration or government that nonetheless tries to elevate its particular policies into a longer-term and truly national commitment.

Among Spain's long-term and permanent interests in Latin America, the following seem particularly important:

• expanding Spain's trade, markets, investments, and economic ties with Latin America. The motives here, however, are at least as much political as economic.

• expanding Spain's cultural, intellectual, scientific (including social scientific), and technical influence in Latin America. Again the motives are as much political as they are cultural.

• expanding the common ties of Hispanic culture, language, sociology, politics, law, and religion. These efforts are currently concentrated on greatly expanded exchange programs as well as on the 500th anniversary of the Spanish discovery of America.

• using its Latin American ties as a point of leverage in its ongoing negotiations with the EEC; using its European ties to increase its influence in Latin America.

• helping augment a greater European presence and influence in Latin America, with Spain as the lead and focal point.

• concomitantly, reducing the U.S. presence and influence in the hemisphere.

• working toward the evolution and creation of a greater Hispanic confederation or commonwealth. Such an arrangement may be a long way off (or perhaps unattainable); nevertheless it is important to begin putting the building blocks in place.

• forging new ground for solidarity by active engagement of Spain in positive campaigns in Latin America, such as the transition to democracy (about which Spain presumably knows a great deal and thinks of itself as a model), the struggle for human rights, and peace initiatives (such as Contadora) in Central America.

It is now more difficult to distinguish Spain's long-term and *national* interests in Latin America from the initiatives of particular regimes or governments. These categories are not easily separable; and since Franco there has developed a major Spanish interest, largely nonpartisan, in democracy and human rights as perhaps permanent objectives of Spanish foreign policy. This of course presumes that Spain remains a democracy and that Latin America wishes to continue its recent experiments with democracy.

Prime Minister Adolfo Suárez was interested in Latin America, but his concerns were primarily domestic: the post-Franco transition to democracy. Latin America was viewed as an instrument to serve Spain's grander international design: entry into the EEC and the European community of advanced, industrial, democratic nations. Now that Suárez is out of office, he is spending more time in Latin America—sometimes in ways not always appreciated there—offering Spain as an example that the sometimes more authoritarian regimes of Latin America could emulate. Prime Minister Calvo Sotelo also had limited interest in Latin America and largely continued his predecessors' policies. It remained for Socialist Prime Minister González to give a new direction to Spanish foreign policy in Latin America and to infuse it with a new activism and ideology.

Under the Socialist government Spain's foreign policy has been oriented more strongly toward the promotion of democracy in Latin America, the defense of human rights, the attainment of peace in Central America, greater economic development for the region, and a grand, joint but Spanish-led, celebration of the 500th anniversary of the discovery of the Americas in 1992. The new Spanish initiatives have been fueled by the special interest of González in Latin America and his extensive work with the Socialist International, by the close attention Spain's transition to democracy evoked in Latin America, as well as by the prestige of the Spanish king. We should not forget that it is a *Socialist* government that has undertaken these initiatives, led by a real Socialist party whose roots and interpretations are still, at least among some of its factions, quite militant and Marxist. Even today some of its beliefs are molded by an intensely ideological socialism stemming from the 1930s (precisely when the party was outlawed by Franco and forced underground or into exile) rather than by the milder forms of European social democracy.

Many within the party (though not necessarily González) see these ideals and objectives as a way of staking out a larger margin of independence for Spain, while simultaneously reducing U.S. influence *both* in Latin America and in Spain itself. The current of anti-Americanism that has been strongly present in Spain historically, particularly since 1898, is visible in many of the new Spanish initiatives. Spain has quasi-officially taken up "dependency theory" as an explanation for Latin America's ills, which conveniently places the blame for Latin America's underdevelopment on the shoulders of the United States and therefore has a powerful attractiveness to Latin

381

American intellectuals whom Spain is assiduously wooing. Former Foreign Minister Fernando Morán referred to the United States as a "hegemonic power" in Latin America and criticized not only U.S. "interventionism" in the hemisphere but also the control exercised by the United States over Latin American culture, the media, and modes of thinking. He would have substituted for the U.S. influence a joint Spanish-French approach to Latin America, presumably based in part on the even more strongly anti-American attitudes of French Minister of Culture Jack Lang and Mitterrand's adviser on Latin America Regis Débray. More objective observers viewed this as a purely romantic and unrealistic vision, which, given French-Spanish animosities over Spain's entry into the EEC among other things, had very little possibility of being effectively implemented.

With regard to human rights, Spain was strongly condemnatory of authoritarian regimes in Argentina, Chile, and Uruguay. Under a Socialist government, as might be expected, the Spanish posture has been more strongly critical of right-wing regimes than of left-wing ones—even while admitting both types are oppressive. The Spanish attitude, however, both publicly and privately, is that the right-wing types are more reprehensible in a moral sense. Hence, although the Spanish government has been quick to condemn right-wing abuses, only recently did it issue its first criticism of a leftist regime (Nicaragua's).

Spain has also been playing a strong role in the efforts to achieve peace in Central America. Both Prime Minister González and the Foreign Ministry have invested considerable time and prestige in seeking to resolve the Central American crisis. They have proposed a "little Helsinki" peace conference for the region, and they believe the best instrument for achieving peace is through the Contadora group (Colombia, Mexico, Panama, Venezuela). They would like to play a major role in bringing together the conflicting parties for a negotiated settlement, an accomplishment that would bring credit to themselves as well as to Spain. Within a few weeks of the regime's taking office, however, these high expectations were considerably dampened, in large part because of the difficulties and realities of big power politics in that part of the world. In short, Spain came to see that no solution in Central America would be possible without the United States (or, likely, the Cubans), and it had to reassess whether its policy on Central America was worth risking its relationship with the United States.

Earlier, Spain had been critical of the U.S. emphasis on the East-West dimensions of the Central American conflict, had criticized the U.S. blockade of Cuba as "ineffective" and "unwise," and had suggested, in González's words, that U.S. leadership "has a negative dimension that is greater than the positive one." These sentiments did not endear Spain to the Reagan administration. Recognizing this and that Spain's relationship with the United States is more important than posturing over Central America, the government opted for a quieter, more restrained, although still vigorous, policy. It also became somewhat disillusioned by the growing Marxism-Leninism of the Sandinistas in Nicaragua, was impressed by Duarte's victory and the steps toward democracy in El Salvador, and warned against continued Sandinista support for ETA (the violent Basque separatist movement) terrorists in Spain itself. The accord of September 1984 between Morocco and Libya similarly sent a shock through the Spanish foreign ministry, pulling Spain still closer to NATO.

All these factors combined to help temper Socialist Spain's foreign policy. González declined an invitation to visit Nicaragua, he no longer seemed eager to receive Castro in Spain as part of a state visit, and he was no longer pushing for a strong Socialist International role in resolving Central America's disputes, in large part because that would exclude the United States as a key actor. The more modest Spanish agenda became to get all the actors committed to the Contadora initiatives, to get the European and NATO councils to support these efforts, and to convince the United States of Spain's usefulness as a potential intermediary.

Spain's Central American policies are not based on any great economic or strategic interests in that area; rather, in keeping with other recent initiatives emanating from Spain, the policy seems to be based more on historic, moral, and political purposes. The government emphasizes it is not seeking to impose a solution but helping to implement initiatives that enjoy the support of the democratic countries of the region. Further, it says it is reacting to specific requests by other countries (Colombia, Costa Rica, Cuba, Nicaragua), political leaders (the late Omar Torrijos of Panama, former president of Venezuela Carlos Andrés Peréz), and groups (Socialist International or the Salvadoran guerrillas) to become involved.

The conclusions that can be drawn (following Spanish international affairs specialist Sánchez-Gijón) regarding Spain's role in Latin America are as follows:

• The policy is based primarily on historic, political, and moral considerations, less on economic or strategic ones.

• Spain's policy was personally conducted by Prime Minister González and implemented by his foreign minister.

• González gravitated from a somewhat idealistic approach to a more pragmatic one.

• After having found resistance to its initiatives in some countries (Panama, Venezuela), Spain is likely to pursue only policies that enjoy consensus among the interested parties.

• Central America is important but not decisive for Spain's pursuit of a longer-term Latin American policy.

• Central America is not sufficiently important to Spain to risk antagonizing the United States.

• Spain's policy is aimed at the creation of a community of democratic nations formed around an evolving Hispanic ideal in which Spain would be a leading member. In this regard the Socialist government's Latin American policy is quite traditional, exhibiting many continuities with the earlier concept of *hispanidad*.

• Spain's Latin American policies must also be seen as a political instrument for enhancing Spain's European possibilities and its transatlantic relations.

Limits on the Iberian Role in Latin America

Spain and Portugal (in earlier years) have played major roles in Latin America. Spain, especially in the past twenty years, has become a significant presence in the region, an actor of considerable importance. Yet factors constraining or limiting its influence and activity are also major and deserve serious attention. These constraints were frankly expressed in a statement by former Spanish Foreign Minister Morán:

> The image of Spain is better than its actions. Spanish influence is greater than Spanish power. I frequently say something I have discovered, something I had foreboded: the great problem of Spanish foreign policy is that it has a lot of influence and very little power.[5]

The main reasons for this impotence, on the part of both Portugal and Spain, are discussed in the following pages.

Portugal. Portuguese foreign policy currently has three main priorities:

• to cement its political ties to Europe and to NATO

• to cement its entry into the European Economic Community (EEC)

• to secure a position for Portugal as interlocutor with its former African colonies, mainly Angola and Mozambique[6]

The first two priorities have a European focus; Latin America is not mentioned at all in the list. If forced to make a choice, Portugal would probably say that its Middle Eastern relations are now more important than its Latin American ones. Latin America does not figure prominently in Portuguese foreign policy.

Portugal has no embassies anywhere in Central America. Its relations with most of the rest of South America are similarly limited. There is quite a bit of interest in Portugal in the Central American situation; every day new stories appear in the Portuguese press about Nicaragua, El Salvador, and the U.S. role there. But that is part of normal media coverage and reflects worldwide interest in the subject, no greater and no less in Portugal than elsewhere in Europe. Portuguese foreign policy, however, is not closely involved in the area. Portugal's role in Central America, when there is one, is due chiefly to the concern of on-again-off-again Prime Minister Mario Soares and his Socialist party, not because of any significant or permanent Portuguese interests there.

Soares's interest in Central America—like that of González—stems from his long-time association with the Socialist International (SI). Because of his experience in the mid-1970s in fending off a power play by the Portuguese Communist party, Soares is also thought to be able to recognize a Communist when he sees one. When Soares served as prime minister, he and the party set policy on Central America; the government and the foreign ministry simply went along with it. It is a personal and party interest that is chiefly involved, not one encompassing major national or *Portuguese* interests. In general, Soares, like González, has been a moderating influence within the SI and in Western European councils. He has been a rock of good sense in European Socialist and social-democratic salons. Other recent prime ministers have shown even less interest in Latin America.

Even with its former colony Brazil, Portugal now has very limited relations. The relationship is based chiefly on history, custom, and nostalgia rather than on many concrete interests. Brazilian television, especially its soap opera-like *novelas*, are flooding the Portuguese market, and there is some resentment about this on the part of Portuguese intellectuals and government officials. But there is little in the way of commercial, political, or trade relations between the two countries. There is more Brazilian investment in Portugal than there is Portuguese investment in Brazil, but on both sides the figures are fairly minuscule. In fact, except for their common history and language, there are few reasons for strong relations between the two countries.

The Portuguese are apprehensive about being replaced by the Brazilians even in formerly Portuguese Africa. After a decade of preoccupation with the domestic economy and politics, the Portuguese are seeking to reestablish ties with their former colonies. The Soares government had high hopes of presiding over a Lusophone, Portuguese-led summit, but it could not deliver on its promises. It had wanted to include Brazil to give the summit greater importance and credibility, but Brazil did not want to play a subordinate role. Brazil also has strong commercial ties there. The Brazilians report that the Portuguese refuse to believe that Brazil's goals in Africa are limited and that it does not want to supplant Portugal.

Other than Soares and the PS initiatives, Portugal's initiatives in Latin America and its presence there have been quite circumscribed. Even in Portugal's area of "special relationships" it has been largely supplanted: Spain is now a larger presence than Portugal in Brazil, and in formerly Portuguese Africa Brazil is playing a larger role than Portugal. Portugal is simply too small, too weak, and too under-developed to be a very large presence in Latin America; and the years of political upheaval and economic decline following the 1974 revolution have forced Portugal to be occupied more with internal than with foreign affairs. Portugal is just now beginning to pursue a more activist foreign policy, but the constraints on its playing a much larger role are strong. Even if Portugal were to or could play a larger role, Latin America would not be near the top of its list of priorities.

Spain. Spain's initiatives in Latin America have been both significant and interesting. It is important to remember, however, that there are major constraints on Spain's playing a larger role.

1. In spite of the rhetorical flourishes about the "fundamental unity" of the Spanish soul and soil, Western Europe and the United States are far more important to Spain than is Latin America.

2. Spain still has limited resources to devote to its foreign affairs. It is the most recent arrival in the camp of the middle-industrial powers; it is not yet as affluent as France or West Germany or most of Western Europe, and its budgets for new foreign initiatives remain modest by comparison.

3. Spain's research on international relations and foreign policy is quite limited. Only one or two small "think tanks" are conducting foreign affairs research on Latin America, and university course offerings and research in these areas are similarly modest. Spain tends to feel it intuitively "knows" Latin America because of its common history and culture, but the serious knowledge base about Latin America is limited.

4. The agency designated to further Spanish cooperation with Latin America, the Instituto de Cooperación Iberoamericana, is still

going through considerable internal uncertainty and upheaval, as well as frequent changeovers in leadership, over its precise direction, goals, and purposes. It has an ongoing dispute with the Foreign Ministry about who should be in charge of Latin American affairs; its budget is sufficient to support only a modest number of programs in Latin American studies and scholarships for Latin Americans to come to Spain; and as a public agency it remains all but invisible.

5. Spain's trade with Latin America is only 10 percent of its total trade and is unlikely to go much higher. These numbers do not portend well for any future greatly expanded political relations with the area.

6. Spain still has limited institutional connections with Latin America. It has no military presence, little economic aid, small embassies in most of the countries, and limited investment and commercial transactions. The institutional base simply is not there for any major new initiatives in the area.

7. Spanish attitudes toward Latin America tend to be patronizing and condescending and are often resented by Latin Americans. These attitudes derive from a general lack of knowledge about Latin America (few Spaniards have ever been to the region) and from still-present notions of cultural, political, and even racial superiority. Spaniards do not yet differentiate clearly among the Latin American countries. They still think of Latin America as exotic, and people from the "Indies," as they were called, tend to be lumped together in one undifferentiated mass. Most Spaniards are not yet inclined to see Latin America as constituting a fraternity of equals; rather the assumption of Spanish superiority—that Spain will "lead" and "teach" Latin America—is widespread. These attitudes in the present context are not guaranteed to endear Spain to the nations of that area.

8. Spain would like to serve as a bridge and intermediary between Europe and Latin America, between North and South, or with the United States. But the Latin American countries believe they are quite capable of conducting bilateral relations with Europe or the United States by themselves; they do not need and often resent Spain's efforts at intermediation.

9. Latin America is far away; the logistics are difficult. Most Spaniards are just not very interested in Latin America. Europe is their interest and preoccupation. Latin America is viewed as having some special claim on Spain's attention, and of course there are historical ties there. But for Spaniards, what happens next door in France or Europe is far more important than anything that happens in Latin America.

10. Another factor hindering a more effective Spanish foreign

policy in Latin America is a division within the Spanish government itself and the governing party. Within the PSOE there are many radical third worlders caught up in Marxist dependency theory and hoping to "liberate" Latin America, both from its own repressive institutions and from the United States. This position is countered by that of González and the moderates who are more pragmatic, see the "big picture," and do not want to have Spain break with the United States over Central America. These ideological battles continue to be fought within the Spanish government over the appropriate position and role to play in Latin America.

11. Spain has posited its Latin American foreign policy no longer on a community of corporate-authoritarian regimes tied together by traditional *hispanismo* as under Franco, but on the basis of a community of *democratic* states. This provides a strong moral and political basis to the policy and represents a grand vision. But there are dangers in such a policy as well. First, Spain has itself not fully consolidated its democracy; democracy in Spain could still be upset; and if it were, Spain's Latin American policy, which is based so heavily on Spain itself remaining a democracy, would be a shambles. Second, Latin American democracy remains very unstable, and hence it is inherently chancy for a country like Spain to tie its foreign policy to any one particular political preference. And third, in both Spain and Latin America, the democracy agenda is by no means unanimously agreed to, either as the only basis for domestic legitimacy and even less so as a basis for foreign policy. There are severe risks in such an ideological foreign policy.

Conclusion

Spain is playing a larger role in Latin America. Its presence there—diplomatically, politically, economically—is growing and has been for some twenty-five years. Moreover, the Spanish presence has been growing irrespective of the political shifts in Madrid or of the particular regime or government of the moment. The growth of serious Spanish interest and interests in Latin America began under the regime of Generalissimo Franco and has continued under each of his successors, under regimes of the right, regimes of the center, and a regime of the left. It is likely that Spain's presence in Latin America will continue and that it will expand, albeit slowly, incrementally, and within the limits and constraints we have enumerated. Spain is a rising and significant presence in Latin America, but neither its presence nor its future possibilities should be exaggerated. Spain is an old—and a new—force in Latin America, but it is not likely soon if ever to supplant the other powers operating there. Nor are the Latin American nations themselves about to embrace Spain particularly closely, and certainly they will not subordinate their foreign policies to that of Spain or of some Spanish-led commonwealth or confederation.

There are a lot of romantic notions abroad, in Iberia and in Latin America, about new power blocs and a realignment of alliance systems. Some Latin Americans would clearly like to use their Spanish and other European connections to break, or at least reduce somewhat, their dependence on the United States. There is a strong streak of anti-Americanism among some Spaniards as well, who would like to get revenge for the War of 1898, to "prove" that Hispanic culture is superior to the Anglo-Saxon one, to erect a new alliance or commonwealth arrangement that excludes the United States, among quite fanciful notions. The evidence accumulated here provides scant support for these romantic possibilities.

Spain is a rising, new (or revitalized), major presence in Latin America, but so far there is little flesh on those bones. Spain is not strong enough politically, militarily, or economically to supplant the United States in Latin America, nor will it be. Its institutional and financial base is insufficient to play the role of a great power in Latin America—a medium power, yes; but not a great power. Moreover, the cooler and more pragmatic voices in both Spain and Latin America recognize this. The global economic depression that prevailed from 1979 to 1984 made it clear to most Latin American leaders that they could not break their economic ties to the United States even if they wished to. The United States is, after all, their dominant trading partner. Indeed, the economic downturn forced them into an even closer economic relationship with the United States—particularly as the U.S. economic recovery demonstrated just how powerful an instrument the locomotive of the U.S. economy is and how dependent Latin America is on it. It revealed that Europe cannot, either as a community or as individual nations, serve as an effective replacement to the United States in Latin America. Financial assistance from Europe has simply not been sufficiently forthcoming, certainly not in amounts to substitute for U.S. assistance, credit, and markets. Even the revolutionary states—Nicaragua, Suriname, perhaps Cuba—have realized that Europe's aid and trade will not rescue them and that, in one form or another, they will have to reach some economic accommodation—and perhaps a political one as well—with the United States.

It is helpful to know that some of the earlier, romantic ideas are now in eclipse on both sides of the Atlantic and in both the northern and southern portions of the hemisphere. But that should not blind us to some of the new realities in the area. Spain (as well as France, Germany, Japan, the Soviet Union, and others) represents a new force in Latin America. Latin America is no longer exclusively a U.S. "lake" or sphere of influence. It has become increasingly a region of multilateralism, not just of bilateralism. The other powers influencing Latin America will not go away, nor can we simply wish them away. We must deal realistically with the increased complexities they bring to our relations with all the countries of the region.

Too often U.S. policy has been simply to react against all new European initiatives in Latin America, including those of Spain. American foreign policy requires more nuance and sophistication in this respect. One can think of far worse possibilities in Latin America than a rising Spanish, French, or West German presence there. Moreover, the idea of Spain offering its good offices or serving as interlocutor is not one that we must necessarily or always react against. Although one can understand why many American policy makers who have traditionally had Latin America all to themselves, without these European and other complications, would prefer to operate in the old ways, times have changed: the United States can no longer function as a policeman throughout Latin America. The Latin American nations are themselves more assertive and independent, and a number of European countries of middle-ranking power—including Spain—have established a significant presence there. It is time to adjust American policy accordingly, to take cognizance of these new facts, and to work with our European allies where that is fruitful and useful rather than simply responding negatively to all European initiatives.

Spain has begun to reforge its historic Latin American ties. How far that effort will go, and whether Portugal too will begin to move away from its internal preoccupations to reestablish its special relationships with Brazil and Portuguese Africa, we cannot know at this time. It seems unlikely, from the analyses presented here, that we will quickly or easily see the organization of a Hispanic commonwealth or confederation or of a Lusophonic one. Still the Spanish presence has become a significant one in Latin America in a relatively brief time, and it is likely that its influence will continue to increase. Spain is not a decisive force in Latin America, but for the first time in almost 200 years it is a force to be reckoned with.

There is not likely to be, as once seemed conceivable, a common

Hispanic development theory, model, and political sociology—one that would borrow from external sources but would also be based heavily on indigenous institutions and practices and that would also be distinctive from both the Anglo-Saxon developmental model and the Soviet one. There are *elements* of such a distinctive Hispanic developmental model present, and those may be nurtured; and there are continuous efforts in both Iberia and Latin America to fashion an indigenous Iberic-Latin model of development. But the issue is by now too divisive, too caught up in partisan politics, with too many associations and heavy baggage, too much tied to nationalistic, ideological, and cultural complexes and deep feelings to offer possibilities of a new, reasonable, culturally specific approach to development. Each Spanish administration, we have seen, has defined these issues in different ways, has had different notions of *hispanismo*, or in the white heat of a political campaign has seen fit to repudiate the approaches of its predecessor rather than search for common ground. The Latin American nations too have had different ideas about these concepts. No one is clear whether such a Hispanic model of development should be based on democratic precepts, authoritarian-corporate ones, or perhaps some still-to-be-invented combination of both of these. Meanwhile, the different Spanish groups and regimes have their reflections and interlocutors in Latin America, with each group or faction reading different interpretations rather than common understandings into the events that take place.

Still we must conclude that there is not only a new Spanish presence in Latin America, but also something serious in the idea of Hispanic unity and commonality.[7] Despite the infinitely varied nuances of interpretation, the politics, and the partisan posturings, there are strong common features between Spain and Hispanic America and between Portugal and Brazil. These common features are likely to remain permanently. There are elements other than history (ties of culture, behavior, sociology, and politics) that both *unite* the Iberian-Latin community of nations and make them *different* from the Anglo-Saxon nations. Whatever their differences, the Iberian-Latin American nations are likely to retain their sense of common destiny and purpose. It would not be entirely surprising if this sense not only persisted but also was strengthened. Similarly, the feeling that they are different from other nations, particularly those of the English-speaking world, is likely also to persist. These feelings of cultural, even spiritual, commonality among the Iberian-Latin American nations may in the long run carry just as many important implications for foreign relations—between Latin America and Iberia, between

Iberia and the United States, and between the United States and Latin America—as the more precise measures of military or commercial ties usually employed in social science analysis.

Notes

1. Fredrick Pike, *Hispanismo* (Notre Dame, Ind.: University of Notre Dame Press, 1971).

2. For a full discussion, see Howard J. Wiarda, *Corporatism and National Development in Latin America* (Boulder, Colo.: Westview Press, 1981).

3. Some of the materials in this chapter are based on the analysis of Antonio Sánchez-Gijón, "Spanish Involvement in Latin America," in *Allied Involvement in Latin America: Background Analyses* (Washington, D.C.: Center for Strategic and International Studies, Georgetown University, Latin American Security Project, 1984).

4. Pike, *Hispanismo*.

5. Quoted in Sánchez-Gijón, p. 5.

6. The material in this section is based on extensive interviews and renewed fieldwork in Portugal and Spain in May-June 1984, July 1985, and July 1987.

7. Fredrick Pike, "Latin America," in Jaime Cortada, ed., *Spain in the Twentieth Century World* (Greenwood, Conn.: Greenwood Press, 1980), p. 208.

12
Afterword

Both Spain and Portugal have made rapid and impressive progress toward democracy in recent years that deserves our support and applause. Their entry into the European Community also merits celebration, not just because it implies closer ties to Europe economically (not without its ongoing problems, however) but because it now finally makes Iberia a part of Europe politically, culturally, and psychologically, rather than apart from it which has been the sad situation for so long. Integration into Europe has brought with it closer ties to the common Western defense as well as admission into the community of modern, Western, democratic nations. That movement now seems to be definitive rather than still open to dispute and negotiations.

But repeatedly we have warned in this book that celebration of Iberia's democratic transitions should not serve to blind us to the hard realities that exist and the need for further analysis. The fact is that Iberia's political culture, its institutions, its socioeconomic problems, and the international environment are still only incompletely supportive of democracy. Although Spain has made far more progress on most of these counts than Portugal, in both countries there are still strong forces, institutions, ambitions, and pressures that are not very democratic, and in some cases are downright antidemocratic.

This book has stressed the importance of the theme of continuity in studying Spain and Portugal. Despite the dramatic developments of the 1970s (the Portuguese revolution and Franco's death) that opened the way for democracy, the break with the past has not been as thorough or complete as is often presented. Many Portuguese and Spanish institutions have continued to function in much the same bureaucratic authoritarian ways as in the past. Political attitudes have shifted toward the support of democracy, but social attitudes have not consistently changed as quickly. And even the political attitudes, if one probes beneath the surface, are not as unambiguously democratic, egalitarian, and liberal as one might hope. In both countries, in social and political institutions as well as personal attitudes and orientations, traditionalist, elitist, corporatist, authoritarian, and hierarchical ideas continue to coexist, often uncomfortably with the democratic ones.

The point has a larger theoretical significance. In much of the development literature, both Marxist and non-Marxist, traditional societies and institutions are thought of as hardened shells bound to crack and give way under the impact of modernization. But we now know that is not usually how development works: rather than crumbling, traditional institutions such as those long existent in Spain and Portugal are often remarkably flexible and accommodative. They typically bend in response to change rather than being overcome by it. They tend to absorb what is useful in modernity and can be readily adapted to local ways and institutions, meanwhile rejecting or filtering out the rest and thereby keeping much of their original essence. That is the experience of Japan, China, and India; it is now being recognized as the experience of Latin America and much of the rest of the third world; and it is also the experience of Spain and Portugal. The Iberian nations are no exception to the rules of continuity amid change or of modernization within tradition; rather they confirm this understanding of the change process, which is becoming the dominant one in the development literature.[1]

The result is that in Spain and Portugal we still see many mixtures, overlaps, and crazy-quilt patterns—"halfway houses" of traditional and modern, of authoritarian-elitist and democratic-egalitarian institutions. That is not unexpected, although few books on the subject take this approach. The existence of such overlaps and mixed patterns as well as the permanence and permeability of traditional institutions and ways of doing things force us to reconsider our understanding of the process of development and modernization. Such factors also force us to rethink our assessments of the completeness of the transitions to democracy in Spain and Portugal. For not only is it mistaken intellectually to think of such transitions as more fully consummated than they are in reality; but it also implies that when one group or ideology in Spain or Portugal seeks to govern by completely ignoring the other, without the necessary accommodations, that can be a political formula for disaster as well.

There also are foreign policy implications for the United States derived from these considerations. Spain and Portugal are now democracies, and in a moral and ethical sense we are pleased and happy that they have joined the camp of Western pluralist democracies. Our foreign policy should be aimed at supporting the newly established democratic institutions and governments in Iberia. We should not—as Secretary of State Alexander Haig once did—say that Spanish democracy is purely an internal matter for the Spaniards to decide. For if democracy were to be upset in Spain and Portugal, it would be disastrous for those two countries and would emphatically *not* be a purely internal matter. The European Community would then face a major crisis, it would add a further extremely disruptive element to NATO's already dangerous disarray, and it would severely strain U.S. relations.

It is therefore incumbent upon the United States, for our interests as well as theirs, to support democracy strongly in Spain and Portugal. But we must also keep in mind that democracy is not our only interest in Iberia. Furthermore, while democracy seems firmly in the saddle now, that could change; and if it does we will need to be prepared in a policy sense—whatever our moral and political preferences—to deal pragmatically, since our interests are affected, with a nondemocratic regime in either of these two countries. Nor should we assume that just because Spain and Portugal have democratic governments all our policy differences with them will magically disappear. They will not, as our continuing differences over NATO, Central America, and the Middle East and the presence of U.S. military forces and bases in both these countries make clear. Hence while the democratic transitions in Spain and Portugal offer a marvelous opportunity to put our relations with these two important nations on a far better basis than in the past, at the same time they also provide an ongoing challenge to American foreign policy.[2]

Notes

1. A. H. Somjee, *Parallels and Actuals of Political Development* (London: Macmillan, 1986); and Howard J. Wiarda, *Ethnocentrism in Foreign Policy: Can We Understand the Third World?* (Washington, D.C.: American Enterprise Institute for Public Policy Research, 1985).

2. For a more complete discussion of these issues in a closely related area see Howard J. Wiarda, *The Democratic Revolution in Latin America* (New York: Twentieth Century Fund, forthcoming).

Index

Eurocommunism and, 220
infiltration by, of unions, 163
influence of, in "red belt," 345
isolation of, 195
labor and, 109–10
and MFA, 108, 136–37
and 1975 elections, 110–13
and revolution of 1975, 89, 106–7
and service sector, 355
and Socialists, 347
and tertiary sector, 353
victories of, 360
voting totals of, 346
Communist party, Spain (PCE), 222–23
Compadrazgo (kinship), 42
Concelhos (districts), 348–49
Concientização (mobilization campaign), 345
Conscript officers, Portuguese, 124
"Consociational democracy," 90
Constituent Assembly, 232–33
MFA and, 111, 342
Constitution of 1822, Portuguese, 72, 73
Constitution of 1824, Portuguese, 73
Contadora, 380, 382
Continuity
in Portugal, 393–94
in Southern Europe, 254–55
in Spain, 393–94
Converse, Philip, 226
Corporate institutions, 166
Corporate pluralism, 90
Corporation
defined, 258–59
dynamic, 167–68
Corporations Ministry, 106, 161, 165
Corporatism. *See also* State corporatism
Aristotelian-Thomistic synthesis and, 302
as controls, 153–59
and corporative model, 301
definition of, 259
dismantled, transcended, persistent, 164–68
dynamics of, 31–33
of Estado Novo of 1930s, 168
fascism and, 26–28
Fascist label for, 25
as feature of Iberic-Latin system, 22
in global context, 169
Iberic-Latin tradition of, 50–51
as ideology, 34–35
impact of, 25
in Italy, 25
in Latin America, 299–305, 375
main currents of Iberic-Latin, 39–43

as manifest system, 149–53
meanings of, 29–31, 254
to neo-syndicalism, 241–88
North American/European disguised form of, 33–34
other forms of, 255–56, 257–59
as other "ism," 333–34
as part of Iberic-Latin political culture, 26
political change and, 90–95
as political tradition, 34–35
politico-cultural sense of, 168
in Portugal, 133–35, 373n.74
Rerum novarum–based conception of, 161, 168, 170
revitalized, 159–64
Schmitter's definition of, 145
sociology of knowledge of, 16–17
as sociopolitical organization, 34–35
Southern European, 244, 254–55, 258–59, 278
as tradition, 143–49
transcendence of, 113–16
variety of forms of, 27–28
"Corporatism of association," 27, 29
Corporatist systems
revival of, 25–26
universality of, 152
Corporatist traditions, 26–31
in Portugal, 143–74
Corporative Chamber, 152, 153
Corporative Council, 152
"Corporative framework," 49
Corporative ideal, corruption of, 99–100
Corporative model. *See also* Corporative tradition
challenges to, 304–5
components of, 302–4
economic factors of, 303
Iberic-Latin, 36–38
politicization of, 305–18
rationale for, 300–302
reception of, in Latin America, 306–7
reception of, in Spain/Portugal, 307–10
sociopolitical features of, 303
Corporative polity
convergence of, with liberal, 33–36
dynamics of, 43–51
Corporative state, Portuguese, 95–104
Corporative system, Portuguese, 143–74
Corporative tradition, as form of corporatism, 30
Cortes, Portuguese, 65–67, 144
Council of Europe, 192
Council of State, 111–12

State systems, Southern European, 266–
70
Statism
  Portuguese economic, 156–59
  tradition of, in Iberia, 7
Strikes, 162–63
Suárez, Adolfo, 194, 200, 217, 236
  corporatism of regime of, 315
  and Latin America, 200, 313–14, 375,
    376, 381
  political analysis of, 40
Suárez, Francisco, 67–68
Subjection, pact of, 67
Succession, question of, in corporatist
  polity, 21
Suffrage, Portuguese, 332, 336, 341, 343–
44
Syndicalism, 49
  as contrast to corporatism, 145
  from corporatism to, 146
Syndicates, 160
Systems
  competition and, 24–25
  convergence of, 21

Talleyrand, C. M., 175, 242
"Tempered monarchy," Portuguese, 72
Tertiary sector workers, 353
Thomas Aquinas, influence of, 259
Thomaz, Admiral, 123
Thomistic philosophy, influence of, in
  Portugal, 61
Thomistic state, 67
Third World
  in Iberia, 10, 11
  Spain as bridge to, 316
Third worldism
  Iberic-Latin dissociation from, 36–37
  Portugal and, 131, 132
Tocqueville, A. de, 7
Torrijos, Omar, 383
Tourism
  economic impact of Iberic, 182
  Portuguese, 82
Trade unions
  under Caetano, 160–62
  and 1926 Portuguese coup, 76–77
  under Salazar, 100, 153
  and Southern European state
    systems, 267–69
Traditional institutions
  development and, 394
  modernization and, 249
Two Portugals, 210, 235, 331
  and third, 365–66
Two Spains, 210, 235

UDC. See Union of the Democratic Cen-
ter
UGT. See Socialist General Labor Union
Unamuno, Miguel de, 295
Underdevelopment, problems of, as po-
  litical implications of socioeconomic
  change, 10–11
União Nacional, 334. See also Aliança Na-
  cional Popular
Union of the Democratic Center (UDC),
  217, 219–20, 229
  network of, 218
  Spanish right and, 225
United Nations
  Hispanic voting bloc, 378
  Portugal in, 192
  Spain admitted to, 191
United States
  applies anti-Communist pressure,
    109
  influence of, 193–94
  Latin America, 317, 318, 379, 381–83,
    390
  news media of, 113
  and 1975 elections, 112
  Portugal, 188, 196, 394–95
  rationale for Iberian support, 11–12
  Spain, 188, 196, 394–95
  and Spínola coup, 110
"Unity committees," 163
Urbanization
  Portuguese voting patterns, 355
  Southern European, 248–49
Uruguay, corporative model, 305

Vargas, Getulio Dornelles, 93, 299, 312
Visigoths, influence of, 59–60
Vitorino, Nuno, 356
Vote distribution, Spain and Portugal,
  229
Voter alignments, Portuguese, 348–64
Voting cleavages, Portuguese, 363–64
Voting patterns, Portuguese, 358–63
Voting percentages, Portuguese and
  Spanish, 228
Voting strength, bases of cleavage and,
  227–30

Wage and Price Board, 34
Wallerstein, Immanuel, 329
Weber, Max, 257
Weltanschauung, Portuguese, 148
Westendorp, Carlos, 198
Western Europe
  Iberian strategy of, 12

About the Authors

HOWARD J. WIARDA, an adjunct scholar of the American Enterprise Institute, is the former director of its Center for Hemispheric Studies. He is professor of political science and comparative labor relations at the University of Massachusetts, Amherst, where he was the director of the Center for Latin American Studies, and a research associate of the Center for International Affairs, Harvard University. He has published extensively on Latin America, southern Europe, the third world, and U.S. foreign policy. Among his publications are *The Communist Challenge in the Caribbean and Central America* (1987); *Finding Our Way? Toward Maturity in U.S.-Latin American Relations* (1987); *The Iberian-Latin American Connection: Implications for U.S. Foreign Policy* (1987); *Ethnocentrism in Foreign Policy: Can We Understand the Third World?* (1985); *In Search of Policy: The United States and Latin America* (1984); and *Rift and Revolution: The Central American Imbroglio* (1984).

Iêda Siqueira Wiarda holds a doctorate in political science from the University of Florida and teaches at the University of Massachusetts. She has lectured in the United States and abroad, has been a course chairperson at the Foreign Service Institute/Department of State, and has written a number of monographs, articles, and book chapters on Latin America, Iberia, and public policy issues.

Acknowledgments

CHAPTER 1, "The Question of Democracy in Iberia," was first published in Howard J. Wiarda, *Corporatism and Development: The Portuguese Experience* (Amherst: University of Massachusetts Press, 1977), chapter 1. The focus here and subsequently is on Portugal, but much of what is said is also applicable to Spain.

CHAPTER 2, "Iberian Background and Political Culture," was first published in Howard J. Wiarda, *Corporatism and Development* (Amherst: University of Massachusetts Press, 1977). Again, while Portugal is the focus of this chapter, many of the more general comments are meant to apply to Spain as well.

CHAPTER 3, "Can Portugal Transcend Its Corporatist Tradition?" was first published in Howard J. Wiarda, *Transcending Corporatism?* (Columbia, S.C.: University of South Carolina, Institute of International Studies, 1976).

CHAPTER 4, "Change and Continuity in the Portuguese Armed Forces Movement," was first published in *Iberian Studies*, vol. 4, no. 2 (Autumn 1975). This paper formed part of a larger ongoing research project dealing with Portugal and the Portuguese Revolution. Field research was conducted in Portugal in 1972–1973 under a grant from the American Council of Learned Societies and the Social Science Research Council, and on briefer research trips in March–April 1974 and May–June 1975. The writing of this paper was completed in August 1975. Although the paper focuses on the armed forces officer corps and particularly on the officers of the Armed Forces Movement as the chief driving force in the Portuguese Revolution, it is apparent that attention should also be devoted to the recruitment patterns and political socialization of enlisted men and noncommissioned officers, particularly as these relate to, overlap, or conflict with the political action of the MFA and its several factions.

CHAPTER 5, "The Corporatist Tradition and the Corporative System in Portugal: Structured, Evolving, Transcended, Persistent," was first published in Lawrence S. Graham and Harry M. Makler, eds., *Contemporary Portugal: The Revolution and Its Antecedents* (Austin: University of Texas Press, 1979).

CHAPTER 6, "Iberia, Latin America, and the Second Enlargement of the European Community," was published originally as Occasional Paper No. 2, Center for Hemispheric Studies, American Enterprise Institute, December

1981. This paper was prepared while the author was a visiting scholar at the Center for International Affairs, Harvard University; the assistance and support of the center and its personnel are gratefully acknowledged.

CHAPTER 7, "Political Parties in Spain and Portugal," was published originally in Peter H. Merkl, ed., *Western European Party Systems* (New York: Free Press, 1980).

CHAPTER 8, "From Corporatism to Neo-Syndicalism: The State, Organized Labor, and the Changing Industrial Relations Systems of Southern Europe," was published originally by the Center for European Studies, Harvard University, Monographs on Europe, No. 4, and in Richard F. Tomasson, ed., *Comparative Social Research*, vol. 5 (Westport, Conn.: JAI Press, 1982).

CHAPTER 9, "Interpreting Iberian–Latin American Interrelations: Paradigm Consensus and Conflict," was published originally in Howard J. Wiarda, ed., *The Iberian-Latin American Connection* (Boulder, Colo.: Westview Press, 1987).

CHAPTER 10, "How Well Institutionalized Are Portuguese Elections and Democracy?" was published originally in Myron Weiner and Ergun Ozbudun, eds., *Competitive Elections in Developing Countries* (Durham, N.C.: Duke University Press, 1987).

CHAPTER 11, "Spanish and Portuguese Foreign Policy in Latin America," was published originally in Howard J. Wiarda, ed., *The Iberian–Latin American Connection* (Boulder, Colo.: Westview Press, 1987); see also, by the author, "The Significance for Latin America of the Spanish Democratic Transition," in Robert Clark and Michael H. Haltzel, eds., *Spain in the 1980s: The Democratic Transition and a New International Role* (Cambridge, Mass.: Ballinger, 1987).

A Note on the Book

This book was edited by Dana Lane
and Janet Schilling of the
publications staff of the American Enterprise Institute.
The index was prepared by Grace D. Egan.
The text was set in Palatino, a typeface designed by Hermann Zapf.
Coghill Book Typesetting Company, of Richmond, Virginia,
set the type, and Edwards Brothers Incorporated,
of Ann Arbor, Michigan, printed and bound the book,
using permanent acid-free paper.